Teaching Oral Traditions

Modern Language Association of America
Options for Teaching
Joseph Gibaldi, Series Editor

Teaching
Oral Traditions

Edited by
John Miles Foley

The Modern Language Association
New York   1998

For information about obtaining permission to reprint material from MLA
book publications, send your request by mail (see address below), e-mail
(permissions@mla.org), or fax (212 477-9863).

Library of Congress Cataloging-in-Publication Data

Teaching oral traditions / edited by John Miles Foley.
     p. cm. — (Options for teaching, ISSN 1079-2562 ; 13)
   Includes bibliographical references (p.   ) and index.
   ISBN 0-87352-370-9 (cloth). — ISBN 0-87352-371-7 (pbk.)
   1. Oral tradition — Study and teaching.   2. Oral tradition in
literature — Study and teaching.   I. Foley, John Miles.   II. Series.
   GR40.T393   1998
   398'.07 — dc21   98-20667

Cover illustration of the paperback edition: King David playing the lyre, as
scribes take down his words; from the facsimile edition *The Vespasian
Psalter: British Museum Cotton Vespasian A. I* (f. 30v), ed. David H. Wright
(Copenhagen: Rosenkilde and Bagger, 1967). By permission of the British
Library.

Printed on recycled paper

Published by The Modern Language Association of America
10 Astor Place, New York, New York 10003-6981

Contents

Part II: Critical Approaches

Part III: Praxis: Oral Traditions in the Classroom

Living Traditions

Texts with Roots in Oral Tradition

John Miles Foley

Introduction:
An Audience for Oral Traditions

This book is for teachers and their students. It offers an avenue into the study of *oral traditions*, an exciting and rapidly expanding area of "literary" studies whose (re)discovery as a widespread form of verbal art is largely a twentieth-century achievement. Relatively recent research has begun to unearth the astounding wealth of oral traditions that have thrived either alongside or entirely without textual forms and that have served as a vital cultural activity for peoples throughout the world, from ancient times to the present day. In what follows, a group of experienced scholar-teachers, from a wide variety of disciplines, works to bring these (re)discoveries from the scholarly forum to the classroom. As a volume, this integrated collection is designed to acquaint generalists and specialists alike with a repertoire of pedagogical approaches to the world's oral traditions, past and present, by providing both an exposition of key issues and a digest of practical applications. Part 1, "Canon or Cornucopia?," is an introduction to the nature and scope of this most extensive of "canons"; part 2, "Critical Approaches," presents a menu of prominent and useful methods for studying oral traditions; part 3, "Praxis: Oral Traditions in the Classroom," is a series of twenty-five brief tutorials on commonly taught works and areas; and part 4, "Courses, Readings, and Resources," gives specific pedagogical examples and audiovisual resources. The overall aim is to offer the nonspecialist undergraduate teacher — and others as well — a pedagogical entrance into a multidisciplinary field of inquiry that now touches on more than a hundred traditions and draws from the methodologies of literary studies, folklore, anthropology, and linguistics.

Need for the Volume

It comes as a surprise even to most professional scholars that writing and texts are relatively recent inventions. Indeed, if we superimpose the history of our species on an annual calendar, the advent of writing occurs only in the month of December. Before that time, cultures had to transact their historical, philosophical, and "literary" business without the aid of letters, never mind the cutting-edge media of mass-market paperbacks and electronic communication that contemporary writers and readers take increasingly for granted. Even in these last few years before the millennium, the greater part of the world's population still conducts most of its cultural affairs without writing, and even the most literate societies — modern Western societies, for example — maintain oral traditions in their repertoires. Since only eighty to a hundred true literatures have ever evolved anywhere in the world, it is dangerous if not misleading to focus as exclusively as our colleges and universities often have done on the literary text as the unrivaled paragon of verbal art. In this field as in so many other fields of study, our assumptions need to be reexamined.

Perhaps aided in some ways by the electronic revolution in communication, a reevaluation of oral and written media has indeed begun. One can glimpse a new attention to oral traditions in the scholarly circuit of research, as many hundreds of studies emerge each year on such various topics as the unwritten roots of the Bible (Old and New Testaments both), the genesis and artistic fabric of the Homeric poems, the narratives performed by numerous Native American peoples, and the vast panoply of oral traditions from various parts of Africa. In these and many other venues, field-workers and analysts alike have begun to wrestle with the fascinating challenge of understanding the medium that served as the exclusive vehicle for verbal art through the first eleven months of our "species year" and that remains the principal channel for artistic discourse for most of the world's inhabitants.

Although the study of oral traditions is most well established as a field for scholarly research, it has now begun to enter the classroom as well. The contemporary attention to multiculturalism and non-Western cultures has certainly spurred interest in the unwritten verbal art of many different peoples.[1] Of course, oral traditions have been a part — if an occasional and marginalized part — of the curriculum for a substantial period of time. Taught most frequently as belonging to the folklore of a given group, they have not usually been granted full citizenship in the polis of literary figures and their texts. In the 1990s, however, particularly with the increased recognition of African American, Native American, and Hispanic American verbal art, in all of which oral tradition plays a major and determinative role, much more attention must and is being paid to the "margin."

In an effort to help further this enterprise, *Teaching Oral Traditions* is intended especially for the vital community of undergraduate teachers of the humanities. The book tries to help instructors formulate new offerings (on oral tradition per se and on oral traditions in specific areas) and to help them update and revise courses that already exist. In both cases the ultimate aim is to raise student awareness of the vast canon of oral traditions that far outstrips our treasured textual record in size and diversity and, one hopes, to deepen student appreciation of the variety of cultures and individuals that have produced these traditions.

Fundamental Issues for Scholarship and Pedagogy

Late-twentieth-century scholar-teachers are to a great extent caught in a web of texts and textual thinking. We were trained through texts to read and explain texts, and we reenforce this hermeneutic loop with every book or essay we read or publish, every student paper we assign and evaluate, and every class we teach. So deeply ingrained is our basic predisposition toward the written, textualized word that we find it difficult to imagine a world of oral tradition where words are primarily if not exclusively sounded and heard and where performance is the chief (and constitutive) medium for artistic discourse. We find it difficult to conceive of performance and sound as primary and of their textualization as a loss rather than a gain. We are particularly hard put to deal with works on the cusp of oral tradition, that is, works that survive only as texts but that we know, through independent testimony or telltale expressive features, have stemmed from prior or ongoing oral traditions. By and large, our training, our values, and even our most mundane daily duties as college and university faculty members insulate us against an understanding of what has become for most a foreign (because nontextual) language of communication.

Thus the first move in acquainting the teacher with oral traditions and works that derive from oral traditions must be to offer some glimpse of the tremendous riches of this kind of verbal art, both through history and around the world in our own day. Instructors need to know that whatever the national or ethnic literature they teach, oral traditions of remarkable depth and resonance are involved, either at the historical beginnings of those literatures or as part of their present-day profile. From the Sumerian *Gilgamesh* and the ancient Greek *Odyssey* through the medieval European vernacular texts and on to the contemporary, living performance traditions of central Asia, China, Africa, Australia, and the United States, conventionally defined "literature" is indeed just the iceberg's tip. The primary responsibility for this volume is therefore to open up a new world of possibilities and to suggest how the world we think we know should in some important and basic respects be remapped.

In closer focus, one of the most salient and consistent features of oral traditions is their lack of textual tidiness, a characteristic that can initially be unnerving—though eventually enlightening—for contemporary Western teachers and students alike. For one thing, this feature means that the currently embattled notion of canon is of little if any use in studying oral traditions. With no one version of a given work ever gaining unique authority until texts intervene, the phenomenon of multiformity — the very antithesis of canon — is the compositional and receptional rule of thumb. Any selection of performances may instance a tradition with more or less fidelity, but no one group can ever be complete or even representative. Theories of intertextuality or "anxiety of influence" are rarely applicable, since we are dealing here not with epitomes but instances, not with singulars but always with plurals. Even for written texts that derive from oral traditions, the authority of text as object is productively called into question, and the relations among performer-writer, tradition, and audience-reader must be reassessed.

Also, as the most recent research has started to show, the old airtight categories of oral versus written amount to a false and misleading typology, actively contradicted by what scholars have encountered in manuscripts and what they report from fieldwork. The mere existence of literacy in a society may reveal nothing about the society's oral art; what matters are the uses to which that literacy is put. Even a generally literate person may resort to the traditional oral medium for certain kinds of artistic discourse. A teller of "Jack tales" in the southeastern United States and an epic poet in Bali may be highly literate, even learned and scholarly, persons who know how to tune their discourse to the appropriate channel. In short, it is fair to observe that as this field of inquiry has evolved, its distinctions and questions have become considerably more difficult and, once addressed in their full complexity, much more revealing. We no longer ask whether a given culture is oral; we ask whether this or that genre of verbal art exists as oral tradition. We no longer question the orality of ancient and medieval manuscripts; we inquire whether the work involved derives from an oral tradition. And once we have reasonable answers to this first tier of questions, we pose the most interesting one: What if any effect does oral tradition have on our reading and our teaching of the given work? It is precisely this final question that has driven the development of *Teaching Oral Traditions*.

Summary of Contents

Part 1, "Canon or Cornucopia?" examines how oral traditions fit into our existing ideas about verbal art. My essay on the impossibility of canon juxtaposes two very different kinds of repositories — the Alexandrian Library, wonder of the ancient world and one of the first canons, and the Internet, incipient wonder of our modern world — and suggests that oral tradition works in some ways very much like the Internet. Lee Haring champions the cause of making comparative literature a truly worldwide enterprise that engages oral and textual forms. He sketches a course he created that allows students to experience the diversity of artistic systems, with special emphasis on non-Western traditions. Katherine O'Brien O'Keeffe opens another pathway into the general subject by studying the intersection of orality, literacy, and gesture, illustrating how performance can be recovered from medieval manuscript texts. Her essay dovetails with Elizabeth Fine's history of how texts have actually been made from oral traditional sources; identifying three different models (anthropological, literary, and performance-based), Fine gives examples of how texts can be augmented to encode and encourage performance.

Each of the five essays in part 2, "Critical Approaches," describes a prominent methodology for the study and interpretation of oral traditions, with a view to giving teachers a repertoire of perspectives that can be usefully employed in the classroom. Rosemary Lévy Zumwalt starts with a historical digest of approaches from the nineteenth century to the present, including discussion of the chief proponents of each school. Her essay should serve as a handy chart to guide teachers as they navigate the sometimes complex web of unfamiliar critical methods. Mark Amodio then focuses on events of the present day, bringing studies in oral tradition and contemporary critical theory into dialogue and showing how both highlight active audiences, textual instability, and authorial absence. The next three essays are guides to approaches that have had substantial effect in various parts of the general field and in many disciplines. Richard Bauman and Donald Braid describe the framing and constitutive role of performance, specifically how the event of performance keys a communication in crucially important ways. Thomas DuBois takes up the role of ethnopoetics, which emphasizes a culture's idiosyncratic expressive style as the touchstone for transcription and interpretation. Nancy Mason Bradbury closes this section with a discussion and illustration of traditional referentiality, a perspective that stresses the role of implied contexts in enriching the work of verbal art.

In part 3, "Praxis," the focus shifts from theory and methodology to a series of small handbooks on particular traditions, areas, or groups in an effort to assist teachers in as many different disciplines as possible. Some caveats should be prefixed to this part. First, the division between "Living Traditions" and "Texts with Roots in Oral Tradition" is meant as an organizational convenience rather than a hard-and-fast distinction;[2] indeed, many living traditions coexist with written or even printed forms, and as always we should be imagining a complex spectrum rather than opposed and discrete categories of orality and textuality. Second, the brief essays on particular areas are meant as introductions; they make a few practical suggestions and do not and cannot aspire to be thorough treatments of the traditions and groups they address. Third, there is the insoluble problem of coverage. This volume, which I believe to be the first pedagogically oriented book in the field, certainly cannot be exhaustive — but with oral traditions, inherently plural in form, the goal of exhaustive coverage is out of the question. With these limitations in mind, the guiding premise for the selection of essays in part 3 has thus been the simple criterion of practicality: we have concentrated on those works and traditions that already have existing resources — editions, translations, scholarship — and that are likely to be the responsibility of the nonspecialist undergraduate teacher.[3] At the same time, we have strived to push beyond this artificial and temporary limitation and to point to traditions and genres that may not as yet be easily accessible in documentary form. In short, we have done as well as we could at this moment in the history of studies in oral tradition. One measure of the volume's success would be an expanded and even more diverse subsequent edition.

Among living traditions, then, the teacher will find assistance in the following areas: Native American (divided into north and south),

African, African American, general Hispanic and Mexican American, Jewish, Indian, Chinese, Japanese, Arabic, South Slavic, British American balladry, the folktale, women's expressive forms, and storytelling. With texts that depend in various ways on prior or once contemporary oral traditions, pedagogical help is included for the Hebrew scriptures, the New Testament, Homer's *Iliad* and *Odyssey*, *Beowulf*, Chaucer, medieval romance, Old French, the Icelandic sagas, and the extremely widespread frame tale. Taken separately and collectively, this smorgasbord of essays should enrich the teacher's concept of how oral tradition plays out in both familiar and unfamiliar instructional contexts.

Part 4, "Courses, Readings, and Resources," provides background and practical support. Lynn Lewis and Lori Peterson synthesize the results of a nationwide survey on the teaching of oral traditions and summarize courses from more than a dozen disciplines, keyed to a series of sample syllabi in an appendix. Their essay thus provides direct assistance for the classroom teacher through models for courses and course units. Beverly Stoeltje and Nancy Worthington make more general and theme-oriented suggestions and focus on strategies for teaching multiculturalism through its natural ally, oral traditions, showing how identity is powerfully expressed in nonwritten forms. William McCarthy adds some specific curriculum advice by walking the reader through a composition course that uses oral tradition as a vehicle for students to discover their own rhetorical voices and improve their writing skills. A highly selective bibliography of audiovisual and Internet resources rounds out this hands-on part of the volume.

The time is right for *Teaching Oral Traditions*. Thanks to the efforts of scholars and field-workers, more and more primary materials, representing numerous different cultures and periods, are appearing every year. Moreover, the critical thinking in studies in oral tradition has matured to a point where it has a particular and significant impact on the understanding of both living and textualized traditions. But as promising as the ongoing scholarly conversation has been, until now there has existed no pedagogical resource, no place where nonspecialist teachers of literature can go to learn how to manage this exciting new addition to "the canon." By providing such a resource and by placing it in the readily available MLA Options for Teaching series, we hope to help both teachers and their students become a better audience for verbal art in all its richness and diversity.

Notes

1. See, for example, the chapter "Oral Literature Today" in the *Harper-Collins World Reader* (Caws and Prendergast 2591–655).
2. Note, for example, that the general Hispanic essay by Zemke, this volume, covers both living traditions and the medieval Spanish *Poem of the Cid*.
3. Practicality and the primary audience of the MLA series have also directed the invitation of authors to submit essays on various traditions and approaches. In an attempt to make this volume as pertinent and useful as possible, I have in all cases chosen scholars familiar with the general curricular design of North American colleges and universities. Foreign scholars might have offered interesting perspectives on many of these traditions and approaches, but for the purposes of this pedagogically focused project an acquaintance with the audience seemed of paramount importance.

Part I

Canon or Cornucopia?

John Miles Foley

The Impossibility of Canon

For among all mortal men the singers have a share
In honor and reverence, since to them the Muse
Has taught the pathways, for she loves the singers' tribe.

Homer, Odyssey

Canon is a loaded term these days, in more ways than one. Etymologically it ultimately derives from the same forebear as does *cannon*, its more transparently pyrotechnic sibling.[1] Cannons have always exploded; now, more and more, the canon is imploding. Most tellingly for humanities curricula on the eve of the new millennium, *canon* has come to designate a battlefield, an intellectual fortress under siege, a primary site for cultural combat. We are told, with good reason, that our selection of literary artifacts for the Museum of Verbal Art is incomplete, even biased, in its parochialism. And, indeed, the relatively few cherished items chosen for public display have been gathering dust, undisturbed on their pedestals, for far too long. We may repackage the exhibits, paste on fresh new labels, shift the viewer's perspective this way and that, but none of these increasingly desperate strategies addresses the most fundamental problem. In assembling the museum collection, generations of curatorial staff have shirked their duty. Relying on unexamined assumptions about what constitutes a proper subject for literary study, they have foreshortened rather than broadened our horizons. An unblinking appraisal must lead one to admit that, until recently, their labors have too often led to tautology: we have continued to celebrate what has always been celebrated, granting pride of place to those very artifacts on which our aesthetic criteria for selection have been based.

In the 1980s and 1990s, however, dramatic and rewarding gains have been registered in many areas. Where are the long-lost women authors, you ask? Nationwide, a generation of scholars labors to bring women's literature into the college and university canon, making tandem strides across the virtual space of anthologies and literary research and across the real space of classrooms throughout the land. Where are the exciting new voices of African American and Native American authors, you ask? Again, the answer is gratifying: today's students and scholars are often as familiar with Toni Morrison, James Baldwin, Leslie Marmon Silko, and Louise Erdrich as with William Shakespeare, Herman Melville, Honoré de Balzac, or Leo Tolstoy. In these and other areas once marginalized by the academy, the boundaries truly are expanding. New voices are entering the discussion, new champions are joining the fray, and for many students and teachers the old guard of authors and texts is also profiting from a revitalized context of human diversity. The Museum of Verbal Art is now a much more interesting place to visit, whether privately or with our students.

How ironic, then, that even the most visionary curators among us have largely failed to tap potential resources that in size and variety dwarf even the museum's expanded holdings. Having taken such brave and important steps to acquire and display lyrics, novels, short stories, and other treasures from the four corners of the known (literate) world, we have tended to ignore the magnificent array of verbal art whose only shortcoming is its preference for the spoken over the written word.[2] Even when the existence of such traditions has been credited, they have seldom been admitted to full partnership with the current contents of the museum.

Our museum has not been much more receptive to rethinking the descriptions and interrelations of its present holdings as new discoveries about the history and provenance of those holdings have emerged. The curator of antiquities has no doubt had the worst of it so far: with the scholarship mounting daily about the influence of oral tradition on Homer, Hesiod, and other ancient Greek authors, recycling the same tired portraits of eminent literati has become measurably more difficult. Nor has the curator of medievalia rested untroubled as the rediscovery of oral tradition has spread from era to era and item to item. The exhibit on the Anglo-Saxon *Beowulf* has demanded refurbishing, as have those on the Old French *Song of Roland*, the medieval Spanish *Poem of the Cid*, and the Old Norse sagas, all of whose identity as uncompromisingly literary monuments once seemed secure. There have even been whispers that high-traffic exhibits featuring elite authors like Geoffrey Chaucer, long recognized for his mastery of texts in many tongues, need a bit of face-lifting. Similar woes have beset the curators of Eastern art, whether Indian, Oriental, or Arabic. Not only do epochal texts like the *Mahabharata* stem from oral traditions, it seems, but some of them also appear to have "lesser" kin still alive in the hinterlands of folk tradition. And this is to say nothing of the Judeo-Christian Bible, whose roots — both Old and New Testaments — turn out to be firmly planted in the realm of the spoken word.[3]

Still, even with the pressure exerted by firsthand observations of living oral traditions and the rediscovery of oral traditions at the root of many canonical texts, the museum has undergone no fundamental change, no major building program or renovation, no paradigm shift. The reason is not far to seek: the canon enjoys historical depth and political power. And when it comes to verbal art that either wholly lacks the culturally indispensable loop of author, text, and readership or whose background consists in part of something besides another text, the chances for a new installation are slim indeed. What is more important for our present purposes, the implications for pedagogy are obvious. No matter how able the docent or guide, any tour through the museum is necessarily limited by the holdings and displays that constitute the itinerary. One cannot consult and interpret what one cannot examine. Even if a visitor is fortunate enough to enlist the services of a guide trained in areas not represented in the museum, that expertise will remain untapped and unapplied. Small wonder that the classroom teaching of verbal art has suffered from, if anything, an agenda and domain even more restricted than the scholarly discussion of verbal art.

How, then, do we begin to remedy this situation? What sorts of curatorial insights and strategies for acquisition are necessary to ready the Museum of Verbal Art for the next millennium? How are we to ensure that visitors to the institution are exposed to a significantly expanded and enriched canon that realistically reflects the many faces of verbal art and in particular the worldwide cornucopia of oral traditions and works that depend on oral traditions?

From the Alexandrian Library to the Internet

As a first step, let us try to place our hoped-for, millennial museum and its canon in perspective by juxtaposing an unlikely pair of "depositories": the great and mysterious Alexandrian Library, wonder of the ancient world, and its present-day analogue and wonder of the modern world, the Internet. These two imposing edifices, bookends to the waning age of inscription and print, represent watershed moments in the technology of storing and communicating knowledge. Underlying their physical differences, however — the one edifice a towering stack of tangible surfaces and spatial representation, the other a web of electronic impulses and virtual representation — lies a more radical distinction. The Alexandrian Library consisted of information; the Internet consists of pathways that lead to information.[4]

Although the history of the library has been plagued by contradictory testimony from earliest times, enough of that history has been reconstructed that we can be sure of the library's central, ongoing purpose: nothing less than to house under a single roof copies of all books ever written.[5] During the library's prime under the Ptolemies, reports were required every year on progress made toward what was considered an achievable goal. How many scrolls were presently in hand? Were there prospects for major new collections? How were the "ship scrolls" coming?[6] Behind this process, fueled by a kind of bibliographical imperialism, lay an astounding conceit: since there must be a limited, finite number of items, let us find them all and make them our own. This aim may not sound entirely unfamiliar to a twentieth-century culture of authors, readers, and objectified works of verbal art; the same spirit has filled old-fashioned library buildings to overflowing, created the need for off-site storage facilities, and perhaps accelerated the advent of the digital library.

The Ptolemies had of course virtually unlimited funds at their disposal with which to pursue their dream of a universal library, but more important to the project than their deep pockets were their deeply held convictions about the necessary relation between, for example, the author and works we call Homer and the numerous scrolls that wholly or partially recorded the *Iliad* and *Odyssey*. One of these convictions, the *illusion of object*, is still very much operative today, although electronic media are daily forcing us to become more imaginative about what constitutes a tangible object. The librarians, let us call them, in effect equated Homer and the scroll; for the purposes of collection, the two were indistinguishable. This equation is all the more remarkable in the light of two related facts. First, oral composition, transmission, and performance were still ongoing in some parts of the Greek world during at least the early years of the library, so that we can hardly speak of any standard text; second, the Alexandrian "card catalog" listed no fewer than 131 separate Homeric texts.[7] Nonetheless, the illusion that the work of verbal art was a collectible object made possible the library's foundation and its continuing existence.

Cognate with the work-as-object assumption was the *illusion of stasis*. Only if the work had the permanence and value of a static object could it merit deposit in the library. This second illusion must have helped relieve the embarrassment of the hundred and some Homers: if something had attained the form of a static object, then its suitability for inclusion in the library's collection was warranted. Once again, the early stages of this process must have taken place even as "Homer" was being performed and reperformed — in different places, by different poets, and certainly with different results (judging by the potpourri of alternate readings and texts).[8] Generations of editors might pore over variant scrolls, excising or exchanging one line or passage with another, but the philological contest they oversaw was open only to manuscripts, sanctioned rivals who had already won admission to the agon, the ritual battle, on the basis of their textuality. From a modern perspective, we can interpret such collective variation as what Paul Zumthor (*Oral Poetry* 51–52) calls *mouvance*, the journey of any work from one textual representation to another. But in their time and place, the most important function served by the static objects so assiduously amassed by the Ptolemies and their agents was simply to create a complete material record, a treasure-house of thought become written word, an archive complete in itself. In this respect the Alexandrian Library also housed the first Museum of Verbal Art, the original canon.

And so was created the model that has reigned for two millennia and more, as significant for what it excluded as for what it included. Everything written was worth collecting; everything unwritten was defined out of existence. The library could aspire to universal coverage because that universality was restricted solely to texts. The canon was conceivable only because of the twin illusions of object and stasis, which also made possible librarianship, philology, and, not least, cultural self-definition. Because performances of oral tradition were neither objective nor static, since in contemporary terms there was no substance to them, they could not qualify as entries in the grand inventory of concrete items. Oral traditions were not so much unwelcome as unshelvable in the library canon.[9]

Now we leap forward to the other bookend, to the incipient construction of the Internet, the modern information superhighway that promises unprecedented access to theoretically unlimited knowledge. In its grandiose aspirations, this claim may seem to echo what the Ptolemies had in mind, and indeed the two repositories have some features in common. While no single site on the Internet can play more than a supporting role, the system in its entirety — as a virtual library without geographical or other physical limitations —

aims at the inclusion of everything. And everything now means more than books. Already, colleges and universities specialize in electronic archives of texts, manuscript facsimiles, and other scholarly tools that it is economically or technologically impractical to publish or own in conventional printed format. Already, scholarly organizations sponsor electronic journals in various disciplines.[10] Already, those at home in the virtual environment write their own identities into the Internet card catalog on personal "home pages." Taken as a whole, this computer-driven system brings a heretofore unthinkable number of items under the same virtual "roof," and its holdings increase daily as more institutions and individuals join the network and as more facilities, often unparalleled, go online.

What makes the Internet much more than an Alexandrian Library is neither the sheer number nor the remarkable diversity of its "scrolls" but, rather, their unprecedented, hands-on accessibility. What sets the Internet apart, in short, are the connections woven into its web — the "hot links" that lead to a universe of immanent knowledge from a single search. How do you get a look at that incomparable medieval masterpiece of manuscript illumination, the *Book of Kells*? Start up the browser program and click on your destination — in this instance, Georgetown University's *Labyrinth* archive (www.georgetown.edu/labyrinth/). Not just the manuscript page in question but the whole medieval period opens before your eyes, as you pass effortlessly, according to your own designs, among different texts, authors, languages, and centuries, fashioning your understanding of the *Book of Kells* against a panoramic background as you go. Compare this procedure to actually visiting Trinity College, Dublin, where the manuscript itself is housed in a conventional university library and where you can examine a single page or two in dim light at the end of a musty corridor. Or perhaps you prefer the free-standing photographic facsimile printed on paper and bound between covers, which will allow you to examine more than a couple of pages, as long as your library is privileged enough to own a copy of the limited edition. But neither a journey to Dublin nor a research expedition to your local library can offer the immediate, proximate, multidimensional context that is a built-in staple of Internet study and research at its best. And it is not so much that Trinity College or your nearby library may lack the information you need (though that may be the case) as that they lack the living web of pathways that make the information instantly and always accessible.

These links or pathways have other characteristics as well, salient features that distinguish an interactive journey through the Internet from a trip to the best-stocked library, even to the Alexandrian Library. For one thing, any route taken through the electronic maze is more than a standardized, repetitive tour of the facilities; according to the interests and judgment of whoever constructed the given sites and their options, the route offers automatic, institutionalized access to myriad ancillary topics as an ever-present reality. The itinerary is never writ in stone but always susceptible to change en route, ever evolving even as the traveler proceeds. Correspondingly, each Internet session is perforce a unique event and experience, providing a fresh perspective for each user each time he or she enters the virtual edifice. Even after many sessions on the same topic, the opportunity to try out new avenues or follow the same links in a different sequence or at a different depth, branching here or there, will always shed new light on the most familiar surroundings. Indeed, the watchword for successive visits to the Internet library is variation within limits rather than rote repetition. As we shall see, with these same observations we could as well be describing oral traditions.[11]

Pathways versus Canon

In conceiving of how the ancient Greek bard navigates through the maze of traditional story, Homer also speaks of pathways (*oimai*). During the great feast among the Phaeacians on Scheria, for instance, he portrays Odysseus as honoring the celebrated singer Demodokos with the choicest cut from the shining-tusked boar and with the equally complimentary words that began this essay:

> For among all mortal men the singers have a share
> In honor and reverence, since to them the Muse
> Has taught the *pathways*, for she loves the singers' tribe.
> (*Odyssey* 8.479–81; my trans., emphasis added)

What the Muse teaches, we should notice, is not texts — that is, items supporting the twin illusions of object and stasis — but, rather, routes, avenues, means for getting there. She is represented not as lending volumes from a story archive but as installing links for the performing bard (and by implication the audience) to click on. Her repository of traditional oral epic consists not of scrolls shelved in an Alexandrian Library but of pathways that provide users access to the stories through a pretextual analogue to our Internet.[12]

Let us pursue this analogy, historically counterintuitive as it may appear. I have already suggested that the Homeric *oimai* are parallel to links on the Internet and therefore that a web or network of interrelated sites is a more apposite cognitive model for ancient Greek oral tradition than anything associated with the world of unitary, physical texts.[13] Modern-day oral traditions certainly bear this out. For example, South Slavic *guslari*, preliterate singers of epics who have been particularly well studied in this regard, focus not on the thing but on the process. For them the song exists in its doing, its performance — its movement from here to there, partially predictable and partially unpredictable; for them the song has nothing to do with the cenotaph of the book.[14] To be sure, by recording one of their performances one can subsequently manufacture a textual item, a durable good, a "scroll" fit for acquisition and deposit by the Ptolemies' librarians. But a second and third recording made the next day or in front of a different audience or even with the same bard in a different frame of mind will reveal inevitable disparities that quickly put the lie to the authority of any one version. The song lives outside any single performance — never mind outside the reduced medium of any one recording or transcription — as a series of potentials, a network of pathways that offers innumerable options at the same time that it connects with innumerable unspoken assumptions and implicit references. Had we the patience to sit through a hundred performances, we would simply confirm the same thesis a hundredfold: none of the recordings would actually *be* "the song," but all of them would in their different ways *imply* "the song." Oral tradition can no more be canonized than the Internet can be forced between two covers.

Thus we come to the first of the major reasons why oral tradition is fundamentally incompatible with the concept of canon. Whereas Petrarch's sonnets, Montaigne's essays, and Gogol's novels have always fit naturally into the Museum of Verbal Art and whereas the recently expanded museum now features new displays on works like Morrison's *Beloved* and Silko's *Ceremony*, there still is no space for oral traditions. Nor can there ever be, at least in the present building. And it is not the curators who are at fault this time, because as contemporary teachers and scholars become more aware of cultural diversity, they are making well-intentioned and innovative efforts to listen to all voices, not just the chosen few that have so long and adamantly claimed exclusive rights in constituting our heritage. The problem lies instead with the very nature of oral tradition as a medium for verbal art, with the incontrovertible fact that any one performance is just that — one performance. We cannot file it, title it, edit and translate it as we would a papyrus manuscript, first edition, or other artifact of literary culture. Oral tradition exists only in its plurality, its multiformity, its enactment, and to reduce that wonderful complexity to a single libretto for ease of shelving is to falsify its art. Proteus exists only in his shape-shifting and resists the captivity of canonical form.

To accommodate the world's oral traditions, our museum will have to undergo some alterations that are more than cosmetic. First and foremost, the staff must find effective methods for representing plurality and what that plurality stands for. Singularity, epitome, and authority are useless criteria for living oral traditions; they bespeak the illusions of object and stasis, not the realities of process and rule-governed change. The many faces of an oral traditional work are what folklorists seek to expose when they insist on publishing multiple performances of a given work, and we can take an initial step by following their lead. Just as any single site pales in importance against the totality of the Internet — since by isolating even the most valuable site we sap its greatest strength — so concentration on any single fossil of a once living oral tradition blurs the focus on that tradition's natural, necessary context. Teachers can sharpen the focus by asking their students to compare two, three, or more performances or versions of a given work, to measure similarities and differences, to see what remains relatively stable from one to the next, and thus to learn how the work can exist plurally in its many manifestations, not as a product but as an ongoing process. Always different and yet always the same, oral traditions can then be understood as *implied and instanced* rather than *uniquely contained* in each separate yet related performance.

There are many other strategies that can be engaged, some of them currently available for use in the classroom and some on the near horizon of our augmented "library science." For example, the approach called ethnopoetics has already begun to restructure our thinking about the faithful representation of oral traditions by insisting on close examination of their transferral to texts.[15] For Native American tales, Dell Hymes asks us to recognize the fundamental expressive units of the original work (often at odds with Western poetics) and to shape the textual representation accordingly (*In Vain* and "Use"). Correspondingly, Dennis Tedlock has argued for reinstatement of the pauses, tone shifts, gradations of volume, and other performance features that text making customarily and parochially levels out or silences (*Finding* and *Spoken Word*). Students can quickly be taught to practice a novice's version of the same worthy craft, restoring life to what would otherwise remain or become artifacts. Additionally, electronic text archives, in whose ready recesses the student and scholar will eventually be able to probe many parallel performances, are coming online; these archives have a hypertext format, which promises to overcome many of the hindrances imposed by spatial limitations innate in the book format. No longer will editors be required to incarcerate a work in one epitomized version, unfairly consigning its siblings to a secondary identity as appendixes, footnotes, or lemmas. With the multimedia revolution, oral traditions can also be presented in more than one dimension; the acoustic and even visual reality of the performance can become part of its transcription.[16]

For living traditions, we thus need nothing less than a new wing added on to the Museum of Verbal Art, an interactive environment in which visitors are urged not just to view but also to become involved in the exhibits, to change their status from observers to participants. The opportunities afforded by such a facility would be many: attending multiple performances; taking part in instantaneous, "face-to-face" exchanges; switching presentational formats to accommodate traditions on their own idiosyncratic terms; hearing and experiencing (as well as reading texts made from) living works of verbal art. In concert with current trends in museology, this new facility would go far toward dissolving the twin illusions of object and stasis, restoring to the works and performances some degree of their original vitality while concurrently transforming a readership into a participating audience, an interactive community.[17] For those works excluded from the old museum on the basis of their nontextual identity, the new wing would represent a uniquely appropriate home — fostering the understanding of pretextual verbal art by posttextual means.

Of course, the kind of museum tour that makes up a world literature survey, for example, may not have access to the resources needed for multimedia experience of the living oral traditions it studies. The challenges associated with procuring actual performances are daunting, and the language barriers are formidable (see Daskalopoulos, this volume, for ways of overcoming these barriers). But even if everyday classroom experience necessarily stops short of the ideal of creating a participant audience, teachers can open the textual record to student involvement by stressing some of the principles that underlie design of the museum's new wing. Performances can be lifted off the printed page and reperformed by the class, according to whatever stage directions are included with the text or can be otherwise unearthed. Different versions of the same work can be queried about their incongruities, and a sense of the work as instanced rather than contained by any one version can be developed. In short, any pedagogical practice that illustrates the multiformity and performance of verbal art from oral tradition will go far toward eliminating the illusions of object and stasis and toward giving students an appreciation of the work on its own terms.

These strategies also have significance for a considerable number of *oral-connected traditional texts* that are already comfortably housed in the old museum collection on the basis of their presumably literary and textual nature but that recently have been shown to be rooted in oral traditions and therefore deserving of additional attention in the new wing. In many ways these works too are more process than product and thus not entirely canonizable. In updating their exhibits, we must take care to discover and convey what we can about the background and foreground of each work. Is their writtenness merely an accident of transmission, a matter of transcription (as with oral performances recorded before acoustic means were available)? If so, they will require certain kinds of treatment (e.g., those described in part 2 of this volume). But even when we are dealing with authored texts, much closer to what most of us have been trained to call literature, we still have a curatorial responsibility to discover what we can about the history behind the work, its possible multiformity (in part or in whole), and the nature and degree of its dependence on an oral tradition. To the examples cited earlier—Homer's *Iliad* and *Odyssey*, the Anglo-Saxon *Beowulf*, the Old French *Song of Roland*, the medieval Spanish *Poem of the Cid*, the Old Norse sagas, the Sanskrit *Mahabharata*, the Judeo-Christian Bible, and even the "literary" genius Chaucer—let us add the ubiquitous and familiar ballad genre, which has long prospered as both oral tradition and text (see Niles, this volume). In fact, the ballad offers the opportunity to emphasize how the worlds of orality and literacy, once thought to occupy mutually exclusive orbits, can and do coexist in myriad fascinating combinations, within the same culture or region and even within the very same person. That is, not only do oral traditional features persist alongside and into written texts, but an individual may be fluent in both expressive media.

The key to understanding the oral-connected traditional text and the variety of channels in an individual's expressive repertoire is to move beyond that untenable first approximation of oral versus literate and toward the finer discrimination of *register*, a linguistic term for a special variety of language used for a particular purpose (Foley, *Singer* 49–53, 82–92). For example, one can clearly distinguish the South Slavic epic register, studded with archaisms and dialect forms native to other (often inimical) geographical areas, from the streamlined, monodialectal, conversational register in vogue in any given city or village at any given time. Teachers can illustrate this important concept expeditiously by asking their students to describe the same incident or problem—perhaps a local political intrigue or an on-campus lecture or concert—in three different performance arenas: by speaking to a parent, to a roommate, and to the dean. By realizing, from the inside out, that our expressive repertoires contain a number of registers among which we code-switch to suit the situation, students can more readily grasp the functional importance of traditional oral ways of speaking. From there it is but a short step to pointing out how such performance registers can in part carry over to written texts. If a particular brand of language, honed over decades or centuries, has proved singularly capable of supporting a certain kind of communication, then why should it be abandoned the moment that texts enter the picture? Indeed, it is a measure of our modern cultural egocentricity as traders in texts that we presume the written idiom to have been an overnight sensation, immediately and forever displacing the old ways of transacting verbal business. Now that we know better, perhaps we will one day be not only wise enough to cease excluding oral traditions and oral-connected works from the Museum of Verbal Art but also imaginative enough to design an interactive wing that allows each tradition and work to project an appreciative, knowledgeable audience and to address that audience on its own terms.

Call Numbers, Addresses, and Traditional Referentiality

If oral traditions and the Internet are more process than product, more pathway than canon, and if they fail the Alexandrian Library tests of object and stasis, then just how does the audience or user navigate their Protean webs? To put it another way, how does the dynamic of implication (as opposed to textual reference) really work? In confronting this challenge, we arrive at the second major reason why oral tradition is fundamentally incompatible with the concept of canon. As already suggested above, any instance or performance of verbal art in oral tradition is necessarily fragmentary in itself; what makes it whole is the implied, unspoken tradition, the proverbial context of the speech act. Thus the key to serving as a suitable audience for oral tradition and oral-connected texts, to completing the communicative circuit, is to understand the special nature of their *traditional referentiality* (Bradbury, this volume; Foley, *Immanent Art* 6–8; Foley, *Singer* 95–97).

To return to our analogy, consider the matter of electronic call numbers in the virtual library. Those familiar with browsing this kind of collection know how to proceed from one address to another, employing a string of characters like "http://www . . ." to open up the next set of *oimai* on an itinerary that is always evolving. Naming is an all-important dimension of the journey. Any boilerplate address, though nominal in itself, must of course be reproduced precisely to open up its treasure chest of possibilities; any minuscule deviation, even a single incorrect character or an extra space, will amount to static on the channel. While we may well locate interesting and useful books simply by walking through contiguous stacks in the conventional library, on the Internet an approximate name for a site will prove meaningless to the system as a whole and cause the desired connection to fail.[18] This is not because the "http://www . . ." phrase itself has anything substantial to do with what one actually finds at the site, since the phrase neither designates a book (as nonelectronic call numbers do) nor demarcates a typical discipline, topic, or area (as spaces within the physical plants of libraries do). But the Internet address serves a purpose no conventional call number can match: it names the site—not descriptively but indexically—by recourse to a highly specialized language. To neophyte browsers such addresses will have little or no heuristic value until they learn the code and can speak the language required for this particular kind of research. Although that strange new tongue may seem imposing at first, a tutorial in the rules that govern it will cause what was initially opaque to quickly and readily "speak volumes."[19]

Addresses in oral tradition work analogously, or at least as much by indexing as by describing. The Grimms' oft-told tales, a book off the shelf of childhood experience, furnish a simple illustration. Many of these stories, which we customarily hear long before we read them, betray their general identity by opening with the magical phrase "Once upon a time"—a narrative switch or pathway that kindles the imagination and points unmistakably toward the arena for the storytelling event that is about to occur. Were we to begin performances to our children with the rough equivalent "Long ago it happened that," we would satisfy the criteria of object and stasis that sustained the Alexandrian Library and its institutional progeny through all these centuries by translating one thing into another, creating a new scroll that derives its authority from a textual relation to an item already enshrined in the collection. But within the system of storytelling, "Long ago it happened that" has little or no meaning: it's not that the substitute phrase is inadequate as a thing in itself; it just doesn't lead anywhere. It is a scroll, not a speech act.

Consider some similar addresses in the oral-connected traditional texts of Homer. The poet commonly resorts to formal, florid-seeming combinations of nouns and epithets—"swift-footed Achilleus," "goddess grey-eyed Athena," "earthshaker Poseidon," and so many more—not because he lacks imagination or is shackled by the demands of his inherited poetic language but because these phrases are pathways to the figures they name. By dialing up the equivalent of "http://Achilleus," Homer, along with his audience, opens the site for this "best of heroes," bringing into play not just Achilleus's fleetness but also his entire mythic history—semidivinity, heel, and all. This is why the great man can be called swift-footed even as he sits sulking in his tent, having angrily withdrawn from battle in his quarrel with Agamemnon, and also why he can be addressed in this way no fewer than thirty times in the *Iliad* without fear of redundancy. If an *oimê* represents a designated pathway to reach a given node in the traditional network of ancient Greek epic, then how can it prove redundant? Cliché is the handmaiden of object, stasis, and canon, not of performance and interactive tradition. For an audience with full command of the special idiom in which the *Iliad* and *Odyssey* are composed, the function of these noun-epithet formulas is not unlike that of the "bookmarks" available in Internet software. By saving the addresses one has previously visited, all subsequent trips to those sites are usefully foreshortened, and this is equally true whether the path in question leads to a virtual archive on the Internet or to a focal character who lives most fully in the story-archive of Greek myth. Clicking on "swift-footed Achilleus" or, for that matter, "Little Red Riding Hood" makes the designated characters come alive in a decidedly noncanonical way, with an inimitable economy of expression. As always with addresses in oral tradition, what counts is not the vagaries of surface but the depths of referential content.

Modern oral traditions are no different on this score, depending less on the address per se than on what that address implies. At times the sign marking the pathway may even seem diametrically at odds with its traditional referentiality, as in the case of a relatively common and otherwise homely formula from South Slavic oral epic, *na Markovac kleti*.[20] With any serviceable dictionary in hand, we arrive expeditiously at what this phrase would signify if it turned up during a conversation on a street in the former Yugoslavia or in a modern novel — to wit, "down by damned Markovac." A direction and location are indicated, in short, and the toponym comes in for some straightforward bad-mouthing as *kleti*, "accursed" or "damned." Imagine our surprise, then, when we learn that Markovac refers to the sacred birthplace of Prince Marko, a major hero in South Slavic song (see Popović), and furthermore that the very singers who celebrate the hero are also aware of the apparent bad-mouthing of his place of origin. I say "apparent" because within the register of South Slavic epic there is nothing at all pejorative implied by *na Markovac kleti*. From the perspective of the ambient tradition, which as we have seen resembles a network of sites much more than a collection of shelvable texts, "down by damned Markovac" not only lacks negative associations but is uniquely brimful of positive implications attributable to its traditional referentiality, its identity as a link. As one singer put it when queried about this disquieting discrepancy between literal and idiomatic meanings, "Pa mora da se rekne" — "You have to say it that way." In Internet language, he was advising that you get there via "http://na Markovac kleti."

———

Canons and oral traditions just don't mix. The one relies on objects, stasis, and shelf space; the other on pathways, performance, and traditional referentiality. The one lives only by "literal" isolation in scrolls; the other only by remaining umbilically attached to an unspoken but always immanent tradition. If our Museum of Verbal Art is ever to house a collection truly representative of human diversity, then we its curators must deconstruct the very notion of canon, reach beyond the etymological limitations of *bibliothêkê*, and teach not just texts but also *oimai*. The Internet, with its links, built-in context, and ever-emergent dynamics, offers both an analogue to oral tradition and a blueprint for the new museum wing. We can begin the renovation by helping our students and colleagues understand that art need not inhere only in a text, no matter how polished and gemlike that text may be. In fact, the time is right for such a discussion, given the flourishing of receptionalism, new historicism, and other text-destabilizing approaches that are so much a part of contemporary critical thinking (see Amodio, this volume).

The verbal art of living oral traditions inheres in the instance of performance and in what that performance implies. As for oral-connected traditional texts — and, as we have seen, there are many crucially important works in this category from all over the world — the instructor's responsibility is to help students gauge the extent to which pathways, performance, and traditional referentiality are still applicable when speech acts take on textual form. In either case, the context and referent for the individual performance or text will always lie in large part outside even the most expansive, comprehensive canon, just as they lay beyond the Alexandrian Library and the most ambitious acquisitions program in library history. Homer had it right when, as he entered the fantastic web of the *Odyssey*, he made this petition to a resource undreamed of by the Ptolemies: "Of these events from somewhere, O Muse, daughter of Zeus, speak also to us" (1.10). What events? All of Odysseus's adventures, from boar hunt to Trojan War and back home to the inevitable reunion "inscribed" in the very speech act of *nostos*, or "return." From where? From within that (untextualized) mythic reservoir. By whose agency? Under the aegis of the Muse, patroness of pathways and the traditional internet. And to whom? Why, to Homer, to the beloved tribe of singers and their audiences, and not least to us and our students.

Notes

I gratefully acknowledge the helpful comments contributed by Mark Amodio, Werner Kelber, Walter J. Ong, Brandon Woodruff, and the anonymous reviewers commissioned by the MLA.

1. Indo-European **kanna* develops two reflexes in ancient Greek, κάννη ("reed") and κανών ("rod, ruler"). The first of these, through Latin *canna* ("reed, reed pipe") and Italian *cannone*, yields "cannon," meaning a large tube or barrel and therefore the weapon that fires projectiles. The second, through late Latin *canōn* ("measuring rod, rule, model") and medieval French, eventually produces "canon" in the original (Latin) sense of an ecclesiastical code and eventually a secular code or standard.

2. A welcome exception to this policy is the recent *HarperCollins World Reader*, which includes the chapter "Oral Literature Today" (Caws and Prendergast 2591–655). See also Haring's essay on a "true comparative literature" in this volume.

3. For a history of the rediscovery of oral traditions behind (and alongside) many canonical textual traditions, see Foley, *Theory of Oral Composition*; for an annotated bibliography, Foley, *Oral-Formulaic Theory*, with updates in the journal *Oral Tradition* and online at http://www.missouri. edu/~csottime. On Homer, see esp. Edwards; Foley, "Oral Tradition." For further information on the monuments cited here, see the contributions to this volume by Martin (on Homer), O'Keeffe and Olsen (on *Beowulf*), Vitz (on the *Song of Roland*), Zemke (on the *Poem of the Cid*), Lindahl (on Chaucer), Parthasarathy (on the *Mahabharata*), and Jaffee and Kelber (on the Bible).

4. I am only too aware that the accelerating pace of media evolution promises to make the details of the following description of the Internet obsolete before long. But apart from the time-bound particulars, the fundamental contrast between data and pathways should persist.

5. For an imaginative recasting of the odd and tantalizing shards of evidence about the library, see Canfora. See also El-Abbadi; Nagy, *Homer*, 61–62; Pfeiffer.

6. By a regulation that makes the Library of Congress's policy on mandatory deposit of all books published in the United States seem liberal, Ptolemy I Soter "gave orders that any books on board ships calling at Alexandria were to be copied: the originals were to be kept, and the copies given to their owners. The collection thus acquired was known as the 'ships' collection" (Canfora 20).

7. Records show that as of 300 BCE the Homeric holdings included at least thirteen texts containing readings adopted by men of letters (*kat' andra*), sixty-six anonymous "city" editions (*kata poleis* or *hai politikai*), and fifty-two vulgate (*koinē*) texts (Foley, *Traditional Oral Epic* 24). We should be careful not to indulge in an anachronistic interpretation of these statistics, however. The existence of texts and of specialists who manage them is one thing; a mass readership, or even a technology that

could support such an enterprise, is still many centuries away. Compare the user-unfriendly environment of the library's papyrus scrolls with the similar vellum-based "textual communities" of the Middle Ages (Stock, *Implications*; more generally, Boyarin) and contrast both those textual economies with post-Gutenberg developments and the mass readership created and sustained by the modern paperback book (cf. also O'Donnell).

8. Of special importance here are the fragmentary texts of early Ptolemaic papyri, which show that, even after the editorial labors of Aristarchus and the other Alexandrian scholars, alternate "tellings" were still being created (West 11–13). Compare the variation inherent in alternate performances of South Slavic oral epic (Lord, *Singer of Tales* 30–98; Foley, *Traditional Oral Epic* 158–200, 278–328) and, yet more significant, in the scribal "performances" of Anglo-Saxon poetry (Doane; O'Keeffe; more generally, Zumthor, *Oral Poetry*).

9. Note that the etymological sense of *bibliothêkê* is of a "place" (chest or shelf, from *thêkê*, ultimately *tithêmi*, "put, place") where one keeps *biblia* ("scrolls"). From this fact Canfora argues that the Alexandrian Library "was thus not a library but a shelf, or several shelves, running along one side of the covered walk" (77). If he is correct, this would be another instance of a modern model anachronistically forced back on to an ancient institution, with confounding results (scholars' inability to locate with certainty a separate library building, etc.). It would not, however, affect our understanding of the library as a collection of tangible artifacts.

10. One intriguing example is *Electronic Antiquity*, an international journal devoted to the ancient world and based at the University of Tasmania (ccat.sas.upenn.edu/~awiesner/ea/contents.html).

11. As Werner Kelber put it in a letter responding to a draft of this essay, "What seems to happen with our experience on the Internet is that centuries of text culture begin to take on the dimension of an interlude that was about to separate us from the living pathways of oral and electronic traditions."

12. Of course, we should observe that the individual (or small-group) construction of an Internet site distinguishes the site from an oral traditional work, which is the product of generations as well as of the latest individual performer.

13. In making this claim, I am not ignoring the important contemporary discussion about intertextuality, which for all the integrating, comparative force of its first element, *inter-*, is still concerned most fundamentally with individual texts physically present as items in the Museum of Verbal Art.

14. One of the clearest indications of this cognitive parallax is the concept of "word" (*reč*) among the South Slavic epic singers, who identify nothing smaller than a whole verse line as a word, although they also use the term — in the singular — to designate a speech, a scene, or a whole story.

For them "word" means "unit of utterance" and "speech act" rather than a dictionary entry. (See Foley, *Traditional Oral Epic* 44–50; cf. Zumthor, *Oral Poetry* 51–52, on *mouvance*.)

15. See the essay on ethnopoetics by DuBois, this volume; of related interest is Fine's essay on editing and translating oral traditional works, also this volume. For a comparative perspective on ethnopoetics and its place in a composite theory of oral tradition, see Foley, *Singer* 11–17, 88–90.

16. For an experiment along these lines, consult the multimedia edition of the South Slavic tale *Udovica Jana* collected by Joel Halpern and Barbara Kerewsky-Halpern (Foley and Kerewsky Halpern).

17. Compare Wertheim on the ongoing contributions of cyberspace and virtual reality to solving problems of representation first posed by medieval scholars.

18. Tellingly, it has been the threatened loss of the ability to walk through the conventional library collection, along with doubt over whether a truly reliable search engine would ever be forthcoming, that has given many faculty members pause over the advent of the electronic card catalog.

19. Browsing software is designed to alleviate the necessity of dealing only with addresses, much as a subject search or a CD-ROM bibliographical search enables users of conventional library facilities to find specific materials.

20. For a full account of this phrase in context, see Foley, *Immanent Art* 244–47.

Lee Haring

What Would a True Comparative Literature Look Like?

Deconstruction, writes Jacques Derrida, must, "through a double gesture, a double science, a double writing — put into practice a *reversal* of the classical opposition and a general *displacement* of the system. . . . Deconstruction does not consist in moving from one concept to another, but in reversing and displacing a conceptual order as well as the non-conceptual order with which it is articulated" ("Signature" 195). When discussions of deconstruction employ such abstract language, scholars forget that its reversals and displacements are political moves. Sometimes you can watch deconstruction happen. In 1968, when I was living in Nairobi, Kenya, three members of the Department of English at the University of Nairobi issued a manifesto that effected the abolition of the department and its replacement by a department of literature. Indispensable to the majors' course would be fieldwork and analysis of oral literature (or folklore, as it is usually called in the United States). The issue raised in the Nairobi manifesto, and the debate that ensued on that campus, exposes the fundamental problem of the teaching of literature. What shall be the center, what the periphery, and how shall the relation of one to the other be determined (Ngũgĩ 94)? By placing Africa at the center, the Nairobi rebels reversed the classical opposition between imperial and colonial literatures. Displacing the curricular system can be carried even farther. On the logic of the Nairobi model, if you can let go of cultural nationalism, a world orientation is inescapable. A true comparative literature begins from acknowledging the universal importance of the art of the word in human societies and organizes its studies to explore that importance.

What Is Comparative Literature?

Comparative literature began by feeling its way toward some such acknowledgment, crossing national and linguistic boundaries, insisting that specific comparisons among literary works in French, German, Italian, and English required knowing those languages. Hence its elitism (Bernheimer 42–43). Then the devaluation of language learning in the United States and the excellence of new translations caused comparative literature's elite standing to decline. Now critics annex new territory for comparative literature by drastically questioning the existence of something called literature and the justification for its canon. English and comparative literature departments have generously taken in reader-response criticism, Lacanian psychoanalysis, structuralism, deconstruction, and postmodernism; they have created courses in the literature of previously unrepresented groups. But they should also respond to the more basic challenges to their assumptions. "What is literature?" asks Terry Eagleton as he prepares to dissolve the entire subject of literary studies (1–16). "It is most useful," he says,

> to see "literature" as a name which people give from time to time for different reasons to certain kinds of writing within a whole field of what Michel Foucault has called "discursive practices," and . . . if anything is to be an object of study it is this whole field of practices rather than just those sometimes rather obscurely labelled "literature." (205)

Eagleton's radicalism reaches most students immediately. Instructors, however, wonder what to do with this paradigm of literary training and how to move their students forward.

What of the literary canon—traditionally thought of as a set of works selected for their excellence and enduring qualities? Like the notion of what literature is, a canon must be agreed on. Then literary theory and pedagogy can justify themselves by adopting the canon as their object of study (Eagleton 197). To reinforce the Anglo-American canon, Harold Bloom offers a theory of poetry that is really a way of structuring literary history. In his theory, "strong" poets wrestle with their predecessors; out of their struggle they make poetry. The later poet (say, Wordsworth) produces in his poem (say, the Immortality Ode) a misreading—Bloom's Shakespearean term is "misprision"—of the earlier poet's poem (in this case, Milton's *Lycidas*) (19–45).

Like any myth, Bloom's has very general application. Any critical approach that illuminates the production of one culture is worth examining for the possible transfer of that approach to other cultures. Why not translate Bloom's theory of literary history into questions a critic might ask about the expressive function of literature in any society? What can be told about the literary artist of a society: age, sex, nationality, motive, attitude? How has he or she learned to practice verbal art? Was there a master to learn from? What is the poet's attitude toward what he or she is performing, and what is the poet's attitude toward his or her precursors? What would be different about the performance event or artistic product if the artist were someone else? In the present state of knowledge, most of these questions cannot be answered methodically. They should be the subject matter of criticism and teaching in coming years, especially because they invite application to oral as well as to literary systems.

The philosophical approach called social constructionism asserts that people's social organization, law, religion, and customs owe their authority to a social consensus. That consensus is validated by referral to a higher power (ancestors, gods) and by its unceasing adherence under the name of tradition. Verbal art production occurs because people agree on the rules for production, publication, and appreciation of poetry, drama, or epic. If literature and its canon are, as critics say, only social constructions, what is the pedagogical consequence of unsettling and demystifying literary studies? What follows from François Jost's remark, "international contextualization in literary history and criticism has become a law" (29)? If comparative literature eliminates elitism and periodization, it is left with my title question (which I owe to the Yale anthropologist John F. Szwed): What would a true comparative literature look like?

The theoretical base for comparative literature, as I see it, is neither Marxism nor an amorphous cultural theory, which are both dismissed by Marjorie Perloff (180). The base is commonsense anthropology: certain human practices sufficiently resemble one another to warrant being studied side by side. What follows is a provocative series of questions. Why do people like what they like? How do they go about creating and apprehending it? How do they produce and consume art? What practices have made a set of people attribute value to certain words? Cross-cultural studies confirm the universality of verbal art (Murdock). All societies practice the arts of the word. What is more, they practice verbal art in literary systems, which are complex wholes including artists, audiences, occasions and contexts of performance, referential content of words, evaluation, genres, publication, and a concept of tradition. Why not study literary systems? Using translations and ethnographies, comparative literature can take as its field both oral and written literatures in literary systems around the world.

Commonsense anthropology will have to agree with contemporary criticism that there are no universal or invariant themes, techniques, or devices of literary art, whether oral or written. Each culture operates differently in the realm of verbal art. The essential dimension of the study of all literature is the study of verbal art in its actual occurrence. It is the communication of verbal art among human beings that contains what is important in literary production and consumption, not any supposed universals. Adapting the formulation by Gilles Deleuze and Felix Guattari, we could say that there is no universal or general abstract mechanism that produces verbal art. There are no "invariable or obligatory rules." Instead, there are what Deleuze and Guattari call "abstract machines," which consist of "optional rules that ceaselessly vary with the variation itself, as in a game in which each move changes the rules" (100; see also Deleuze and Parnet). Here is a plausible working assumption: variation is a constant of literary systems. Any system of literary production and consumption is defined not by homogeneity but by "a variability whose characteristics are immanent, continuous, and regulated in a very specific mode" (Deleuze and Guattari 93–94). As an instance of that variability, Stanley Fish argues that communities construct authoritative interpretations of literary texts through a process similar to what the philosopher Richard Rorty calls the social justification of belief (Fish 303–71). Since interpretive communities are people in history, some of them have been observed; their activities of creation and performance, as well as of interpretation, can be discovered (see also Renza).

A Course on Literature and Society

Believing that these considerations from critical theory are perfectly suited to the teaching of a true comparative literature, I initiated a graduate course at Brooklyn College titled Literature and Society. My department gave it that title, by the way, to open the topic to several different teaching approaches. Mine attempts the semantic and stylistic characterization of literary and folkloric systems. Other titles might have been Ethnopoetics (the study of the poetic system of a single community), Comparative Criticism, or Anthropology of Literature (Merriam; Armstrong, *Affecting Presence* and *Powers*). Or, on a de Man model, Poetics, Rhetoric, and the Production of Verbal Art (P. Brooks 99). Prototypes for the course have been created in other fields. One was Barbara Kirshenblatt-Gimblett's survey on speech play; many of her sources are relevant to the course. A second prototype was a cross-cultural study of riddles (a literary form easily neglected by students of high culture) that shows that riddles correlate with training for responsibility and have other significant social functions (Roberts and Forman). A third forerunner of the study of comparative literary systems was the work of Brian Sutton-

Smith in children's play and games (Sutton-Smith and Roberts; Sutton-Smith, Roberts, and Kendon). Perhaps the most imposing prototype of all has been Alan Lomax's map and characterization of musical styles around the world (*Folk Song Style*).

But what about a textbook? Without one, I had to formulate questions that would elicit the rules of production of various societies. Take genre, for example. In a given society, what genres of verbal art are found? Speech, song, story, drama? What are the attitudes toward genre mixing or genre shifting (or is there such a concept)? Questions like these must be asked, because genre systems are entirely socially constructed, qualitative, and subjective. In the words of a leading folklorist, Dan Ben-Amos, "the logical principles that underlie this categorization of oral tradition are those which are meaningful to the members of the group" ("Analytical Categories" 225). One can say the same for any culture. The compilers of the First Folio separated Shakespeare's comedies, histories, and tragedies in the native taxonomy of their period. The genre system is a good place to start. Plenty of information is available (Ben-Amos, *Folklore Genres*; Orsini).

Among other questions I ask my students, about several societies in turn (the questions are adapted from D. Hymes, "Objectives"; Bauman, *Verbal Art*), are questions about the artist:

> What can be told about this person: age, sex, nationality, motive? High status, low status? A special class, or coming from any class? Attitude toward the conditions under which performance or publication takes place? Is the performer also the composer and poet, or is the performer separate from the composer? Life histories of performers or authors? How is performance learned? Who were the performer's models? What is the role of manuscript collections and printed books in the learning process? To what extent and in what ways is the artistic product thought to be related to the artist's personality (e.g., through a concept of creativity)?

Here the most useful course materials come from outside Western culture (Rothenberg and Rothenberg). For example, in her study of an Egyptian *hilali* oral epic poet in performance, Susan Slyomovics precisely observes the details of the performer's socially ambivalent position (*Merchant*). Slyomovics also narrates the phases of her relationship as a Western female to this performing man of a strongly male-dominated culture. Gender issues could be further emphasized through a reading of Regina Harrison's cultural translation of Quechua women's songs.

Related to the place of the artist is the topic of how one learns to be a poet or performer, a pivotal subject in Albert Lord's classic *The Singer of Tales*. I ask my students these questions about performance or publication:

> How is verbal art brought to an audience? What are the rules and variations governing performance or publication? What keys exist to signal that performance is happening (repetition, parallelism, special lexicon or formulae, an appeal to tradition, audience behavior)?

In criticism, much attention has been given to self-referentiality, in studies of the work of John Barth, Italo Calvino, and many other novelists. An essay by Barbara Babcock, "The Story in the Story," provides a way into this topic. Babcock defines *metacommunication* in narrative performance as "any element of communication which calls attention to the speech event as a performance and to the relationship which obtains between the narrator and his audience" (66)—the kind of interruption Thackeray is famous for in *Vanity Fair*. Another term for the device is "metaperformance," those bits of a performance that draw attention to the performance itself. The finest and most detailed explication of metaperformance for students is Gary Gossen's study of the Chamula of Mexico, which also explains their genre system.

I ask my students questions on these topics also:

> Context: What is the scene of the artistic event (a theater, a coffee house, a library)? How would changing the location alter the event? What social and physical factors affect performance?

> Audience: Is the audience physically present or imaginary? Age, sex, nationality? What does an audience do in response to the artistic event? To what extent and in what way is the relation between artist and audience an index of the

associated culture (for example, outcast/majority, servant/ master)? How do performer-hearer relations affect performances of folklore or publication of literature? To what extent and in what ways is verbal art thought to be related to the personality of an audience? What would be different if the audience were different (rewriting of folktales for children, for example)?

Content: What objects or memories does verbal art refer to? To what extent and in what ways is this society's body of verbal art related to the worldview of performers and audiences? To what extent and in what ways is a system of verbal art related to the social structure of those who perform in it and receive it? Are certain genres performed or appreciated only by women or only by men? What is the relation between the customary or expected behavior of the people of the society and the behavior of characters in fiction or myth?

Tradition: In this society, what is the meaning of tradition? How is it preserved, extended, and renewed? What do people do to make poetry or narrative "traditional"? Do they uphold a concept of traditional purity or authenticity?

If these questions are to be answered through discussion and analysis, students will need readings that show how literary or folkloric texts are embedded in their social context. I begin with a discussion of Eagleton's *Literary Theory* and a statement of my principle, that the diversity of artistic systems is an irreplaceable laboratory for an understanding of the nature of verbal art and hence for an understanding of something of the nature of humanity. Sometimes I refer students to Ruth Benedict's introduction to *Zuni Mythology*, because of her attention to variation and to the constraints within which narrators operate.[1]

The first case study that students encounter, by Carol M. Eastman, identifies the poetics of performance in an East African coastal society, examining genre, setting, participants, purposes, the sequence of acts of the communication, the tone or manner in which the communication takes place, its channels and codes, and the norms of interaction and interpretation. Eastman also explains the method she is using: it is the ethnography of speaking developed by Dell Hymes (*Foundations*). Eastman's topic headings can be quickly transposed onto the literary world. For instance, the work of Flaubert can be seen most clearly not as a transhistorical phenomenon but as a production in a literary field, among currents, movements, schools, groups of authors, and norms of interpretation. This is the subject of Pierre Bourdieu's *The Rules of Art*, which graduate students might read. Eastman's essay provides a model for students to use in independent study projects and papers. And the essay, like all the sources I use, presents texts in context.

To ensure continual comparison, I have students read case studies from other non-Western societies (Gossen; K. Basso). Indeed, the account of a literary system that often stimulates them most is James Peacock's study of Indonesian popular drama. Budding playwrights are exhilarated to find that drama is importantly imbricated in the lives of Javanese; one student referred continually to Peacock's book as the course went on. Peacock suggests that the *ludruk* drama influenced Javanese to move away from older life patterns and toward modernization. He concretely shows the ways in which an artistic system, like a language, is "a cultural way of communicating about much, but not all, of the culture" (D. Hymes, "Objectives" 281). Moreover, students observe that universal authors are not universal. In Indonesia, there is no parallel to Shakespearean drama, and Euramerican culture has no parallel to the *wajang kulit* of Indonesia.[2]

After this discussion of a performed genre, I present the general theory of folklore and literature as performance (Bauman, *Verbal Art* 3–58), with references to more detailed studies (Falassi; Cosentino, *Maids*; A. Burns; Glassie, *Passing*). Richard Bauman gives a list of the means whereby people know that performance is taking place — a list that transposes nicely onto as much of the literary world as any student or instructor knows. These means include figurative language and parallelism; special paralinguistic features, formulas, and codes; an appeal to tradition; and a disclaimer of performance. Once the general framework is clear, a case study based on performance should come next. Unfortunately, Roger Abrahams's typology of speech acts and performance events in the West Indies (*Man-of-Words*) has been allowed to go out of print. Equally commanding, however, is Charles Briggs's ethnographic account of traditions of discourse in a New Mexican society (*Competence*). By explaining the relation between people's competence and the genres they choose to perform, Briggs helps students understand how verbal art comes into existence.

Having both a special personal interest in Africa and numerous students of African background, at this point I focus on African performances (Slyomovics, *Merchant*) and genres (Scheub, "Review"). Another instructor might make a different choice. The most challenging ethnography I have assigned is Steven Feld's account of the connections among environmental facts, sounds of nature, and social relations among the few hundred human beings of a face-to-face society in Papua New Guinea (*Sound*). These domains, totally separate for a Westerner, are interwoven in Kaluli thinking. In Feld's presentation, structuralist anthropology is an invitation to bring nature and culture together and study the contexts of artistic expression. Thus an important topic in criticism is revealed, and playing Feld's field recordings (*Kaluli*) in class is a revelation.

Now it is time to bring students' attention back to the West (though comparison has never stopped). Raymond Williams, writing in *The Long Revolution* of British culture and literature from the industrial age to the 1960s, proposes the concept of the "structure of feeling" — an inherently social domain of life comprising experience, feeling, and "the personal." He shows that literature is visibly affected "by the nature of the communication system and by the changing character of audiences" (241). Some new historicist criticism explores this domain (Armstrong and Tennenhouse). After seeing the juxtaposition of African folktale performance, Indonesian popular theater, Egyptian epic performance, and industrial Western society, a student understands the structure of feeling better than Williams explains it. And Williams's passionate assertion of the universality of creativity is a constant inspiration.

For examination questions, I prefer the most naive: Are the genres of verbal art the same in all societies? Kafka's "Metamorphosis" portrays the alienation of an artist; does the artist everywhere have to be alienated? Compare audience behavior in two societies we read about.

For paper topics, I have suggested examining (1) what distinguishes verse from prose in Native American literature as compared with standard Anglo-American literature (D. Hymes, *"In Vain"*;

Tedlock, *Spoken Word*); (2) audience behavior in Caribbean and African performances (Abrahams, *Man-of-Words*; Ricard; Seitel); (3) epic performance in Egypt today (Slyomovics, *Merchant*) and in 1930s Yugoslavia, with a glance at Homer (Lord, *Singer of Tales*; Foley, *Singer*); and (4) the contrast between the genre system in Chamula (Gossen) and in Saint Vincent (Abrahams, *Man-of-Words*). Students have invented more adventuresome topics: oral and "literary" literature in Guyana; oral literature of Native Americans; the emergence of Black English in literature; the Harlem Renaissance seen through the concepts of Raymond Williams; the arrival of harmony in Western music between the fourteenth and sixteenth centuries, as seen through concepts of Max Weber; Tibetan lamaism as performance; Q. D. Leavis versus Raymond Williams on the reading public in nineteenth-century Britain; an ethnography of speaking in slave narratives; praise poetry in Africa and the African-American blues song as contrastive kinds of social commentary. The variety of these topics reminds us that "the slightest exercises in bringing together two literatures, two authors, or two documents of literature (perhaps even two passages, such as Gonzalo's pillaged lines from Montaigne's essays in *The Tempest*) demand acceptance as comparatism" (Clements 21).

The course Literature and Society, then, responds to fundamental questions of literary theory with a world orientation, within the constraints of what is teachable. Its approach can settle, with facts, some vague assertions of literary theorists, for example, the denials that women ever practice a distinctive dialect (cited by Higonnet in Bernheimer 161) or find an audience for their distinctive artforms (Spivak 241–68). I admit I know no one qualified to teach the course, but experimentation with it will ensure learning. What difference does this approach make to curricula and student experience? It makes two marginal academic fields, comparative literature and folklore, central to the study of verbal art. It turns students and instructors into what Willfried Feuser calls compulsive poachers. "Border transgressions and forays into uncharted lands," Feuser writes, "are in fact the essence of [comparatists'] calling, which is the discovery and constant renewal of cultural relativism in literature"

(380). And, having a world orientation, comparatism retains the terms in which cultures comprehend their own symbol systems. On that principle, not only graduate students but also undergraduate and high school students can experience as vividly as possible the diversity of artistic systems.

Notes

Thanks to Nancy B. Black and John Miles Foley for advising me on this essay.

1. Once, it seemed useful to have a session on cultural relativism (see Spiro) and discuss readings by Lomax ("Appeal"), Geertz (*Interpretation* 33–64 and *Knowledge* 55–70), and older anthropologists (Herskovits 61–78; Kluckhohn and Kelly; Bidney 423–29). In retrospect, that session, and indeed the whole course, had more to say about cultural diversity than about relativism.
2. I add relevant writings on drama by Artaud, Kirby, and Schechner (Rothenberg and Rothenberg 235–40, 257–69, 311–24), Abrahams's survey of folk drama ("Folk Drama"), and studies of mumming by Glassie (*Silver*) and Handelman.

Katherine O'Brien O'Keeffe

The Performing Body on the Oral-Literate Continuum: Old English Poetry

Until fairly recently, scholarship on oral traditional poetry has emphasized the circumstances of composition — the singer-poet's competence, deployment of theme or type-scene, and mastery of formula and formulaic system. Such emphasis was necessary in the early history of the argument: those advancing the Parry-Lord hypothesis for Homeric texts (and later for medieval texts) had to argue, against current belief, that these texts in manuscript not only *could* have been oral in their origin but actually *had* to have been. In these arguments, the focus on competence stemmed from the need to demonstrate that in an oral tradition the illiterate singer composed his piece as he sang it. As a result, performance and its significance were subsumed under composition.[1] Present work on oral traditional poetry has moved away from this strong version of the oral traditional hypothesis to consider the survival and function of oral traditional texts in cultures where various forms of orality and literacy coexist. Concomitant with this move has been a renewed interest in performance, particularly in the ways performance (as a collaboration between performer and audience) mediates the reception of the oral traditional work. Since the study of reception and performance is always historically specific, my essay examines the nature of performance as it has been studied, and as it may be pursued, within the corpus of Old English (OE) poetic texts.

In modern American culture, ceremonies, commands, plays, and music are all brought into being by performance. The performer of an action makes something happen, something that exists theoretically apart from the performer but that requires the performer's action to be fully realized (see Bauman and Braid, this volume). A ready illustration is the ceremony to inaugurate the president. The ceremony itself is a tradition, existing apart from the participants, but their enacting of it is a unique event that changes the status of the person taking the oath. In this performance, the principals and the audience work together to produce the effect of the ceremony — those on the platform by their words and their bodily gestures, those in the audience by their witness to and approval of the enactment.

Our experience of concerts or the theater offers another venue in which we recognize the efficacy of performance. A piece of music (whether classical or rock) or a play exists apart as a score or a script and becomes realized uniquely only in the event of performance. No two performances are identical. The crucial elements of performance, then, are a preexisting "text," a set of expectations, an individual whose task is to bring the text to life, and an audience who witness and approve (or disapprove). Modern texts are often marked to indicate some crucial elements in performance. Such directions attempt to compensate for what is missing from these written texts — the performing body that makes them live. But what about texts whose traditional communities are long dead? Can any notion of performance be recovered for them? In what way is the idea of performance important to understanding them?

Background

Performance has always assumed some role in modern investigations into the earliest English poetry, though it has not always figured prominently. When in the sixth edition of *The History of the Anglo-Saxons* (1836) Sharon Turner imagined the circumstances of Anglo-Saxon social life, he painted the people a convivial lot: "They loved the pleasures of the table. . . . At their cheerful meetings it was the practice for all to sing in turn" (58). Song had its professionals even in those days, and Turner distinguished between the performance of "bards" ("rude exclamations of a rude people, with a rude language, greeting their chieftains. . . . The bards . . . retained and appropriated [the old rude style] because more instrumental to their professional advantages" [274]) and that of "ambulatory glee-men" who "at one time . . . tumbled and danced, showed their bears, and frolicked before the people in the dresses of various animals, at others they may have told little tales to interest the mob, from whose liberality they drew their maintenance" (285). There is little in such an account that today we could verify as "factual," but such notions with various nuances would persist. To describe the activities of a Germanic household, Francis Gummere used *Beowulf* as his source, from which he drew his picture of communal performance, where a heroic deed might be "sung amid the enthusiasm of the warriors and their guests, with shouts of applause and remembered delight of battle, with copious flowings of the ale" (114).

Unfortunately, we have little solid information about the physical circumstances under which singers performed OE poetry. A number of disapproving references in Latin refer particularly to monastic entertainments. Few passages in OE poetry itself reflect the activity of the traditional poet, but even these are extraordinarily difficult to interpret. In *Widsith*, an OE catalog poem, a scop (singer) recounts his travels and fate as an itinerant performer:

> And then Ealhhild, Eadwine's daughter, the queen of the people, gave me another [gift]. Her praise extended through many lands, whenever I was to say in song where below the sky I best knew a queen ornate with gold, bestowing gifts. Whenever Scilling and I with clear eloquence upraised a song before our victorious lord and my voice rang out melodiously and loud to the lyre, then many people high-mettled of mind, those who were well informed, have said they never heard better singing. (Bradley 339; *Widsith*, lines 97–108)

In Widsith's account, the poet's task is to praise the powerful in song accompanied by a harp. But Widsith tells of travels to an impossible number of lands and courts, impossible both geographically and chronologically, and it is difficult to take the elements of his account as good social history. *Beowulf*, too, offers tantalizing glimpses of performance.[2] At the completion of the great hall Heorot, a poet sings of creation (Klaeber, lines 86–92; Donaldson 3) and sings at other points in the story; after the fight with Grendel, Danish warriors ride to the mere on horseback, and one of their number commemorates Beowulf's deeds and those of the Germanic hero Sigemund (Klaeber, lines 864–915; Donaldson 16). Whether his performance (obviously given on horseback) was in prose or verse, accompanied by a harp or not, is a continuing matter of dispute. Beowulf's report to Higelac of his triumphs at Heorot include mention of *gomela scilding*, either *the* old Scylding (i.e., Hrothgar himself) or *an* old Scylding (someone else, perhaps his scop) performing to the accompaniment of a harp (Klaeber, lines 2101–14; Donaldson 37). There are other mentions.

Interpreting these references is fraught with danger: the passages are often allusive, assuming the contemporary audience's knowledge of the activity; specific words or expressions are on occasion highly ambiguous, admitting mutually exclusive interpretations. OE verse is poetry, not social history as such; it represents rather than reflects the society it portrays. One important work that has interrogated the available evidence for the practices of oral performance in OE is Jeff Opland's *Anglo-Saxon Oral Poetry*. Opland constructs his argument from an array of evidence — from the poetry itself, from contemporary references, from Latin writers' descriptions of Germanic custom, and by analogy with the practice of modern Xhosa and Zulu traditional poets. He works from the presupposition that there were two types of performers: a scop, who was a praise poet attached to an individual king, and a *gleoman*, who was an itinerant performer who accompanied himself on a harp. While Opland adduces a number of references in both Latin and OE prose to suggest that the scop was a respected performer and the *gleoman* rather disreputable, both *Beowulf* (1160a) and *Widsith* (136a) use *gleoman* in a completely neutral context. Opland's book is valuable because it carefully examines the evidence in the light of modern research into oral traditional poetry. Nonetheless, a century and a half after Sharon Turner's sketch, we are still not much farther advanced in obtaining a picture of OE performance.

Opland's work was aimed at historical reconstruction, amassing and interpreting whatever evidence was available to build a picture of the social circumstances of the earliest poetry in Anglo-Saxon England. But as he admits, the evidence is fragmentary and at times contradictory. The fictions of OE poetry—especially the nostalgia that marks *Beowulf* or the antiquarianism that marks *Widsith*—are awkward supports for descriptions of actual social behavior among Anglo-Saxons of whatever period. The poetic traditions that have been offered as analogies to OE poetry—most frequently, those of the Muslim singers of the former Yugoslavia and, in Opland's book, those of the Xhosa and Zulu praise poets—are living oral traditions. Most scholars agree that the body of Old English poetry surviving is oral-derived, not oral (Foley, *Traditional Oral Epic* 5–8). This refinement of definition indicates that lying behind the poetry is an oral tradition from which the poetry draws its language, much of its style, and habits of thought. Though we cannot hope to assess the historical particulars of performance in the oral tradition that lies behind the manuscripts of OE poetry, it is still possible and profitable to discuss the poetry in relation to performance.

Current Approaches

Starting in the 1980s, a more productive approach to performance in an oral context has been developed, particularly by Paul Zumthor in his work on Old French narratives. In "The Text and the Voice," Zumthor makes a number of claims whose implications must interest us. "The question of 'orality' in the *chansons de geste* or in any other poetic genre can . . . be raised only in terms of *performance*, not of origin. . . . 'Orality' is the historical authenticity of a voice" (67, 69). In such claims, the text in performance is vocalized, and voice and gesture are what move the audience. Zumthor's approach "*consider[s] on principle every text* earlier than the thirteenth century . . . *as a dance*" (89). Subsequently, in *La lettre et la voix*, Zumthor explains *vocalité* as "l'aspect corporel des textes médiévaux, leur mode d'éxistence en tante qu'objets de perception sensorielle" (21; "the bodily aspect of medieval texts, their mode of existence *qua* objects of sensory perception" [my trans.]).

In forefronting vocal and physical performance in the production of medieval texts, Zumthor of necessity restricts his field of inquiry to gesturing, singing, chanting, and acting (*La lettre*, ch. 11), modes of performance that are of little analytic help to students of early English texts. By focusing on the performing body, Zumthor attempts to evade both the putative oral-literate dichotomy and the asserted dominance of the textual over the oral in surviving written evidence. This maneuver produces a valuable corrective to previous assumptions that a work, when written, is "fixed," "dead," in short, "textual." However, there are consequences to this maneuver that remain to be explored.

In his emphasis on vocality, Zumthor replaces an essentialist reading (which says that whatever exists in writing is textual in its essence) with a different totalizing one. When he redefines a work composed before 1300 as "vocalized" (regardless of the work's written or oral origins), he divorces it from the page and claims it as the province of the body by way of performance. Hence his emphasis on the dance and on the work as object of sensory perception. In this reading, the textual is an object, the oral (or the vocalized) an event. Despite his concession to Derrida of the possibility of arche-writing even in purely oral works ("Text" 69; see Derrida, *Of Grammatology* 56–62), Zumthor's reading of the early medieval work through vocality is a deliberate move to reclaim presence for the vocalized work by focusing on the evanescence of the event in performance. In his emphasis on the affective elements of performance, the vanished meaning of an early medieval work, forever beyond our grasp, lies in the effect of the performer's body on the audience. Zumthor's consideration of the body is, however, secondary to his efforts to carve out an unbreachable territory for the oral as opposed to the textual.

In the concept of performance Zumthor claims the body for

orality in the name of the speaking voice, a strategy that both defines the dominant site of *vocalité* (the mouth) and extends it. But performance is more multifaceted than Zumthor's argument will allow, and in the following argument I examine the emergence of the body in two further metonyms—the hand and the text. The role of the body lies in the realm of the production of the text: in Zumthor's formulation what is uniquely oral is a performer's bodily mediation of the text, a mediation that produces meaning. But in an early written tradition (here the corpus of surviving OE texts), the scribe's body also mediates the production of a text. Zumthor's silent erasure of the scribe diminishes the rich complexity of performance on the oral-literate continuum.

John Miles Foley attempts to recuperate performance from another direction in an approach to the meaning of the oral traditional text that draws on reception theory and the ethnography of speaking. His extension of the concept of performance asks not just what but how words mean. In *Immanent Art* he examines the ways an oral traditional text works through traditional referentiality. Traditional referentiality "entails the invoking of a context that is enormously larger and more echoic than the text or work itself, that brings the lifeblood of generations of poems and performances to the individual performance or text. . . . Such a process of generating meaning I call *metonymy*, designating a mode of signification wherein the part stands for the whole" (7). Foley takes this line of thought further in *The Singer of Tales in Performance*, arguing that meaning is inherent in oral traditional texts, that each instantiation of an oral or oral-derived text calls on the larger tradition, and the metonymic meaning of the text is encoded in a particular register (82). For oral texts, performance is the enabling event. But Foley goes on to argue that for oral-derived texts we must look to the performance arena, "the place wherein the expansion of nominal metonymic integer to ambient traditional meaning is not only a possible but a prescribed mode of interpretation" (48). In this definition, the performance arena is a "dedicated forum" (49) where the audience, steeped in the tradition, may interpret the immanent meaning. And the elements of the register that trigger the audience's appeal to the tradition include archaisms (for

OE, the poetic lexicon), special codes, figurative language, parallel-ism, and special formulas (82–92).

Foley, shifting the attention away from the moment of bodily actions that engender traditional performance, develops "perfor-mance" as an interpretive concept: the power of the performance arena derives from the tradition of bodily performance. Writing does not alienate a text from traditional meaning immediately—early written texts will still appeal to immanent meaning despite their writ-ten condition. And the elements of the register in oral-derived texts provide us some limited access to the traditional meaning of these texts: "No, the manuscripts are not performances, not experiences; but yes, they do retain not only the mere linguistic integers that constituted the meaning-laden idiom of the actual events in oral tra-dition, but, even more crucially, the implied array of associative metonymic signification which that medium or register was uniquely licensed to convey" (292).

Foley is correct that a manuscript is not a performance, if our understanding of *performance* is limited to the discrete bodily media-tion of a text by a singer before an audience. However, if we extend his concept of performance arena to include the manuscript itself (the crucial medium for oral-derived texts), we must include the scribe whose bodily performance makes the manuscript possible and pro-duces the event of the text. Indeed, a consideration of performance requires us to look not merely at performing mouths but also at per-forming hands and performing texts. The key to performance is the bodily event. In the interrogation of performance on the oral-literate continuum, in the attempt to understand its role in the creation of meaning in a setting where oral and literate folkways meet, it is as distorting to privilege one mode (orality) as the other (literacy). Pre-cisely because purely oral medieval texts cannot be recovered, we cannot afford to regard surviving manuscript texts as mere damaged incarnations. In fact, for the very reasons that Foley suggests that we may interpret these texts through a performance arena, we should be able to read, through these texts, the body in various stages of performance. For truly oral-derived texts, each manuscript instanti-ation is an event whose performance has drawn on the immanent tradition lying behind the manuscript.[3] And the performer is the scribe who has written it. Our focus therefore cannot be solely on the body of the singer; rather, in a culture with a substantial oral-literate mix, we must look at two other performing bodies, the body of the scribe and the body of the text.

Scribal Performance

For scribal performance the audience is deferred in time and space. If the communal intimacy of purely oral tradition is absent, the scribe's performance nonetheless may be characterized as an event by its unique evocation of the tradition in the circumstances of its copying. When scribes complain about their task, they often do so in terms of the bodily effect it has on them. The scribe of London, British Library, Royal 6 A. vi, an English manuscript of the early eleventh century, copies a traditional complaint about how little the trouble in writing is recognized: "Three fingers write, the whole body labors. / Whoever does not know how to write thinks it is no labor" (*Colophons*, item 23,684; my trans.). An eighth-century scribe enumerates with visceral particularity the bodily consequences of his art: "Who does not know how to write thinks this is no labor. Oh how grievous writing is: it oppresses the eyes, weakens the kidneys, and at the same time afflicts all the limbs. Three fingers write, the whole body labors" (*Colophons*, item 13,323; my trans.). Implied in these complaints is the realization that the oral performer may be seen to work — singing, gesturing, moving — but the scribe's body, though silent and (effectively) invisible, is also wholly involved in the task at hand. When these scribes complain that those who do not understand writing cannot comprehend the physical toll writing takes, they invite us to consider the hand as equal to the mouth in mediating oral-derived texts. Their colophons elegantly connect for us mouth, hand, and text.

A number of facsimiles illustrates graphically that each manuscript is both performance and event. The volumes of the Early English Manuscripts in Facsimile series provide large-scale facsimiles of whole manuscripts. Their plates make it easy to illustrate the uniqueness of each instantiation of a text in formatting, spacing of words, punctuation, choice of script, and amount of information a contemporary reader had to bring to each page. For *Widsith* and the OE riddles the only facsimile is *The Exeter Book of Old English Poetry* (Chambers et al.), though it is not widely available. For *Beowulf* the circumstances are quite different. Facsimiles of the complete manuscript have been edited by Kemp Malone and by Julius Zupitza. The latter facsimile, though printed on a small scale, is readily found in most college libraries. For those with access to the Internet, the *Labyrinth* offers stunning images of a variety of manuscript pages from *Beowulf* and other poems.[4] The texture of these pages offers the interested reader an unmatched glimpse at scribal performance. There modern readers can see the text as an object, examine the scribe's strategies in dealing with holes in the vellum, with problems with space, and with corrections (by erasure, expunctuation, and insertion). They may also begin to see both the difficulties confronting a medieval reader and the unkindnesses of time to the manuscript itself. The images of the manuscript event make a useful counterpoint to the poem's own accounts of textual performance discussed above.

Performing Texts

In the early study of oral traditional verse, narrative poetry dominated scholarly attention. In OE, however, this genre gives us little direct help in understanding performance. If we turn to somewhat humbler kinds of verse, for example OE charms, we find for some of them rudimentary directions for their performance. The charm "Æcerbot" ("For Unfruitful Land"; Storms 173) gives lengthy directions for performing the charm, involving the removal of pieces of turf from the field, the recitation of formulas and prayers, the bringing of the turf to church, and so on. The occasion for the performance of this charm thus crosses ceremony and poetry, and efficacy in performance of the charm relies not merely on the power of the words but also on the correct physical enactment of the directions. Similarly, "Wiþ Dweorh" ("Against a Dwarf") has explicit prose instructions for preparations and for the way the charm is to be recited for the afflicted person:

> One must take little wafers, such as are used in worship, and write these names on each wafer: Maximianus, Malchus, Johannes, Martimianus, Dionisius, Constantinus, Serafion.
>
> Then the charm that is mentioned hereafter must be sung, first into the left ear then into the right ear, then over the crown of the man's head.
>
> And then let a virgin go then to him and hang it on his neck. And do so for three days. He will soon be better.
>
> (Storms 167)

The performance of this charm combines oral and literate elements, reminding us not simply of the coexistence of orality and literacy but also of their complicated interactions. The charm's implication in the world of writing is not limited to its having been copied into London, British Library, Harley 585, though even in its copied state the directions refer to the charm set out in the manuscript as "mentioned" (the Old English is *cwæð* ["said" rather than "written" or "copied"]. But the writing of the names is part of the charm, which relies equally on three modes of bodily performance: singing, writing, and ritual action. The meaning of the charm (substantially resident in its action) thus lies in the world of performance, where iteration and gesture are the efficient cause, a world that crosses mouths, hands, and texts. The charms in Godfrid Storms's edition offer much scope for exploring the function of performance in the creation of meaning.

The charms, in both prose and verse, are a body of texts that offer directions for their performance. And while scribes may appear to produce their effects without bodies, certain poems, in the absence of performers, draw on the tradition ironically, and delightfully, to perform themselves. These are talking-object poems, most notably the OE riddles of *The Exeter Book*. The riddles often speak directly to the reader of the text, as in this example, "Shield":

> I am one on my own, wounded by weapon of iron, scarred by sword, wearied from the actions of the fray, exhausted from the edges of the blade. Often I see battle and fight the

foe. . . . Never have I been able to find in town the kind of physician that has healed with herbs my wounds; instead, the sword-gashes upon me grow bigger through mortal blows by day and by night. (Bradley 372)

The object, speaking in the first person, describes its various characteristics and asks the reader to identify its name. The misdirection of the speaking text suggests that the "I" is a human being instead of a shield. Similarly, the riddle "Gospel-Book" challenges the reader to identify it after a series of misdirections:

A certain enemy robbed me of life, took from me my mortal powers, then doused me and immersed me in water, took me out again, and set me in the sun where I was violently despoiled of the hairs that I had. Then a hard knife's edge dissected me, buffed clean of blemishes. Fingers folded me and the bird's delight [i.e., the quill] repeatedly made tracks across me with lucky droppings. . . . If the children of men are willing to make use of me, they will be the healthier and surer of victory, the bolder in their hearts and the blither of mind and the wiser in spirit. . . . Inquire what I am called, a thing of advantage to people. My name is renowned, and I myself am bountiful to men, and holy. (Bradley 374)

Here the misdirection is the information that the "I" began its life with the death of the body from whose skin the gospel book's parchment would be made. Does the "I" refer to the animal, now dead, or to the book, for which dousing would spell death? Such first-person addresses draw on oral traditional performance in which the performer becomes the character the performer embodies. But in the speaking book riddles (and even more particularly in the OE Metrical Prefaces), the division of the subject engendered by a text that performs itself asks further investigation of the performing body. Broadening the scope of performance to include hands and texts as well as mouths helps us to see that traditional works are not imprisoned in their manuscripts; they are embodied in them.

Notes

1. See, for example, Lord, *Singer of Tales* 14, 16, 25, where performance fades before a discussion of the training of an apprentice *guslar* ("singer").

2. For ideas on various aspects of teaching *Beowulf*, see Bessinger and Yeager; for special reference to oral tradition, see the essay by Olsen, this volume.

3. On the influence of oral traditional formulas in the copying of OE verse, see O'Keeffe, especially 40–41, 190–94.

4. These are available at http://www.georgetown.edu/labyrinth/library/oe/oe.html.

Elizabeth C. Fine

Leading Proteus Captive: Editing and Translating Oral Tradition

Imagine trying to catch the Greek god Proteus, who shifts his form in myriad ways, from bird to horse to crashing ocean waves. Once grasped, he would free himself by changing shape. It is no less difficult to capture oral tradition and preserve it in print for others to read. For like the mythical Proteus, each teller and each performance change the shape and texture of a story. Variations in tellers, audiences, plot, words, rhythm, facial expressions, gestures, and vocal tone all work together to make the telling of even a fixed and traditional text a unique, lively, and ephemeral event. When one compares the static, two-dimensional, visual, and linear nature of print to the multisensory nature of a live performance of verbal art, then one can begin to appreciate how difficult it is to capture an oral tradition in print.

Just as a map is not the territory it represents and is not always a satisfactory guide, neither is a printed text necessarily a satisfactory or even competent representation of an oral tradition. What students might assume are accurate records of oral traditions may in fact be

59

paraphrases, rewritten versions, or simple reports about a storytelling event. A good printed text is a record of performance or, to use a more illuminating word, a translation of the performance to a different medium, that of print. Helping students understand how folklorists have chosen to translate oral traditions into print is a first and critical step in helping them appreciate and understand verbal art. After assessing the history of text making in the United States, I examine some principles for translating oral traditional performances to print.

History of Text Making

When the American Folklore Society formed in 1888, it brought together different groups of scholars with different interests in oral traditions. Ethnologists were interested in the myths and lore of American Indians, writers and historians were searching for a distinctive American culture, and international literary-comparative folklorists were tracing the diffusion of tradition from the Old World to the New World (Bauman and Abrahams 361–62).[1] These scholars had different ideas about what oral tradition was and how it should be recorded in print; they formed two camps, the anthropological and the literary. The literary folklorists, following the accepted nineteenth-century European definition of folklore as the "unwritten popular traditions of civilized countries" (Dundes, "American Concept" 228), wanted to restrict oral tradition studies to American immigrants. The anthropological folklorists, including William W. Newell, the founder of the American Folklore Society, wanted to include the traditions of the American Indians.

Under Newell's leadership, the society defined folklore broadly as "oral tradition — information and belief handed down from generation to generation without the use of writing" (Dundes 229). The definition included American Indian traditions and thus incorporated anthropological approaches into the study of American folklore. The anthropological folklorists dominated folklore studies from 1888 to the mid-1930s, when their interest shifted to more abstract questions of function. In the late 1930s, literary folklorists came to dominate the field but showed a growing appreciation of anthropological methods. From the 1940s on, a number of intellectual influences broke down the boundaries between these two branches and eventually led to the performance approach, which called new attention to the need for texts that would better record the context and performance style of oral traditions (see Bauman and Braid, this volume).

The Ethnolinguistic Model of the Text

In general, texts published by American anthropological folklorists follow an ethnolinguistic model. This type of text serves as an accurate, verbatim transcript of discourse that aids in linguistic analysis of native languages and records vanishing cultural traditions. The early texts conveyed little if any information about the informant, setting, or cultural significance of the tale. Nor did they record many nonverbal performance features. Since such texts were frequently collected through the dictation process (before the advent of recording equipment) and through a translator, they represent more a report to an outsider than a traditional cultural performance in a native context. The basic format for the ethnolinguistic text was established by two leaders in early American anthropology, John Wesley Powell and Franz Boas.

The hallmark of the ethnolinguistic text is the use of multiple, serial translations of the same performance. The *First Annual Report of the Bureau of American Ethnology* (1879–80) includes "Illustration of the Method of Recording Indian Languages," by J. O. Dorsey, A. S. Gatschet, and S. R. Riggs. This article recommends printing three different versions of a text: the native language transcription, an interlinear translation, and a free translation, in which the text is presented in standard English. The native and interlinear versions would be useful in linguistic research, while the free version would provide a more accessible record of cultural traditions.

Folklorists working in the ethnolinguistic tradition have produced texts of widely differing quality, depending on the text maker's recording techniques, knowledge of the language, and interest in and appreciation of the aesthetic features of a performance. In the 1880s, Garrick Mallery pioneered the use of phonographs and cameras to record nonverbal features in an effort to understand the sign language of American Indians. In the early 1900s, in *Wishram Texts*, Edward Sapir recorded whispered phrases, very high-pitched sounds, and some gestures, and he occasionally described performance style, within parentheses, in the native language transcription. In the 1930s, the British anthropologist Bronislaw Malinowski argued passionately for recording more performance and contextual features, realizing that "ambiguity and confusion appear when we project words on paper after having torn them out of their context" (*Gardens* 36). Malinowski thought that the ideal study of language in context should use a complete sound and film recording of the speaking situation.

Two anthropological folklorists, Ruth Bunzel and Ruth Benedict, recorded Zuni Indian oral traditions in the 1920s.[2] Both worked with the same narrator, Nick, who told "Deer Boy," a tale about an abandoned infant who is raised by deer and later captured and returned to his village.[3] But although both Benedict and Bunzel recorded "Deer Boy" from the same narrator, Benedict's version, collected in 1923, is shorter and stylistically less elaborate. For this 1923 performance Nick narrated the tale in English rather than in his native language, so many of the stylistic features common in Zuni fictional tales were probably eliminated. No ideophones or sound effects, opening or closing formulas, or archaic greeting interchanges occur in this version. Dialogue is sparse, and there is little of the four-patterning (repetition of a feature four times) that Nick so skillfully uses in the version collected by Bunzel. The English translation is particularly flat; the sentences are short and jerky, and not one exclamation point appears to mark an exciting passage. Here is a sample:

> The only deer they saw were the mother deer and her two fawns. The people ran after them, but they could not overtake them. All the horses were worn out except those of the

four uncles. When only his uncles were left in the chase, the little boy no longer ran fast. The uncles killed the three deer; the rest of the people only killed rabbits. So all the deer went to that house. The eldest took the little boy captive.

(Benedict, *Zuni* 2:18)

In contrast to this stylistically barren text, Bunzel's version is much richer. Although Bunzel also used dictation to record the tale, it does not seem to have interfered greatly with a dramatic performance. Nick did his own translating, and another informant aided with the revision of the text. Without doubt, having Nick narrate in Zuni rather than in English accounts for the stylistic superiority of this performance and text. Bunzel's text retains the opening and closing formulas, archaic greeting interchanges and ideophones, specific place-names, and four-patterning—all of which are characteristic genre markings of *telapnaawe*, the Zuni category for fictional tales. Consider this selection from the second version:

They went one by one on one side and one by one on the other side, and so made a circle. After they had made a circle they closed in towards the east. He came to White Rocks. There he turned around and came back. He went by Yellow Rocks. He went along. He came to Black Rocks. Here the people's horses got tired. They were tired and now the boy was far ahead. He went on. He came to where the pine trees were standing and here the people's horses were really used up. The boy turned around. His uncle mounted on the white horse was far ahead. And another uncle mounted on a bay horse was also far ahead. Then the boy made out that he was tired, but he just pretended. One of his uncles caught his mother, and another caught his sister, and another caught his brother. The boy alone came almost to the woods. There his uncle jumped down and ran after him. He ran after him and caught up with him and threw his arms around him. As he clasped him in his arms he struggled. "Oh dear, my boy, stand still, whoever you may be," he said to him. But he did not speak. He just looked into his eyes. Then the people came there. They caught him.

(Bunzel 108–09)

The Literary Model of the Text

The dominant historical orientation of the literary folklorists led to a text model that neglected to record many contextual or nonverbal performance features. The literary model, assimilating the medium and qualities of performance into the conventional form of literature, takes two forms, scholarly and popularized. In 1945–46, the American Folklore Society reviewed the state of folklore research in America. Assessing the quality of the literary text collections in 1947, Herbert Halpert found that these scholarly compendia followed an "unfortunate publishing practice" influenced by "the now outmoded view that folklore consisted only of 'survivals.'" Many of the collections were arranged "in tabular form with annotation but little comment." Folk beliefs were printed in a "numerical listing in colorless terms, occasionally with a few references in footnotes to other parallels." Accuracy was not common, nor was a discussion of the meaning or function of beliefs and tales (Halpert 359–60).

As an alternative to bare, dry, scholarly texts, many folklorists popularized their texts, rewriting tales to add more life. Not only literary but also anthropological folklorists such as Frank Cushing published versions adapted to the tastes, values, and conventions of the mass reading public. These rewritten tales, however, obscured and distorted the stylistic features of the original performance. In the same 1947 review, Halpert also criticized popularized collections for handicapping scholarly research.

Cushing's 1901 publication of *Zuñi Folk Tales* contains a version of "Deer Boy" that follows the literary model. No information appears about the storyteller or performance situation, and Cushing may have attempted to popularize the tale by altering certain details to suit the moral tastes of his audience. The most striking alteration is his treatment of the impregnation incident. In all other versions that mention the magical impregnation of the priest's daughter, the act simply occurs, with no motive given. But Cushing says that the "Sun loved her exceedingly," and, changing into a "glorious youth, . . . he looked upon her gently and lovingly; she looked upon him not fearfully; and so it came about that she loved him and he loved her, and he won her to be his wife" (132). Cushing also seems to have tampered editorially with the deer-hunt incident. In the four other versions in which deer are slain, both the twin fawns and the mother deer are killed. But Cushing says the uncle and sons "merely caught" the mother deer and let her go, observing, "Faithful to the last has she been to this youth" (143). Since Zuni tradition holds that slain deer, if ritually treated, will live again and since even in Cushing's tale the kachinas tell the deer that after the deer's death the deer will sport "ever-living" (141), sparing the mother deer's life seems out of place.

The Performance-Centered Model of the Text

Beginning in the 1930s, a number of intellectual forces began to bring anthropological and literary folklorists together in a common effort to record the context and aesthetic style of oral traditions. The contributions of the Prague school of linguistics, Milman Parry and Albert Lord's oral-formulaic theory, the ethnography of speaking and ethnopoetics in the 1960s, the performance approach in folklore studies, efforts to retranslate and supplement existing ethnolinguistic texts, and experimentation with notational systems and photography created a new concern for capturing the nonverbal aesthetic features of a performance in print.[4] During the early 1970s, Dennis Tedlock published two influential works — "On the Translation of Style in Oral Narrative" and *Finding the Center: Narrative Poetry of the Zuni Indians* — demonstrating that much more could be done, in a readable way, to present performance features in print. He and the poet Jerome Rothenberg subsequently initiated the journal *Alcheringa: Ethnopoetics* (published in the 1970s), which provided a forum for experiments in translating oral traditions.

In the introduction to *Finding the Center*, Tedlock describes the typical performers, situations, and native categories for Zuni tales and myths. He also describes characteristic stylistic devices, norms of interaction and interpretation, and genre markings. Notes at the end of each tale contain comments on the tale by the narrator, audience, and translator. To record performance style Tedlock uses three techniques largely undeveloped by previous text makers: line breaks, ellipses, and spaces to indicate pauses; changes in typography (font size, orientation) to represent modes of speaking; and italicized comments for other vocal and nonverbal elements.

Influenced by free-verse poets who experimented with line breaks defined by breath pause, Tedlock employs two types of pause units. The first type, marked by the end of a line, represents a pause of one-half to three-fourths of a second. The second type, marked by a dot between strophes, represents a pause of two to three seconds. Longer intervals are marked by spaces larger than those between strophes. In his translations, he tries to approximate the Zuni contrasts in line length. To capture elongated vowels, he uses a long dash, as in "he went o———n."

Since Zuni storytellers vary the volume of narration from almost a whisper to almost a shout and since punctuation marks in English are ambiguous, Tedlock uses smaller type for quiet passages or words, larger type for middle-level passages, and capitals for loud passages. He also employs split lines to represent the two-pitch chanted lines. For example, he translates "TON^{AA}WAANA TON-^{HE}SHOTAWASHNA" as "WHEN YOU HAVE ^{GONE} THERE YOU WILL BUILD ^{HOU}SES" (*Finding* xxii). The final technique, italicized comments, describes special voice qualities and metanarrative or nonverbal elements such as gestures, laughter, or sighs. Since Tedlock's tape recorder was not equipped with a counter, he did not work out a system of correlating these features with the texts, and thus few gestures or movements are preserved.

Turning again to the "Deer Boy" tale and to the same deer-capture incident recorded by Cushing, Benedict, and Bunzel, we can see that Tedlock's translation preserves many more performance features in a dynamic and readable way. Note how he manages to retain the Zuni language ideophones and how the emotional impact finds expression in the typography and parenthetical description. Having students read this passage aloud will help them appreciate the Zuni storyteller's dramatic effects:

The deer saw the people.
They fled.
Many were the people who came out after them
now they chased the deer.
Now and again they dropped them, killed them.
Sure enough the boy outdistanced the others, while his
      mother and his elder sister and brother
still followed their child. As they followed him
he was far in the lead, but they followed on, they were
      on the run
and sure enough his uncles weren't thinking about killing
      deer, it was the boy they were after.
And ALL THE PEOPLE WHO HAD COME
      KILLED THE DEER
                    killed the deer
                              killed the deer.
Wherever they made their kills they gutted them, put them on
      their backs, and went home.
Two of the uncles

               •

then
went ahead of the group, and a third uncle
(*voice breaking*) dropped his elder sister
his elder brother
his mother.
He gutted them there
while the other two uncles went on. As they
      went ON
the boy pretended to be tired. The first uncle pleaded:
      "Tísshomahhá!
STOP," he said, "Let's stop this contest now."
That's what he was saying as the little boy kept on running.
As he kept on his bells went telele.
O———n, he went on this way on until

               •

the little boy stopped and his uncle, dismounting
caught him.

After evaluating a range of ways to translate performances into
print, I concluded in my book *The Folklore Text: From Performance to
Print* that the typographical approach used by Tedlock was one of

the most effective. Since Tedlock concentrated only on recording acoustic features, however, I extended his method to record body and facial movements as well. In the following section, additional suggestions for translating performances to print are examined.

Translating Performances to Print

Information about a performance can be recorded in print in at least two different ways: through a report or a record. A performance report simply describes the content or form of a live performance in one's own words; it does not attempt to re-create the performance in another medium. A performance record attempts to preserve the formal features of the live performance in another medium, such as film, video, audio, or print. I limit the term *text* to records of performance in a written or print medium. To respond aesthetically to a text, readers must have knowledge about the culture and context from which it emerges, or what Arnold Berleant calls "the aesthetic field." The oral traditional text can rarely stand alone without some accompanying report about the participants, situation, and cultural background.

Today more and more folklorists are realizing the fallacy of artificially separating text and context. As Charles Briggs has argued, performers embed their interpretations of social interaction within their performances through a process he calls "contextualization." It is important, for example, to record the audience and performer interchanges, or what Briggs and others call "back-channel" talk, such as "uh huh," "yes," and "really?" because such interchanges provide "invaluable means of understanding the contextualization process" (*Competence* 16). Gestures and vocal modifications can also contain cues to the way performers contextualize discourse.

Transcribing a live performance into print is an act of translation between two different media or sign systems. The translation theorist Eugene Nida argues that an adequate translation has four characteristics: it makes sense, it conveys the spirit and manner of the original message, it is natural and easy to read, and it produces a similar response (162–63). Texts that best meet all these criteria use a combination of natural language descriptions and iconic signs (signs that resemble in some way what they represent). For example, an up-turned arrow (↑) to represent a falsetto voice or a wavy line (~~~) to represent a rasp or guttural vocal quality are easy for readers to inter-pret because the arrow and the line are iconic. Descriptive words and phrases, arranged in special ways on the page, can record vocal and nonverbal features. In my system, the larger, easily recognized, goal-directed movements appear in the right margin and accompany all the underlined words in the discourse to the left. When the same action continues on succeeding lines, I use the symbol (- - -). The subordinate, modifying movements, which accompany only a few words, are placed directly below the words they accompany. Audi-ence responses appear in brackets. The larger vocal features, spanning a line or lines, such as vocal characterizers and qualifiers, appear in the left margin. Smaller features, such as a falsetto or rasp or an elongated vowel, are recorded with the words they accompany. A rising dash at the end of a line indicates a rising juncture; the pitch on the last phoneme rises slightly. A level dash at the end of a line indicates sus-tained juncture; the pitch of the last phoneme is retained. Certain repetitive stances or particularly complex movements that require an explanation too long to fit alongside the discourse are abbreviated and described further in an attached performance report. Where the narrator and a character speak on the same line, only the character's vocal qualities and characterizers are described, leaving readers to as-sume the narrator's typical vocal qualities as described in the perfor-mance report. Myriad micromovements such as eye blinks and finger positions within gestures are not translated, since such detail would overwhelm readers and contribute little to the perception of stylistic patterns.

To illustrate this performance-centered text, I have translated a student performance of an African American toast, "Stagolee." The performer, James Hutchison, learned his version from imitating an-other student on the playground and from a handwritten text made by that student. The handwritten version originated in a literary text published by Julius Lester in *Black Folktales*. The two versions are quite similar, but when Lester's literary version returned to oral

---

"Stagolee": Literary Text and Performance-Centered Text

Lester's Text (125)

Now on this particular day, Stagolee was sitting on the porch, picking the blues on the guitar, and drinking. All of a sudden, he looked up and saw this pale-looking white cat in this white sheet come riding up to his house on a white horse. "We ain't never had no Klan in the daytime before," Stagolee said.

Hutchison's Performance (Fine 190)

Stagolee was still sittin' on the porch

shuckin' some
hip swing

    BLUES on the GUItar   *mimes playing*
hip swing   *hip swing*   *guitar*

    Stagolee looked up—   *still holds guitar,*
                                    disbelieving
                                      expression caused
                                      by slight head
                                      turns- -

crescendo   saw this BI- -G old white HO- -SS⟋   *(- - -)*

crescendo   with this LI- -ttle old WHI- -TE MA- -N⟋   *(- - -)*

crescendo   dressed in this LO- -NG old WHITE   *(- - -)*

        SHEE- -T⟋

loud,   Stagolee say, "MA- -N, we NEVer had no
surprised   KLANS in the DAYtime befo'!"
        [laughter]

steps back in
surprise, both
hands emphasis

---

tradition, it took on more features of black oral speech, as the figure illustrates. Instead of using the formal literary style of attributing dialogue lines by following the quoted material with "he said," Hutchison follows the characteristic black oral style of preceding dialogue lines with "he say." In addition, he employs falsetto and rasp, common in the performance tradition of toasts, to emphasize attitudes and emotions. Furthermore, his balanced lines, achieved through a combination of parallel constructions and rhythmic stresses and pauses, seem much easier to recite, and the rising pitch patterns add to the suspense.

In addition to the typographical methods described above, photographs can be invaluable aids in representing the context and nonverbal style of a performance tradition. For example, Harold Scheub uses visual media effectively in his collection of Xhosa oral traditions, as performed by Nongenile M. Zenani (*Storyteller*). His photographs, illustrating how the storyteller conveys a variety of characterizations and attitudes through her gestures and facial expressions, help the reader appreciate the rich artistry of Zenani and the oral performance tradition.

In closing, let me note that one effective way to introduce students to the importance of finding or creating accurate and richly contextualized texts is to assign them the task of collecting and comparing existing texts of a given tale or of making their own texts of a performance. Comparing a videotaped performance to a simple transcription of the words alone, as well as adding appropriate signals to restore some of the reality lost in the reduction to text, will help them recognize the importance of evocative representations of verbal art from oral tradition.

Notes

1. What follows is drawn from Bell, "Newell"; Colby and Peacock; Dundes, "American Concept"; E. Fine. On the history of editing works that stem from oral traditions, see also Foley, "Folk Literature."
2. For a collection of scholarship on the Zuni and others, see E. C. Parsons (*Pueblo Mothers*), whose many publications of oral traditional tales include stories collected from the Sea Islands of South Carolina (*Folklore*), from the Tewa (*Tewa Tales*), and from the Kiowa (*Kiowa Tales*).
3. The tale is variously entitled "The Foster Child of the Deer" (Cushing), "Deer Boy" (Benedict, *Zuni Mythology* vol. 2), "Deer Youth" (Bunzel), and "The Boy and the Deer" (Tedlock, *Finding*). For convenience only, I use Benedict's title "Deer Boy" to refer to the tales as a whole.
4. See E. Fine 30–45; also, in this volume, Bauman and Braid on performance, Bradbury on traditional referentiality, DuBois on ethnopoetics, and Zumwalt on various approaches.

Part II

Critical Approaches

Rosemary Lévy Zumwalt

A Historical Glossary of Critical Approaches

It is appropriate that this examination of critical approaches to oral
tradition should be termed a glossary, since *glossary* has as its root
glōssa, the ancient Greek for the tongue and language, and is defined
as "a vocabulary giving the words of a book, author, dialect, science
or art" (*Webster's*). Thus my endeavor is to give the *glōssa*, the tongue
and the language, of approaches to oral tradition, from the perspective of science and art. My focus is on the theories developed by
twentieth-century folklorists in their study of oral tradition.[1]

I begin with the early assumptions about the importance of the
text itself—the folktale, myth, legend, or ballad apart from the
people who told it or sang it—and then with the early reconstruction
of the text's origin and route of diffusion (in the chart that follows
this essay, these are the twentieth-century "mechanical" approaches
that include the Finnish historic-geographic method and the age-area
hypothesis). After discussing these early text-oriented searches for origins, I examine the cultural approaches, which look at oral tradition
from three perspectives: where oral tradition provides a reflection or

an inventory of what is in the culture (culture reflector), where oral tradition reflects both what is in the culture and what the people wish were in the culture (culture and personality), and where the emphasis is on how oral tradition fulfills certain cultural needs (functionalism). I then consider the patterning of the text itself: the oral-formulaic approach, which aims at uncovering the underlying units that allow the narrator to remember and re-create complex texts, and the morphological approach, which focuses intensively on the internal patterning of a specific genre, that is, on the morphology of the folktale, riddle, or proverb. I move to the broader sweep of structuralism, with its concern for the universal aspects of the human mind—for what is referred to as the underlying or deep structure—and the way this structure is manifested in oral tradition. From the universality of structuralism, I shift to the expression of meaning through symbols as studied in the symbolic-interpretive, structural-interpretive, and psychoanalytic approaches. Tightening the lens through which these theoretical concerns are viewed, I next discuss ethnopoetics, which deals with the artistic rendering of oral tradition, and performance theory, which highlights the process of creation, the event itself, the performer, and the audience. From performance I turn to the feminist approach, which traces issues of power and gender in oral tradition. Finally, I discuss the concerns of authenticity, which involve an examination of the assumptions made about oral tradition and the reasons for them.

Eighteenth- and Nineteenth-Century "Grand Theory" Approaches

Before I trace the paths taken by the study of oral tradition in the twentieth century, let us look back, if only briefly, at those scholars of the eighteenth and nineteenth centuries who set the stage for the vexing study of origins. In the three main approaches—*Romantic nationalism, cultural evolutionary theory*, and the *solar mythological* approach—the central question was, Whence did the oral tradition arise? The adherents of Romantic nationalism answered the question in this way: From us, from the soul of our people, from our fatherland. Johann Gottfried Herder, who inspired the movement, linked national character or national soul to folk poetry, which he referred to as "the archives of a nationality" (Wilson 28).[2] The folk poets were those "organically one with their culture—those most in tune with the national soul." Folk poetry retained the "national language." Since upper classes had abandoned their national culture for things French, Herder saw the peasants as preservers of folk poetry and the national language (Wilson 28–29). Romantic nationalists were not concerned with arriving at the origin of oral tradition for all peoples of the world; they were, instead, possessive about their traditions. The *Kalevala* compiled by Elias Lönnrot in 1835 belonged to the Finns; the tales published in 1812–15 by Jacob Grimm and Wilhelm Grimm in *Kinder- und Hausmärchen* belonged to the Germans; the tales published in 1845 and 1848 by P. C. Asbjørnsen and Jørgen Moe in *Norske Huldre-eventyr og Folkesagen* belonged to the Norwegians. In the language of Romantic nationalism, our turf, our land, gave rise to the blood and soul of our people and to the *Volksgeist* (folk spirit) of our literature.

In nineteenth-century cultural evolutionary theory, the answer to the question of origins involved assumptions about the development of social stages that went from savagery to barbarism to civilization. In savagery, peoples' lives were guided by myths; in barbarism, people wove the vestiges of the myths into folktales; in civilization, the educated, who had lost all but the most fragmented traces of oral tradition, turned to the peasants and to children to study the quaint remnants of the past. Thus while social groups evolved toward higher levels of complexity on the ladder of evolution, their oral tradition devolved; that is, while social groups went from simple to complex, oral tradition went from complex to simple.[3] For the anthropologists Andrew Lang and Edward Burnett Tylor, cultural evolutionary theory not only explained the origin of oral tradition but also provided the framework for classifying the customs, beliefs, and practices of all peoples and for compiling a history of the development of humankind. In the two-volume *Myth, Ritual, and Religion*, Lang presented his ideas about the universal, shared base of "savage lore" and its survival in Greek myths and European peasant lore. In *Primitive Culture*, Tylor traced the survival of the oral tradition from the early stages of humankind to the beliefs and practices of European peasants and to the rhymes and games of children. Tylor wrote that children's folklore reproduces "in what are at once sports and little children's lessons, early stages in the history of child-like tribes of mankind" (1–74). This broad, sweeping system was the panacea that provided order for all of oral tradition and all of anthropology.

In direct opposition to the cultural evolutionists stood the solar mythologists, who argued that the folktales told by peasants were not vestiges from a savage state but, rather, the remains from a glorious and elevated past when all peoples communicated in eloquent metaphors before "the disease of language" destroyed their understanding. Nature was the central focus of life, and the people of the mythopoeic age spoke in lyrical fashion to describe the wonders of the sun's rising and setting, of its rays shining through diaphanous clouds. Using comparative philology, Max Müller, the central proponent of the solar mythological approach, traced the origins of mythology back to the Aryan peoples and to their sacred Veda. Müller determined that the Greek god Zeus was equated to and derived from Dyaus, the Vedic sky god, and by extension that the pantheon of Greek divinities was a disguised form of the Vedic pantheon. Assuming this elevated origin for oral tradition, Müller explained the barbarous elements in Greek myth. For instance, the elements of incest and cannibalism in the Greek tale of Uranus's marrying his daughter Gaea and Cronus's devouring his offspring as soon as his sister-wife, Gaea, gave birth were for Müller a camouflaged version of a sacred Veda. Such stories really told of the union of heaven, in the form of Uranus, and earth, in the form of Gaea, and of the movement of the clouds in the sky, in the guise of Cronus's swallowing and spewing forth his children (Dorson, "Eclipse" 64).

Twentieth-Century "Mechanical" Approaches

The sweeping and passionate aspirations of the nineteenth-century scholars of oral tradition were tamed by those scholars of more sober concerns in the early twentieth century. In the *Finnish historic-geographic method* and in the *age-area hypothesis*, the focus was on documenting the spread of a tale. Folklorists were adherents of the first approach and anthropologists of the second: the primary distinction between these two approaches was the presence or absence of written texts. For the followers of the Finnish historic-geographic method, the date of the earliest recorded text established the beginning of the literary treatment of the text. Anthropologists who used the age-area hypothesis, such as Franz Boas, were working in cultures without writing; they thus had no record of written texts by the people themselves. They therefore relied on the geographic spread of the tale. Both approaches assumed that a tale diffused from a central point, like the circles of water that widen from the place where a pebble is thrown. The more widely a tale was dispersed geographically, the older it was; the tale's ur-form would be found at the center. For both approaches, the focus was on a laborious recording of all appearances of the tale or text. Antti Aarne, a Finn, and Stith Thompson, an American, were the major proponents of the Finnish historic-geographic method. To document the path of a tale, first Aarne and then Thompson recognized the need to create reference tools that would allow scholars to standardize their citation of narratives from many different literary and cultural sources. This realization resulted in Aarne and Thompson's *Types of the Folktale* and in Thompson's six-volume *Motif-Index of Folk-Literature*. Save as a mouthpiece for the spread of oral tradition, the tellers of the tales were nowhere to be found in this focus on the paths of diffusion.[4] If nineteenth-century scholars embellished where detail was lacking, these early twentieth-century scholars pared their study down to the bare bones of the narrative in an attempt to establish the illusory origin of the tale. In the process, they lost the tellers and the tellers' purposes for passing on the stories.[5]

Cultural Approaches

The cultural approaches filled the social gaps left by the Finnish historic-geographic method and the age-area hypothesis. In the *culture reflector, culture and personality,* and *functionalism* approaches, the emphasis was on oral tradition as an information system that encoded cultural meaning and served the needs of the members of the society. During his fieldwork with Northwest Indian cultures, Franz Boas discovered that the narratives of the Tlingit, the Tsimshian, and the Kwakiutl reflected details of their culture, such as aspects of kinship, information about hunting and the preparation of food, and religious beliefs. Since Boas was working in societies that had undergone drastic change during the previous two decades and since he was interested in reconstructing precontact culture, he used the narratives as one of the sources of information about these cultures. In *Kwakiutl Culture As Reflected in Mythology,* Boas remarked that the tales "reflect the mode of life and thoughts of the people . . . [and] probably contain all that is interesting to the narrators. . . . In this way a picture of their way of thinking and feeling will appear that renders their ideas as free from the bias of the European observer as is possible" (v). While for Boas this method was linked to his interest in what he called historical reconstruction of past cultures, the focus need not be on the past. Rarely referred to in contemporary analysis as the culture reflector method, this approach remains important in the study of oral tradition.

While the culture reflector method holds a mirror to a culture, showing what is present in it, the culture and personality approach emphasizes the things *not* found in the culture that are present in the oral tradition. Ruth Benedict, one of the major proponents of this approach and a student of Boas, built on the concepts developed by her mentor and others. In *Zuni Mythology* (1935), she discussed aspects of traditional culture present in narratives but no longer present in the life of the Pueblo. For example, people in the tales enter their homes by climbing up a ladder to the roof and climbing down a ladder through an opening in the roof. According to Benedict, this is a "cultural lag" from earlier times (1:xv). While her discussion of cultural lag is in keeping with Boas's approach to historical reconstruction through the texts of narratives, Benedict did not stop with a literal reading of the stories. She argued that the tales fulfilled psychological needs such as wish fulfillment, fostered emotional identification with the wronged party, and allowed for projection of suppressed desires. Most important for Benedict, and for others in the culture and personality school such as Cora DuBois and Abram Kardiner, the tales were at once a reflection of the ethos of the culture and a means for shaping the ideal personality of its members. As Benedict argued in *Patterns of Culture*, "A culture, like an individual, is a more or less consistent pattern of thought and action" (46), and oral tradition is one means for culture to manifest this patterning.

The functionalist approach stressed how oral tradition is used for the social good. Drawing from his fieldwork (1915–16, 1917–18) with the Trobriand Islanders, who live off the coast of New Guinea, Bronislaw Malinowski emphasized how myth has "the normative power of fixing custom, of sanctioning modes of behavior, of giving dignity and importance to an institution" (*Argonauts* 328). In short, myth serves as a sociological charter for belief. The Trobrianders justify their rituals and beliefs by reciting associated mythological narratives. The oral tradition links them to time past — indeed, the narratives are called *libogwo*, or "old talk" (298) — and insure the perpetuation of life in the future. Thus, according to Malinowski's functionalist approach, oral tradition has real, pragmatic work to do for a people: it undergirds their view of the world, their sense of reality; it gives them a sense of security in an insecure world. Expanding on Malinowski's approach, William R. Bascom carefully examined what folklore does for people. While acknowledging that oral tradition provides amusement, Bascom identified the following four functions: oral tradition provides an escape from reality through the creation of a fantasy world; it validates culture and strengthens tradition, as Malinowski had discussed; it educates people, "particularly, but not exclusively, in non-literate societies" ("Four Functions" 293); and it fosters social conformity through messages of support for accepted patterns of behavior and messages of ostracism for aberrant patterns of behavior.

Pattern of Text

The pattern approaches to the study of oral tradition directed attention to the text itself. Axel Olrik delineated principles or laws that, he maintained, apply to all forms of folk narrative, which he called

Sage (including myths, songs, heroic narratives, and local legends). Among these *epic laws* are the following:

> Law of opening and law of closing: "The *Sage* begins by moving from calm to excitement, and after the concluding event, in which a principal character frequently has a catastrophe, the *Sage* ends by moving from excitement to calm" (131–32).
>
> Law of repetition: "There is intensifying repetition and simple repetition, but the important point is that without repetition, the *Sage* cannot attain its fullest form" (133).
>
> Law of two to a scene: "Two is the maximum number of characters who appear at one time" (134).
>
> Law of contrast: "The *Sage* is always polarized. . . . This very basic opposition is a major rule of epic composition: young and old, large and small, man and monster, good and evil" (135).

Olrik argued that these epic laws constrain the teller of tales: "We call these principles 'laws' because they limit the freedom of composition of oral literature in a much different and more rigid way than in our written literature" (131).

In the *oral-formulaic approach*, Milman Parry and Albert Lord identified the patterning in the text as primarily a memory device. From their study of South Slavic epic poets over a period of years — together in the 1930s and Lord alone in the 1950s and 1960s — the two were able, as Lord reflected, "to observe singers working in a thriving tradition of unlettered song and see how the form of their songs hangs upon their having to learn and practice their art without reading and writing" (*Singer of Tales* 3). Parry and Lord proposed that the epic singers of tradition — including Homer in his performance of the *Iliad* and the *Odyssey* — used oral-formulaic phrases to aid in the recollection and enactment of detailed, lengthy narratives. Through a study of epic performances and texts, Parry and Lord identified certain lines and half-lines as formulaic because "they follow the basic pattern of rhythm and syntax and have at least one word in the same position" (Lord, "Yugoslav" 47). To this basic notion of formula — defined by Parry as "a group of words which is regularly employed under the same metrical conditions to express a given essential idea" (*Making* 272) — Lord also advanced the concepts of theme (a recurrent narrative pattern such as feasting or assembly) and story pattern (a tale type that underlies an entire epic), thereby developing a multiform theory of oral composition applicable to all levels of epic verse. Whereas Olrik had stressed the constraint placed on the teller of tales by epic laws, Lord stressed the productive tension between tradition and creativity: "And the picture that emerges is not really one of conflict between preserver of tradition and creative artist; it is rather one of the preservation of tradition by the constant recreation of it. The ideal is a true story well and truly retold" (*Singer of Tales* 29).[6]

In *The Theory of Oral Composition*, John Miles Foley points to "the healthy variety of approaches and applications" that have grown from Parry's and Lord's influential work (111). While much research has continued the original focus on Greek and South Slavic epics, scholars have branched out to "more than one hundred separate language areas . . . Old English, Old French, the Hispanic traditions, medieval German, African, Turkish, Chinese, Japanese, Irish, Russian, Native American, and numerous others" (xiii).[7] One outcome of this diversification has been the development of a more flexible concept of the formula and other traditional structures that not only takes into account such issues as the diversity of individual traditions but also allows for a better understanding of the oral traditional poet's artistic strategies and effects.[8]

With the *myth-ritual approach*, ritual provided the model for the patterning of the text. In "The Hero of Tradition" and *The Hero: A Study in Tradition, Myth, and Drama*, Lord Raglan identified twenty-two incidents that appear in the life stories of literary, mythological, and religious personages such as Oedipus, Romulus, Dionysus, Moses, Elijah, and Arthur.[9] These incidents range from the early stages of the figure's life to his marriage and kingly rule to his fall from favor ("Hero" 145). For example, the hero traditionally comes from royal parentage, although the exact details of his conception are often obscure and unusual; this ambiguity ordinarily leads to an assassination attempt from which the child narrowly escapes, spirited away at birth to be reared by foster parents in a far country. Raglan maintained that this narrative scheme is based on "ritual incidents in the career of a ritual personage" (150). The hero pattern, for Raglan, stems from mythological accounts that in turn are based on the ritual high points of the hero's life: birth, marriage, accession to the throne, and death. The life stories of historical figures were shaped to fit this sequence. As Raglan wrote, "The pattern career for a hero was generally known, and that either from flattery, or from a genuine belief that the career of a hero must conform to type, mythical incidents were introduced into the story of genuinely historical heroes" (157).

With the *morphological approach*, Vladimir Propp redirected the focus of text patterning to the internal structure of the folktale. In *Morphology of the Folktale*,[10] Propp defined the units, or functions, that make up a folktale as "act[s] of a character" expressed by a noun, for example, interdiction, violation, reconnaissance, delivery, trickery, complicity, villainy, lack; these units focus on the "significance for the course of the action" (21–65). He determined that the number of functions in a folktale is limited to thirty-one and that the sequence of the functions is always the same, though some might be missing in a particular tale. For Propp, the incidentals of the tale were not crucial: the names and attributes of the characters might change, and even the number of characters might vary greatly. "Functions of characters serve as stable, constant elements in a tale, independent of how and by whom they are fulfilled," he wrote (21).

Structural, Symbolic, and Interpretive Approaches

In the *structural approach*, Claude Lévi-Strauss maintained that oral tradition reveals the underlying or deep structure of the human mind. Unlike Propp, Lévi-Strauss was not focusing on a single genre, the folktale in one society; rather, he considered all aspects of culture, from kinship terminology to mythological narrative, as manifestations of the underlying, universal aspects of the human mind. He made a distinction between the *syntagmatic*, or surface structure, which was Propp's concern, and the *paradigmatic*, or deep structure, which was his own concern. Using the analogy of the digital computer, Lévi-Strauss argued that human beings perceive the world in terms of binary opposites such as night/day, dark/light, man/woman, right/left, up/down, and so forth. These perceptions are structurally embedded at a deep, cognitive level; aspects of culture provide symbolic means to bridge, or mediate, the opposites. For example, mythological narratives allow for mediation of binary opposites that are present in the culture itself. In "The Story of Asdiwal," Lévi-Strauss analyzed a Tsimshian narrative according to four levels or sequences — the geographic, the techno-economic, the sociological, and the cosmological — that provide the chronological account. He also studied *schèmes* (schemata), following the same four categories that, he said, exist "simultaneously, superimposed one upon another" (17). Through a complex analysis, Lévi-Strauss arrived at a "global integration" of the schemata that yield, he assured the reader, "the structure of the message" (21).

Rejecting the formalism of the morphological approach and the arbitrary intellectualism of the structuralist approach, the *symbolic-interpretive* approach stresses the importance of the cultural meaning system "from the native's point of view," as Clifford Geertz phrases it. In expressive culture, which includes oral tradition, art, festival, ritual, music, and games, people are telling a story about themselves for themselves. The challenge for the student of oral tradition, then, is to find out what is revealed in the intricate symbolic layering. Geertz acknowledges that this approach will not allow one to range widely in cross-cultural fashion but, rather, will demand an adherence to what is being said within the specific culture ("Thick Description"). The context of meaning is localized in one cultural setting. The universality of Lévi-Strauss's approach is replaced by the emic, or the native, categories of thought.[11]

Eschewing the view that pits one theory against another, Steven Feld combines structuralism and the interpretive approach (*Sound* 225). He provides a composite analysis of the myth "The Boy Who Became a Muni Bird":

> To summarize, a structural analysis of the story organizes the episodes into sequences that embody provocation, mediation, and metaphor. Structurally, the argument is that social *sentiment*, mediated by *birds*, is metaphorically expressed in

sound. . . . Mythically these forms are reached through the mediation of becoming a bird. They are then culturally activated by turning weeping into song, and song into weeping, both of which involve the canon of the performer becoming a bird. (42–43)

Feld also draws on the ethnography of communication, which deals with the cultural rules for the social use of language. His work shows that one does not have to choose between structuralism, with its universal orientation, and the interpretive approach, with its culture-specific focus; rather, one can combine the two in a deeply sensitive analysis of myth, song, and emotion.

Psychoanalytic Approach

In the *psychoanalytic* approach, oral tradition serves as a symbolic projection for unconscious desires, or, as Freud put it, myth is "psychology projected to the outer world" (qtd. in Dundes, "Earth-Diver" 273). This projection might be straightforward, as when anxiety is translated to another form of expression, or it might be inverse projection, which involves, as Dundes explains, "a transformational shift" ("Psychoanalytic Study of Folklore" 29). In this more complex form of projection, an individual's desires or emotions are attributed to another, who "is the object of those feelings" ("Psychoanalytic Study of the Grimms' Tales" 60). Thus, in "The Maiden without Hands" (Aarne and Thompson 240–41; tale type 706), it is the daughter who desires her father; but by projective inversion, this is rendered as the father wanting to marry the daughter (60–62). As Dundes stresses, oral tradition provides "a socially sanctioned means of expressing one's anxiety." Often the social sanction itself requires the disguise of humor, because one "can joke where one cannot speak directly" ("Ways" 44). In *Cracking Jokes: Studies in Sick Humor Cycles and Stereotypes*, Dundes writes of this disguise: "It usually is essential that the joke's meaning *not* be crystal clear. If people knew what they were communicating when they told jokes, the jokes would cease to be effective as socially sanctioned outlets for expressing taboo ideas and subjects. Where there is anxiety, there will be jokes to express that anxiety" (vii). Thus joke cycles and other forms of oral tradition allow people to express a whole gamut of repressed emotions and regressive wit (see, e.g., Dundes and Abrahams).

Ethnopoetic Approach

The *ethnopoetic* approach focuses intensely on the recording and translating of poetry in a manner that is faithful to its artistic performance.[12] In *Finding the Center*, Dennis Tedlock writes of the challenges and difficulties of translating Zuni Indian narratives called *telapnaawe*, or "tales," and *chimiky'ana'kowa*, or "The Beginning" (xvi). Trained in linguistics, Tedlock said that at first he lost "the subtler qualities of the speaking voice" and was mired in the tediousness of "the precise notation of phonemes." Referring to the initial phases of translation, he remarked, "I saw this task as largely a matter of polishing the rough translations done in the field, but I was unhappy with the flat prose format which had always been used in presenting such narratives" (xviii). Influenced by Munro Edmonson's translation of *The Book of Counsel: The Popol Vuh of the Quiche Maya of Guatemala* entirely into couplets, Tedlock decided that the Zuni narratives were poetry and not prose. He observes:

> What makes written prose most unfit for representing spoken narrative is that it rolls on for whole paragraphs at a time without taking a breath: there is no silence in it. To solve this problem I have broken Zuni narratives into lines: the shorter pauses, which average three-fourths second and almost never drop below one-half second, are represented here by simple changes of line; the longer pauses, which run from two to three seconds, are represented by strophe breaks. (xix)

For Tedlock, the poetic words alone do not convey the meaning of the narrative. A translation must attempt to encapsulate the living performance. Tedlock therefore "combines poetic and dramatic features" (xix). He has devised means of indicating loudness or softness of delivery, pitch of voice, manipulation of voice quality, and pace of delivery. He uses italicized notations for events other than narration, "as when the performer clears his throat, sighs, breaks into laughter, turns his head to make an aside, or gestures" (xxiv-xxv). In this way Tedlock creates a sensitive poetic translation of performance elements that breathes life into narratives of oral tradition.

Performance Theory

Performance theory shifts the focus to the dynamic process of creation, the performer, and the audience (see Bauman and Braid, this volume). As Richard Bauman details in *Verbal Art as Performance*, "The term 'performance' has been used to convey a dual sense of artistic *action* — the doing of folklore — and artistic *event* — the performance situation, involving performer, art form, audience, and setting" (4). With links to the interpretive approach and to the ethnography of communication mentioned above, this approach involves a reorientation to the material that has the effect of a kaleidoscopic twist. The detailed study of the text itself — whether morphological, structural, or psychoanalytic — is gone. In its place is a detailed study of the communication of oral tradition. As Bauman explains:

> Performance is a mode of language use, a way of speaking. The implication of such a concept for a theory of verbal art is this: it is no longer necessary to begin with artful texts, identified on independent formal grounds and then reinjected into situations of use, in order to conceptualize verbal art in communicative terms. Rather . . . performance becomes *constitutive* of the domain of verbal art as spoken communication. (11)

Bauman identifies seven keys to performance: special codes (such as archaic expressions; for an artful example of archaic language in storytelling, see Toelken, "Pretty Language"), figurative language, parallel structure, special paralinguistic features (such as forms of delivery and voice tone), special formulas, appeal to tradition, and disclaimer of performance (16–22).

In *Storytellers, Saints, and Scoundrels: Folk Narrative in Hindu Religious Teaching*, Kirin Narayan sets performance theory in motion. Through her words she brings to life the Hindu ascetic with whom she studied, Swamiji, and his stories. In transcribing, Narayan captures a sense of what Swamiji himself calls his "topsy-turvy language," composed as it is of Kannada, Hindi, Sanskrit, Marathi, and some English words:

> As I have transformed tapes into written English translations, I have tried to capture the flavors I discern in Swamiji's varied use of languages, but I only separate out English itself. English words are all distinguished with an asterisk—for example, "photo,*" "procession,*" "income tax,*" and so on. Sometimes trying to speak English, Swamiji drolly enunciates wrong words. When he had a bad bout of arthritis, for example, I heard him informing people, "I myself am happy, but this body* is suffering. What to do, it's an old body.* It got arithmetic.*" (20)

Narayan conveys the storytelling context not only by informing the reader about who is present but also by weaving the audience into Swamiji's narratives. She includes in brackets comments that Swamiji directed to the people present: "['You might have heard this story,' Swamiji looks up at Govindbhai standing at the foot of his chair]" (22); and observations on Narayan's and others' reactions to Swamiji's stories: "[Kirin explodes into laughter at this droll image of a buffalo contemplating its God. Swamiji grins and continues]" (32). Narayan also describes Swamiji's gestures as he tells the stories: "[Swamiji rolls his head to one side, then straight up, the gesture of a young man ready to take on anything]" (50); "[Swamiji straightens up in his chair, sententiously fluttering his eyelids, flexing his arms bent at the elbow first upwards, then down]" (134).

Feminist Theory

Feminist theory brings to the study of oral tradition an examination of the intersecting issues of class, race, ethnicity, power, and gender (see Weigle, this volume). In "Absent Gender, Silent Encounter," Debora Kodish identifies "one purpose of feminist scholarship" as the deconstruction of "male paradigms" and another as the reconstruction of "models attentive to women's experiences" (44). Susan

Slyomovics offers one such model for the telling of women's experiences in "Ritual Grievance: The Language of Woman?" She writes of the *zar*, an exorcism ceremony of the Middle East and Africa in which a woman is possessed by a male spirit:

> She calls to the spirit inhabiting her body, speaks of her imprisonment, and the walls that surround her. In the following example she says only the wind, which is freedom and freshness, reaches her in her domestic prison through the tiny aperture, the *taqa*, of the Egyptian peasant home:
>
>> They imprisoned me took away the keys
>> And the wind comes from the tiny aperture
>> Who takes care of me
>> Who takes care of me
>> I am the one who calls, I call, I am calling
>> I am the one who calls, I call, I am calling
>> It is time, it has been a long time, Welcome
>> I am the sick one. (56)

Slyomovics concludes that the *zar* raises questions about the manner in which ceremonial language articulates, and perhaps through its performance actually shapes, social relationships between men and women (see also Hollis, Pershing, and Young).

Authenticity

The study of *authenticity* delineates assumptions made about oral tradition and more specifically about the concept of tradition. This critique of authenticity, a concept widely accepted and firmly embedded in the approaches to the study of oral tradition, is part of the postmodern, reflexive approach. In an examination of the Romanticism that shaped the concept of the authentic folk, Regina Bendix speaks of "a reflexive historiography of the field" (104). From this critical vantage point, the focus is on the part the collector-scholar plays in the process of recording, studying, and theorizing about oral tradition and thereby defining and creating that tradition. Instead of denoting a body of material passed intact from generation to generation, tradition itself becomes a contested term. As Richard Handler and Jocelyn Linnekin argue:

Tradition cannot be defined in terms of boundedness, given-ness, or essence. Rather, tradition refers to an interpretive process that embodies both continuity and discontinuity. As a scientific concept, tradition fails when those who use it are unable to detach it from the implications of Western common sense, which presumes that an unchanging core of ideas and customs is always handed down to us from the past. (273)

As befits a postmodern approach, this critique of authenticity calls into question categories long held to be at the core of approaches to the study of oral tradition.

———

This glossary of critical approaches to the study of oral tradition has moved from the wide sweep of Romanticism to the minutiae of the Finnish historic-geographic method to the introspection of the critique of authenticity. There is in the variety of approaches an underlying complexity linked with philosophical concerns (Who are the folk? What is the nature of language? What is tradition?) and with issues of power and control (Who gets to decide which group are the savages and which the civilized?). To echo, then, my opening reference to *glōssa* as tongue and language, this glossary speaks with many tongues of the varied and widely divergent approaches to the study of oral tradition. Am I to close, now, on such a cacophonous note, with different tongues speaking in different registers? Possibly this is the only true note on which to end, since history often offers continuity only to those who strive, sometimes arbitrarily, to order the past. Still, there are tones that sound harmoniously in these various registers. There is a concern with what is passed on orally and with what assumes a recognized format, often labeled "traditional." Perhaps stretching the author's original intent, I will suggest that Foley's concept of word power courses through a number, if not all, of these approaches. Word power, Foley says, is a "particular mode of meaning possible only by virtue of the enabling event of performance and the enabling referent of tradition" (*Singer* xiv).

The Study of Oral Tradition

Categories of Approaches	Specific Approaches and Theories	Assumptions about Oral Traditions	Major Proponents
Eighteenth- and nineteenth-century "grand theory" approaches to the study of origins	Romantic nationalism	Expression of *Volksgeist* of a people	Herder
	Cultural evolutionary theory	Survival from savage or barbaric state	Tylor Lang
	Solar mythology	Disease of language since original mythopoeic age	Müller
Twentieth-century "mechanical approaches" to the study of origins	Finnish historic-geographic method	Literary texts documenting geographic dispersion	Aarne Thompson
	Age-area hypothesis	Oral texts documenting geographic dispersion	Boas
Pattern of text	Epic laws	Oral tradition generated from textual laws	Olrik
	Oral-formulaic approach	Patterning in the text as memory device and traditional referentiality	Parry Lord Foley
	Myth-ritual approach	Patterning through ritual incidents in life stories	Raglan
	Morphological approach	Focus on internal structure of the genres of oral tradition	Propp
Structuralist and interpretive approaches	Structural approach	Oral tradition as manifestation of deep structure	Lévi-Strauss
	Symbolic-interpretive approach	Oral tradition as portrayal of self	Geertz
	Structural-interpretive approach	Oral tradition as deep structure and individual performance	Feld
Psychoanalysis	Psychoanalytic approach	Oral tradition as projection of psyche	Dundes
Ethnopoetics	Ethnopoetics	Translation of oral tradition to convey poetic and dramatic features	Tedlock D. Hymes
Performance	Performance theory	Oral tradition as process of creation	Bauman Narayan

(continued)

The Study of Oral Tradition *(continued)*

Categories of Approaches	Specific Approaches and Theories	Assumptions about Oral Traditions	Major Proponents
Feminism	Feminist theory	Oral tradition as articulation of power and gender issues	Hollis Mills Pershing Slyomovics Young
Authenticity	Authenticity	Examination of assumptions made about tradition	Bendix Handler Linnekin

Notes

I thank John Miles Foley for his gentle and insightful suggestions for the revisions of this article.

1. For other surveys of critical approaches to folklore and to oral tradition, see Dundes, "Ways" and "Oral Literature"; T. Burns.
2. For a feminist interpretation of Herder and Romantic nationalism, see J. Fox. For a critical appraisal of assumptions made about the folk and folk poetry, see Bendix.
3. See Dundes, "Devolutionary Premise." For an application of cultural evolutionary theory to children's folklore, see Zumwalt, "Complexity."
4. For an example of how the *Motif-Index* is used to identify motifs in a particular tale and to determine its possible origin, and of how *The Types of the Folktale* is used to identify a folktale, see Dundes, "Ways" 38–41.
5. For an examination of the development of the Finnish historic-geographic method and the age-area hypothesis, see Zumwalt, *Scholarship* 107–11. For examples of the application of the Finnish historic-geographic method, see A. Taylor; Thompson, "Star Husband Tale."
6. For an exquisite examination of issues involved in the performance of tales and the connection between performance and the oral-formulaic approach, see Foley, *Singer*. See also Lord, *Epic Singers* and *Singer Resumes*.
7. See, in this volume, Bradbury on traditional referentiality, Martin on Homer's *Iliad* and *Odyssey*, Olsen on *Beowulf*, O'Keeffe on Old English poetry, Zemke on Hispanic traditions, Herrera-Sobek on Mexican American traditions, Toelken on Native American traditions (North), McDowell on Native American traditions (South), Alexander on South Slavic traditions, Cosentino on African traditions, Vitz on Old French literature, Quinn on Japanese traditions, and Bender on Chinese traditions.
8. On history and methodology of the oral-formulaic theory, see Foley, *Theory of Oral Composition*; for its bibliography, see Foley,

Oral-Formulaic Theory, with updates in the journal *Oral Tradition* (Tyler, Dilevko, and Foley; L. Tyler), and the entire bibliography available at www.missouri.edu/~csottime. For evolution of the theory, especially its relation to artistic issues, see Foley, *Traditional Oral Epic, Immanent Art*, and *Singer*.

9. While Raglan does not include Jesus in the examination of patterning in the life of the hero, Dundes does so ("Hero Pattern"). For myth-ritual theory, see Dundes, *Study* 142–44 and "Hero Pattern" 229–40; Zumwalt, *Scholarship* 125–30.

10. *Morphology* was originally published in Russian in 1928, translated into English in 1958, and reissued in 1968. Propp focused exclusively on Russian fairy tales that fitted Aarne-Thompson tale type 300–748 (Aarne and Thompson 88–254; "Tales of Magic"). Other scholars extended the morphological approach to other genres of oral tradition and in so doing formulated definitions of those genres based on the morphological structure; see Abrahams and Dundes; Dundes and Georges; Dundes, "On the Structure" and "Making."

11. For a brilliant analysis of the native genres of classification, see Gossen.

12. A major contributor to this approach is Dell Hymes; see his *"In Vain."* See further the essay on ethnopoetics by DuBois in this volume.

Mark C. Amodio

Contemporary Critical Approaches and Studies in Oral Tradition

Beginning with the rise of New Criticism and formalism in the early decades of this century, literary theory (an umbrella term for a wide range of often competing theoretical schools) has come to occupy an important position not only in the published work of scholars but in most graduate classrooms and in a growing number of undergraduate classrooms as well.[1] While as recently as ten to fifteen years ago courses devoted to the teaching of literary theory were still relatively rare, today they occupy an increasingly central position in postsecondary curricula as students and their instructors come to see literary theories less as arcane and threatening dogmas and more as useful tools for understanding and interpreting all types of literature.[2] Contemporary literary theory has called into question, among other things, the stability of texts, the ways in which texts mean, the ways in which readers receive texts, the authority of authors and their control over the texts they produce, and the degree to which texts reflect the social realities and political ideologies of the cultures in which they are produced. In doing this, literary theory has mounted, with much continuing (and generally productive) controversy, a serious challenge to the dominant, largely New Critical view of texts as the reified, stable repositories of the monolithic meaning with which their authors imbued them.

Oral Theory and Contemporary Criticism

From Milman Parry's early and widely influential formulation in the late 1920s, oral theory has spoken, and continues to speak, directly to many of the issues that occupy contemporary theorists. But for reasons ranging from the general inaccessibility of the ancient Greek, medieval English, and South Slavic texts that have served as its primary proving grounds to a widespread misunderstanding of its principles, aims, and procedures, oral theory has sometimes been relegated to the margins of contemporary critical discourse.[3] Oral theory's entrance into the mainstream of that discourse has been further impeded because for many years oral theory has been seen as synonymous with the theory of oral-formulaic composition, a groundbreaking but ultimately narrow approach that applies unproblematically only to those poems that meet its rather restricted criteria for orality.[4] However, over the past ten years oral theory has moved steadily away from many of the limited tenets of the theory of oral-formulaic composition, so that today there are few, if any, oralists who would classify themselves as oral-formulaicists, and one would be hard pressed to find many who subscribe to the hard Parryist position that dominated the field for so long.[5] In considering oral theory's relation to contemporary critical theory, we thus need to distinguish carefully between the Parry-Lord theory, with its heavy emphasis on composition-in-performance and its fundamental belief in the mutual exclusivity of the oral and written modes of composition,[6] and the more supple and nuanced oral theory currently being developed by scholars such as A. N. Doane, John Miles Foley, Katherine O'Brien O'Keeffe, Alain Renoir (*Key*), and Brian Stock (*Implications* and *Listening*), a theory that acknowledges that orality and literacy exist along a continuum and are deeply interrelated and interdependent cultural forces (see also Amodio, "Introduction").

Although oral theory has already proved to be a powerful tool for investigating oral poetics not only in demonstrably oral texts but in oral-derived and written texts as well,[7] it remains fair to ask what a theory that attempts to explain the highly specialized types of poetic composition and reception found in ancient, medieval, and contemporary oral cultures might possibly have to say to those theories concerned with investigating the vastly different compositional and receptional processes that prevail in literate cultures. The answer, to put it telegraphically, is a great deal. Oral theory and contemporary critical theory share many basic principles, engage many similar issues, and ask many closely related questions. But it is in the challenges they have mounted to the dominant, largely New Critical understanding of the complex interactions within the text-audience-author triad that the concerns of oral theory and contemporary criticism have dovetailed most clearly and importantly.

The New Critical Model

Central to the New Critical perspective, and consequently to the way in which many students and their instructors still approach the business of reading and interpreting literature, are some well-defined and very stable relations among the producer (author), her or his product (text), and the consumers of that product (audience): the author possesses absolute authority and invests his or her unique creation with a meaning that is then always readily available to an audience trained to read the text closely and objectively. Misinterpretations may (and do) frequently arise, but they result solely from a reader's misreading the text or in some other way failing to "get" the author's meaning. The many interpretive failures that may arise during a reader's negotiation of a text are easily corrected by one who already has discovered the "correct" path through the text, because in the New Criticism "interpretation of a text is envisaged as being rather like many people climbing a single mountain, confident that, on its sun-kissed summit, they will all meet, shake hands and reconcile their differences, discussing (often wryly, for some took wrong turnings) the relative merits of the several routes to the top, but now united in the conviction that they share the secret of F6 (or whatever)" (Minnis xvi–xvii).

The Active Recipient

Along with arguing against the New Critical view that texts are fixed repositories of the meaning with which an author — or, to use Roland Barthes's memorable and unsettling phrase, an "author-God" — invests them (143), contemporary critical theory has mounted a serious challenge to another of the New Criticism's tenets, namely, that readers must be largely passive and ideally objective recipients of the author's text if they are to arrive at a successful interpretation, one that is correct because it uncovers the author's meaning. Stanley Fish, one of the early proponents of that branch of subjective criticism known as reader-response theory, touched off considerable controversy by suggesting that literature can exist only *in* the reader, that "the objectivity of the text is an illusion" (43), and that readers actively engage in creating (or, less extremely, cocreating) the text and its meaning(s). While remaining controversial in some quarters, Fish's assertions fit comfortably into oral theory because oral literature, in the most absolute sense, exists always and only in the poet and audience (see Foley, *Singer* 136–80 and *Immanent Art* 38–60; Finnegan, *Literacy*; Ong, *Orality*). Because oral texts have no existence independent of their reception, their audiences necessarily serve as their dynamic cocreators, just as, according to Fish and many others, contemporary readers do for the printed, physically stable, but nevertheless always shifting texts they read. Despite the truly ephemeral nature of oral literature and the physicality that characterizes written literature, the difference between oral and written texts is not nearly so great as many often surmise it to be. In oral cultures one gains access to the world of texts only through the singer's or poet's public performance, while in literate cultures one need only be able to read to have such access; nonetheless, the unheard song is no different from the unopened book: without a recipient, neither truly exists. The active recipient's role finds powerful confirmation in the field studies that Lord, Foley, and Ruth Finnegan have undertaken in the former Yugoslavia and Africa. As they discovered, contemporary audiences of oral poetry actively exert subtle and not so subtle pressures that help determine the poem's narrative contours, length, emphases, and so forth.

Textual (In)Stability

In contrast to the New Criticism's view of texts as self-sufficient, stable artifacts that witness their authors' unique and idiosyncratic creative abilities as well as their absolute authorial control, oral theory and contemporary critical theory argue that texts are best understood as radically unstable entities subject to pressures and readings that their creators could in no way predict or control. Printed texts are undeniably stable in that the words on the page do not physically change position from one perusal to the next. As someone trained in a highly literate culture, I should be greatly surprised and confused on picking up a copy of *Beowulf* to discover that the poem begins with a word other than the Old English interjection "Hwæt" ("Lo"). In contrast to the poem's physically fixed text, however, the abstract, internalized text that I must reconstitute every time I read the poem and that provides the foundation for my interpretation of *Beowulf* undergoes continual alteration as my understanding of a particular word, phrase, sound pattern, or story pattern comes newly into focus as a result of my connecting it with something inside or outside the poem or even simply through my noticing it for the first (or hundredth) time. As I always point out to students in my *Beowulf* seminar, *how* the poem means remains stable while *what* it means remains interestingly (and perhaps, at times, vexingly) in flux as new ways of reading and thinking about it merge (or sometimes collide) with older ones.[8]

The realization that texts in an oral culture exist only as multiforms that all lay equal claim (despite their varying degrees of aesthetic accomplishment) to their traditional foundations ranks among the more important contributions of the theory of oral-formulaic composition and offers strong support for the view of texts as slippery, shifting entities that lies at the heart not only of oral theory but of much contemporary critical theory as well. As Lord noted in *The Singer of Tales*, oral poetry is both ephemeral and highly protean. In an oral culture, once the reverberations of the poet's voice die, the poem exists only in the minds of those who were present at its performance. Since oral cultures have no need or desire to preserve a single performance of a poem in writing in order to establish it consciously (or unconsciously) as *the* version against which all subsequent versions can be examined for deviations, it is not surprising that multiformity should be a distinguishing characteristic of oral poems. The largely nonliterate South Slavic oral epic singers (*guslari*) whom Parry and Lord interviewed and from whom they collected thousands of lines of oral poetry did not, despite the poets' stated beliefs to the contrary, ever sing the same song the same way twice.[9] Unlike literate authors, the *guslari* were not particularly troubled by variations between versions of a song or seeming narrative inconsistencies within a given song. The idea that there is, or even can be, a single correct, authorized version of a song against which the fidelity of all other versions can be measured did not have the hold on them that it does on those of us imbued with literate, textual habits of mind. It is only to literates, who have the ability to leaf back through their texts in order to verify a narrative matter and so clarify their memories, that the idea of a fixed text has become paramount.

Authorial Presence, Absence, and Authority

Turning now to the third element of the audience-text-author triad—the author—we discover that oral theory appears to depart significantly from contemporary critical theory because oral theory holds that oral poetry depends on the poet's presence (without the poet physically in front of his or her audience, there can be no poem), while contemporary critical theory contends that texts produced in a literate culture are universally marked by the author's absence. Especially in the days before electronic sound amplification and recording became possible and common, the number of people who could experience oral literature was subject to a variety of limitations. Most simply, members of the audience had to be contemporaries of the poet, and they had to be physically present during and in earshot of the poet's performance. A written text, in contrast, is subject to no such physical or temporal restrictions and may be read by hundreds of thousands of readers from very different cultural backgrounds over the course of several centuries.

The difference between an ephemeral, unique, nonreproducible, and performance-dependent oral text and a physically fixed and mechanically reproducible written one is considerable. A significant difference also exists between the theories that have been developed to assist us in understanding the mechanics and aesthetics of these two kinds of texts. But oral theory and contemporary criticism do work toward very similar ends in one way: they both demand that we free critical inquiry from the belief that a text's explanation can be found "in the man or woman who produced it, as if it were always in the end . . . the voice of a single person, the author confiding in us" (Barthes 143; emphasis deleted). Oral theorists, especially those who work with ancient and early medieval literatures, have out of necessity long deemphasized the figure of the author and have instead focused their investigations on what would be called the author-function in contemporary critical terminology. Because the authors of most of the extant texts from these periods tend to be either anonymous or little more than empty names and because oral poets are often seen as indistinguishable (and perhaps interchangeable) conduits for the articulation of traditional, inherited material, oral theorists have by default excluded the author from their consideration and have focused instead on the author-function, the text, and the text's reception. Whereas contemporary criticism, in the view of many, has attempted to free critical inquiry from the tyranny of the author (Barthes 142–48), oral theorists have warned against the dangers of injecting an authorial presence into what has long been believed to be a highly deterministic tradition. As Donald Fry puts it, because the "traditional poet performs with diction and structures borrowed from others, within inherited patterns[, i]solating the traditional poet within his own corpus smacks of Romantic and post-Romantic notions of poetry and unique genius" ("Old English" 3). But in its treatment of the author, oral theory departs from contemporary critical theory. To take but one example, scholars have only recently begun to pierce the blanket of sameness cast upon early medieval English oral-derived poetry by the traditional oral register in which most (if not all) Old English poetry is composed; as a result, the individual talent and idiosyncratic behavior of the artists responsible for creating even the most thoroughly traditional Old English poems are beginning to come into focus.

The *Beowulf* poet's treatment of the traditional theme of the beasts of battle illustrates just how distinctively the author has stamped even what is widely regarded as the most traditional of Old English poems. Francis Peabody Magoun, Jr., first described this theme as "the mention of the wolf, eagle and/or raven as beasts attendant upon a scene of carnage. They seem to appear in nine poems on twelve occasions, where their presence serves to embellish a battle scene or a reference to warfare" (83). As Magoun and others went on to note, the theme's shared narrative elements and the verbal correspondences among its occurrences point to the theme's roots in oral tradition.[10] We will probably never be able to judge whether the theme is given its most or least traditional articulation in *Beowulf*, but in the poet's handling of the theme, especially when the poet gives the raven the power of speech and defers the theme's usual complement of a bloody martial engagement to a point outside his narrative, we can recognize the individual accomplishment of the *Beowulf* poet and perhaps even gain a clearer sense of his genius.[11]

Although writing is a technology of alienation that, as contemporary criticism demonstrates, has weakened the author's authority (if not led to the author's extinction) and that has created a reader who actively and subjectively (co)creates literature, authors and readers in literate cultures share many similarities with singers and audiences in oral cultures. As his poem's introduction illustrates, Lawman, the author of the late-twelfth-century *Brut*, goes about his business in ways that are strikingly familiar to moderns. Not only does he name himself, but he also announces his occupation (he is a priest), the place where he lives (outside Worcester in Redstone), and his father's name (Leovenath). Most important, he also cites the three *written* sources of his poem (two of which are extant), calls our attention to his editorial acumen, and explicitly comments on the methods and technology he employed to produce the poem. After traveling far and wide to gather his sources, Lawman spreads them before himself and, after leafing through them, announces that

> Feþeren he nom mid fingren? Ᵹ fiede on boc-felle.
> Ᵹ þa soþere word? sette to-gadere.
> Ᵹ þa þre boc? þrumde to are.
>
> (Brook and Leslie, lines 26–28; 1: 2)

> Quill pens he clutched in fingers, composing on his parchment,
> And the more reliable versions he recorded,
> Compressing those three texts into one complete book.
>
> (Rosamund Allen 1)

His authorial self-consciousness, his endeavor's demonstrable inter-textuality, and his undeniably literate mode of composition clearly situate both Lawman and his poem within a highly literate poetics whose contours remain identifiable and familiar even at the remove of some eight hundred years. The *Brut* has much to teach us about the medieval roots of contemporary compositional practices, but because it depends as heavily on oral as on literate poetics (for a fuller discussion of the *Brut*'s oral poetics, see Amodio, "Introduction" 13–21), it speaks directly and powerfully against the still widely held view that insurmountable differences separate medieval from modern and oral from literate cultures.

———

Both the application of contemporary critical approaches to early oral and oral-derived literatures and the application of oral theory to literature produced in literate cultures by literate authors have been fore-stalled by the belief that orality and literacy are distinct and mutually exclusive categories, a belief fundamental to what Finnegan labels the "Great Divide" (*Literacy* 12–14). In this brief and highly selective survey, I have tried to outline some of the more important points of contact between oral theory and contemporary critical theory in the hope that the examples offered may prove helpful in further challenging the false dichotomy oral/literate to which many oralists and nonoralists alike still cling. I have further tried to show that recognizing and exploring some of the parallels between oral theory and other contemporary critical approaches and then carefully and judiciously applying insights from each will prove extremely beneficial to both oralists and contemporary critical theorists. Some of the most radical and unsettling contentions of contemporary critical theory find powerful support in oral theory, where textual multiformity, authorial absence, and subjective, active recipients are not simply theoretical postulates but essential and, most important, demonstrable components of the reception of oral and oral-derived texts. Similarly, the theoretical framework for much of the groundbreaking work being done in oral theory has already been laid by contemporary critical theory, where the unstable nature of physically fixed texts, the limitations of authorial control, and the role of the recipient have long been central concerns. Acknowledging that the distance between oral theory and contemporary critical theory, like the supposed distance between the oral and written worlds, is not nearly so great as many have postulated will enable us better to understand the mechanics and aesthetics of texts and cultures that lie at various points along the oral-literate continuum.

Notes

1. See Groden and Kreiswirth for a thorough overview of the various schools of contemporary literary criticism and theory. For a detailed discussion of the development of oral theory, see Foley, *Theory of Oral Composition*.
2. For generally useful discussions of strategies for bringing contemporary theory into the undergraduate classroom, see Sadoff and Cain.
3. That the term "oral theory" appears nowhere in Groden and Kreiswirth's recent compendious guide to contemporary theory and criticism illustrates just how thoroughly marginalized oral theory continues to be, despite the impressively large, and continually growing, body of scholarship produced by oralists. For a comprehensive list of works in oral theory up to the mid-1980s, see Foley's *Oral-Formulaic Theory and Research*, a volume that contains references to more than 1,800 articles and books in ninety-odd languages (with updates in the journal *Oral Tradition*).

4. According to oral-formulaic theory, which rests ultimately on an absolute dichotomy between the oral and the literate modes of composition, only those texts composed during performance by demonstrably nonliterate singers or poets can be considered oral. The classic articulations of the theory of oral-formulaic composition can be found in Parry (*Making*) and in the work of Parry's student and successor, Albert Lord (esp. *Singer of Tales* and the posthumously published *Singer Resumes*).

5. For a recent, important, and spirited defense of the theory of oral-formulaic composition, see Lord, *Singer Resumes* 187–202.

6. As Lord made clear in some of his later writings, composition-in-performance is not to be confused with improvisation. The type of traditional oral composition Lord is concerned with is "not improvisation, if by improvisation we mean that which is impromptu, without premeditation or preparation" (*Singer Resumes* 101). Further, as Lord continues, "Each performance results in a 'new' text, . . . but that 'new' text is made up of formulas, blocks of lines, and themes of preceding performances," in short, of traditional compositional elements. See also Lord, *Epic Singers* 76–78.

7. On the term "oral-derived" and for an important discussion of oral-derived texts, see Foley, *Immanent Art*.

8. See Bessinger and Yeager for approaches to teaching *Beowulf*; for pedagogical approaches to Old English poetry from the perspective of oral tradition, see Olsen, this volume; O'Keeffe, this volume. See also Amodio, "Affective Criticism."

9. We must note, of course, that the nonliterate *guslari* interviewed by Parry and Lord during their field trips in then-Yugoslavia had their own concept of "word," one that differs greatly from our literate one. The *guslari*, from their perspective, reproduce works accurately, because they work in a tradition in which the basic element of composition, what we would call a word, is in fact a multiform, substitutable element that ranges in size between a poetic line and an entire epic. For a more detailed discussion of this issue, see Foley, *Traditional Oral Epic* 39–51 (esp. 44–45).

10. For more on the theme in Old English poetry, see Olsen, "Research . . . I"; Lord, *Singer Resumes* 137–66.

11. *Beowulf* is the only poem in which any of the beasts of battle speak and the only poem that fails to present an explicit account of slaughter following the appearance of the beasts of battle. See further Olsen's discussion of this theme's treatment in Cynewulf's poetry (*Speech* 45–50). Donoghue makes an important contribution to our understanding of the individual talent of Old English poets by arguing that the poems generally attributed to Cynewulf do not exhibit the uniformity of syntax that we might expect among the works of the same poet.

Richard Bauman and Donald Braid

The Ethnography of Performance in the Study of Oral Traditions

Orientations

The ethnography of performance is a term that refers not to a specific theory or analytic method but to a general approach to the study of oral traditions. At the heart of performance-centered approaches is a reorientation from a view of oral traditions solely as textual objects to a conception of oral traditions as manifestations of a special mode of communicative action and as resources for the conduct of social life.[1]

From the first emergence of the modern concept of folklore in the late eighteenth century until very recently, oral traditions have been conceived of as textual items — collectively shaped, traditional texts that could diffuse across the landscape, persist through time, fill up collections and archives, or reflect culture. Viewed in these terms, oral traditions appear to have lives of their own, subject only to impersonal, superorganic processes and laws. But this view is an abstraction, founded on memories or recordings of tales as told, songs as sung, spells as chanted. Approached in terms of performance, the symbolic forms we call oral traditions have their primary existence in the action of people and their roots in social and cultural life. The texts we are accustomed to viewing as the materials of oral traditions are merely the thin and partial record of deeply situated human behavior. Performance-centered approaches seek to go beyond a conception of oral traditions as disembodied textual items and to view those traditions contextually and ethnographically, in order to discover the individual, social, and cultural factors that give them shape and meaning as part of lived experience.

Under the stimulus of this reorientation, the term *performance* has taken on several interrelated meanings that reflect the concerns of this approach. Most generally, performance is used in the sense of "doing" or "practice," centering on the active use of verbal art forms in context (see, e.g., Paredes and Bauman; Ben-Amos and Goldstein). Identifying performance as practice deepens our understanding of oral traditions by emphasizing their dynamic and creative qualities as "equipment for living" (Burke).

Conceptualizing performance as social practice, however, does not directly address the dimension of artfulness that we associate with performance as a special mode of communication. Not all doings of oral traditions display the same artistry and virtuosity. For example, some may only report or quote or summarize artistic performance. Building on the conception of performance as practice, a second, more restricted meaning of performance has emerged from related work in folklore and linguistic anthropology (Bauman, *Verbal Art*; D. Hymes, "Breakthrough"). Here, performance is understood as a distinctive mode of communication, resting on an assumption of accountability to an audience for a display of skill and efficacy. Performance highlights the artful way communication is carried out, above and beyond the other features of the communicative act. From the point of view of the audience, the act of expression is thus laid open to evaluation for the skill and effectiveness with which it is accomplished. In performance, the act of expression is also marked as available for the enhancement of experience; the intrinsic qualities of the act itself are enjoyed. The explicit inclusion of an audience in this formulation makes clear that this approach to performance is social-interactional. The performer-audience interaction has a formative—indeed, a constitutive—influence on performance. A performer fashions his or her performance to affect—move, persuade, enlighten, entertain—an audience and anticipates evaluation by that audience in return. Likewise, the responses of the audience have a reciprocal effect on the unfolding course of the performance (Briggs, *Competence*).[2]

We use the term *ethnography* in identifying our approach to performance in order to emphasize that performance, as cultural behavior, is patterned within each society in culture-specific, cross-culturally and historically variable ways, and that the forms, patterns, and functions of performance in a given culture are to be discovered empirically, not assumed a priori. As we employ the term, ethnography is a sustained investigation into the unique dynamics and cultural patternings of cultural behavior in a given community. While ethnography is primarily oriented toward field research, the same process of sustained empirical investigation can be extended to the exploration of historical cases or written literature (e.g., Bauman, "Performance"; Foley, *Singer*; Martin, *Language*).

In this essay, we first develop the basic assumptions and concepts of performance-centered approaches to oral traditions by concentrating on performance as an artistically marked way of speaking, a view of performance that incorporates the more general sense of performance as practice. We then discuss some implications of performance-centered analysis for notions of context, traditionality, textuality, and genre. Finally, by examining a specific instance of oral storytelling, we suggest how narrative performance may be approached from a performance-centered perspective.

Foundations

Identifying performance as an artful mode of communication suggests that performance involves a way of using language, a way of speaking, that is available as a communicative resource to the members of a given speech community. The frame of reference for this understanding derives from the *ethnography of speaking* (D. Hymes,

Foundations; Bauman and Sherzer), an approach to the study of language in society and culture that has transcended the approach's origins in linguistic anthropology to guide investigations in a wide range of disciplines, including folklore, literature, classical studies, linguistics, speech communication, social history, and religious studies. In contrast to linguistic approaches that focus exclusively on grammar as an abstract, autonomous formal system or on language as a vehicle of thought, the ethnography of speaking seeks to discover the culturally specific patterns and functions of speaking, of language in use. It therefore places emphasis on the act of speaking in the act's situational context and on the competency of individuals to speak (and interact) in culturally and situationally appropriate and interpretable ways. By situational context, we mean the culturally defined scenes or events in which the conduct, interpretation, and evaluation of speaking take place. The speech event is a central unit of description and analysis in the ethnography of speaking. The classic questions, 'Who says what? to whom? how? for what purpose? under what circumstances?' all point to essential components of the speech event and, by extension, of the performance event as well.

Drawing on these insights, performance-centered studies of oral traditions consider the knowledge and ability required to accomplish a performance in the ebb and flow of social life. To the extent that skill and efficacy of expression may become the focus of attention in any act of communication, the potential for performance is always present. Performance must therefore be understood as a variable quality, relatively more or less salient among the multiple functions served by a communicative act — to inform, to persuade, to entertain, to make contact, and so on. The relative dominance of performance will depend on the degree to which the performer assumes responsibility to an audience for a display of communicative virtuosity as against other communicative functions. That responsibility may range along a continuum from sustained, full performance to a fleeting breakthrough into performance. In certain instances, the calibration of performance may be signaled overtly. Compare, for example, the kind of hedging introduction one commonly hears from a less than fully confident joke teller (such as, "I'm not very good at telling jokes, but . . .") with the assured preamble of an eyewitness to a memorable event telling a story that he has recounted many times ("Yes, that I know is true. That I saw him do. I sat right, right in the shop and saw him, saw him do that" [Bauman, "Disclaimers" 193]).

To understand how performance may be differentiated from other modes of communication, it is useful to invoke the idea of *interpretive frames* (Bateson; Goffman). The notion of frame rests on the recognition that every communicative act incorporates elements that serve to convey interpretive guidelines, signals that suggest how the act is to be understood. Consider the wink that signals, "Don't take this seriously," or the raised voice that indicates, "I'm really mad!" The wink or shout serves as a kind of communication about the act of communication of which it is a part, that is, it serves as *metacommunication* (Briggs, *Learning*). Such metacommunicative signals frame the communicative act by guiding listeners' interpretations of it.

The performance frame, in effect, signals, "I'm on! Watch this display of verbal virtuosity! Take account of how skillfully and effectively I render what I say." The specific means that signal or key the performance frame will vary from culture to culture; an essential part of the ethnography of performance is to discover how performance is keyed in a speech community. Nevertheless, certain keys to performance seem to turn up frequently in the world's cultures, though in varying combinations. A brief inventory of these commonly employed devices might include:

Special framing formulas ("Once upon a time," "Did you hear the one about . . . ?")

Formal patterning principles or devices (rhyme, grammatical parallelism, meter, intonational patterns, taking on voices)

Special speech styles, or *registers* (archaic speech, indirect or allusive speech, "salty speech," jargon)

Figurative language (use of metaphor, simile, irony, other tropes)

Appeals to tradition ("The old people say . . .")

Special kinds of bodily movement (standing up, pacing, bowing the head, mimetic gestures)

>   Special settings conventionally associated with performance (the
>   nightclub stage, the lectern, the liars' bench)
>   Disclaimers of performance ("Unaccustomed as I am to public
>   speaking . . . ," "I'm not as good a storyteller as my grand-
>   father, but . . .")

This is not a checklist. The means of keying performance, as well as
the patterns, functions, and meanings of performance as a way of
speaking, will vary from culture to culture and from historical period
to historical period; they must be discovered empirically as part of
the ethnography of performance.

At least some aspects of the formal construction of the message,
that is, of *poetics*, will always be relevant to the performance frame,
insofar as performance focuses attention on the intrinsic qualities of
the act of expression, on how the utterance is constructed. This
makes it all the more important to emphasize that performance does
not reside in the formal organization of the text alone. Good form is
a necessary but not sufficient element of performance. Even a finely
wrought verse or story may be quoted, relayed, or reported by a
speaker who is nevertheless unwilling to take responsibility for a full
virtuosic display, open to evaluation by an audience. Accountability
is essential to performance in our sense of the term. Performances are
judged for efficacy as well as skill, that is, how well they are fitted to
the situation at hand and how effective they are in achieving their
ends, whether entertainment, persuasion, instruction, evocation of
emotion, or any other.

Recognizing performance as an artful way of speaking directs
attention to the interdependence of text and context by placing the
situated act of speaking at the center of investigation. The identification of situational context as a shaping factor in oral performance
focuses attention in turn on the organization of the events in which
oral performance characteristically occurs. Situational contexts may
have a formative influence on the texts that emerge in them, as when
a slumber party encourages the performance of scary stories, like
"The Ghostly Hitchhiker" or "The Hook" (Brunvand, *Vanishing
Hitchhiker*), that so often seem to have happened to a friend of a
friend of someone at the party. At the same time, the stories help

make the slumber party what it is; they are constitutive of the event. One might say, "It just wouldn't *be* a slumber party if we didn't tell scary stories." The performance of oral traditions, therefore, is not simply the presentation of traditional texts in conventionally organized events. A focus on performance as artistic communication suggests that both text and context must be understood as situated accomplishments. Both are emergent in performance. The models provided by generic norms, standard scenarios, and prior renditions of traditional items stand available to participants as a set of conventional expectations and associations, but these models may be used as resources for creative manipulation, shaping the emergent text and context to the conditions of the moment.

Situational context is not the only point of reference for contextualization. In performing a narrative, for example, the storyteller might link his or her performance to elements of the physical setting ("It happened on a rainy night just like this"), to cultural beliefs and values ("It's dangerous for boys and girls to go out parking in remote places"), to participants in the event ("This really happened to a friend of a friend of mine"), to past experience ("The last time I babysat for someone, I was scared to death"), to other narratives ("That's just like the time that . . ."), to past performances of this narrative ("I heard this from my sister"), and so on.

Contextualization of a performance by reference to past performances, as in "The old people used to say" or "I got this story from my uncle," is of special interest to students of oral tradition. We are accustomed to thinking of traditionality as a quality that inheres in a cultural form that originated in the past and has been handed down through time. It is useful to recognize, however, that the attribution of traditionality to a song or story or proverb in communicative practice is an interpretive construction carried out in the present, as performers actively invoke links between their own and prior performances. This is *traditionalization*, the creation in the present of ties to a meaningful past that is itself constructed in the act of performance (D. Hymes, "Folklore's Nature"; Bauman, "Contextualization").

Thus far this essay has argued that the form, function, and meaning of oral traditions cannot be fully comprehended by conceiving of them as static, disembodied texts, that oral traditions are anchored in the process of production and reception. What is it, then, that allows us so readily to treat texts as self-contained, autonomous objects despite all these anchoring counterforces? What prompts us to separate them from their social, cultural, and discursive contexts? At the heart of the decontextualization process is the closely related process of *entextualization*, of rendering a stretch of discourse extractable, of making a stretch of verbal production into a unit that can be lifted out of the contexts in which it is grounded (Bauman and Briggs; Silverstein and Urban). This process of text making brings us back once again to form, to those formal devices and patterns that serve to render stretches of speech production discontinuous with the surrounding speech and internally cohesive. For example, in Bahamian storytelling (Crowley, *I Could Talk* 32–40), the opening sequence

> "Bunday!" + opening formula (such as "Once upon a time, a very good time, monkey chew tobacco and he spit white lime")

and the closing sequence

> closing formula (such as "If you don't believe my story is true, ask the captain of the longboat crew") + "Bunday!"

serve to separate the narrative from what comes before it and what comes after. In between the opening and closing, such additional formal devices as taking on voices, onomatopoeia, the use of distinctive pronunciations and idioms, and the repetition of short songs provide internal ties that organize the performed tale into a cohesive unit and make the text a bounded object susceptible to decontextualization. Performance, as a highly reflexive mode of communication that heightens awareness of the act of speaking, that puts the act on display, objectifies it, and to some degree lifts it from its situational surroundings, strengthens this susceptibility still further.

The possibility of decontextualization from one context implies recontextualization in another, whether in another performance or in an archive, folklore collection, storybook, or novel. Decontextualization and recontextualization may be understood as two aspects of the same process, though time and other factors may mediate between them. Because the process is transformational, insofar as the anchoring of a text in a new context will alter at least some aspects of its form, function, or meaning, recontextualization directs attention to what a text brings with it from earlier contexts and what emergent form, function, and meaning it acquires in its new contexts. Attention to the process of decontextualization and recontextualization introduces a historical dimension into performance analysis by focusing on the *intertextual* links in the chain of situated uses of oral traditions that take place over time (Bauman and Briggs; for an example see Bauman, "Nationalization").

While from more traditional perspectives intertextuality may appear to rest on demonstrable relations among cognate texts (versions, variants), from a performance-centered perspective intertextuality is once again a creative accomplishment. Intertextual links are *created* in performance, as the performer fashions a song or a story by reference, implicit or explicit, to prior performances. But intertextuality does not need to be restricted to recontextualization of traditional texts; it can apply productively also to genre (Briggs and Bauman). Genre is commonly used as a classificatory concept, a way of grouping oral traditions into normative typological categories — fairy tale, legend, myth, ballad, riddle, and so on — each with its conventional defining attributes. In terms of performance, though, genre is better understood as a socially provided and culturally shaped framework for the production and reception of discourse, a model (or frame of reference, or set of expectations) that serves as a guide for the fashioning of an appropriately formed, intelligible utterance. It is the system of generic discriminations employed by the members of the performance community that we seek here, in our ethnographic frame of reference, not the more universal analytic categories formulated by scholars for comparative purposes (Ben-Amos, *Folklore Genres*; Briggs, *Competence*).

Two *Corridos*

A Mexican American singer on the Texas-Mexico border who wants to recount in song a memorable incident of conflict or crisis is likely to draw on the traditional *corrido* ballad form as a model.[3] Thus, a *corridista* composing a song about the assassination of John F. Kennedy will produce a *corrido* that may echo a song recounting an episode from the Mexican Revolution a half-century earlier, because the new composition employs the same generic conventions as the earlier one. Note the resemblances between the opening and closing stanzas of two such *corridos*:

La Toma de Matamoros

Voy a cantar estos versos
pongan mucha atención
    todos,
voy a cantar la tragedia
de la Heroica Matamoros.

Día martes tres de junio
de mil novecientos trece,
a las diez de la mañana
Lucio Blanco se aparece.

. . . .

Ya con ésta me despido,
me compadezco de todos,
y con tristeza les digo
que perdimos Matamoros.

The Taking of Matamoros

I am going to sing these
    stanzas,
everyone pay much attention;
I am going to sing the ballad
of the Heroic Matamoros.

On Tuesday, the third of June
of nineteen hundred thirteen,
at ten o'clock in the morning
Lucio Blanco makes his
    appearance.

. . . .

Now with this I say farewell,
I feel compassion for all,
and with sadness I tell you
that we lost Matamoros.

(Paredes, *Texas-Mexican Cancionero* 83–85)

En Honor a Kennedy

Voy a cantarles señores
sólo así puedo expresar
el dolor de mis dolores
mi gran pena y mi pesar.

In Honor of Kennedy

I am going to sing for you
    gentlemen,
only in this way can I express
the pain of my grief,
my great sorrow and heavy
    heart.

Año de sesenta y tres	The year of sixty-three,
del veintidós de noviembre,	on the twenty-second of
entre la ciudad de Dallas	November,
mataron al Presidente.	in the city of Dallas
	they killed the President.

. . . .

Aquí termino señores	Here I end, gentlemen,
la tragedia que escribí,	the tragedy that I wrote,
con dolor de mis dolores	with the pain of my grief
en honor a Kennedy.	in honor of Kennedy.

(Dickey 88–89; some changes in trans.)

Both songs open with reflexive references to the singer, the audience, and the act of singing itself, that is, to the communicative nexus of the *corrido* performance. Information follows about the location of the ballad action in time and place and about the identity of the central figure in the narrative. Both songs close with a *despedida* ("leave-taking"), in which the singer sums up the emotional weight of the ballad and takes leave of the audience. "The Taking of Matamoros" and "In Honor of Kennedy" are thus linked by a series of traditional framing devices that are conventions of the *corrido* genre.

Old Chief Goes Fishing

As an example of the kinds of insights afforded by performance-centered analysis of oral traditions, we present here a brief look at one narrative performance. Because of space limitations, our analysis is intended to be suggestive rather than exhaustive.

The following narrative was recorded by Donald Braid during a field interview with Duncan Williamson on 6 February 1993. Williamson is one of the Travelling People of Scotland, sometimes called Tinkers because of their former association with the making, selling, and mending of tinware. The Travellers maintain a separate cultural identity in spite of legal and social pressure on them to abandon their way of life, a way of life that includes, prominently, the itinerancy referred to by the designations "gan aboot folk" ("going about folk") or "Travelling People" (see Gentleman and Swift; Rehfisch). The interview focused on aspects of Williamson's genealogy. For many of the relations Williamson identified, he offered characterizing stories that carried the interaction beyond mere genealogical information, serving among other things to enhance the interview experience through performance. As he talked about Maggie MacLearen, a distant relation, Williamson commented that she was a good storyteller. He told two of her stories; we transcribe the second of these here.[4]

1 She was telling me another story.
    Old Sandy Cameron, she said,
    her man's father, Old San — Old Chief,
    he was a great fisherman.
5 He liked to fish.
    And he was fishing in some private loch, see? [uhuh]
    She was a great story —
    she could tell you stories about anything.
    And she says Old Sandy,
10 God rest his soul —
    And she'd swear'r life away
    trying to make you believe it was true.
    Maybe it was.
    And she said Old Chief was fishing, she said,
15 with a bit of stick and a line.
    And she said he was casting
    some kind of private river somewhere.
    Some estate out in Perthshire.
    On —

20 Along came a big gentleman, you know? [mhmm]
    Gentleman.
    Big waders, you know? [mhmm]
    And the basket on his back,
    and the landing net, you know?
25 Real gentleman.
    And he's casting away and casting away.
    And Old Sandy pulled in (gesture) a big sea trout,
    about that size. [mhmm]
    And the gentleman was watching him.

30 He hooked it off
    and threw it back.
    Gentleman's staring at him.

Casting away with a cast of flies.
Old Sandy's casting the worms he had.
35 And he's cast again, see?
He knew he was in trouble, you see? [mhmm]
Cast again.
And the gentleman's watching him.
Because he, he thought it was the laird, you see?
40 He could have done with a fish, but —
And he hooked another one about this size (gesture). [mhmm]
And the gentleman's watching him again.

It was close together.
He's hooked it off.
45 "Away you go, you fishie."
And he put it back again.
And the gentleman come up.

"Excuse me, sir," he says.
"Why are you fishing here?"
50 And he said, "I'm fishing in the river," he said.
"Don't you know," he said,
"you are on private property?"
"I didn't know it was private property," he said.
"I'm one of the Travelling folk," he said.
55 "I'm just trying to get a fish."
"But what's the sense of —
You see, I've been here for an hour,
and I can't catch anything.
What's the secret?"
60 "Well," he said,
(brusque voice) "just a handful of worms, mister," he said to
        him.
You know the way the Travellers speak, [mhmm]
kind of rough.
(brusque voice) "A handful of worms."
65 "Well, I saw you putting two nice fish back,
didn't you?"
He says, "Why did you put them back?"
He says, "I'll tell you why I put them back."
"Why did you put them back, then?"
70 He says, "My pan's only that size." (indicates a size smaller than
        the two fish he caught) [laugh]
And he pulled in his line and walked away.
Gentleman watched him.

Never said a word. [laugh]
That's the only way he could get out of it, you know? [uhuh]
75 He was going to charge him for fishing.

He said, "My, my, my wee frying pan, mister,
is only that size," he says,
"and they're too big for my pan,
so I'll no bother more today."
80 And he walked away.
The gentleman looked at him, the laird,
fishing the stream,
private river.

Narrative performances like this one are particularly interesting as a site for exploring the interrelation between oral traditions and social life because they are multiply anchored in human events. Narratives are grounded in the narrative event in which they are told and simultaneously in the narrated event(s) that they recount (Bauman, *Story*). Williamson's performance, as transcribed above, actually interrelates three events: the interview with Braid, Maggie MacLearen's earlier recounting of the story to Williamson, and the story of Sandy Cameron ("Old Chief") and the laird (the "gentleman"). Let us examine some of the salient dimensions of contextualization Williamson uses to endow his narration with social meaning.

Observe first, in the opening line of the transcript, that Williamson relates the story he is about to tell to the story he has just told, thus establishing the new story's relevance to his ongoing interaction with Braid. He develops this relevance further by noting (line 3) that Old Chief was MacLearen's husband's father, because kinship is the central focus of the genealogical interview. In addition, Williamson links the story both to MacLearen's repertoire and to the occasion in which she told the story to him; the second link amounts to an act of traditionalization, relating this telling to a prior telling of the same story, a recontextualization of it.

In general terms, the portion of the encounter recorded in lines 1–19 is framed as a report of MacLearen's recounting of the story. Lines 14–19 are transitional: the narrative action commences in line 14, and the major complication on which the story turns is foreshadowed in the identification of the river as being on a private estate.

These are relevant parts of Williamson's own telling but still framed as a report of MacLearen's narration. With line 20, however, Mac-Learen drops out and Williamson takes full control of the narration, introducing the gentleman who is to be the foil to Old Chief as the action unfolds and emphasizing the gentleman's importance by citing him twice again in the next three lines.

The body of the narrative, from line 20 onward, is a tightly cohesive and complexly crafted performance, in which Williamson skillfully employs a range of formal devices in the service of textual organization and artistic effect. A full formal analysis would far exceed the scope of this essay, so we confine our discussion to a few selected features.

Note the effectiveness of the parallel constructions built on line 29, "And the gentleman was watching him": lines 32, 38, 42, 47, 72, and 81. These parallel lines divide the narrative into segments that establish Old Chief as the agent of the significant actions in the story and the gentleman as one who largely watches things happen. Line 47 stands out in this series; instead of watching, "the gentleman come up." This change marks an important structural point in the narrative, where Williamson switches from narrative description to quoted dialogue that leads up to the denouement.

Note too the finely tuned use of physical gestures (lines 41, 70), which underscore the importance of the size of the fish to the point of the story. These gestures, together with the quoted dialogue that makes up the bulk of the action from line 45 to line 79, are important elements of performance, in that they represent the mimetic reenactment of the narrated action rather than a discursive recounting of it. This embodiment of the action draws the narrated event into the narrative event, merging the two and creating an effect of immediacy and presence.

The quoted speech in line 70 is the climax of the narrative, the critical utterance by which Old Chief prevails in his encounter with the gentleman. Williamson conveys its climatic importance in multiple ways: first, by accompanying Old Chief's words with a dramatic gesture; second, by establishing that the effect of these words is to bring the gentleman to silence (line 73: "Never said a word"); and finally, by replaying them in elaborated form as a narrative coda (lines 76–79), which allows the final breaking off of the encounter.

Old Chief's clever escape from the difficult situation of being caught red-handed poaching fish on a private estate has special significance in the larger context of Traveller life, beyond what is captured by the transcript. The Travelling People all too often find themselves at or outside the margins of the law, in part because of deliberate policies designed to marginalize them, in part because opposition to mainstream society serves as a potent basis of self-definition. Travellers thus pride themselves in their ability to gain the upper hand in their dealings with others, especially with people of privilege. Not surprisingly, then, their narrative repertoire is filled with stories that celebrate such victories (Braid, "Traveller," "Negotiation," "Construction"). In the story before us, Old Chief is doubly successful. First, he bests the gentleman at fishing, his humble "bit of stick and a line" and "handful of worms" prevailing over the fancy fly-fishing gear of the laird. Then, he silences the laird and wins the day with his quick-thinking strategy of throwing back the large fish he hooks and ultimately with his verbal wit, a prized skill among the Travellers.

It is also telling that Old Chief's climactic statement in line 70 draws the response of laughter from Braid, signaling the success of the performance, its effect in moving the audience. Indeed, Williamson is assiduous in attending to his audience throughout the performance, monitoring Braid's understanding and interest and eliciting his participatory involvement with metanarrational tag questions such as "See?" and "You know?" that anchor the performance in the storytelling event and draw back-channel responses such as "Uhuh" and "Mhmm." Williamson offers further metanarrational guides to interpretation in lines 62–64 and 74–75, lines 62–66 underscoring the central significance of "the way the Travellers speak," which prefigures the punch line of line 70, and lines 74–75 summarizing the punch line's effect in accomplishing the resolution of the problematic encounter between Old Chief and the gentleman.

There is much more we could say about the poetics of Williamson's performance — the cohesive and measuring effect of additional parallel constructions (lines 30 and 44; 51–53; 67–69); the repetition of key phrases (lines 26 and 33; 61 and 64), quotative frames (lines 50–54), and metanarrational tag questions (lines 35, 36, 39); the use of series of grammatical variants of key words (lines 4–6); and so on. Instead, we invite the reader to join us in the discovery process by reading the transcript aloud, restoring the living voice of performance. We are confident that this experience will enhance appreciation of Williamson's performance. Perhaps, too, reading the transcript aloud will enhance the persuasiveness of our argument that performance offers a powerfully illuminating vantage point on the form, function, and meaning of oral traditions.

Notes

1. On the historical place of performance studies, see the glossary of approaches to oral tradition by Zumwalt, this volume.

2. Another sense of *performance* focuses on cultural performances, symbolically resonant public events such as festivals, spectacles, dramas, or fairs, in which the central meanings and values of a community are embodied, acted out, and laid open to examination and interpretation. As the scenarios of such events frequently include the performance of oral traditions, they are of interest to students of verbal art. But the elucidation of cultural performances in all their semiotic and cultural complexity demands analytic perspectives that extend well beyond the focus and scope of this essay (see Abrahams, "Shouting Match"; Bauman, "Performance"; M. Singer; Stoeltje and Bauman).

3. On the *corrido* and other genres from Mexican American oral tradition, see Herrera-Sobek, this volume.

4. In transcribing the narrative, we have set it out in lines based in part on syntactic structures, in part on breath pauses. Salient gestural and paralinguistic features of Williamson's performance are indicated in parentheses; back-channel responses by Braid are given in square brackets. Our primary concern in preparing this transcription has been to bring to the fore a range of significant formal devices and patterning principles employed by Williamson in the crafting of his performance. Transcription takes on special heuristic significance in the analysis of performance because of the centrality of form to an understanding of how a performance is accomplished and how it achieves its effects (see DuBois on ethnopoetics, this volume).

Thomas DuBois

Ethnopoetics

In 1970, the journal *Alcheringa: Ethnopoetics* appeared. Its statement of purpose framed a new scholarly enterprise: the examination of poetics in cultures throughout the world, particularly nonliterate ones:

> By exploring the full range of man's poetries we hope
>
> - to enlarge our understanding of *what a poem may be*
> - to provide a ground for *experiments in the translation of tribal/ oral poetry* and a forum for the discussion of the *problems and possibilities of translation* from widely divergent languages and cultures
> - to encourage poets to participate actively in the translation of tribal/oral poetry
> - to encourage ethnologists and linguists to do work increasingly ignored by academic publications in their fields, namely to present tribal *poetries as values in themselves* rather than as ethnographic data

- to initiate cooperative projects along these lines among poets, ethnologists, performers, and others
- to emphasize by example and commentary the relevance of tribal poetry to where-we-are today.

(Rothenberg and Tedlock 2; italics added)

Like most new journals, *Alcheringa* was created to fill a need. Literary journals saw oral poetry as primitive and wanted no part of it; anthropology journals saw oral poetry only as data, not art. In time, through the efforts of many researchers, particularly Dennis Tedlock and Dell Hymes, ethnopoetics — and the goals of *Alcheringa* — became established as legitimate, even central. Two and a half decades later, when ethnopoetics has become a standard term in the study of oral traditions in general, it makes sense to take stock of where the field has been, what it has discovered, and where it is moving. New vistas for ethnopoetic research opened up in the 1980s, but some of its original goals remain unrealized even today. I examine this approach with an eye to its usefulness to the teacher of literature. By problematizing the nature of textual presentation, accentuating the expressive and rhetorical aspects of oral communication, and grappling with issues of cross-cultural aesthetics, ethnopoetics offers teachers valuable tools for understanding expressive communication and awakening student interest in the wealth of literature that relies on oral transmission.

What a Poem May Be

Few distinctions carry as much weight in the study of literature in English as the poetry/prose dichotomy. Whether it is words or form that makes the difference, we generally view poetry as something greater than prose: a finer, more intricate, decidedly more expressive mode of communication. To call someone's writing poetic is to offer it high praise; to label someone's work prosaic is to diminish its value.

At the outset of the ethnopoetic enterprise, a few scholars began to question the placement of Native American narratives on the prose side of the prose-poetry dichotomy. The style of such oral storytellers had always been described as artless, monotonous, prosaic. Myths recorded from Native American narrators were usually translated into stiff, formal English, laden with grammatical explanations or philological notes. Alternatively, narratives were translated freely as prose, with little attempt to capture and reproduce the original's form or even to translate the same word in the same way consistently. Both these methods of textual presentation robbed the original narratives of much of their expressive potential and grace (D. Hymes "Some North Pacific Coast Poems," "Particle"). And since few readers, scholarly or generalist, could readily avail themselves of the original texts, which were written in phonetic transcriptions and in languages seldom studied outside tribal or linguistic circles, the artistry of these texts remained beyond the reach of most.

It was the first goal of ethnopoetics to present anew narratives from Native American cultures as poetry, accentuating the form and expressive aspects inherent in many collected texts and sound recordings. Such an act, of course, calls into question both how we conceive of poetry and prose in English and how we recognize each in other cultures. For theoretical foundations, the researchers turned to the Prague school linguists, particularly Roman Jakobson, who had pioneered the study of poetics within linguistics. Also fundamental to the enterprise were the writings of earlier American scholars of Native American cultures, especially Edward Sapir (*Language*) and Melville Jacobs; an emerging subfield of linguistics called sociolinguistics; and the ethnography of communication. To this scholarly foundation were added the presentational innovations of modern poets in English and the expanded potential of modern print. In claiming the exalted title of poetry for the texts they translated and in presenting the translations as poetic texts, these scholars maintained that narratives in cultures marked by primary orality possessed a formal artistry that previous scholars had missed. Although a text may not show a strict adherence to a traditional meter or other recognizable marker of poetic identity, it may still prove poetic in structure as well as delivery. By reading, translating, and presenting the work as poetry, then, the expressive aspects and formal features of the text itself are recovered for the reader.

Experiments in the Translation of Tribal/Oral Poetry

Alcheringa, like the field of ethnopoetics itself, owes much to Ted-lock, whose many works focus on ways to present oral narration that integrate into the texts as much of the style and sounds of the original as possible, even in translation. Loud words can be capitalized, whis-pered words reduced to fine print. Pauses in speech can be repre-sented by line breaks. Expressive tone and length of pronunciation can find demarcation on the printed page. In his anthology *Finding the Center: Narrative Poetry of the Zuni Indians* and in his seminal theo-retical work *The Spoken Word and the Work of Interpretation*, Tedlock creates evocative, expressive texts that capture much of the flavor of Zuni and Quiché Mayan oral narratives (see Fine, this volume). Here, as an example, is Tedlock's translation of the opening of An-drew Peynetsa's Zuni myth "Coyote and Junco" (the bullet marks a very long pause):

SON'AHCHI.

   SONTI ^{LO}————NG A _{GO}
   •

AT STANDING ARROWS
OLD LADY JUNCO HAD HER HOME
and COYOTE
Coyote was there at Sitting Rock with his children.
He was with his children
and Old Lady Junco
was winnowing.

(Finding 77)

The very sight of Tedlock's text makes one want to read it out loud—which is, of course, the point. Several observations about this type of ethnopoetics should be made.

First, ethnopoetic innovations in how to present the text on the page reveal by comparison the relative lack of expressive information conveyed in conventional written layouts. A text before us, de-pending on the orthographic system, may or may not do an adequate job of representing the sounds of a language that make a word a word. But the sounds of a language that express stylistic or emotional

content—although that content is present in nearly every human utterance—seldom find representation on the printed page. The few
markers of emotion that exist in written English (e.g., the exclamation point, italics) are stretched in numerous ways to convey an array
of tones, sentiments, and verbal actions. For the most part, however,
such features of communication are simply ignored. This choice of
what to record textually reflects deep-seated cultural values and derives in part from a writing system that has its roots in practical record keeping and trade rather than in poetry or drama. The choice
also reflects profound differences between oral and written communication in resources and tendencies. What ethnopoetic presentations offer, by contrast, is an intriguing way of representing that
entire side of verbal communication to which our ears are attuned
but to which our eyes are unaccustomed. When we have practice in
reading and exercise some patience, ethnopoetic translations provide
the basis for readings of oral narratives informed by the intricacies of
human emotion and expressive style.

Second, such translations remind us that textual presentation itself is a mode of analysis. By presenting oral performance as poetry,
deciding how to break and place the lines on the page, and deciding what other features of the performance to include, the editor-
translator creates an analysis, an interpretation. These editorial
decisions are problematic, as any editor of premodern texts would
admit. For many readers of Native American translations, however,
the problems of textual editing have seemed inconsequential. The
ethnopoetic translation awakens us not only to the sounds and structures of the original narration, then, but also to the interpretive eye of
the scholar-presenter. Such awareness provides for a more informed
appreciation of the text at hand.

The Problems and Possibilities of Translation

While ethnopoetics experimented with the practical means of representing oral narratives in print, theoretical debate emerged over what
features to translate. Whereas Tedlock and scholars working in the
same vein wished to express above all else the poetic nature of tone,

pause, and tempo, others — like Hymes — focused on other poetic features of the oral performance, such as verbal patterns, parallelism, and rhetorical structure. Privileging one set of expressive features over another can lead to widely divergent interpretations of a given text (see D. Hymes, *"In Vain"* and "Use"; see also Toelken and Scott; Langen; Swann).

At the outset of the 1980s, a decade after the creation of *Alcheringa*, Hymes took stock of his work in ethnopoetics and advanced it further with his book *"In Vain I Tried to Tell You": Essays in Native American Ethnopoetics*. Restating his view that Chinookan narratives are poetic, not prosaic, Hymes systematically analyzes their rhetorical and aesthetic features. Fundamental to his approach is the realization that Chinookan oral performance is organized in units of lines rather than sentences. Lines are recognized through their rhetorical function as well as their outward form. Parallelism between lines is created by various devices, including repetitions of words or particles, syntax, content, and usage. Repetition and parallelism turn the linear flow of discourse into a layered succession of lines, creating in the mind of the conversant audience member a rhetorical and aesthetic structure. Lines may group into verses, verses into stanzas, stanzas into scenes, and scenes into acts, each grouping signaled through instances of repetition, parallelism, and contrast.

These patternings often correspond to the pattern numbers of the culture in question.[1] In a culture with a pattern number of three, for instance (like most European cultures), ethnopoetic structure will often occur in groupings of three or (somewhat surprisingly) five. In cultures that rely on the pattern number five (like Chinookan), groupings of both five and three will occur. In cultures where the pattern number is two or four, groupings of both two and four predominate in narrative structure (e.g., Zuni). The reason for the co-occurrence of five and three as one set of patterning options and two and four as another set is unclear, although a correlation has been demonstrated for a substantial number of different languages. A typical example of such patterns and analysis is Hymes's representation of a portion of Clackamas myth, recorded from Victoria Howard by Jacobs in 1958 (*"In Vain"* 364):

In the morning,
> now they got ready,
>> the very first is Water Bug;
>>> she went,
>>>> she hid in the canoe.

They went to the river,
> they got in their canoe,
>> they went.

Grizzly turned and looked,
> she saw her,
>> she said,
>>> "Dear oh dear! I told you not to come."

She pays *no* attention to her there.

They went,
> they arrived,
>> they went ashore.

Howard's narrative is presented as a series of interrelated lines grouped into five verses; the five verses make up one of the three stanzas in this portion of the story. Hymes recognizes lines and verses through his familiarity with characteristic rhetorical patterns in other Chinookan texts. Typical, for instance, are the three-part, onset-ongoing-outcome sequences of action inherent in several of the verses above. The fifth verse, "They went, / they arrived, / they went ashore," becomes in Hymes's analysis not artless redundancy (as earlier translators might have viewed it) but an instance of recurrent, culturally significant attention to the initiation, development, and completion of action. With the help of the text's presentation on the page, it becomes easy to see this fifth verse as exactly parallel to the second: "They went to the river, / they got in their canoe, / they went." Interwoven with these two verses are two verses, also parallel, that introduce characters—the villainous Grizzly Woman and her nemesis, Water Bug—each of which initiates an action that opposes the other. In the first verse, Water Bug, suspicious of her kinswoman's uncharacteristic helpfulness, insists on going along. In the third verse, Grizzly Woman, aware of her kinswoman's rightful suspicions, is upset to find her in the canoe. Pivotal to the stanza is the terse fourth verse, "She pays *no* attention to her there"—a one-line verse that contrasts in length with the others of the stanza but parallels similar verses elsewhere in Howard's narrative. Textual presentation, then, aims not solely to evoke in the reader the sounds and delivery style of the original but also to convey the rhetorical structuring of the text as a whole. The relation of form to other aspects of the narrative (plot, tone, suspense) emerges from this re-presentation.

Poetries as Values in Themselves

In his epilogue to *"In Vain I Tried to Tell You,"* Hymes concludes, "If one finds a degree of genuine imaginative life [in these translations], then the rest, the laying of foundations, erecting of scaffolding, sifting and sorting of detail, will have the justification I most desire" (382). Ethnopoetics serves the end of revealing the artistic merit and aesthetic achievements of formerly disparaged narratives and narrators. Analyzing recorded texts along ethnopoetic lines, scholars often perceive further aesthetic features, unnoticed in earlier translations but made apparent by the analysis. In his study of Howard's narrative, for instance, Hymes demonstrates how attention to ethnopoetic contours and a subtle alternation between different noun prefixes helps clarify the plot, characterization, tone, and theme of the myth (342–81). Ethnopoetic patterning creates a rhetorical architecture that is apprehensible to the audience member conversant in the tradition. Such patterning reflects a set of expectations shared between narrator and audience, which the skilled performer may then satisfy, delay, or subvert for artistic ends. An unusual pattern may signal a pivotal moment or some powerful "literary" effect (e.g., irony, suspense, humor).

Widening Arcs of Research

To date, aspects of ethnopoetic research have been applied to many oral traditions.[2] Some studies stay close to the issues of presentation and analysis discussed in this essay; others combine the methods and insights of ethnopoetics with other types of analysis, for example, the examination of rhetoric, style, and community. A trend toward methodization is well under way, in which ethnopoetics becomes a tool or foundation for another kind of inquiry. Such a trend reflects the acceptance of the importance of both Tedlock's and Hymes's findings. Ethnopoetics reaches toward fundamental features of oral communication and reveals the wealth of artistry and formal complexity sometimes sensed by earlier scholars but seldom demonstrated.

Ethnopoetics and the Literature Teacher

What are the lessons to learn from ethnopoetics, and how can teachers use ethnopoetic research profitably in the classroom? I offer a few suggestions as someone acquainted with the benefits and challenges of introducing this kind of material to students. I hope my words will serve as springboards for other teachers' efforts and innovations, in keeping with the collaborative, experimental nature of ethnopoetic research since its inception.

All oral communication is interesting. In previous eras, Western cultures made much of the distinction between highly valued written literature and the seemingly ephemeral, artless oral communication of everyday life. Today that distinction is no longer so easy to make, in part because we have realized the ethnocentrism and foolhardiness of excluding from consideration works that derive from nonliterate traditions. Oral communication, too, can be artful; some oral performances, at their finest and most evocative, invested with communal recognition and a sense of lasting significance, may rightly be designated as literature. But in cultures where primary orality has held sway, we cannot easily discern the artistry of oral narratives through analytical means developed for the study of literate Western narrative. Rather, we must look to approaches such as ethnopoetics as methods for recognizing and appreciating oral artistry on its own terms.

I sometimes make this point to students by playing a short recording of an old woman speaking to a baby. As the woman croons, her monologue becomes recognizable as artful, structured verse.

Although few of the students understand her language (Finnish), they come to understand the force and beauty of her words through a transcription and ethnopoetic translation. The artistry, the patterning, was there for the students to notice even before they had a clear idea of what she was saying; the translation then deepens that comprehension. Other teachers may find similar sources — the words of an elderly person in the community, or someone familiar to students as a good storyteller or speaker. The piece need not be long — in fact, the shorter the better for ease of repetition and analysis — but it should be complete enough to represent a coherent kernel of communication. Most issues of *Alcheringa* include sound-sheet recordings of selected texts included in the issue, any of which would work in the classroom. Recognizing the aesthetic merit of oral communication does not debase the high ideal of literature; rather, it creates the basis for a feeling of common ground and appreciation between the performer-author and the student. Only when students understand the worth of their own words can they fully enjoy the worth of others' words.

The study of form belongs in the literature class. A clear lesson of ethnopoetics is that the literature teacher should, and indeed must, talk about form as well as plot, theme, and characterization when dealing with works created and performed in an oral context. After all, traditional narrative performance often revolves as much around performance style as around plot. This is the crux of what John Foley terms *immanence*: the intimate, taken-for-granted familiarity with plot, characters, and other details that allows the performer to invoke whole images or scenes with a few carefully chosen words (*Immanent Art*; *Singer*). In this kind of highly coded system, form provides valuable clues to meaning and merit (see Bradbury, this volume).

Ethnopoetic translations should be included in literature courses. In a literature course that spans the world's traditions, or even in a course that attempts to narrow the scope (e.g., to Native American literature), no teacher can ever hope to master all the languages and literary practices involved. It was for just this reason that ethnopoetics was developed: to give the earnest reader the benefit of an informed, formal analysis apprehensible through the reading of the work in translation. Teachers can use ethnopoetic texts in the classroom just as they use other anthologized poems or narratives, reading the (sometimes technical) ethnographic and ethnopoetic commentary as essential background.

Ethnopoetic analysis can be tied to other concerns of literary analysis. Such other concerns might be themes, characterization, or the arousal and satisfaction of expectation. As one gains familiarity with ethnopoetic analysis and works repeatedly with a given oral or oral-derived text, one begins to see ways of combining ethnopoetic insights with other aspects of literary analysis.

Poem 29 of the *Kalevala* illustrates how an unexpected structural device can relate to narrative and thematic features. The *Kalevala*, Finland's national epic, was created on the basis of oral epic and lyric songs collected and arranged by Elias Lönnrot in the nineteenth century.[3] In poem 29 (lines 79–402), the incorrigible hero Lemminkäinen has fled the wrath of his enemies, heading to the seas for adventure. He arrives at an island inhabited by many women but few men. Anxiously, Lemminkäinen asks if he can ground his boat, to which request the women generously accede. With one affirmative answer under his belt, Lemminkäinen presses further, asking whether a smallish man can hide on the island. Again he receives a positive and very welcoming answer. With two positive answers behind him, Lemminkäinen now asks with confidence whether he can have some land to farm. Here, crucially, our expectations—borne of the tendency to organize such series of questions into culminating patterns of three in Finnish oral tradition—is subverted: the women answer negatively, explaining that no land whatsoever is left unclaimed on the island. This negative response leads Lemminkäinen to try an underhanded alternative, by asking, in a fourth question, whether he can find a place to sing. Singing soon turns to lovemaking, and the hero has his way with nearly all the island's women, until he is forced to beat a hasty retreat before the island's enraged menfolk. Lönnrot has allowed a traditional means of managing and manipulating audience expectation to come through in this poem. The structural alteration of an expected pattern — the unexpected negative response — serves a double function: it prefaces as well as justifies the bawdy interlude that follows. To a peasant audience of the nineteenth century, Lemminkäinen's act is poetic justice for an island community with no available land or with women too miserly to divulge the existence of land. The tragic lot of the landless and the cruelty of the inhospitable recur as important themes throughout Finnish epic and lyric songs, justifying all kinds of narrative acts. Problems of misleading or unwelcoming words mark Lemminkäinen's adventures in particular. The subverted pattern serves as a stylized, coded means of signaling future events, inscribed expectations, and received interpretations. It helps us understand the characters, their situations, and the text's tone.

Ethnopoetics has much to offer the literature teacher. It makes texts available for use in the classroom in a form that attempts to do justice to their formal and rhetorical artistry. It addresses and alleviates some of the problems of translation that can make a text or tradition seem remote. And it provides an analytic framework that allows for insights into both the formal workings and the other literary characteristics of the text. Two and a half decades after the founding of *Alcheringa*, ethnopoetics has made progress toward achieving its initial goals. Much work is needed, however, before the deeper goals of this approach can be realized: to engage people of all sorts in the consideration of literature and to underscore the relevance of once forgotten works to where we are today.

Notes

1. As anthropologists have shown, many if not most cultures possess a pattern number: some number that recurs over and over again in the myths, practices, and verbal art of the culture. English-speaking readers may think of all the recurrences of the number three in English-language culture — everything from the tale "Three Little Pigs" to the song "Three Blind Mice" to the proverb "three's the trick" to the three

divisions of the United States government. Other cultures depend on other numbers. See D. Hymes (*"In Vain"*) for further discussion of pattern numbers.

2. See, for example, analyses of narratives from Upper Chehalis (Kinkade), Karok (Bright), Sahaptin (V. Hymes), Quechua (Hornberger), Spanish (Briggs and Vigil), Herati Persian (Mills, *Rhetorics*), Hiberno-English (Glassie, *Passing*), Finnish (T. DuBois), biblical Greek (D. Hymes, "General Epistle"), and Kuna (Sherzer), to name but a few.

3. Francis P. Magoun, Jr., provides a good prose translation of the *Kalevala* (Lönnrot), but without ethnopoetic analysis. For further discussion of ethnopoetics in this text, see T. DuBois.

Nancy Mason Bradbury

Traditional Referentiality: The Aesthetic Power of Oral Traditional Structures

Paul Zumthor describes medieval texts as "flattened, crushed onto the paper or parchment by the heavy weight of centuries." What these texts expect from us, according to Zumthor, "is that we give them back their volume" (*Speaking* 79). Any reader's task is to give a written text back its volume — any reader must animate the potential voices and prospective meanings encoded on the page. But, like the contributors to this book, Zumthor argues that restoring a poem's or story's volume requires special skills when what survives to us is the echo of an oral performance rather than a silent communication between author and reader. If the text in question arose from a culture in which books were few or nonexistent, if their production was time-consuming and expensive, if writing was a highly specialized skill and verbal art was regularly experienced aurally, then that work's written state is itself a critical issue. Giving such a text back its volume may require tools that are more familiar to the ethnologist, anthropologist, or folklorist than to the teacher of literature.

The first two essays in part 2 of this book give overviews of past and then present critical work on oral traditions; the last three map out in some detail current approaches that hold real promise for classroom teaching. Since the two essays that precede this one emphasize living oral traditions, I focus on written texts whose ancestry is wholly or in part oral traditional. Often we know very little about the circumstances under which works of this kind were committed to writing. John Miles Foley has proposed the term "oral-derived" for works like the Homeric poems or *Beowulf* in order to emphasize the way in which writing fixes and transforms the oral and to acknowledge clearly that we do not know how much or how little the surviving text resembles the vanished performances (*Traditional Oral Epic* 5–8).[1] In cases where we lack concrete information about performance, we can either disregard the influence of oral traditional modes of thought and expression or we can seek critical methods that will help us understand that influence. My purpose is to make one such method available to literature teachers interested in expanding both the array of texts they offer and the critical tools with which they equip their students.

Oral Theory and Traditional Referentiality

Proponents of oral traditional theory have generally identified a work's constituent elements as phrases, themes, and (for narrative genres) story patterns. To begin with phraseology, students are likely to be struck by the amount of repetition in an oral or oral-derived text. They have labored to avoid repetition in their own written work and, having been warned sternly against clichés, may justifiably think of repeated or commonplace phrases as aesthetic failings. Yet in many oral genres and traditions, formulaic phrases, along with familiar themes and story patterns, are the poet's means of composing spontaneously at performance speed. An oral singer is not composing new phraseology word by word, like an author using pen or word processor, but is speaking in a traditional idiom built up over time through many retellings. Is the formula, then, mainly a mechanical aid to rapid composition, a necessary aesthetic flaw? If so, why does formulaic language persist in written compositions even after the exigencies of performance have been removed? What might formulaic language have to offer an author writing and a reader reading? As early as 1955, Stanley Greenfield argued that the formula has an aesthetic function: "The association with other contexts using a similar formula will inevitably color a particular instance of a formula so that a whole host of overtones springs into action" ("Expression" 205). That is, for listeners familiar with a tradition, a formulaic expression can convey with impressive economy a freight of associations or "overtones" from other narrative contexts in which they have heard the same phrases.

In written as in oral compositions, formulaic language activates for the audience a field of recollections that are laden with meaning and charged with emotion for the particular culture whose traditions the formulas encode. Both Foley and Alain Renoir have seen the importance of this function, especially for critical interpretation of oral-derived texts. We find formulaic language in written works because, even in increasingly textual environments, the use of traditional structures, in Foley's words, "still holds the key to worlds of meaning that are otherwise inaccessible" (*Immanent Art* 7). Foley has given this special evocative power the name "traditional referentiality."[2]

How does traditional referentiality differ from literary allusion, which may also involve a host of connotations called up by one's previous encounter with a phrase? Both are species of intertextuality, which I take to be a broad umbrella term for any instance in which one text "quotes" another. A literary allusion recalls a specific written source and makes use of the source text's network of meanings, its cultural prestige, and perhaps its unique verbal aptness. These effects rely on a sharp distinction between the alluding text and the text to which it alludes. The formula differs from the literary allusion in that an audience experiences a formula not in relation to a specific earlier text from which it is wholly distinct but in relation to the multiform tradition of which it is a part. A literary allusion in this sense is like a metaphor: it relies on a relation of similarity between two separate entities. A formula, Foley argues, is metonymic: it offers us a small part of a traditional field of reference as representative of the whole field (*Immanent Art* 7–8). The formula's referent is located not in a prior written text but in the prior verbal experience of poet and audience, a distinction not insignificant from the perspective of reception. The point is not for the audience to recall the particular place in which it last heard the formula but for the audience to use its familiarity with the tradition to grasp the formula's supranarrative meaning, accumulated in the course of many occurrences.

Formulaic Language and the British Ballad

While Renoir has worked primarily with Germanic epic and Foley with epic traditions in ancient Greek, Old English, and South Slavic, I use the British ballad to illustrate the implications of traditional referentiality for the reception of oral-derived narrative. Among the various scholars who have studied the oral aspects of the traditional ballad, Flemming Andersen in particular has worked toward conclusions closely parallel to the theory of traditional referentiality. The extent to which we can think of the ballad as orally *composed* has always been a debated subject, though of course its oral *performance* is a given. Francis Child's monumental collection of ballad texts mingles the products of eighteenth- and nineteenth-century oral traditions with a wealth of literary compositions, the orally transmitted ballads often influenced by written versions and the "literary" ballads sometimes amounting to transcripts of oral traditions. Memory, limited improvisation, and writing have all helped shape the ballads that survive to us from earlier centuries, and sorting the genuine expressions of tradition from the literary impostors has come to seem a more and more quixotic task. But the ballad fits comfortably within Foley's definition of an oral-derived genre: the ballads passed down in early collections are "works of finally uncertain provenance that nonetheless show oral traditional characteristics" (*Traditional Oral Epic* 5).

As an illustrative text, I take the widely anthologized Scottish ballad "Tam Lin" (number 39 in Child's collection, which includes nine versions lettered A to I). Like any narrative with an oral as well as a written past, it is difficult to date. One literary historian judges it likely to have taken its present form in the second half of the eighteenth century (Fowler, *Literary History* 279), yet we have references to "The Tayl of the yong Tamlene" from 1549 and "a ballett of Thomalyn" from 1558 (Child 1:336). We simply do not know what relation the surviving versions bear to the earlier, lost ones. The versions of "Tam Lin" show the whole range of the genre's oral and literary affiliations: we have field recordings from traditional ballad singers as well as versions collected and probably reworked by important literary figures, including Sir Walter Scott and Robert Burns.[3] The powerful Burns version of "Tam Lin" (Child A) illustrates perfectly the dilemma posed by the oral-derived text: Burns may have written down the words verbatim from the lips of a ballad singer, or he may have altered every line. The truth probably lies somewhere in between. This version is by no means a pristine expression of folk consciousness, yet its formulaic language, its themes, and its overall story pattern are widely attested within the surviving corpus of ballads; its art is largely the oral-derived art of a folklore genre.

Like many instances of oral-derived poetry, even Burns's version of "Tam Lin" (Child A) may at first strike a student as repetitive, thin in its verbal texture, and curiously lacking in inventiveness, intricacy, or narrative depth:

1. O I forbid you, maidens **a'**,   *all*
      That wear **gowd** on your hair,   *gold*
   To come or gae by Carterhaugh,
      For young Tam Lin is there.

2. There's nane that gaes by Carterhaugh
      But they leave him a **wad**,   *pledge, forfeit*
   Either their rings, or green mantles,
      Or else their maidenhead.

3. Janet has kilted her green kirtle
      A little aboon her knee,
   And she has broded her yellow hair
      A little aboon her **bree**,   *brow*
   And she's awa to Carterhaugh,
      As fast as she can hie.

                    (Child 1:340–41)

The stanzas are in fact impressive in their narrative economy: already we have a prohibition issued to the listener, justified by the speaker, and broken by a character in the ballad. We have an ominously sexual male presence and a willful female one, who makes for the prohibited Carterhaugh "as fast as she can hie." Although "Tam Lin" is named for its hero, the action turns on the courage and fidelity of its heroine, in many versions named Janet. Because ballads are so condensed, whatever details they offer tend to signify powerfully. All we know about Janet from the initial three stanzas is that she makes directly for a spot forbidden on account of its association with robbery and illicit sexual encounters, behavior that would not seem to speak well of her character, especially to premodern audiences. We have only one other piece of information, that she hikes up her skirts and ties up her hair, details that seem to run in the same direction, characterizing her as brazenly immodest as well as in an unseemly hurry to reach a forbidden destination.

The lines about skirts and hair, the first four lines of stanza 3, constitute a ballad formula in Andersen's definition: "a recurrent, multiform unit expressing a significant narrative idea, with more or less pronounced supra-narrative function" (37). This supranarrative function of the formula corresponds to Greenfield's "whole host of overtones" and to Foley's traditional referentiality. Anyone familiar with ballad narrative will many times before have come across this action of kilting up the skirts and binding up the hair, and the more contexts in which the listener has known it, the more potently it will signal not just rashness in Janet — tucking up her skirts so that she can run faster into danger and temptation — but also a force of character that might not be suspected from the literal account of her actions so far. As Andersen's compilations show (242–49), a woman who kilts up her skirts in a ballad is most often a determined woman of action preparing either to follow a lover who is cruelly abandoning her or to set off in search of one who has failed to return.[4] The formula allows the singer to carry over into the present song the pathos and the daring of the many ballad women who, setting aside the limits of gender by tying up loose skirts and loose hair, set off to find or to protect a loved one. In this first instance of the formula, the heroine's determination is to pursue an amorous adventure or simply to defy convention, but later in this ballad the same formula will amplify her steadfast devotion to her enchanted and imperiled lover, Tam Lin (version A, stanza 17).

Interestingly, Andersen's analysis shows that the evocative Burns version of "Tam Lin" is no less formulaic than other extant versions. Far from rendering the ballad trite and unimaginative, the formulas of Child A contribute strongly to the ballad's aesthetic power, if one knows how to interpret them. A sung ballad goes by quickly; it operates by outline and implication. Thus its formulas play a significant role in reception by providing important clues to character, action, and meaning. The tying up of skirts and hair in Child A (and many other versions) deepens a narrative resonance implied in other ways by the text. It foreshadows the courage and endurance we will see in Janet, at a point in the ballad when she could simply sound promiscuous. "Tam Lin" is of course accessible to audiences unaware of the field of supranarrative associations discussed here, but it is enriched when we try to emulate the listener ideally steeped in the tradition.

While skirt tying heightens our sense of Janet's daring and resolve, another formula — flower picking — enhances the atmosphere of erotic expectancy that also forms a part of her character and interest. In Child A, Janet "had na pu'd a double rose, / A rose but only twa" (stanza 5), when her lover appears. Andersen's collected instances confirm the thinly veiled allusion to deflowering that lies behind the plucking of flowers: "The formula primarily serves as forewarning of a violent act, typically sexual in nature" (119). The ballad's next narrative move begins with another formula, this one more uncommunicative or even seemingly irrelevant on the literal level but again significant in its traditional connotations. At home, after her first encounter with Tam Lin, Janet is described as "playing ball" (stanza 9). The flower-picking formula can signal a kind of complicity in the upcoming sexual encounter: warned against doing so, the heroine insists that she will pluck flowers if she pleases. Playing ball, however, puts Janet into a more innocent company, that of faithful wives and even little children who will be singled out for abduction. Andersen's compilations show that it is the rare ballad that uses both flower picking and ball playing: more frequently, one is enough to characterize the heroine and initiate the action. It is likely, as E. B.

Lyle argues, that "Tam Lin" A and the other versions employing both formulas have annexed one of their two action-initiating formulas from another ballad ("Opening").

But the artistic result of combining the three formulas we have noted (skirt kilting, flower picking, and ball playing) is an increased depth and complexity: rather than settling definitively on subconscious complicity or untroubled innocence, Child A and its close analogues create an ultimately heroic Janet who enters into adulthood with a convincing mixture of girlish innocence and womanly desire. The ballad's climax, a symbolic enactment of a lifelike emotional struggle, requires her to hold on physically to her lover as he goes through a series of terrifying changes beyond his control. In the A version, he becomes an adder, a grim bear, a lion, a hot piece of iron, a burning coal, and finally himself, a "naked knight" (stanza 35). A possessed figure is saved by the courage, love, and endurance of an independent, passionate, and unconventional mate. This song underscores its point by its formulas, so commonplace in their surface meaning and yet so resonant in their traditional referentiality.

Examples from Other Traditions

Ballad scholars have tended to find the concept of formula more useful than that of theme or typical scene, the larger compositional unit posited by oral traditional theory. The ballads are so short, David Buchan has argued, that we may best think of the singers as combining individual commonplaces or formulas rather than as combining clusters of such units, that is, themes (58–59). But in narrative traditions where the songs are much longer, scholars have found that themes function in much the same way as formulas. A well-known theme from Germanic heroic poetry, for example, is the beasts of battle. With a battle threatening, predators such as a wolf, a raven, and an eagle gather in anticipation of a feast. The beasts are most often shown on what will be the winning side, and thus, like the ballad formulas that carry more than their surface meanings, this theme conveys important supranarrative information. Renoir uses the Old English *Elene* to illustrate how a traditional structure can be set to work in an individual literary context yet retain its traditional referentiality ("Rhetoric"). In *Elene*, the poet Cynewulf contrasts the small Roman army with the fearsomely large troop of invading barbarians. As we would expect, the beasts of battle accompany the barbarians, who appear to be the inevitable victors. But the Roman leader, Constantine, has a revelation that leads to his conversion on the spot to Christianity, and the opportunistic beasts of battle now appear on the side of the Romans. Thus the poet uses the theme to mark the religious conversion as the crucial turning point. For an audience of initiates, the theme serves as a "poetic pivot," in Andersen's words (290), by accentuating the underlying forces that create the tale's drama.

Renoir advocates the continued scholarly recovery of such contexts in the belief that it can help us experience formulaic poems "as live works instead of embalmed corpses" ("Rhetoric" 247). Foley too recommends that we try to grasp the poetic techniques that shape oral and oral-derived works rather than condemn the works' deviations from literary canons of taste. His methodology requires one "to gather instances of the given phrase or narrative pattern and then to inquire what extrasituational connotations they share" (*Immanent Art* 247). As a final illustration, we may look briefly at the Homeric formula *physizoos aia* ("life-producing earth"). Modern readers of the *Iliad* have long noticed contexts in which this description of the earth seems somewhat incongruous. Unaware that her brothers have died, Helen speaks of them as alive, and the poet comments, "Thus she spoke but *the life-producing earth* already held them fast" (3.243–44). John Ruskin found the passage ripe with "high poetical truth," expressing the poet's love for the earth our mother at the same time that he acknowledges the sadness of human mortality. Milman Parry took the opposite position: stressing the functional utility of the formula, he argued that *physizoos aia* was simply the poet's mechanical way of saying "earth" in a given metrical position (Ruskin and Parry qtd. in Foley, *Immanent Art* 248). Foley suggests that we interpret the formula with reference to the common ground among its three occurrences in Homer: "All three episodes share a fundamental concern with a mysterious duality of life and death," with "the earth as both beginning and end, as both the fertile mother who bears and nourishes all humanity and at the same time the bloodless leveler who will one day hold us all fast—'even the strong man'" (251). Thus Foley mediates between Parry and Ruskin, arguing that by no means must the formula's compositional utility render it merely mechanical.

The concept of traditional referentiality productively redefines the old debate between the mechanistic and the aesthetic views of a formula's function. It offers a useful methodology for the reader of oral-derived texts who wishes to move beyond deploring "tags," "clichés," or "unnecessary repetition" as aesthetic failings. It opens the way for a wider consideration of how and why traditional, oral-derived works seem to favor the metonymic rather than the metaphoric axis of language,[5] and it moves us another step toward a poetics that will illuminate rather than obscure whatever aesthetic value oral-derived texts may possess.

Notes

1. See further the essays in part 3 of this volume. For helpful general information on teaching Homer and *Beowulf*, see, respectively, Myrsiades; Bessinger and Yeager.
2. For full and useful syntheses of his theory with the work of numerous scholars across many different cultural traditions, see Foley, *Immanent Art*, esp. 6–17; and *Singer*, esp. ch. 1.
3. For accounts of the versions, see Child 1: 335–40 and John D. Niles, "*Tam Lin*," esp. 338n5. Niles offers an illuminating reading of "Tam Lin," as does Lyle ("Ballad").
4. Among the other instances of the formula are the following, by Child number, version letter, and stanza: 41.B.2, 63.E.7, 71.36, 77.A.11, 103.A.13, 110.A.7, 182.A.4, 214.I.12, 215.F.8, 218.A.7, 226.C.12.
5. See Lodge for the adoption into literary theory of Roman Jakobson's linguistic distinction between metaphor and metonymy. Brewer argues that metonymic relations are more basic to medieval poetry than metaphoric relations.

Part III

Praxis: Oral Traditions in the Classroom

Living Traditions

Barre Toelken

Native American Traditions (North)

Keeping in mind that there are an estimated 150 different Native American languages (not dialects) in daily use today north of Mexico and that each of these languages represents a different culture, we must recognize that few observations can cover the tremendous range of expressive possibilities we encounter in Native American oral traditions. Even so, some generalizations can be made in this brief treatment, provided the prospective teacher is willing to follow the leads further into the oral traditions of any particular tribe that may come into discussion.

Moreover, since the serious consideration of Native American languages and literatures did not get under way until many eastern tribal languages had already disappeared or become moribund, most of our reliable material today comes from the Midwest, the Great Basin, the West and Southwest, and the Northwest (including western Canada) and Alaska (including the arctic coastal Eskimo cultures, the interior Athabascan groups, and related coastal peoples like the Tlingit and the Tsimshian). Nonetheless, some of the eastern tribal languages have been maintained and are in a state of resurgence, and other tribal oral traditions have survived the transition into English. In all cases, the teacher will want to obtain reliable texts from oral performances (wherever possible) that are accompanied by full cultural, linguistic, and literary discussions. Some solid examples are provided in this essay.

Genre and Culture

Conventional European terms for oral genres are only partially useful for discussing Native American materials, but their lack of fit is an instructive way of approaching the unique qualities of our subject. For example, it is most common today for folklorists and anthropologists to define *myth* as a sacred narrative, *legend* as a third-person story about an event believed to have occurred in the present (not the mythic) world, and *folktale* as a fictional narrative in which people or animals act out culturally meaningful plots. *Memorates* are first-person narratives about striking, often supernatural occurrences that happened to the narrator. In a typical Native American oral narrative, however, all these elements may combine or intersect in one performance.

For example, in a Coquelle story from the coast of Oregon, Old Man Coyote jumps into the mouth of a whale, later kills it by cutting its heart out, and exits between its ribs when it is deposited on the beach by the ocean waves (Wasson). As a coyote tale, the story provides one of many dramatic accounts of a humorous character who acts out the moral and ethical dilemmas of human life. But it also coincides with and makes reference to mythic narratives about why and how whales are deposited on the shore as sacred tokens of deep family relationships between human beings and ocean beings (Wolgamott). The story also mentions accurately a number of places that still exist in the historical world, and it describes an event that is believed by many Coquelle people actually to have occurred on the coast of Oregon. Further, since the Coquelles live their lives in this rich legendary context, they walk along the beach and see many of the same features described in the old story, including occasional beached whales. If a striking occurrence befalls someone on this beach, it takes place in a culturally constructed environment that inevitably lends intense meanings on all levels—mythic, legendary, fictive, and personal.

Cultural Dramatization

For this reason, it is important for us to know as much as possible about the context in which a certain oral performance takes place before we can explore the range of its possible meanings. Seeing the story of Old Man Coyote as an explanation of the everyday relationships between whales and coyotes according to the Coquelle Indians would be absurd to begin with and would not lead us very far into the rich literary and cultural experience available even to outsiders in such a complex narrative. Just as "The Three Little Pigs" is not a story of explaining or illustrating pig behavior but, rather, a dramatization of cultural values that allow human beings to save their families and "keep the wolf from the door," so most Native American stories are dramatizations of culturally constructed abstractions, performed by knowledgeable speakers to informed audiences. Far more than enjoyable entertainments—which they are, of course—they encapsulate and make accessible important aspects of worldview that otherwise usually remain unarticulated. A close examination of them will reveal a set of cultural attitudes not only about language and creative expression but about cultural meanings as well.

Among many of the southwestern tribes, the most common contemporary oral legends are about witches ("skinwalkers," "dog-people," "*brujas*"), people who are thought to dress in canine animal skins—or turn themselves into dogs and coyotes—and try to gain power for themselves by injuring or killing others (Brady). The epitome of egoism and personal competitiveness gone wild, these witches dramatize and personify the kind of behavior that tribal peoples have always considered culturally destructive and personally sick. It is no surprise to find that the narrators are often teenagers who feel the discrepancy between their culture's demand that they cooperate unselfishly and their schoolteachers' insistence that they compete individually. But older people tell the stories, too, especially when unexplained sicknesses, injuries, or disasters occur. Sickness and accident are thought to be the symptoms of imbalance and disharmony, brought about either by one's own cultural mistakes and moral mismanagement or by the malevolent actions of a witch. The witch stories bring moral and cultural assumptions together into dramatic constellations that articulate the fears, concerns, and values of people living in a spiritually hazardous world, surrounded by other cultures who promote negative behavior. Again, these stories do not explain (or explain away) witchcraft; rather, they make it culturally experiential through dramatization in live narration.

The myths or sacred stories dramatize the larger, universal issues that focus on creation or formation of the world, processes by which the world came to be organized as it is today, and dramas that embody basic principles. A myth that starts, "At the beginning, the world was covered by a great, warm lake; in the lake floated a log, and in the log was a woman, and she was pregnant," is obviously proclaiming a female basis for life and fertility; it does not address other questions, like, Where did the log come from? or, How did she get pregnant? The Zuni emergence myth (like those of most other Pueblos) starts with all living things far underground, described much like insects and reptiles (Tedlock, *Finding* 223–98). The Sun (male) creates twin sons out of muddy foam and sends them deep into the earth to bring the other beings up to the light. This dramatization combines the image of male penetration of the female earth with a slowly articulated birthing of all living things. Life does not begin with magical creation from nothing but is potential, inherent, needing only to be brought forth. The Blackfoot buffalo dance myth details a marriage between humans and buffalo, which entails — as all marriages do — the development of reciprocal relations between the two groups: the buffalo supply food, and their human relatives supply the ritual dance that brings buffalo back to life (Grinnell 229–30). The Kathlamet Chinook "Sun's Myth" depicts a chief who abandons his duties to go in search of the sun, contrary to his wife's advice. He finds the sun (who is female), breaks a number of taboos, and returns to his people only to destroy them all with a stone ax (D. Hymes,

"Folklore's Nature"). The cultural assumption is that egoism leads to personal and social destruction. The function of such myths is not to explain or rationalize a moral concept but to dramatize it in such a way that every time the myth is articulated, it becomes palpable, experiential, culturally alive.

In addition to narratives that dramatize either in sacred or in everyday terms the culturally assumed normal behaviors and responsibilities of people and animals, Native American oral traditions also include oral histories (often recitations of striking events and weather phenomena that have affected the tribe), oratory (heard mostly at funerals, powwows, and other ceremonial events), rumor and gossip (excitedly creative expressions about contemporaries), and jokes (one of the most prominent of the modern oral genres).

Humor and Culture

As is true of jokes generally, Native American jocular traditions express anxieties and concerns about discrepancies and abnormalities in the surrounding world (Toelken, "Culture"). Native jokes focus on relations with other tribes, frictions with whites and white institutions, and embarrassing interactions with other cultures. In addition, many tribal customs include the development of joking relationships between friends and allies; joking often occurs as a prelude to political discussion, as a way of mitigating embarrassment among acquaintances, as a way of demonstrating clan or adoptive reciprocities, and as a way of denigrating oneself on behalf of group solidarity. For this reason, a Native American joke text can seldom have a full meaning outside the context in which it orally dramatizes some important aspect of shared cultural value. Since orally delivered jokes are thus heavily coded, in most tribes it is considered impolite to joke in front of strangers. This reserve has probably contributed to the stereotype of the stoic Indian. But Native American jokes—like gossip and rumor—are close to Western categories of humor and, since they are part of the interplay of everyday life, may be readily overheard and appreciated by the sensitive listener. The author Leslie Silko has commented on the importance of humor and gossip in the content and style of her fiction (*Running*).

Oratory

Oratory refers to a more formal level of declamation in contexts where words articulate and actually shape political and social relationships, sacred processes, commitments, and acknowledgments. Oratory is less likely to be heard by the outsider but may still be encountered on formal occasions like tribal meetings, potlatches, festivals, and other large gatherings. It is characterized by formulaic openings and closings, by lengthy pauses between utterances (in many tribes, the pause lasts longer than the preceding spoken phrase), by repetition in four or five parallel phrases, by elevated volume, by special posture (usually standing), and by formal accoutrements (special clothing, a speaker's staff or "talking stick"). Unfortunately, some of the most powerful of early orations are preserved for us only in written texts taken down by military interpreters; much of the richness of tone and coloration has been lost in the translations of people who had distinctive agendas, smothered by storage in the enemy's archives. Even so, the eloquence of Chief Joseph, Red Cloud, and other great orators comes through vividly enough to suggest their original power (Vanderwerth; on the importance of how an oral performance is textualized, see DuBois, this volume; Fine, this volume).

History and Reality

Oral history is made up of the anecdotes and reminiscences of people who have shaped their accounts of the events they lived through, adding them to the lively oral traditions that came before. The Kiowas tell about emerging from the forests at the headwaters of the Yellowstone River, traveling out into the Great Plains, and passing the formation we now call Devil's Tower (Momaday). The Navajos recall coming on foot into the Southwest at a time when the Anasazi ("ancient people") still lived in cliff dwellings: "We used to throw stones at them so they'd go back up into the cliffs, and then we'd take the vegetables from their gardens" (Tsinααbααs Yazzie). Oral history is thus more than an account of lineal movement through time; it is an ongoing recollection of "our real-life adventures." That among most tribes these stories are passed along into contemporary times in the first-person plural indicates that one of the functions of oral history is to engage the listeners as actors in their culture's accumulating history. There is far less focus on prominent individuals than on the welfare and identity of the tribal or clan group. *We* occurs far more commonly in these narratives than *I*. Thus, while personal experience may indeed be involved, it is almost always subordinated to cultural experience.

Just as many people today have no difficulty in accommodating both sacred narratives from the Bible and secular scenarios from history and science, Native Americans also combine oral history with sacred stories (often learned from neighboring tribes) into a richly textured expression of their sense of identity and place. For example, the Navajo mythic narrative about where all life came from was learned from the Hopis; as is common among agricultural peoples, the myth has everything emerge from the earth like plants. The Navajos, former Athabascan hunters and fishers, having wandered thousands of miles from their homeland in interior Alaska, encountered a new reality in the southwest deserts about five hundred years ago and captured it in the oral traditions they learned from their new neighbors—apparently along with practical and life-saving advice on how to practice agriculture in the desert (Zolbrod). Although their sacred story thus dramatizes a new life paradigm based on the wonder of emerging plants in an arid landscape, their oral history recalls the human adventures at the end of their long migration. In more recent years, some medicine men (actually the nongendered Navajo term for medicine man is *hataałi*, "a singer") have included sheep and horses among those animals that emerged from the sacred earth navel at the beginning of time, for, even though they know that historically these animals came along later, with the Spanish settlers, the singers also believe that their sacred story should account for everything in the world, or else it will not be true.

Levels of Meaning

In dealing with any of these traditions, the teacher should address the relation between expression and meaning on a number of levels. First, of course, any oral performance needs to be interesting and engaging to its narrator and audience, or it will not survive long in an oral culture that expects good stories. Thus discussion could begin with the question, What is interesting or entertaining about this story? Since many of the stories are tied to features in the real world, discussion might also focus on how a story refers to nature, natural processes, relations among parts of nature (Is nature made up of our resources or of our relatives? Is nature mute or does it speak to us? If animals are our relatives, how will the human characters in the story act toward them?). Perhaps the most engaging level of discussion grows from the realization that most of these traditions embody and dramatize complex cultural abstractions: values, logical assumptions, worldviews. A key question should always be, What idea is being dramatized by this narrative? and not, What does this story explain? Anyone growing up surrounded by these stories will absorb many dramatic constructions of culturally systematic but unstated assumptions. Therefore, what are the assumptions in this story, and how does this story then function in the teaching and maintenance of a cultural worldview?

Style and Performance

Of equal importance to the dramatic content of an oral performance are the features of style, structure, occasion, and propriety that provide powerful signals of meaning and usage. In most tribes, coyote stories (in other tribes the character is a raven, a rabbit, an old man, or a spider) are told only in the winter months, since the very oral articulation of the narratives is thought to be so powerful that it can affect the weather. But when does winter start and end? For the Navajos, winter ends with the first lightning and thunder; for the Flatheads, winter ends when the first snake is seen: in both cases, nature, not the human calendar, determines and announces when stories can or cannot be told. Most tribes prefer that those of us who listen to or read and discuss their stories do so during the appropriate time of year, even though they have no way of enforcing the rule.

In some tribes, the narrator must be teased to tell a story, bribed with snacks and gifts, flattered and begged by younger listeners. In others, the narrators will perform regularly during the proper season because (as with the Navajos) they believe children will grow up unbalanced if they do not hear the stories. In some tribes (like the Tlingit), stories are owned, often by families and clans, and may not be told by others without permission (Dauenhauer and Dauenhauer 24–29). Among the Hopi and the Zuni, listeners are expected to respond every now and then with a word or phrase that shows they are paying attention; not hearing this sound will cause many narrators to stop immediately or to ridicule their audience for being lazy and inattentive (Tedlock, *Finding* xxv; Sekaquaptewa). Among the northern Athabascans in Alaska and western Canada, the job of listening is thought to be as demanding as the act of narrating and is referred to with the same phrase they use to describe gleaning the last bits of meat from a bone (Scollon and Scollon).

In some Native American cultures, moral approval of a character's actions is indicated by laughter, while in others, laughter shows an awareness that the character has done something so far out of line that listeners would be embarrassed to have done the same (Toelken and Scott). Clearly, in the best of all worlds, we would want to study live performances in natural contexts so we could consider how these various responses provide indications of meaning and nuance. Failing that, we would want to obtain tapes and videotapes of a real (not an induced) performance. At the least, we would seek printed texts that provide us with as many of these features as are recordable on paper.

Some stylistic elements do come through in print, of course. If a text is accurately and fully transcribed, we will be able to see the parallel phrasing and the repetition that characterizes much of Native American oral performance. An important action or idea will be repeated four times (which in many tribes also suggests circularity or surroundment — that is, a sense of completion and balance — because of the four primary directions), or five times (which in most of the northwest tribes indicates fullness, completeness). But in a printed text we cannot hear the pauses between the utterances, even though the pauses are equally important aspects of meaning. Just as Native American orators usually pause between sentences to indicate the gravity of the passage, storytellers use pauses and a pacing that is quite different from the comparatively excited onward rush of Euramerican stories.

Structure and Meaning

Many mythic narratives have a double structure that can be perceived by a careful reader (Bierhorst, *Red Swan* 10–14). The same story sequence will be told twice, not always in parts of equal length but usually in a way that uses one part to reflect on the other. In the first part of the Kathlamet Chinook "Sun's Myth," the male character desires to travel, travels to his goal, arrives and responds to the situation, then settles down. In the second half, he goes through the same sequence, except that instead of being outward bound he is homeward bound; instead of attaining riches, he destroys his villages; instead of settling in a large, opulent house with a new mate, he settles in a small house and is entirely alone. The ironic contrast, brought about by the man's willfulness, is stunning.

Language and Power

For most Native Americans, language is thought of not simply as a medium of information but also as a creative force (Witherspoon). For many tribes, prayers are not so much petitions as they are articulations of a desired condition. The oral presentation of a coyote story causes the listeners to engage vicariously in behavior they are culturally expected to avoid. Performance of a myth — often accompanying a ritual or a healing ceremony — allows the audience to reexperience a sacred event or process. The oral performance of a narrative, then, and not the hypothetical text of it or the later printed fossil of it, is the central feature of Native American oral tradition, and this fact should be considered whenever a story is being discussed. Oral tradition is not simply the absence of writing or a condition previous to the inevitable invention of visible characters; it is not to be dismissed as preliterature. Rather, like all "immanent art" (Foley), it exists and persists in and of itself through the dynamic act of creative interchange between tradition bearers and their culturally knowledgeable audiences. Since this is the process by which Native American concepts and values have been articulated, maintained, conveyed, and internalized, it is no doubt the best medium for understanding Native American thought, creativity, and culture. Therefore the study of Native American oral literature inevitably entails the discussion of the cultures in which the traditions are contexted; it cannot be limited to the consideration of literary conventions and generic categories.[1]

Note

1. Roemer may be a helpful aid in understanding the tradition informing Momaday's *The Way to Rainy Mountain*. For a more general overview, see Ruoff.

John H. McDowell

Native American Traditions (South)

In the introduction to a recent anthology entitled *Native South American Discourse*, the editors observe that no South American Indian has ever won the Nobel Prize "for his oral performances of myths, legends, or political oratory" despite the fact that

> every day and every night members of societies in remote areas . . . are creating and performing a remarkable diversity of verbal forms characterized by metaphorical richness, complex poetic and rhetorical processes, and intensely personal styles, all of which are an intimate part of the replication and transmission of their cultural and esthetic traditions.
>
> (Sherzer and Urban 3)

The South American continent is host to a wealth of highly refined oral traditions cultivated by specialists and verbal artists in the native communities. A growing body of ethnographic accounts makes this treasure trove increasingly available, if people accept the invitation to experience verbal artistry in association with its social and cultural settings. This proviso no doubt contributes to the reluctance of Nobel judges to venture afield from the familiar confines of the international literary canon.

Think for a moment of the vast panorama of living oral tradition across the South American continent. It is no accident that Claude Lévi-Strauss, the foremost mythologist of our times, centered his research in Native South America, for the peoples of this region have been prodigious in their cultivation of mythic narrative. Working outward from the Bororo Indians of central Brazil, Lévi-Strauss traces a web of mythological thought that encompasses all of South America and the native peoples of North America as well (see esp. *Raw, From Honey, Origin,* and *Naked Man*). An extensive ethnographic literature reveals in Native South America a stock of mythic narrative unsurpassed in any world region. But that is far from the whole story: Native South American oral tradition is justly celebrated for highly evolved forms of political oratory and ceremonial speech making, for songs and ritual chants of native doctors, for recitals of ceremonial genealogies. Documentation of these and many other verbal forms has earned Native South Americans recognition as among the most verbally accomplished of the world's peoples (see, e.g., McDowell, "Mission"; Seeger; Bastien; Urban, "Dialogues"; Hill).

The student who would encounter the oral traditions of indigenous South America will find performances imbued with patterned aural textures, complex grammatical and syntactic profiles, and innovative modes of reference. All the delights attaching to the experience of literature are readily at hand in the oral performances of Native South Americans. The student disposed to encounter these performances on their own terms can observe the literary impulse at the service of social process and cultural reproduction. In contrast to the detached literary production of learned elites, the oral poetry of Native South Americans displays verbal art harnessed to practical needs such as accomplishing rites of passage, instructing neophytes in the mysteries of the cosmos, and effecting cures through spiritual channels. This is not to deny the presence of a more contemplative oral art in Native South America, as in the emergence of folktale from myth in settings where the indigenous religion has lost its hold on the people (for further information on Native American narrative tradition, see S. Niles).

Approaching Oral Tradition

What, then, is required to enter the magical world of Native South American oral tradition? Full comprehension would entail competence in the language of expression and in the local systems of belief and practice, an ideal beyond the reach of all but a few dedicated researchers. But the situation is not desperate. A partial, mediated, yet genuine appreciation can be obtained through serious exploration of the appropriate resources. Let us begin by rejecting the isolated text in translation, a chimera that can deceive or dispirit the reader. Such unnatural contrivances are the product of a sequence of severances: first, from the social scene of the actual performance; second, from the original expressive medium, the spoken (or chanted, or sung) word; third, from the rhythms, syntax, and lexicon of the original language; and fourth, from the cultural systems that undergird meaning. These texts suffer a devastating alienation to become only pallid reflections of their originals.

The student of oral poetry should seek a closer encounter with the source: the actual telling of a mythic narrative, the actual performance of ceremonial speech, the actual chanting of healer. Important dimensions of indigenous discourse can be retained or recovered in scholarly treatments that have a strong commitment to ethnographic validity. Let me present a checklist for proper handling of oral tradition. To start, we should know the particulars of the performance occasions: Who is the artist? What kind of event is it? How does the audience respond? It is helpful to learn something about the lives and cares of the performers, about their relationship to members of the audience, about the motives and expectations people bring to events of this nature. The point is that the performance of verbal art is situated, or anchored, in social interaction, and social factors influence the style, duration, and content of the performance.[1]

From Speech to Writing

Most performances of indigenous South American oral tradition evince a significant patterning of the acoustic signal. Ritual chants are highly organized in this aspect, but even casual narrative tends toward phrases of some regularity. Straight prose transcription does violence to these structures and nuances of vocal production. Scholars working in Native South America have developed a range of solutions to this problem, typically using poetic lines and stanzas to capture the flow and "chunking" of speech production (Gumperz) and supplementing these devices with additional codes to retrieve expressive features such as pacing, intonation, voice quality, and others. The result is a transcription that visually suggests something of the acoustic quality of the spoken performance, accompanied by explanatory notes and codes allowing for the recovery of additional dimensions of vocal sonority.

The implacable problems of translating from one language to another are well known and not by any means restricted to the domain of oral tradition. Still, the requirement to translate oral poetry from a source language to a receiver language introduces another disruptive juncture, one that must be handled with care if the integrity of oral tradition is to be preserved. Some oral traditions of Native South America are natively rendered in the national languages, Spanish or Portuguese, but the greater part of this corpus occurs in the indigenous languages of the continent. Although there is debate among the experts about classification and other matters, it is clear that Native South America exhibits as much linguistic diversity as any region of the world. Recent estimates indicate the persistence of at least two hundred native languages representing perhaps one hundred different language families and isolated languages. Some of these languages are flourishing, like Quechua (its forms Quichua, Runa Simi, and Inga), the language of the Incas and their descendants, but many others are stagnant or moribund, and not a few lie at the door of extinction. The native languages of South America provide a fabulous linguistic environment for the creation of verbal performances drawn from oral tradition.

Whenever possible, the native language text should be consulted in conjunction with translations into a major world language. Scholars of Native South America have found ways of incorporating native language texts so that readers can tune into details of grammar, syntax, and lexicon even in the absence of competence in the language. For those readers who are inclined to make the effort, such information offers additional possibilities for contact with the source and confers insights regarding the arrangement and patterning of linguistic forms. In narrative speech, for example, one can monitor the appearance of sequencing morphemes or the distribution of morphemes that express the speaker's attitude toward the events narrated. In ceremonial speech, one can appreciate the construction of especially complex words and phrases, among other features. There is another reason to present native language texts: to preserve languages that are endangered, making the texts available to members of communities engaged in grass-roots efforts to promote usage of their native language.[2]

Finally, we come to the alienation of oral tradition from its cultural moorings. Performances drawing on oral tradition in indigenous South America are deeply embedded in local contexts of meaning. Separating these performances from their settings leaves them floating without purpose on an ocean of potential signification. Any image, referent, or pattern could mean anything or nothing. It is imperative to provide sufficient cultural background to permit decoding of meaning in terms congruent with native understandings. This is not to suggest that one transparent explication should be sought, for Native South Americans tolerate and even crave ambiguity as much as anyone does. Instead, what is needed is supplementary information that sketches the interpretive templates used by members of the community to assess the meaning of oral performances. A crucial aspect here is a profile of the genre of performance as it is recognized, named, and employed by members of the society.

Resources

Careful attention to these factors can inhibit if not dispel completely the disruptive effects introduced when oral performances are alienated from their natural habitats. Although at critical stages on the journey from performance to presentation a set of interventions threatens the vitality and integrity of the result, many scholars of Native South American oral tradition have fortunately made important advances toward providing authentic experience of this invaluable store of verbal artistry.

The teacher might want to consult Joel Sherzer's *Kuna Ways of Speaking: An Ethnographic Perspective*. The Kuna, residing in Panama and Colombia, are absorbed with talk and possess a rich and diversified repertoire of speech styles and speech genres. Sherzer provides background on the social and linguistic environment of Kuna talk and then discusses in detail several forms of Kuna speech: the chanting of chiefs in the "gathering house," the "counseling of the spirits" used in curing events, the chanting associated with puberty rites, and "everyday speech" including conversations, lullabies, laments, humorous talk, and stories. Comparing these different speech forms, Sherzer notes that "the more ritual the speech, the more fixed is the syntactic structure and the more pervasive is the syntactic and semantic parallelism" (186).

Another important resource for the teacher of oral tradition is the work of Ellen Basso with the Kalapalo Indians, a Carib-speaking community residing in the Upper Xingu region of Brazil. In *A Musical View of the Universe: Kalapalo Myth and Ritual Performance*, Basso provides texts of narrative performances and ritual enactments and locates these materials in the context of Kalapalo culture and worldview. The narratives "evoke an illusionary past" in order to "clarify the conditions of the present world" (8). The transcriptions are true to the performances, even recording the contributions of the "what-sayer," a coperformer who provides a vocal counterpoint of assent. Basso argues that the highly patterned vocalizations in ritual events depict and control the different orders of "animacy" associated with Kalapalo cosmic entities (see also E. Basso, *Last Cannibals*).

Janet Wall Hendricks explores a Shuar narrative in *To Drink of Death: The Narrative of a Shuar Warrior*. The Shuar, a Jivaroan people, inhabit the lowland regions where Ecuador meets Peru. Hendricks presents the life history of the legendary warrior Tukup', as delivered in his own words. She views this life history as a valuable linguistic document, as a source of information on Shuar warfare and culture, and as a story shaped by the circumstances of its performance. She aims "to discover aspects of the language/culture relationship through close analysis of texts recorded in their natural settings" (27).

Two anthologies of essays provide a useful overview of approaches and resources in this area of research: *Native Latin American Cultures through Their Discourse*, edited by Ellen Basso, and *Native South American Discourse*, edited by Joel Sherzer and Greg Urban. Many scholars active in the ethnographic approach to Native South American verbal art have papers in these volumes, and the volumes' contents literally cover the continent in terms of geographical location and genre.[3]

The reader might also consult the two volumes I have published on speech forms of the Sibundoy peoples of Andean Colombia, *Sayings of the Ancestors: The Spiritual Life of the Sibundoy Indians* and *"So Wise Were Our Elders": Mythic Narratives of the Kamsá*, where I have developed the procedures for handling oral tradition that I recommend here. An example taken from this research follows.

Corn-Planting Day

The Santiagueños, a Quechua-speaking community, live in and around the Sibundoy Valley of Putumayo territory, Colombia. Included in their extensive repertoire of oral traditions are proverblike expressions used to convey kernels of wisdom. These sayings, though utilitarian, are appreciated for their tight acoustic textures and their efficient metaphorical linking of propositions. Initially I encountered them as verbal art miniatures, and only with growing awareness of the language and culture did I begin to piece together their connection to Santiagueño cosmology. As miniatures, they offer a convenient lens through which to inspect the benefits of a scholarly approach like the one advocated in the previous paragraphs.

Let us confine our discussion to one sample text, given in the original Quechua and English translation (see figure). The Quechua original is given as three separate lines conforming to the phrasing

---

Corn-Planting Day:
An Ethnographic Presentation of a Quechua Text

sara tarpu-sca puncha micha-mi,
(corn to plant-*hist* day bad-*aff*)

sara cuta-ngapa, pullitu-cuna-ta cara-ngapa,
(corn to grind-*purp* chick-*pl-acc* to give-*purp*)

atahualpa-ta sita-pu-ngapa, maqui-ca huaglli-mi.
(hen-*acc* to dig-*ben-purp* hand-*foc* to ruin-*aff*)

On corn-planting day, it is bad
to grind corn or give it to the chicks:
the hen will dig up the corn seed for you, your hand is ruined.

Key to Grammatical Abbreviations

hist	historical past	*acc*	accusative marker
aff	affirmative marker	*ben*	benefactive marker
purp	purposive marker	*foc*	focus marker
pl	plural		

Source: McDowell, *Sayings* 75–76

---

of the saying in performance; this same three-part arrangement is preserved in the English translation. To make the Quechua text more accessible, I provide a parsing of the words into roots and suffixes. As a consequence, it is possible to point out some interesting features of this Quechua expression. For example, note the parallel structures in line 2 based on the purposive form, which works like an infinitive but implies action oriented toward a specific goal. This form returns with a twist in the subsequent line: The hen will dig it up for you. Here the addition of the benefactive morpheme drives home the effect of violating the advice conveyed in this saying.

In addition, we can see the play of the affirmative marker *-mi*, one element in the Quechua evidentiary system that obligates the speaker to take a stand regarding the truth of each statement. The affirmative contrasts with the reportative *-si*, which has the force of "they say" or "it is said," and with the interrogative or dubitive *-chu*.

In a strong show of conviction, the speaker here endows her assertion in lines 1 and 3 with the affirmative marker. Finally, the single occurrence of the focus marker, -ca, calls attention to the hand as the most important referent in the saying. This brief lesson in the workings of Quechua grammar is hardly enough to make anyone a connoisseur of the language, but it does provide some insight into the expressive medium and its deployment as verbal art. Methods like these decrease the negative effects of committing speech to print; they also make visible the act of translation and thereby render it subject to inspection and questioning.

What about the setting of performance? "Corn-Planting Day" was elicited from a mature woman, doña Margarita, who had planted corn successfully for many years and who was known for her "good hand" for planting. This saying is normally addressed by an older woman to a younger one, perhaps by a mother to her son's wife, especially if the younger woman is preparing to work with corn inside the kitchen on planting day. As is usual with these sayings, the performance venue is the intimate circle of the immediate or extended family, and the occasion is typically one of routine social interaction in the household. In this setting, the wisdom of the sayings is brought to bear on the practical tasks of daily life in an effort to live in harmony with the divine plan.

A Good Hand

Our text is drawn from an oral tradition known in Quechua as *ñugpamandacuna imasa rimascacuna*, literally, "how the first people were accustomed to speak," or, more loosely, "sayings of the ancestors." The Santiagueños believe that their ancestors possessed a level of spiritual power that is no longer possible today. Fortunately, the ancestors left behind these sayings, passed from one generation to another, as pithy formulations of their spiritual knowledge. It is a prominent element of Santiagueño philosophy to follow in the footsteps of the ancestors, because adherence to this path protects the individual, the family, and ultimately the community from the many sources of spiritual danger that surround and constantly threaten to intrude.

"Corn-Planting Day" cautions women to avoid grinding corn or feeding corn to the chicks on the day corn is planted, lest the hens come and dig up the seeds and, most significant, lest the women ruin their good hand for planting. As doña Margarita explained:

> The women who plant corn either stay away from corn that day, letting someone else attend to the grinding or the feeding of the chicks, or else they will thoroughly scrub their hands with soap after the planting. If you grind corn, you will have to break it down into flour, and that ruins the hand. (McDowell, *Sayings* 76)

The Santiagueños speak of a symbolic contamination that links the breaking or spreading about of corn to the summoning of the hens to dig up the newly planted corn seed. If the corn is spread or broken, a woman's good planting hand will be ruined, which means that any subsequent planting will not result in a high yield of flourishing corn plants.

This item of Santiagueño oral tradition rests on the concept of *alli maqui*, "a good hand." A woman who possesses a good hand will plant corn seed with success. The seed she lays into the ground after turning the soil with her digging stick will not be disturbed by birds, mice, or insects but instead will grow into lush clusters of cob-bearing plants. But the good hand is not an innate possession; nor is it an attribute that remains constant once obtained. It is, rather, a vulnerable, transitory condition that must be achieved and maintained. A good hand is acquired through a spiritual cleansing performed by a native doctor. As doña Margarita put it:

> In the old days they cured everything, the house, the field, the animals, the children, the people. The doctor goes, he takes *yagé*, he does the ritual blowing, he dances, he chants, like that. In order to have good corn, my father would have my hands cured, to keep the birds, mice, and everything else from digging up the seeds. And so corn grows well for me, they don't dig it up when I plant. (76)

The cleansing or curing ceremony is performed by the native doctor with the aid of *yagé*, a psychoactive substance used by doctors and their patients to enter the realm of the spirits and ancestors.

Text in Context

On inspection, we find that the text of the saying is but an ephemeral surfacing of an entire sustaining cosmology. Our encounter with the text would be a paltry one in the absence of the appropriate cultural grounding. My own experience with the sayings of the ancestors traced this progression from surface to underlying system, when what I first took to be isolated proverbial expressions eventually came into focus as elements in a pervasive Andean folk religion. A whole spectrum of oral tradition interacts with dimensions of belief and practice associated with a spiritual edifice. Sayings of the ancestors convey nuggets of ancestral wisdom that can be applied to situations of daily life; mythic narratives rehearse the pivotal role of the ancestors in making the world safe for civilization; ceremonial speeches renew the social contract through dedication to the example of the ancestors; ritual chanting known as "singing to the spirits" makes direct contact with the spirit realm.

The Santiagueño example is instructive for any encounter with Native South American oral traditions. Employing the procedures recommended and exemplified above, the student of oral tradition moves from a tentative glimpse of verbal artistry to an appreciation of oral performance as an articulation of ambient social and cultural habitats. A rich world awaits the teacher and student of oral tradition in Native South America who adhere to these guidelines for mitigating the alienation of oral tradition from its natural habitat. Some effort is required in moving beyond surface manifestations to the text in context, but this effort is amply rewarded by entry into one of the world's great storehouses of oral tradition.

Notes

1. For further information on Native American oral poetics, see Jacobs; D. Hymes, *"In Vain"*; Tedlock, *Finding*.

2. For further information on Native American languages, see L. Campbell; Manelis Klein and Stark; Campbell and Mithun; Rowe; Key.
3. Other important scholarship may be found in Bierhorst, *Mythology*; Michael Brown; L. Graham; Perrin; Reichel-Dolmatoff; Salomon and Urioste; Schultes and Hofmann; Urban, *Approach*.

Donald J. Cosentino

African Oral Narrative Traditions

African oral narratives constitute an archive for the inherited wisdom of traditional society and a repository for those precepts of common sense that Clifford Geertz has called local knowledge (*Local Knowledge*). These stories are paideia for the young and, as Marshall McLuhan famously observed of Homeric epic, encyclopedias for everyone else in the traditional Africa of countless villages. More than enfolding static wisdom, oral narratives are also a subtle vehicle for speculation on everything from correct ways of sharing food to correct dispositions toward God, beast, and human being.

Oral narratives are available for intellectual manipulation because of their flexible structures. Although performers can craft them into seemingly immutable works of art, oral narratives are by nature ephemeral. They are constructed out of a repertoire of smaller plot units variously termed motifs, images, blocks, moves, gross constituent units — scholars do not concur on the terminology. Thus, in creating their unique oral narratives (for each performance is unique), storytellers fulfill the role of artist as well as sage.

The classroom teacher of African oral narratives must somehow convey their sweetness as well as their light. At the same time, the teacher must bridge the "quaint" gap—the prevalent assumption that African oral narratives are nursery tales or just-so stories meant finally for Maurice Sendak's (or, worse yet, Walt Disney's) charming treatment. Strategies for teaching African oral narrative traditions might best be discussed by unpacking the terms of the title. What do we mean by each of its defining words?

Africa

This term is far more than a geographic designation, though even as geography the division of Africa is a hot topic across the disciplines. Do we teach the whole continent or just black Africa, as the sub-Saharan region is often called? To divide the continent by a line through the Sahara establishes the Arab north as part of another world, whose focus is the Mediterranean or the Middle East. Such a division is contested by those scholars and cultural nationalists who insist on the indivisibility of continental African cultures. That same line also cuts off from consideration the oral traditions of Egypt, a nation that for many Africans is the fountainhead of their culture. The question of whether or to what degree classical Egypt was black heats up academic controversy (see Bernal) as well as popular scholarship. For most teachers the question of geographic range will be settled by the availability of existing anthologies, which by and large do not include North African tales (Scheub's *The African Storyteller* is an exception; it includes the pharaonic classic "The Two Brothers" as well as tales from the Sudan). The implications of including and excluding certain areas of the African continent should be considered by teachers and students alike.

Diaspora narratives are also excluded from most African folktale anthologies in print, though the persistence of African oral tradition in the Americas problematizes any easy continental categorization of black narrative (see Prahlad, this volume). Folklorists William Bascom and Richard Dorson spent the last years of their careers debating each other over the connection between diaspora and African traditions. Bascom countered Dorson's thesis of a Euro-American origin for most African American tales by collecting narratives common to oral traditions on both sides of the black Atlantic. His collection was published posthumously as *African Tales in the New World*. Reference to the debate over the nature of diaspora oral tradition and inclusion of cognate African American tales ought to be considered in the syllabus of any course on African narrative traditions.

Oral Narrative

Students of African folktales must grapple with texts that are really transcriptions of oral performances. That these texts are also translations, and sometimes translations of translations, can be an opportunity to introduce students to Plato's shadow parable. For indeed teachers, students, and scholars alike must deal with shadows on the wall of the cave when they open a collection of African folktales. When Frances Herskovits and Melville Herskovits collected their Dahomean narratives, they heard stories performed in Fongbe. The Fongbe was then translated into French by an informant and simultaneously transcribed into English by the Herskovitses. A dubious enterprise, yet one that produced one of the very best published collections of African oral narratives.

If word sense is sometimes lost in the process of transcription and translation, the danger to narrative structure is even greater. In her preface to *The Mantis and His Friends*, a classic collection of Khoisan tales from southern Africa, Dorothea Bleek assures her readers that the repetitions that Europeans find tedious have been removed. Now we have come to appreciate that "tedious repetition" is the structural basis of the oral performance. But editorial ignorance of African aesthetic principles continues to plague narrative collections. Thus in Roger Abrahams's anthology *African Folktales*, the magnificent *Mwindo Epic* of the Banyanga people is retold with many of the repetitive metaphors ("He made himself as clean as the anus of a snail") removed. This is the editorial equivalent of penciling out "wine-dark sea" or "rosy-fingered dawn" from the *Odyssey*. Plot edits are even more serious. Mwindo's heartless murder of the pygmies who protest the killing of the dragon sacred to Nkuba, the lightning god, is simply wiped from Abrahams's edition, leaving Mwindo's subsequent chastisement in the sky (the very climax of the epic) unmotivated.

Teachers should avoid edited texts when possible. An unedited *Mwindo Epic* is available in print, fully annotated by Daniel Biebuyck, the collector, who has appended the original Nyanga text. When such editions exist, they should be preferred. Methods of collection and translation need to be discussed in the classroom and taken into account in narrative analyses. Provenance demands the same intense scrutiny as courtroom evidence. After all, it is the art and philosophy of Africa we are examining. We need to know how the written evidence was collected and preserved.

The dramatic implications of performance should also be suggested. Students are not reading short stories; they are reading transcripts of performances that have no real equivalent in written narrative. In fact, by their radical juxtaposition of images, oral narratives often seem more akin to poetry than to prose. Comparison to other nonwritten dramatic forms may also be useful. Movies, particularly those that rely on the techniques of montage or on the cumulative horror of the Hitchcock technique; trickster formulas in a Bugs Bunny or Road Runner cartoon; self-reflexive ironies in the electronic narratives of soap opera or the telenovela; the function of lyric in a Broadway musical; the startling synchronicities on MTV or in contemporary performance art — reference to these and other alternative dramatic forms may help break the mold of literary expectations that sometimes makes the reading of oral narratives bewildering or boring. The Nigerian scholar Isidore Okpewho has explored the dramatic nature of these narrative traditions in *African Oral Literature*.

The casual reader cannot be faulted for approaching the oral narrative like a short story, since it is usually written down as such. Redactors such as Peter Seitel and Harold Scheub have devised other modes of transcription. Seitel, borrowing his system of typography from the linguist Dennis Tedlock, plays with fonts and formats to suggest dramatic dimensions to his collected Haya tales, *See So That We May See*. Seitel's experiment created interesting if peculiar-looking texts, but they have inspired no imitators. Scheub, who devised a theory of "core clichés" to account for the role of memory in oral performance (*Xhosa*), did inspire a generation of his University of Wisconsin students to account for the dramatic structures of narrative performance in their written texts. Publications by these scholars (e.g., Cancel; Cosentino; Foster; La Pin; Tanna) carefully note such dramatic circumstances as time and place, performer and audience data; verbal techniques such as prologue, epilogue, ideophones, interjections, asides; and lyric patterns of call and response to account for the developing performance.

It is these dramatic elements, too often obscured in conventional transcriptions, that offer an oblique passage into the heart of the narrative. They also allow for a bit of ham acting on the part of instructor and students. If students are taught the choric response, the teacher may assume the storyteller's call. The results can be surprisingly lively. Some narratives, which seem boringly repetitive in the reading, fairly skip off the page if they are chanted by leader and chorus. For example, consider Leopard's aria in the Yoruba tale "Monkey Steals a Drum":

> *What's your trouble, Warrior*
> Yeeye, Iranmatekon
> *He said, "Everybody made a drum,*
> Yeeye, Iranmatekon
> *And Monkey took my drum away*[. . ."]
> Yeeye, Iranmatekon . . .
>
> (La Pin, "Monkey" 47)

Classroom opera of an enthusiastic, if not brilliant, order may be fashioned out of this delightfully translated song.

Of course, video will likely change everything, in both the collection and the teaching of oral narratives. Where field video exists, it should be used to teach performance. Likewise, ethnographic films such as *Angano, Angano*, which records the narrative performance of several raffish, charming, and talented Malagasy storytellers, or John

Marshall's minimalist classic, *Bitter Melons*, which records lyrics and glimpses from the hard life of a Khoisan singer of tales, animate an anthology of narrative texts in a way no lecture can duplicate. I have also had some success inviting African student storytellers to perform narratives in their own languages. On one such occasion a Yoruba student at UCLA performed a narrative that he had earlier collected as my student in a folklore class in Nigeria and that he and I had later collaborated on for a popular publication.

Each oral performance is unique. There are no generic storytellers or generic folktales. Each tale is created by a performer whose name, though known to an audience, is often ignored by a collector. The anonymous folk narrator is therefore an invention of literate scholarship, not a condition of oral performance. Individuality in story performance should be acknowledged in the classroom, even if a name, as most often happens, cannot be attached to a tale. In more recent anthologies, some names and character sketches of narrators have been recorded. Biebuyck has given us a sharp picture of Shekarisi, the master of the *Mwindo Epic*. Scheub has edited a volume dedicated to the genius of Nongenile Masithatu Zenani, a Xhosa diviner and *ntsomi* ("narrative") performer (Zenani). I have described Mariatu Sandi, Manungo, and Hannah Samba as the competing shrewish narrators of Mende *domeisia* ("narrative performances") in "A Competition of Lies" (Abrahams, *African Folktales* 89–104).

Those three Mende women narrators remind us of yet another important social fact: oral narrative performance exists both as text and context. The folklorist Robert Georges has acknowledged the social matrix of narration by describing it as "storytelling event." But older (and more felicitous) descriptions of the sociology of storytelling are to be found in the frame narratives of *The Canterbury Tales* and *A Thousand and One Nights* (Dawood). Since field-workers have been lax in recording frames, teachers may choose to reference these two classic examples of the storytelling frame (see further Irwin, this volume). Or they may refer to frame passages in novels such as Chinua Achebe's *Things Fall Apart* or Zora Neale Hurston's *Mules and Men*, in which the social conditions of Igboland and south Louisiana are seen as coordinates of story performance.

Tradition

What does tradition mean in the context of contemporary African cultures? There still persists the Africa of a million isolated villages, where quarreling cowives tell stories on one another around the cook fires. In places like The Congo Republic, where the nation-state has palpably failed, that Africa is actually expanding. But there is also the urban Africa of Lagos, Kinshasa, Nairobi, and Soweto — a continent of TV stations, movie houses, and universities, of motor parks, mansions, and brothels. Both Africas flourish, side by side, in social reality and narrative fiction. The juxtaposition of these radically different ways of life appears also in the wild anachronisms found in many contemporary folktales. Thus in "A Defiant Maid Marries a Stranger," Mariatu Sandi tells of a werewolf who gives his fiancée a golden ring "so shiny white people turned it into electricity" (Abrahams, *African Folktales* 93). Werewolves, gold rings, electricity, white people — this narrator happily mixes up traditional and modern images to create her version of a classic Mende tale of marriage gone wrong.

For us to discuss accurately this symphony of tradition and invention, the surface of the narrative must be separated from its deep thematic structure. Despite the plot anachronisms, folktales persist because their concerns are fundamentally timeless (see Jones, this volume). As scholars and storytellers both understand, folktales are about two things: blood relations and the problems of growing up. These are also the twin preoccupations of the dream, whose surrealistic landscapes are mirrored in the fantasy sequences that recur in most oral narratives.

Redefining what we mean by tradition in contemporary Africa also allows us to set oral tradition within a broad range of narrative types — oral, written, and electronic — that are all flourishing simultaneously in modern Africa. Just as village, forest, and city coexist, so do folktales, novels, movies, and TV, which together mirror the fabulous complexity of modern African life. These diverse media also influence one another: telenovelas in Nigeria play out folktale themes, Senegalese movies re-create epics, Sierra Leone folktales include airplanes and taxicabs. Shekarisi, the Nyanga epic singer of *Mwindo*; Wole Soyinka, the Yoruba nobel laureate playwright; and Papa Wemba, the Congolese pop movie star, are all contemporary African narrative artists. If we were to imagine a parallel complexity in Western art, then Homer, Shakespeare, and Francis Ford Coppola would all be contemporaries and all be performing today.

Ethnicity is a final crucial component of tradition. There are overarching themes in any collection of African tales, common cosmopolitan perspectives that give a recognizable feel to narratives from the continent. But in the last analysis there is no "African" ethnicity (or "European," for that matter). There are instead Yoruba, Zulu, Chaga, Khoisan, and Mende stories, each rooted in distinct customs and beliefs. Thus the Tanzanian Chaga tale "Mrile," in which the flower-child hero escapes his overpowering mother by sinking into the earth, can be explicated only against the rigid gender classifications defined and enforced by Chaga initiation rites (Scheub, *Storyteller* 282–91). "Umxakaza Wakogingqwayo," the tale of a vain South African princess, suggests parallels between her grotesque rites of passage and the grotesque political extravagances of the Zulu military state presided over by her rapacious father (473–90).

In like manner, the tension between the mallams (religious teachers) and pre-Islamic wise women in Hausa tales such as "The Town Where None May Go to Sleep" or "The City Where Men Are Mended" (Radin 247–53), the rules of the Sande female initiation society that structure Mende concepts of romance in "A Competition of Lies" (Abrahams, *African Folktales* 89–103), or the effects of matriarchy on central African marriage customs in "Wonder Worker of the Plains" (Radin 229–34) all open up to ethnographic glosses. Unfortunately, this sort of cultural information is missing from most anthologies. In order to fill the gap, teachers may consult the original collections from which these tales were borrowed. Folktale collections made in the field usually begin with an ethnographic chapter and are sometimes annotated. The information they offer can move us from an initial bewilderment to an empathetic appreciation of the human predicaments that motivate all storytelling.

Syllabus

The first part of any course on oral traditions should be concerned with the problems of reading an oral text. These are really problems of translation: from African languages to English, from the conventions of oral performance to the contingencies of the written page. Complex patterns of repetition, which reiterate the same theme in various keys and move protagonists along predictable geographic axes from village to bush to village, are templates that structure the whole of African oral tradition. These templates should be located and described before the variations that create myths, epics, and folktales are analyzed.

Myth

The best place to begin a survey of African oral narratives may be with myth. The narrative repertoire of most oral tradition is classified into categories of "truth" and "fiction." Within that dichotomy, folktales with merely human protagonists are called lies, but lies cunningly devised around some essential truth. Myths dealing with the acts of gods and heroes, however, are always "true," though their truth is obscured by the rich language of metaphor. Myths speak of the origin of things: of the separation of the earth from the sky and of people from beasts; of the origin of kingdoms, lineages, and customs; of proper gender and familial roles; of the good and terrible things that sustain culture and nature and enforce the division between the two.

A few widespread myths define key aspects of traditional religion throughout Africa. One such myth is the separation of God from creation. The Fon people of West Africa say that in those days Mawu-Lisa, the androgynous sun-moon god, floated only a few meters above the earth. She/he was clearly visible to all the people of the village, including an old woman who would toss her pan of dirty water into the air each morning, wetting the sacred toes. In disgust at such slovenly manners, Mawu-Lisa drew meter by meter away from the earth, until now she/he is entirely withdrawn, communicating with creation through Legba, the divine trickster, who alone knows the languages of the *vodun* ("gods") and people.

In one form or another, many African myths entertain a similar idea of a distant high god and intermediate spirits who maintain communication through divination or sacrifice. The plots of the myths embody a sort of uncertainty principle that holds to the random nature of creation, usually through the actions of an energetic, unconscious creator. For the Khoisan of the Kalahari Desert that agent is Mantis, perhaps the most casual creator in world mythology, who makes the eland from the shoe of his son and the moon from an ostrich feather he tosses in the sky (Radin 79–80). Kintu is the culture hero for the East African Baganda. Wandering into their lake country with only one cow, Kintu manages to wrest from Gulu the Sky God his daughter, the agricultural goddess Nambi, along with her brother Walumbe, the personification of death (69–72). Herding and farming, growth, decay, and rebirth are all suggested by this myth, which serves as the political charter for Bantu royalty, epitomized in the divine cowboy Kintu.

Mantis and Kintu exist at the opposite ends of the African spectrum of myths. The Khoisan creator blunders and bumps in a shadowy world just before the beginning of time. Through his random actions, the world of the Kalahari becomes fit for Khoisan habitation. Kintu comes to rule over a political kingdom very much like modern Buganda, transforming it from a Garden of Eden to the exigencies of modern life. The contrastive nature of these myths reminds us how inaccurate it would be to present either as typical of African mythology. No such monotype exists. It is just as important to stress differences as similarities, to avoid creating a (Joseph) Campbell soup of myths that loses all local flavor.

The Trickster

There are more tales told of the trickster than of any other character in oral tradition. At one level his tales (for the trickster is almost always a male) seem a world removed from the lofty concerns of myth. He is usually an animal: spider, tortoise, rabbit, hyena, mongoose, mantis, monkey, mouse—living at the margins of the human world he somehow always manages to define. Driven by needs for food, sex, or prestige, he pulls off some dumb ruse or other, which often blows up in his face. Yet everyone loves him for his antics, especially children, who may well see themselves in the trickster's bumbling attempts to copy the adult world.

All the major African folktale anthologies (Abrahams, *African Folktales*; Radin; Scheub, *African Storyteller*) contain trickster sections that should be read and discussed in class. After the students survey continent-wide traditions, it may be useful to concentrate on a single trickster figure such as Ananse the Spider, from the Akan tradition of Ghana. Ananse is a complex trickster, mediating relations between humans and Nyame the Sky God, creating everything from the moon to jealousy to storytelling itself, getting a big butt by clapping his head on his rear end during a ghost dance. Helter-skelter, Ananse is all over the place, reappearing as a figure in school texts, in a popular cartoon film, and throughout the African diaspora as the folk hero of Jamaica, Belize, the Mosquito Coast, even the southern United States, where he persists as "Aunt Nancy" in Gulf Coast tales. Ananse tales were thoroughly collected early in this century and reprinted in many anthologies. They are the subject of excellent analyses in Robert Pelton's *The Trickster in West Africa*.

Surveying trickster traditions will also uncover anomalous characters like the Great Dikithi from southern Africa (Abrahams 218–22) or Musa Wo from Sierra Leone (Cosentino, "Charters"). These are men-children who combine the physical strength of adult men with the manic selfishness of small children. Their powers seem magical, for they project an "omnipotence of thought" that Freud has described as the hallmark of childish mentality. Boundless in amoral energy, the man-child is full of potential for good or evil. Channeled by appropriate rites of passage, he may develop into a hero such as Son-Jara (aka Sundiata; John Johnson; Johnson, Hale, and Belcher) of Mali, Mwindo of the Nyanga, or Sikhuluma of the Xhosa, all of whom began their royal careers as tricksters. Or, left unchecked, the man-child may degenerate into the sort of bad man celebrated in African American ballads such as Shine or Stagolee (see Prahlad, this volume; see also the focused study of this ubiquitous figure by Roberts).

The example of Shine or Stagolee reminds us of the universal appeal of the outlaw. "Violence is as American as cherry pie," said H. Rap Brown, the 1960s activist. And indeed, considering the role of this important miscreant in African oral traditions, the teacher might draw comparisons between him and parallel characters in our culture. Bandits of traditional American legend (Jesse James, Pretty Boy Floyd, Bonnie and Clyde) have yielded pride of place to the romanticized drug lords of rap lyrics, the antic mayhem of *Pulp Fiction* gunmen, or genuine docudemons like Charles Manson or the Oklahoma City bombers. Character traits of African tricksters might be delineated in class discussion and compared to those of other tricksters operating in the multiringed circus of popular culture throughout the world.

Rites of Passage

Growing up is the great theme of fairy tales throughout the world: the transition from childhood to adulthood, marriage, and the responsibilities of the married state. In Africa, this theme classically takes the form of initiation. A youth is separated from his or her cohort and forced to undergo some frightening ordeal in a foreign place. The place of trial is the bush or forest, and the taskmaster is a beast or monster. If the youth endures this trial successfully, he or she is conducted back to the village: older, wiser, and ready for marriage — often to the very monster, who turns out to be a comely human in disguise. The movement of the protagonist from village to bush to village is also a movement from culture to nature and back to culture. It is the universal trail first described by Arnold van Gennep in his seminal study *The Rites of Passage*.

In many African societies tales of growing up are closely correlated to rituals of initiation. Thus the Mende women of Sierra Leone maintain their own sorority, known as Sande, which all adult women are obliged to join. Sande ceremonies are frequently the focus of stories that ponder appropriate gender roles in marriage. These stories, often about an everywoman named Yombo, reach no consensus as to whether marriage is properly dominated by a strong wife or strong husband. There are as many opinions as there are storytellers. Some say Yombo should accede to the demands of her monster-husband Kpana, others that she should use her wits to triumph despite him (Cosentino, *Maids* 144–63). Yombo's fate remains a hot topic around the porches and cook fires of Mendeland because it touches the most personal part of everyone's life. Though a woman will undergo only one Sande initiation in her life, she may relive that magic time over and over again within the frames of narrative performance.

Not everyone makes the transition into adult life. Marriages fail. Famines kill. The forest may eat you up. African oral narratives are not romantic. They are matter-of-fact about hard things: "Stark realism, the insistent emphasis upon man in all his moods, the emphasis upon the contemporary scene, and a high degree of sophistication [pervade] the whole of native African oral literature. Rarely has man been depicted as more completely and inextricably anchored in this world, more obsessively earthbound" (Radin 4). The Ila tale of the Old Woman is a haunting example of this realism. Having outlived all her children and grandchildren, a poor woman inexplicably begins to grow younger. Desperate to learn the reason for her strange fate, she sets out to find Leza Shikakunamo, the high god. Moving to the very ends of the earth, the woman finds neither an answer nor Leza. Finally she cries out to the people who question her motives:

> "My brothers, you ask me! Here in the nations is there one who suffers as I have suffered?"
> And they would ask again, "How have you suffered?"
> "In this way, I am alone. As you see me, a solitary old woman. That is how I am!"
> And they answered, "Yes, we see. That is how you are! Bereaved of friends and kindred? In what do you differ from others? Leza Shikakunamo sits on the back of every one of us, and we cannot shake him off."
> She never obtained her desire. She died of a broken heart.
> (Radin 305–6)

There is a straightforwardness to the old woman's encounters with fate that makes even Job's trials seem trivial and contrived. From this tale one might deduce an African philosophy akin to existentialism; it would indeed be hard to find a more unrelenting view of tragedy in Beckett or Sartre. Ila storytellers of course know neither of these French writers. Their existentialism grows of out a perception of life embedded in African oral narrative tradition.

Old Heroes, New Media

Paul Radin appends the Ila tale as epilogue to his volume *African Folktales*. It might also serve as epilogue to an entire course. There would be a danger, however, in ending the course on so elegiac a note. The end of the tradition would be implied in the death of the woman. But oral traditions are not dying; they are only changing. So a course on oral tradition should end on a note of change. We should ask, Whither folklore? What's becoming of the old heroes in the new media? Who are the current monsters? Where do we locate the modern bush?

We have noted contemporary African artists who carry these oral themes into writing and electronic scripts. But in truth there is no formal line of transmission between their stories and oral narrative performance. Artists in written and electronic media cannot tell stories in the same way, to the same audiences, with the same effects, or for the same meanings. Writers like Chinua Achebe, the great Igbo novelist, can write about Igbo traditions, even include Igbo folktales in their novels, but that is not the same as creating such tales for a live audience (for general ideas on teaching Achebe's *Things Fall Apart*, see Lindfors). Albert Lord's *The Singer of Tales* helps explain why. The rules of oral composition, as he discovered among South Slavic bards, are in many ways opposite to those of creative writing. Qualities that define an excellent oral performer, such as the skillful use of repetition in established plots and themes, are dismissed as hackneyed clichés in a writer.

So a course on oral traditions must confront disjunctions as well as continuities. It must juxtapose oral tradition and written literature, avoiding comforting assumptions about the evolution of oral narrative forms that literary evidence does not support. Reading a "novel" by Amos Tutuola, the self-taught, eccentrically literate author of *The Palm Wine Drinkard* and *My Life in the Bush of Ghosts*, may serve to make that point. Tutuola does bridge the gap between orality and writing. He writes extended rite-of-passage tales, in which his young heroes confront all the monsters of the Yoruba bush dolled up with television hands, light-switch eyes, and factory-whistle noses. The form of the oral narrative still remains: it is the hero's quest. But the hero's adventures in the bush are now developed by a writer, not a storyteller.

There is a free-flowing idiosyncrasy to Tutuola's developing images unconstrained by a live audience or a finite tradition. And yet these constraints are what define the storyteller's art. So Tutuola is a genuine hybrid, creating old heroes in new media. His books are immensely engaging, but they are also culs-de-sac. The forms of the novel and the short story will generate new heroes and a new tradition that does not grow out of the old. But that is material for another course. Like his heroes, Tutuola stands at the crossroads, one arm pointing to an oral tradition that will never die, the other to new narrative forms that other writers will develop. This busy intersection is a good place to end a journey that is only the starting point for another.

Sw. Anand Prahlad

African American Traditions

The relative newness of African American traditions distinguishes them from the other traditions in this volume. Whereas many oral traditions preceded the evolution of writing, the African American materials are as recent as the colonialization of the Americas and have thus evolved in relation to print and other American popular media. There exist no epics of the breadth of the *Panchatantra* in African American oral lore, and so far no writer has compiled a representative collection of African American tales in the fashion of the *Arabian Nights* or undertaken a nationalistic project with the scope of the *Kalevala*. In fact, many elements of modern American society work against such efforts. The richness of African American oral traditions lies instead in their diversity and reciprocity with mainstream America.

Connections to African Traditions

The link between African and African American oral traditions is an important, if sometimes debated, one (see Cosentino, this volume).

189

While it has been established that the major portion of African American materials are of European origin or were developed in the American context, at least a small percentage derive directly from African traditions (Crowley, *African Folklore*). The tale called "The Talking Skull That Refused to Talk," for example, is certainly of African origin (Bascom, "Talking Skull"). As the tale goes, a slave comes across a skull in the woods and the skull says to him, "My mouth brought me here, and your mouth will bring you here too." The slave reports the incident to the slave owner, who threatens that if the skull doesn't talk, the slave will be killed. When the skull fails to speak in the presence of the owner, the slave is put to death. The skull then replies to the dead slave, "I told you your mouth would bring you here."

The most important African influence on African American traditions, however, lies in performance styles rather than in content. The vocal and musical style of rural blues singers is at times almost indistinguishable from that of West African folk musicians. The calls known as field hollers, the styles of spirituals, and the songs of vendors such as those selling fruit or dispensing their wares along urban streets are also highly reminiscent of African vocal performances. The same can be said about the kinetic and vocal characteristics of other urban forms, for instance toasts, which are bawdy poems recited most often in bars. Toasts, in fact, provide a good illustration of the synthesis that often occurred between an African style of performing and forms that were largely European. It has been suggested that the toasting tradition came from England and Scotland and was adapted in style and content to the needs of African Americans (Abrahams, *Deep Down* 109–10). A similar synthesis is evident in the preaching styles of many Baptist ministers, which incorporates the evangelical fervor of early American preaching with African rhythms and poetics. This sermon tradition is reflected in the oratory of prominent leaders such as Jesse Jackson and the late Martin Luther King (B. Rosenberg, "Message").

It has been argued quite convincingly that genres of African American speech are connected by the practice of signifying, which has roots in African culture (Gates). Signifying refers to an indirect, often critical manner of speaking, in which words have double meanings. This is apparent in narratives that may seem innocent on the surface but that contain veiled criticisms. Signifying is just as obvious in spirituals and work songs, which by necessity had to veil some critical comments about European Americans. Signifying often characterizes the telling of jokes, phrases in blues songs, portions of sermons, and even the use of proverbs. For instance, a speaker might use a proverb such as "One monkey don't stop no show" as a form of retaliation in a verbal dual (Prahlad, *Proverbs*). While few specific African proverbs have survived among African Americans, ways in which proverbs are used have certainly been influenced by African aesthetics.

Thematic Organization of Materials

African American materials lend themselves particularly well to thematic organization, and this approach can help connect otherwise separate genres. Largely because of the historical context in which these traditions have evolved, they often reflect particular concerns, some of the most prominent being survival in bondage and the quest for freedom. Countless legends tell of the extreme difficulties that slaves and later generations of African Americans have had to overcome to survive and to maintain strong community bonds and personal self-esteem. Legends are generally accepted as narratives that are believed to be true by those who tell them. Although the motifs of such legends are similar over time and geography, they often circulate and are given particular twists or embellishments within families (Morgan). Common motifs in such legends include attempted escapes, evasion or endurance of punishment, and creative mechanisms for dealing with interactions with European American society. This branch of African American folklore gave rise to the written tradition of slave narratives (e.g., Douglass), which contain the same motifs as the legends, and in more recent times to works such as *Roots* (Haley) and *The Autobiography of Miss Jane Pittman* (Gaines). African American legends have also exerted a tremendous influence on many works of fiction.

The study of legend could also be extended to include figures such as John the Conqueror, who was said to possess magical powers and who in one version induces a field of slaves to fly back to Africa. From such heroes sprang the bad man tradition (Roberts). This tradition encompasses toasts and blues and usually depicts a man who has many qualities of the American outlaw, who is feared but admired and celebrated. Some of the most popular bad men in the African American tradition are Stagolee and Railroad Bill. Occasionally, these heroic figures were based on real people: Railroad Bill, for example, was Morris Slater. As the story goes, Slater walked into town one day with his guns strapped to his sides, and when the sheriff asked him to surrender his guns, he refused. In the shoot-out that followed, the sheriff was killed and Slater became a fugitive. The legends tell of a man who consistently outwitted posses, threw food from passing freight trains to poor people gathered near the tracks, and turned himself into a tree to elude bounty hunters.[1] Other legendary figures are also based in history; however, legends tend to exaggerate their abilities and deeds. Such legends include notable persons from Sojourner Truth and Nat Turner to contemporary heroes like Muhammad Ali.

Many folktales, which are narratives recognized as fictional, also reflect the themes of survival and struggle for freedom (see Jones, this volume). Although the characters of folktales are usually far less virtuous than those of legends, folktales often reveal concerns with resistance, rebellion, and negotiation with European American society (Levine; Roberts). Some of the better known tales are those whose main characters are animals, such as Brer Rabbit. They offer commentary about the ethics of behavior and conflicts between individual and community needs. They might also offer the instructor opportunities for conversation about the importance of trickster tales in the context of an oppressed group. But other tales fit thematically with the struggle for freedom. A cycle involving a main character, John, for instance, centers on the dynamics between a slave owner and a slave who often insists on certain rights or privileges (Hurston, *Mules* 87–90).

Spirituals are another traditional form that lends itself well to this thematic topic. Sometimes referred to as sorrow songs, spirituals were sung by slaves and succeeding generations of African Americans in many contexts, most notably in the fields while working or in private religious gatherings. Although there has been some debate about the origin of these songs, they undoubtedly bear the mark of African American musical and poetic influences. Numerous scholars have suggested that although spirituals are filled with biblical symbolism, they primarily concern gaining freedom here on earth. Many Old Testament characters, such as Daniel, Moses, Jonah, Samson, and David, figure prominently in these songs. The appeal of the songs lies in the metaphorical comparison that African Americans traditionally drew between their own social circumstances and those of these characters. For example, African Americans have compared themselves to the Israelites in bondage and identified with the story of Moses leading his people out of slavery and into the land of freedom. Thus songs like "Go Down Moses" referred to the slaves' desire and determination for freedom (Lovell). Without question, spirituals also addressed freedom on religious and existential levels. Many of the motifs found in spirituals are common in the black sermon tradition; popular sermons often focus on the same stories to which spirituals allude (B. Rosenberg, *Bones*).

A lesser known traditional form is the conversion narrative. These narratives recounted visionary experiences leading to the denunciation of a sinful life and the embrace of a religious one (C. Johnson). In some communities such experiences and reports, the culmination of a period of isolation in which visions were sought, served as initiation into church membership. The stories tell, among other things, of dying and being reborn, crossing pits of fire on tightropes, and meeting and speaking to God in heaven. No African American narrative tradition is more colorful or compelling than this one.

Finally, other musical traditions cannot be overlooked. Blues and gospel music are two of the most pervasive oral traditions, having had a major impact on American culture in general. Gospel music, in contrast to spirituals, is an urban phenomenon and typically includes musical accompaniment such as piano, organ, and sometimes drums, guitars, and other band or orchestral instruments. The lyrics of gospel, which focus more on the New Testament than do those of spirituals, often concern survival and freedom. As this form has developed, it has changed significantly, moving from a more raw presentation by quartets or other small groups to a more sophisticated one by larger groups and choirs. Accordingly, the lyrics in earlier gospel music are different from those of more recent songs. The essence of the tradition, however, remains constant (Levine). Because gospel music, like conversion narratives, is focused primarily on spiritual and psychological freedom, it may present a more complex challenge for teachers.

Although the blues has myriad themes, its songs can be chosen to facilitate the thematic approach. Blues can include early country blues, urban blues, or jazz. A strong undercurrent in the lyrics of all types of blues is a concern with freedom. This theme is often expressed in terms of the relationship between a man and a woman but also reflects conflicts between African Americans and the dominant society. It has sometimes been said that the essence of blues is a cry for freedom. Like sermons, both blues and gospel present compelling interactions between orality and literacy (Evans, *Blues*). On the one hand, they are both often composed by songwriters; on the other, they are based on a well-known tradition of formulaic lines, phrases, and verses.

Developing Teaching Units

The teacher focusing on African American oral traditions would probably want to plan lessons around three basic objectives. The first is to give students an aesthetic appreciation of oral performances, written transcriptions, and the process by which orality is rendered in writing. This appreciation includes the poetic characteristics of the forms, structural differences between genres, features of the contexts in which texts are naturally situated, and ways in which African American traditions differ from the traditions of other groups. The first objective also entails sensitizing students to issues associated with regional dialect; dialect might otherwise be a barrier to student comprehension and appreciation of various narratives. Exercises to achieve such sensitizing would depend on the ages of the students, the philosophical orientation of the particular institution, the student-teacher ratio, availability of enrichment materials, and the amount of time that can be devoted to this topic. Teachers should point out that while a mastery of standard English is necessary and desirable, all of us speak some form of dialect. Furthermore, it should be emphasized that variations in dialect can be valued rather than maligned. This simple shift in perspective is one of the most important steps in learning to appreciate oral traditions. But the step can prove a difficult one. Most students are socialized and educated to value the speech of the mass media and educators and to ridicule or be embarrassed by regional or ethnic dialects. Therefore they are not accustomed to listening closely to ordinary speech or considering it to be artistic. An instructive exercise is to have students tape-record conversations or stories told among themselves, friends, or family members and transcribe portions of the recordings, attempting to capture the actual way language is used in conversation (see Zeitlin, Kotkin, and Baker). Not only will this exercise sensitize students to subtleties of spoken language, it will also raise the level of awareness about language as performance and about the problems involved in collection and transcription of oral narration.

From there the teacher could move to recorded presentations of African American oral traditions. There is an abundance of audio and audio-visual recordings of many types of African American oral traditions — for example, storytelling, blues, gospels, spirituals, sermons, work songs — and in most parts of the country there are performers in the African American communities who will gladly make classroom visits to share their knowledge and skills.[2] I recommend that teachers immerse their students in the oral performances, drawing attention to the aesthetic qualities of orality before bringing in written texts. There are a number of excellent printed collections (Hamilton; Dorson, *American Negro Folktales*; Dance; Abrahams, *Afro-American Folktales*) and works that discuss the artistic construction and performance styles of various genres (e.g., Smitherman; Evans, *Blues*; B. Rosenberg, *Bones*) that can be used when teachers wish to include written texts.

The second objective is for students to gain an understanding of the historical context out of which African American traditions emerged. Attention should be given to the development of the slave trade and to the social forces that were current at the time that the genres in question thrived. Such a unit would fit well with chapters on American history; however, since many textbooks do not give adequate coverage to the experiences and perspectives of African Americans, teachers may need to consult additional works (Levine; Genovese; Segal). Fortunately, many of these works consider the role of oral traditions in the lives of African Americans as well as in the reconstruction of their history.

The third objective is for students to gain an understanding of the functions that these traditions have served in the day-to-day lives of African Americans. Many folktales and legends, for instance, have helped provide a sense of hope and reaffirmation. Figures like John the Conqueror, as heroes in many traditions, gave communities a model of admirable traits. Stories of heroes with strength, determination, and courage inspired community members to live up to such standards. The narratives also raised and maintained self-esteem, since the heroes were symbolic representations of African American culture in general. Humor, another important element in many genres, often gave African Americans a subversive way to criticize aspects of the society that oppressed them. It also allowed them to release some of the tension that resulted from living in an oppressive environment. As one can see, units on oral traditions can complement the study of psychology or sociology.

A number of developments in African American culture, and in modern American society in general, facilitate the teaching of black oral traditions. There are now many audio and video recordings of oral performances available. Teachers should take advantage of these because, as has been noted, performance style is an important and distinctive feature of African American folklore. A teacher could plan a unit, for instance, around sermons. For such a unit, the teacher would want to play several recordings of sermons by C. L. Franklin, discussing with the class the stylistic elements that determine how the sermon is evaluated within its natural context. Such elements include the intensity of the "singing" portion of the sermon, repetition of formulaic phrases, and the relevance of the topic to the social concerns of the congregation. It would also be pertinent to discuss the nature of impromptu performances and Franklin's specific preparation for his sermons. Of course, it would be helpful to obtain a recording of one of the sermons transcribed in the Franklin book, so that students could have a copy of the transcription to refer to.[3] One possible exercise is to compare the poetry and vocal delivery of a sermon preached by Franklin (Franklin and Titon) with that of the same sermon preached by another minister (Davis). The sermon would be an ideal focus for a unit because of the strong influence of preaching styles on other forms of African American folklore, such as blues and gospel. It would also serve as a springboard for discussions about formulaic phrases and how they assist performers in their performances. Sermons from earlier periods could also be compared with more contemporary examples from speakers such as Martin Luther King (B. Rosenberg, "Message," with an emphasis on the same kind of features that were discussed in the Franklin performances; Hill et al. 184–210, 821–22, 1104, 1408, 1420). A final suggestion is to discuss the themes and motifs found in sermons and to relate them to the historical and social concerns of the African American community. For example, why have sermons such as "The Dry Bones in the Valley" remained popular while those based on other biblical stories have not (Franklin and Titon 80)?

The close connection between African American literary and oral traditions also offers many opportunities for study. As I have noted, the genre of slave narratives has a direct relation to legends. But oral traditions have a strong influence on most areas of African American literature; it is practically impossible to fully appreciate most written texts without some knowledge of the oral foundation from which they spring (T. Harris; Gates). Black novelists have always relied on the structures, rhythms, and content of oral traditions in composing their works. Zora Neale Hurston's classic *Their Eyes Were Watching God*, for instance, is structurally based on motifs from the blues. The flood, which can be considered one of the defining events in the novel, is a popular one in blues. Hurston also goes to great lengths to incorporate into the novel proverbs, storytelling, boasting, signifying, and, in general, numerous ways of speaking that characterize the oral performances of rural African Americans. Because her work is so full of humorous interactions, it can also be used as an aid in exploring the social functions of oral traditions.

Later novelists, such as Ralph Ellison in his *Invisible Man*, do much the same thing, although the writing is more complex and less folksy. Especially prominent in Ellison's work is the theme of the displaced African American who journeys from one region to another, which can be linked to legend and slave narratives mentioned earlier. This theme, in fact, can be said to dominate African American fiction. James Baldwin relies heavily on the stanzas of spirituals and on the timbre and voice of sermons and blues in developing the structure and voice of his novels. Toni Morrison's *Beloved* provides another excellent illustration of a modern fictional work that is greatly indebted to oral traditions. In recasting the true story of a mother who kills one of her children rather than have her returned to captivity, Morrison uses motifs that are commonly found in African American legend and tale traditions (T. Harris). The novel *Mama Day*, by Gloria Naylor, is as rich in folk speech, proverbs (Prahlad, "Chickens"), ceremony and ritual, and folk belief as any that have been written.

Teachers could approach these and other fictional works in a number of different ways. They could focus on the direct comparisons between motifs in oral narratives and written texts, or they might instead want to consider the relation in a more general sense, looking at themes that connect the two traditions. Undoubtedly, they would want to spend some time discussing the textual features of the written texts that are derived from oral sources. Many works (Hurston, Morrison, etc.) evolve as characters tell stories to other characters or to the reader. Such examples are easily compared and contrasted with legends taken from folklore books, recordings, or live performances. Moreover, attention should be paid to how the performances and audiences of literature and oral traditions differ.

African American poets have been even more active in drawing from oral sources than have writers of fiction (S. Henderson). Paul Lawrence Dunbar, for instance, inspired by sermons and storytelling, composed numerous poems modeled on these genres. James Weldon

Johnson's *God's Trombones* (Johnson, Douglas, and Falls) remains one of the classic works of poetry based on the folk sermon. Not only does Johnson emulate the sermon style and form, but he also borrows from oral tradition in choosing the topics or subjects of his poems. Langston Hughes is well known for forging a poetic tradition that draws primarily on blues and jazz for its texture, meter, form, content, and voice. A possible exercise would be to examine the lyrics of a singer such as Blind Lemon Jefferson[4] in much the same fashion that the poems by a literary author are examined. What are some of the singer's favorite motifs and phrases? How does the singer use features such as intonation and metaphor? What comparisons can be made between the singer's lyrics and the more formal verse of literary poets?

Beginning with the Black Arts movement of the 1960s, African American poetry developed further in this direction. Poets such as Amiri Baraka became outspoken advocates of a shift in aesthetic focus away from European poetic forms and toward a reliance on the oral traditions of African American culture (a video of Amiri Baraka reading is available from the Lannan Foundation, Los Angeles, CA). Since that time a strong tradition has developed that is often philosophically distinct from the more canonical European-derived traditions. These differences in philosophy can provide interesting points of focus for teachers.

Often, in this tradition of jazz poetry, there is as much emphasis on the context of performance as there is on the written texts (for good examples of jazz poetry, see Feinstein and Komunyakaa). Poets like Quincy Troupe and Sonia Sanchez frequently perform their poetry using the same styles for which preachers or blues singers are known. Along these same lines, the performance of poems is not always true to the letter of the written texts. Two major points are of interest here. First is that although jazz poetry may be evaluated as written texts, it is also judged on its merit as oral performance. Second is the fluid relation that exists between the written and spoken word. These added dimensions represent a radical departure from the aesthetic standards of the mainstream American academic poetic tradition. There are many audiovisual programs available that highlight some of these features of African American poetry, including recordings, tapes, and videos of most modern poets performing their work.[5] These materials can be used in a number of ways by teachers to facilitate a better understanding of the close association between the written and oral traditions.

A final element of African American oral tradition should be considered in the context of this volume: the oralization of biblical text. The importance of biblical symbols has already been noted, but it is also of interest that texts once circulated in oral tradition and then written down have passed again into oral currency (see Jaffee, this volume, on the Old Testament; Kelber, this volume, on the New Testament). This development presents an excellent opportunity for focusing on how variation figures so characteristically in folklore and in literature based on oral tradition. What are some of the differences, for instance, between those stories in the Bible and those African American sermons, spirituals, or other oral forms that feature the same figures? What are some of the cultural factors that might contribute to such differences? Does the existence of a written text inhibit the oral process in any way? These would make engaging questions for students concerned with the organic and dynamic relations between oral and written traditions.

Notes

1. For versions of the traditional song "Railroad Bill," see Taj Majal, *Oooh so good 'n blues* (Columbia Records, LP AL 32600, 1973) and the late Bill Williams, *Blues, Rags, and Ballads* (Blue Goose Records, LP BG-2013). For a literary version see Reed 9–15.

2. For help in identifying such performers, instructors might try contacting their state or local historical societies, arts councils, cultural centers, or folklore offices.

3. An excellent series of recordings of sermons by Franklin is available from Chess/MCA, Universal City, CA. Franklin (Aretha Franklin's father) was a prominent minister at the New Bethel Baptist Church in Detroit, MI. Written texts and discussions of some of his sermons can be found in Franklin and Titon.

4. Recordings by Jefferson and others are available from Shenachie, P. O. Box 208, Newton, NJ 07860; and Rounder Records, One Camp Street, Cambridge, MA 02140.

5. Sources for videos and tapes include Smithsonian Folkways (e.g., the recording *An Anthology of African American Poetry for Young People* and a

reading by Langston Hughes); the Audio Prose Library, Inc., Columbia, MO (featuring interviews with and readings by such authors as Toni Morrison, James Baldwin, and Alice Walker); the American Poetry Archive (e.g., the recording *Color: A Sampling of Contemporary African American Writers* and a reading by Gwendolyn Brooks); the audio companions to *The Norton Anthology of African American Literature* (Gates and McKay) and to *Call and Response* (Hill et al.); and the San Francisco Poetry Center at San Francisco State University, San Francisco, CA.

John Zemke

General Hispanic Traditions

Oral tradition in Hispanic and Portuguese literatures comprises those verbal arts in peninsular Romance languages whose chief purpose is to convey and inculcate community values. Such arts include both narrative poetry (epic and ballad) and nonnarrative poetry (ritual songs, songs for dancing, love songs, laments, lullabies, and nursery rhymes). They also include the folktale, proverb, riddle, and joke, further indication of oral tradition's broad social and cultural domain extending in the Hispanic world from antiquity to the present day.[1]

In this essay, I describe Hispanic oral tradition generally, its time, place, and manner; outline basic critical perspectives; and point briefly to instances of how it has produced verbal expressions possessing a specific beauty and universal appeal. Because we stand as outside observers and because some of the manifestations of Hispanic oral tradition are now only historical, patience may be required to appreciate fully its scope and sophistication. By the very nature of that tradition, its long and uninterrupted operation emerges in proper perspective only with reference to historical literary sources and, what seems a paradox, to modern-day field collections.

Neo-Individualism and Neotraditionalism

Scholarly approaches to Hispanic oral tradition can be summarized in the positions of two competing theoretical schools concerning the Spanish epic. The schools diverge on questions of authorship and historicity of the epic and disagree over what constitutes legitimate evidence of the epic's continuity. Broadly stated, the neo-individualist school believes that the 3,730 verses of the one almost complete Spanish epic, the *Cantar de mio Cid* (*CMC*), were composed in 1207 by the copyist of its one extant manuscript, an erudite clerk named Per Abbat, who thus invented Spanish epic poetry. Neo-individualism considers historically accurate information in the *CMC* to be evidence of a learned author's research in chronicles for details that would confer historical versimilitude on his composition. Having literate authors only imitate or borrow from a narrow band of written sources, neo-individualism thus effectively precludes oral tradition from an essential role in the historical development of the epic and from Hispanic literary history.

By contrast, the neotraditionalist school understands the *CMC* to be a product of a multisecular tradition of oral epic poetry. First conceived by a single *juglar* (poet or minstrel), the epic narrative was subsequently refined and reelaborated by a succession of *juglares*. In this regard, Per Abbat's manuscript is no more or less than "one in a chain of successive versions" (Webber, "Cantar" 66). The neotraditionalist viewpoint accommodates a wider range of evidence into its theoretical underpinnings because it considers both written historical record and modern testimony about or from oral tradition pertinent to developing a clear concept of Hispanic epic poetry. Accurate historical detail is taken as an inevitable residue of the fictionalization of events, not an attempt to endow a fiction with historical credibility. In opposition to neo-individualism, neotraditionalism believes an understanding of oral tradition and its role in the formation of

vernacular literatures is vital to an accurate interpretation of Hispanic literatures.

Neotraditionalism's chief proponent and the twentieth century's
foremost scholar of Hispanic oral tradition, Ramón Menéndez Pidal,
realized that traditional poetry lives in variants and that this quality
distinguishes it from popular poetry. That is, a traditional song or
story is not a fixed entity but, rather, a dynamic, open structure that
generates variants at all levels, from phraseology to narrative pattern.
In its fixity, the written transcription of an oral performance is an
object removed from oral tradition. Menéndez Pidal's observation
that traditional poetry lives in variants has rigorous application to all
the genres of oral tradition mentioned below. Oral tradition has
given the nonnarrative, narrative, and other folk genres a specific texture and acts as a substrate in which a complex network of synchronic
and diachronic intertextual relations has developed. Broadly stated,
oral tradition underlies and enmeshes lyric, epic, chronicle, ballad,
and folktale, and its dynamics are perceptible in exemplars of those
genres.

Diglossia and the Variety of Oral Traditions

Diglossia, the coexistence of two language varieties, each with its
own set of social functions, is an essential characteristic of Hispanic
literary culture. It is evident in medieval collections of oral and written stories such as the *Disciplina clericalis* (*The Scholar's Guide*),
which offered preachers a handbook of ready-made cautionary tales
for their sermons, and in frame tales such as *Calila e Dimna* (*Kalilah
and Dimnah*), whose narrative situation, a dialogue in which questions receive answers in the guise of stories, structures don Juan
Manuel's fourteenth-century masterpiece, *El Conde Lucanor* (*Count
Lucanor*; on the frame tale, see Irwin, this volume). The diglossic
literary culture of the Spanish Golden Age (1500–1700) witnessed
an unparalleled vogue for *cancioneros* (songbooks), whose contents
included *romances viejos* (old ballads) from oral tradition. Erudite poets invented a *romance nuevo* (new ballad), and the printing press
flooded the incipient market of a reading public with *romances* in

libros de cordel (chapbooks). These ballads were vulgarized in *pliegos sueltos* (broadsides), which as *romances de ciego* (blind man's ballads) endured into recent times. Oral tradition's presence is clearly felt in the Golden Age theater as well. Lope de Vega's *Peribáñez y el Comendador de Ocaña* ("Peribáñez and the Knight Commander of Ocaña") quotes a *romance* and an *estribillo* (refrain) at key moments in the action. That individuals trained in an oral tradition develop an impressive capacity for memorizing and retaining long narrations or series of information is plain from the complaints Lope de Vega made against two individuals (*el Memorilla* and *el Gran Memoria*) who gained a livelihood by listening to several performances of a *comedia* (drama) and later writing out the three thousand or so verses that were then sold for unscrupulous editorial purposes. *Burlas* (jokes), *refranes* (proverbs), and *cuentecillos* (folktales) from oral tradition appear in the early novel *Lazarillo de Tormes* (1554). Cervantes's masterwork, *Don Quixote* (1605, 1615), in one sense critiques the encounter of oral and textual cultures. The Romantic movement, entranced by nationalism, "rediscovered" the oral tradition and set about collecting examples that the movement then imitated. In the twentieth century, Machado, García Lorca, and Alberti independently chose traditional lyric forms as the vehicle of their respective poetic geniuses. This brief list illustrates erudite literary culture's historical practice of sampling Hispanic oral tradition.

Awareness of oral tradition provides a paradigm for understanding underlying connections between seemingly disparate literary genres and for understanding the human situations they represent and appraise. For those of us who are only literate, whether we know Portuguese, Spanish, or Catalan, oral tradition challenges us to learn again how to read a text and challenges us to reappraise our tenets of what constitutes literature. But oral tradition also has an existence autonomous from written culture that merits attention.

It is axiomatic that wherever speakers of Portuguese, Spanish, Catalan, and Judeo-Spanish live, a vital oral tradition is found. The Hispanic tradition survives and flourishes in those communities as long as what the tradition tells and how it does so are considered meaningful. When those conditions wane, the tradition lapses and disintegrates. Just as the handiwork produced by craftsmen — barns, plows, looms, or spinning wheels — typically varies from region to region in size, shape, and material, so the verbal artisans of the Hispanic oral tradition possess specific knowledge and techniques that they employ when elaborating their product. The tradition dictates generic specifications to which every performance of song or story conforms, yet each performance is ultimately unique; even the same performer cannot duplicate a performance. The larger community's acceptance, use, maintenance, and repair of these verbal artifacts and its ability to vouchsafe the artisan's techniques for future generations guarantee the tradition's continued survival. The continuing process is not unlike a relay race run at the speed of a generation's passing. Certain individuals compete actively — a medieval *juglar*, an expert singer of *romances*, or a skillful raconteur — while the larger community's knowledge of the ground rules, of the genre, allows that community to act as an informed and discerning audience. Each genre in the oral tradition operates with a specialized vocabulary, grammar, and syntax that competent speakers learn and use as a separate code. Those individuals who learn the most — and use what they learn most fluently — become the tradition's active purveyors, its experts, but all community members acquire a rudimentary knowledge sufficient for participating in or appreciating a performance.

Oral tradition relies not on print for storage of or access to its contents but on a network of individuals, often socially or geographically marginalized, who have fully assimilated the tradition's language and perform as the tradition's authors, editors, and readers. The products of oral tradition therefore exist in a fundamentally different way from, say, a short story by Borges. They are a reality of the memory, and their telling has a particular immediacy.

The pervasive nature and multisecular vigor of Hispanic oral tradition rapidly become apparent when we realize two salient facts. First, all the earliest literary expressions in the peninsular vernaculars either quote or imitate oral traditional forms, like the lyric *kharja* and *cantiga de amigo*; embody features of oral-formulaic composition, like the epics *CMC* and *Roncesvalles*; or have survived for centuries in a latent state without recourse to written record, like many *romances*.

Second, modern Hispanic oral tradition operates in and across a vast geographical area that subsumes multiple cultural groups.

The Renaissance maritime expansion and colonization undertaken by the Portuguese extended their Lusophone culture and oral tradition to Madeira and the Azores islands, Cabo Verde, Príncipe and São Tomé, Angola, Mozambique, Goa, Macau, and Brazil. Contemporaneously, the other peninsular language groups emigrated to Spanish crown possessions in the Canary and Caribbean islands, North, Central, and South America, and the Philippines. The adaptation, transformation, and survival of peninsular oral traditions has accompanied these language groups' movement into previously unknown areas and new cultures. Propelled by different events, the Sephardic Jews exiled in 1492 took refuge in North Africa, the Ottoman Empire, Holland, and England, bringing their oral tradition into contact with new cultures. They enriched and sustained that tradition and later carried it to the Americas and Israel. Thus one finds enclaves of Hispanic oral tradition on five continents.

In marked contrast with the situation that existed into the early twentieth century, the number of skilled participants in Hispanic oral traditions has considerably diminished because of the cultural leveling by mass media, a consumerism that degrades traditional handcrafts, and the abandonment of rural agrarian life. A century of fieldwork recording the Hispanic oral tradition proves its surprising resilience; its eventual demise, however, appears inevitable.[2]

Women's Song and Lyric Poetry

The oldest recorded fragments of Romance poetry are the medieval *kharjas*, versions of women's songs first written down in mid-eleventh-century Andalusia. Their literary genesis underscores learned Hispanic culture's diglossia and its tendency to appropriate the language, themes, and forms of oral tradition. An erudite poet may borrow a meter, incorporate a fragment of song into his own poem, or rework a poem without altering its form or theme. The *kharjas* probably came into existence under a scenario akin to the following. A ninth-century poet trained in classical Arabic at the caliph's court in Cordoba, Muhammad ibn Mahmud al-Qabri the Blind, heard a young woman in the Christian quarter singing a love lament in her native Mozarabic dialect. The song's plaintive refrain attracted his attention:

> Tanto amare, tanto amare, ‖ ḥabib, tant' amáre:
> ¡Enfermeron welyos nidioš ‖ e dolen tan male!

> So much loving, so much loving ‖ my lover, so much
>   loving
> Has made bright eyes grow dim ‖ and suffer so much!
>   (Wilhelm 238)

In this song Muhammad al-Qabri perceived the kernel of a new Hispano-Arabic poetry, the *muwaššaḥa* (girdle song), which quotes a vernacular Mozarabic song as the Arabic poem's conclusion. The song, called a *kharja*, sets the *muwaššaḥa*'s rhyme pattern, determines and condenses its theme, and by its terminal place, switch of language code, and change to a feminine voice disrupts the classical Arabic poetry. For the *kharja* of their Arabic or Hebrew *muwaššaḥa*, poets quoted variant versions of traditional Mozarabic songs, thus documenting a body of fragments that testify to an oral tradition of women's songs.

The *kharja* copied above, the earliest known example, is taken from an eleventh-century Hebrew *muwaššaḥa* written by Yosef al-Katib. Although its theme is universal, the song shares interesting features with other traditional peninsular songs. Naming the beloved *ḥabib* ("friend") parallels or translates the *amigo* ("friend") convention of the medieval Galician-Portuguese *cantiga de amigo* ("friend's song"). The *welyoš* ("eyes") image signifies the beloved, the radiance and joy the beloved brings the lover, whose absence occasions catastrophe. Easily passed over by an outsider, the *welyoš* image resonates strongly in Hispanic oral tradition and would have been instantly recognized in the eleventh century; indeed it remains current today. Moreover, this *kharja*'s metrical pattern reflects one type of *seguidilla* (8-6-8-6), a highly productive form throughout the Golden Age and into the twentieth century. The song's binary construction, vowel repetition, and parallelism reveal oral traditional techniques for maintaining cohesion. Copied here as the *kharja* of an erudite panegyric, this Mozarabic woman's love lament illustrates the fusion of an oral traditional artifact into Andalusian literary culture; it is also a specifically Hispanic manifestation of a pan-Romance oral traditional lyric.

Galician-Portuguese poets recorded or sampled a second facet of peninsular women's song, the *cantiga de amigo*. Preserved in fifteenth-century courtly *cancioneiros*, this genre's poetic style of reiteration and parallelism suggests a likely origin in earlier group dances in which two choruses sang alternately or one chorus responded with a refrain to a soloist. Subsuming several different types, the *cantiga de amigo* represents the largest group of early Hispanic lyric, and its similarities in form and content with the *muwaššaḥa* and Spanish *villancico* suggest a common oral tradition.

Two strophes from a *cantiga de amigo* by King Denis I of Portugal (1261–1325) show the binary, reiterative parallelism and refrain of this form. If one considers them as regional or temporal versions of a single strophe, the simple variants — branch for pine, love for friend — provide a model of how the dynamic of memorization and re-creation in Hispanic oral tradition proceeds by small innovations:

> O flowers, yes flowers of the green pine,
> Do you have any news about my friend?
> > *O God, where is he?*
> O flowers, yes flowers of the green branch,
> Do you have any news about my love?
> > *O God, where is he?*

> (Wilhelm 250)

A third example of early Hispanic lyric, the *villancico*, is also more ancient than the fifteenth-century texts that preserve it. A predominant medieval and Golden Age lyric form, this type of women's poetry, often a love lament, is distinguished from the *kharja* and *cantiga de amigo* by its humor. The *villancico*'s initial two-, three-, or four-verse refrain is glossed in a series of longer strophes, each of which concludes with a return to the refrain; this pattern suggests, again, an alternating chorus-soloist performance practice.

Epic Poetry and the *Cantar de mio Cid*

A few brief observations will suffice to establish the general outline of oral tradition in the Castilian epic and to insist on the musicality of the epic, which was undoubtedly performed to a repeating melody played on a rebec, or other accompaniment. Some 132 Romance epics in poetic form are extant: 9 Provençal, 120 French or Franco-Italian, and 3 Spanish texts — the *CMC*, the *Mocedades de Rodrigo* ("Youthful Adventures of the Cid"), and a fragmentary but uniquely Spanish version of *Roncesvalles*. The lack of Spanish manuscripts in no way justifies characterizing medieval Spanish epic as an anemic genre merely imitative of French models, nor does that lack disprove the epic's orality.[3]

The Castilian epic's historical development may be conveniently divided into four phases: (1) formation, from origins until circa 1140, one date given for the *CMC*; (2) splendor, from 1140 to 1236 (1236 is the date of Lucas of Tuy's *Chronicon mundi*, which integrates epic legendary material into its narrative), a period characterized by increasing length and perfection of the epic and a notable French influence; (3) prosification, 1236–1350, during which chronicles and clerical poetry amplify and adapt epic materials to their respective styles; and (4) decadence, 1350–1500, in which the epic loses its mythic status and is replaced by the novel of chivalry and the romance. It is the uniquely Hispanic romance that eloquently confirms Castilian epic poetry's oral tradition, to which it is a multisecular witness.

Although Castilian epic is not now a living oral tradition, reading the *CMC* today from the viewpoint of oral tradition helps one appreciate how epic language, poetic tradition, and cultural practices were fused into an extraordinary experience of the story: a *juglar*'s performance re-created the epic action in such a way that an audience's experience of the epic reaffirmed the rightness of the hero's deeds and the goodness of the values and ideals embodied in it. The three *cantares* (songs) of the *CMC* relate the exile of the Cid, a petty noble, from Alfonso VI's kingdom, the Cid's victories over the Moors, the king's pardon, the wedding of the Cid's daughters to the infantes of Carrión, the infantes' treachery, the infantes' failed judicial test and punishment, and the daughters' remarriage into the royal houses of Navarre and Aragon. The poem's frequent repetitions and summaries, its language of physical images and heroic epithets portray the hero's integrity, military cunning, physical bravery, moral virtue, and religious belief—cultural values that he embodies and that are endorsed by the successful completion of the heroic tests put to him. In the heroic pattern of exile and return, the plot of the *CMC* unfolds ironically: the actions of the Cid's antagonists yield the opposite of the intended effect.

The verses cited below illustrate the Spanish epic's two-part verse of irregular length—the *CMC* may be recited with two beats per half line or hemistich—and the Spanish epic's final, sometimes internal, assonant rhyme. The poem, with its euphonic and repetitive language, its vocabulary of visual imagery, and its absolute verbal economy, evokes the action of a battle, placing the audience inside a struggle that each listener braves—the initial engagement, the blows and shattered defenses, the wounded and the dying, the protectors invoked—through the *juglar*'s performance:

> Veriedes tantas lanças premer e alçar,
> tanta adágara   foradar e passar,
> tanta loriga falsa[*r*] [*e*] desmanchar,
> tantos pendones blancos   salir vermejos en sangre,
> tantos buenos cavallos sin sos dueños andar.
> Los moros llaman Mafómat   e los cristianos Sancti Yagü[e];

> Who could say how many lances rose and fell, how many shields were pierced, coats of mail torn asunder and white pennons stained red with blood, how many riderless horses ranged the field? The Moors called on Muhammad and the Christians on St. James.

> (Michael 60–61)

What the oral tradition accomplishes is not the listener's apprehension of a set of objective facts but, rather, the creation of a sense of wonder in which the audience defines its subjective identity. Although there is general agreement that a single poet first composed some part of the *CMC*, the version preserved in Per Abbat's copy possesses an artistic sophistication that probably results from successive reworkings of the *CMC* by many singers in the epic oral tradition.

Romances

Romances are essentially songs held in the collective memory of the Portuguese, Spanish, Catalan, and Judeo-Spanish speaking world (Valenciano). Like other traditional genres, the romance is conservative and variable, an open structure diffused through time and space. This open structure makes for a potentially limitless variability that the tradition, or community, holds in check. Field-workers note that bystanders may help a singer by prompting forgotten lines or may reject what they consider incorrect and that informants may disagree as to the accuracy of any given version.

The romance is generally a brief narrative poem in monorhyme verses of sixteen syllables subdivided into two octosyllabic hemistichs with assonant rhyme in the even-numbered verses. As the medieval epic's popularity waned, certain dramatic scenes from epic songs continued to be sung and eventually became the hallmarks of the romance's peculiar style. The romance is genetically related to the epic, but its thematic range is much broader, including material from Spanish and French epics, tales of frontier encounters with Moors, classical and biblical stories, and pan-European ballads. Some romances fictionalized and dramatized recent events, a function that endures now in the *corrido*, a strophic ballad derived from the romance and the *décima*, a local narrative song (on the *corrido*, see Herrera-Sobek, this volume). Fragmentary and highly compressed, the romance uses a poetics of implication that dramatically expresses the range of human emotion.

The music of the romances forms an essential part of their oral tradition and both characterizes and transcends the genre. Renaissance composers identified romance melodies for polyphonic settings, and Sephardic prayer books sometimes cited their titles in order to set prayer melodies. Today, many informants interviewed by field-workers recite romances without music; but for others and in other places—Trás-os-Montes in Portugal or La Gomera in the Canary Islands—the music's vitality remains intact and the tunes vary according to performance context (work song or domestic recreation). Ballad tunes, which vary from region to region and have changed through time, often contain a repeated movement from tension to resolution reflective of the ballad stanza's two-part form.

In contrast with those oral traditional forms that improvise or tailor a performance to immediate circumstances, the romance is a memorized model that integrates formulas, motifs, plot, and action into a circumstantially stable narrative. Using a language of concrete images, it visually implies a series of events that transform the dramatic characters from a time "before" to a time "after." A performance embodies the singer's reproduction of a memorized model that she (women are frequently the custodians of this oral tradition) considers her own and is faithful to. Nevertheless, variability defines the romance, and the reorganization of a ballad's components produces identifiable regional forms. Change, usually accommodating new aesthetic or ethical values, is slow, inexorable, and apparently occurs during the process of memorization. An innovation that one person introduces, even a superficial innovation, may transform a ballad or contaminate it with another ballad. If accepted by the larger community, that changed version becomes the tradition. Because a romance is dynamic and variable, it is not to be confused with static written records. It is at once the sum of all its versions, an abstract entity, and that abstraction's concrete realization as performed by a participant in the oral tradition.

Diego Catalán has identified the romance's basic unit as the formula; the formula's purpose, he says, is to dramatize the narration by visualizing key events of the plot (Catalán 12–13). Formulas from diverse regional versions of *Belardo y Valdovinos* (*Belardo and Valdovinos*) all relate the same basic message—that the subject is mortally wounded—while illustrating one aspect of the romance's variability. The different formulas may be paraphrased as follows: I see the horse drinking water, and blood is running from my veins; I see the horse grazing, and blood pours from my wounds; I see clear water pour from the fountain and a crow that drinks my blood; my wounds are dressed with an orange peel; I have three mortal wounds—wind enters one, air leaves another, and through the smallest passes a hawk; I have seven wounds — the smallest is mortal, and through the tiniest a hawk passes back and forth, its open wings not touching flesh (Catalán 13). Such variability occurs at all levels of the romance and is a distinctive feature of the genre.

Proverbs, Jokes, and Riddles

Dichos (proverbs) and *refranes* (sayings) are essential to many of the greatest works of Spanish literature. Their occurrence in multiple variants denotes an oral tradition, and there is evidence that some were sung. The earliest collections of the fourteenth and fifteenth centuries simply enumerate *refranes*, while the Renaissance humanists compiled vast numbers of examples of "vulgar philosophy" on which they commented extensively. The *refrán* often figures as an illustration of usage in the first dictionaries. Proverbs and other paroemiological forms compiled in Arabic, Latin, and Romance collections entered into the medieval poetic idiom, where they played a key role in such masterpieces as Juan Ruiz's *Libro de buen amor* ("Book of Good Love"). Like other genres of oral tradition, the proverb figures notably in Golden Age theater. Today, Hispanic proverbs retain a vitality that is unusual by American standards; it endows a well-timed utterance with a rhetorical force sufficient to cement a position. The generic line between proverbs, lyric songs, ballad verses, and folktales is unclear; reciprocal borrowing among the types emerges as a defining feature of these folkloric expressions (Armistead 125).

The *adivinanza* (riddle) is an ancient form in Hispanic oral tradition and its erudite counterpart is recorded in Greek, Latin, and Arabic compilations. Vernacular literatures integrated the riddle into prose and poetic pieces, and it remains a vital traditional form today, as this example from Louisiana shows: "A little sack of hazelnuts: / By day they're gathered up / and at night they're scattered (The stars)" (Armistead 112).

These examples merely touch the surface of Hispanic oral tradition's functional system and the tradition's influence on literature. One finds themes, motifs, and poetic structures that are rooted in temporal performance rather than in written documents and that belong to a community rather than to an individual. Hispanic oral tradition poses interesting questions about the reciprocal influence of poetic text and musical phrase, a subject worthy of consideration by musicologists and students of literature. Finally, the physical, temporal, and cultural spaces the oral tradition encompasses make plain the efficiency of communicative models that generate, appraise, discard, and accept variations.[4]

Notes

1. For an anthology of Hispanic poetry from the Middle Ages to the twentieth century, see Cohen. On the lyric, see Cummins; on the musical dimension, see Katz. For a collection of essays on Hispanic oral tradition, see Webber, *Balladry*.
2. For a general and exhaustive source of collections that bear out the eventual demise of Hispanic oral tradition, see Romeralo.
3. Beyond the three Castilian epics in manuscript, the operation of a robust oral tradition is substantiated in medieval Latin and vernacular chronicles, among them the *Cronicon mundi* ("Chronicle of the World") and *Primera crónica general* ("The First General Chronicle"), which reproduce prosifications of epic verse passages. Romances from modern oral tradition give ample testimony to a larger epic corpus that included, among others, *Los siete infantes de Lara* (*The Seven Lords of Lara*), *La condesa traidora* (*The Treacherous Countess*), *Cantar de Fernán González* (*The Song of Fernan Gonzales*), and *Cantar de Sancho II* (*The Song of Sancho II*).
4. A useful starting place for further study would be to listen to recordings of performances from the Hispanic oral tradition. See Daskalopoulos, this volume, for suggestions.

María Herrera-Sobek

Mexican American Oral Traditions

The Mexican American or Chicano population has been blessed with a multiplicity of cultural influences that have had the positive effect of making their oral traditions rich and complex. Mexican American folkore is basically derived from two very different cultural strands: Native American culture (mostly from Mexico and the southwestern United States) and peninsular Spanish culture. When the Spaniards arrived on the continental mainland in the early 1500s, they found two major groups of native peoples in power, the Aztecs and the Mayas. In addition, hundreds of other Mesoamerican Indian nations existed side by side or had already merged with one another.

Moreover, as the Spaniards expanded their empire and explored the territories that make up the southwestern United States today, they found numerous Indian tribes and nations whom they colonized and with whom they intermarried. Hispanic colonial society was thus enriched during the 1492–1848 period by the hybridization process that the various cultures in contact were undergoing. After 1848, with the colonization of the Southwest by Anglo-Americans, the new Anglo-Saxon cultural group also began to influence Chicano folklore.

Nevertheless, since the Spanish empire was the political entity governing New Spain, it was the Spanish language and Spanish culture that had the strongest influence on Mexican American folklore and oral traditions. Thus most of the various genres discussed below have been orally transmitted in Spanish, with their roots firmly anchored in Spanish Mexican culture (for general bibliography, see Heisley; Tully and Rael).

The genres I want to highlight in this brief survey are the *corrido*, or Mexican ballad; prose narratives; folk speech; proverbs and proverbial expressions; folk drama; children's songs and games; and riddles.[1]

The *Corrido*

The *corrido*, or Mexican ballad, encompasses the lyric, epic, and narrative within the thousands of texts in existence and stems ultimately from the Spanish *romance* (ballad). According to Américo Paredes, the *corrido* tradition crystallized in the latter half of the nineteenth century in south Texas and the northern part of Mexico ("Folk Medicine"). He attributes the rise of this genre to the clash of cultures resulting from colonization by Anglo settlers after the Mexican American War of 1848. The Treaty of Guadalupe Hidalgo, signed by both the Mexican and the United States governments after the war, guaranteed the Mexican American population the rights of American citizenship. Nevertheless, Mexican Americans began to lose their lands and their culture and were treated as second-class citizens. It was in response to these inequities that Mexican American men rebelled and fought against injustice, and it was in honor of these men that *corridos* were sung celebrating the deeds they had accomplished in defense of their rights. The lyrics of the ballads "Gregorio Cortes," "Joaquín Murrieta," "Jacinto Treviño," and many others immortalized these heroes.

The *corrido*'s success derives from its flexibility in both poetic structure and thematic content. *Corridos* feature a variety of rhyme schemes (ABCB being one of the most common), stanzas of two to fourteen lines, and variable meter (the most frequent being octosyllabic). With regard to thematic content, they basically tell stories: any event or situation of interest to the general public, or even to a small audience, can be treated. Common topics have been the Mexican Revolution (1910–17), the Cristero Rebellion (1926–30), the immigrant experience, tragic love, earthquakes, floods, outlaws, train derailments, horses and horse racing, and various newsworthy topics. For example, *corridos* were composed about the newspaper heiress Patty Hearst and in honor of the star baseball pitcher Fernando Valenzuela.

Prose Narratives

The categories subsumed under the broad umbrella of prose narratives include myths, folktales, legends, *casos*, memorates, and jests. There are no true Chicano mythic narratives as such; myths in Chicano literature derive mainly from Aztec and Mayan sources. Nevertheless, these narratives proved vitally important in the Chicano quest for self-definition and identity since the turbulent 1960s.

The folktale, however, bears the stamp of both an Indian and a Spanish heritage and is a rich source of Chicano folklore. The European Spanish background surfaces in the fairy tale or märchen type of narrative. "María Cenicienta," "Caperucita Roja," "Blancanieves," and other tales are obviously of European origin, having migrated with the Spaniards to the New World. But contact with a large Native American population eventually led to syncretism. Thus an important number of animal tales, such as those pertaining to the Coyote cycle, originate from Native American stock.

A similar statement can be made about the legends. Although many came from Europe, particularly the religious legends, a substantial number derive from Mesoamerican Indian lore. Others demonstrate a decided syncretism in motifs and structure. A good example of this combinatory process is evident in the La Llorona legend (Kraul and Beatty). La Llorona was a woman who supposedly murdered her children and was punished by being sentenced to roam forever along and through waterways, railroads, and forests in a fruitless search for her lost children.

Recently, scholars have been grappling with the new concepts of *casos* (narratives related to folk beliefs and legends) and memorates (personal family narratives). These two new terms are designed to meet the ever-increasing problem of defining more precisely the large corpus of prose narrative present in all cultures, the older categories of märchen, folktale, and fairy tale having shown themselves to be inadequate. The term *caso* refers to those stories that relate personal experience of supernatural events. Examples of this genre are bewitchment and sighting of the devil, La Llorona, or some other supernatural being. The *caso* is closely related to folk beliefs and folk medicine. A memorate refers to a family story remembered and passed on through a series of generations, for instance, the discovery of buried treasure by some relative or an unusual event at a wedding.

Another significant area of Chicano folklore is the *chiste*, or jest. Paredes undertook seminal research on this genre and has provided a theoretical construct for understanding the basis of much of Chicano folklore in general and jokes in particular ("Folk Medicine"). His basic thesis is that cultural conflict is the principal force generating folklore. There exists a cycle of *chistes* in which a Mexican immigrant is the butt of the humor. In their portrayal of the linguistic difficulties of newly arrived Mexicans, these jokes, often told by immigrants, serve the cathartic function of relieving the stress and anxiety people experience when they move to a foreign country. In fact, bilingualism characterizes many Chicano jokes, which often require fluency in Spanish and English to be appreciated.

Folk Speech

Chicano Spanish dialect has recently been the focus of intense study, particularly by linguists and those interested in bilingual education. The realization by American schools that the Spanish spoken in the Southwest differs markedly from that spoken in Spain, Mexico, and other Latin American countries has led to a flurry of research. For example, the speech of pachucos (inner city youth who dress and

speak in a particular manner) has been shown to serve a social function—to differentiate an in-group from an out-group. Some of the
words belonging to the pachuco argot are *carnal* ("brother"), *jaina*
("girlfriend"), *chante* ("house"), *ruka* ("girl"), *birria* ("beer"), *cantón*
("house"), *chale* ("no"), *lisa* ("shirt"), and *simón* ("yes").

Proverbs and Proverbial Expressions

A proverb may be defined as a short, succinct expression that encompasses a kernel of philosophical wisdom, for example: "Vale mas pá-
jaro en mano que ver un ciento volar" (English equivalent: "A bird
in the hand is worth two in the bush"). Proverbs and proverbial expressions, intimately related to folk speech, form an integral part of
Chicano folklore. Although they are used most frequently by the
older generation, a recent study undertaken by Shirley Arora demonstrates that young people are also aware of proverbs, having been
raised by a mother, father, or other family member who spiced their
speech with these colorful expressions (*Comparisons* and "Proverbs").
Like other folklore genres, the proverb provides yet another important area in which the philosophy or worldview of a people can be
profitably explored. Valuable information regarding the Chicano experience can be gleaned from careful research on proverbs and their
use in Chicano households.

Folk Drama

Chicano folk drama, like its Mexican and Latin American counterparts, traces its roots to the Spanish conquistadores and their religious plays. The early missionaries, interested in converting the
Indians of the New World, discovered that, due to the language barrier, the representation of biblical and religious stories through dramatic enactments provided an effective way to indoctrinate the local
population into the Catholic faith. Thus early theatrical works in the
Western hemisphere consisted of religious plays in which the Indians
themselves played major roles and which were extremely popular
with the faithful. These plays generally took place in the church

atrium and were presented to the populace on holy days such as Christmas or Easter Sunday. When New Mexico was settled in the seventeenth century, works that had been successful in Mexico migrated with the Spanish and Mexican settlers into what is now the American Southwest. Traditional folk drama includes the shepherds' plays (*pastorelas*), Los Matachines, and *Los Comanches* (*The Comanches*; see Campa, *Comanches*).[2]

Children's Songs and Games

Like most of the other Chicano genres, children's songs and games reflect Spanish origins in both overall categories and individual specimens. A rather flexible categorization of songs and games played or sung by children or for children is as follows: *canciones de cuna* (lullabies), *canciones de manos y dedos* (hand and finger songs), *rondas* (rounds), *retahilas* (series), songs, *conjuros* (hexes), and miscellaneous. Paredes made a revealing observation about children's songs and games and cultural conflict, pointing to a basic thread that runs throughout Chicano folklore: as innocuous and free from anxiety and conflict as children's games may appear, close analysis reveals that children often express their fears and anxieties through play ("Folk Medicine").

Riddles

Riddles, defined by Archer Taylor as "questions that suggest an object foreign to the answer and confound the hearer by giving a solution that is obviously correct and entirely unexpected" (qtd. in McDowell, *Children's Riddling* 18), constitute another area of Chicano folklore. But although *adivinanza*, as this genre is called in Spanish, constitutes an integral part of the expressive culture of the Chicano, few studies have been undertaken on riddling habits. An exception is John H. McDowell's *Children's Riddling*, an in-depth study that examines the function of this genre in children's ludic activities and the processes of developing synthetic and analytic thinking, finding commonalities, and evolving other cognitive skills. Riddles offer an excellent series of linguistic challenges, such as bringing into play rhyme schemes, disconnecting and connecting various morphemes, and construing metaphorical images and alliterative, onomatopoeic sounds.

———

This short introduction to Chicano oral traditions provides the reader with a bird's-eye view of the richness of Chicano verbal culture. The wide spectrum of genres and thousands of recorded works make this area a rich field that can be mined for different pedagogical purposes. For example, folk speech, aspects of bilingualism, and code switching can be discussed for their linguistic features. The *corrido* is particularly useful for classroom instruction at all levels of the educational hierarchy. Since the *corrido* is basically a poem that tells a story with music, it lends itself well to teaching structural components of poetry such as rhyme, meter, syllabification, imagery, metaphor, metonymy, alliteration, personification, and so forth. And because these songs tell a story, they can be used for teaching the elements of prose composition related to narrative writing. The *corrido* has a beginning, a middle, and an end; it features a protagonist and secondary characters. There is a particular time and setting to the stories told and a message embedded in the narrative. The *corrido* text also provides a rich source of vocabulary linked to a rural, peasant world.

An important aspect of the *corrido* is its historical content. Thousands of these folk songs are based on historical events, such as Mexican immigration from the 1850s to the 1990s (see Herrera-Sobek, *Northward Bound*). The *corrido* can explore periods of Mexican history, like the Mexican Revolution (1910–17), or episodes in the lives of Mexico's revolutionary heroes, like Francisco Villa and Emiliano Zapata. It can treat of unionization efforts in Mexico or in the United States; for the United States, the *corridos* about César Chávez and the United Farmworkers Union are particularly pertinent. Ballads can be used in drama classes by bringing to the stage a *corrido* or a series of *corridos*, as Luis Valdez and the Teatro Campesino have done, or in film and video classes. In addition, the social issues portrayed in these texts can be investigated. These include gender relations, drug smuggling, incest, patricide, and political assassinations (e.g., the John F. Kennedy or Luis Donaldo Colosio *corridos*).

Many of the same pedagogical strategies described for the ballads can be employed with folk narratives in the classroom. Folktales are prose narratives and as such encompass all the structural elements of storytelling. Of particular interest are the jest or joke narratives, which afford an excellent venue through which social issues can be explored. Many jokes deal with contemporary political tensions, such as those related to the ex-president of Mexico, Carlos Salinas de Gortari. Jokes about immigrants or race relations, for example, shed light on the thinking and worldview of various communities. But extreme sensitivity is required when discussing such jokes in the classroom.

Riddles and proverbs normally take poetic form, and their typical structures of rhyme, meter, and other prosodic elements can be analyzed in a manner similar to that employed in studying the *corrido*. Riddles and proverbs also demonstrate a wide spectrum of vocabulary. Students can be asked to collect them from friends, family, and acquaintances; this activity provides the class with an enjoyable and profitable exercise based on fieldwork. Riddles and proverbs, because of their repertoire of stylistic features and because of their succinctness, are particularly useful in Spanish language classes. The proverb genre especially offers opportunities to explore gender, family relations, social issues, politics, religion, work, and other areas.

Because of the thousands of texts collected from each of the major genres in Chicano folklore, it is also possible to teach each genre as a separate course. The *corrido*, for example, can be organized by topics: Mexican immigration, gender issues, and so on. For such a course, the instructor must supply historical background and encourage the analysis of ballad texts for both poetic and ideological content. Acoustic recordings of Mexican ballads can be played in class or, if proximity permits, collected through fieldwork. If possible, live singers can be brought to class. In short, Chicano folklore is an excellent pedagogical resource. Whether for general cultural enrichment or specific curricular tasks, the multiplicity of texts available in all its genres makes it a splendid classroom teaching tool.

Notes

1. More-focused studies include: for the *corrido* or ballad, Paredes, *With His Pistol* and *Texas-Mexican Cancionero*; Herrera-Sobek, *Mexican Corrido* and *Northward Bound*; Peña; for folk drama, Campa, *Sayings* and *Folktheatre*; Marie; Rael; for folk belief, Hand; Roeder; for folk speech, Arora, *Comparisons* and "Proverbs"; for folktales, Kraul and Beatty; E. Miller; for legends, Robe; for riddles, McDowell, *Children's Riddling*.
2. The semireligious dance drama called Los Matachines is a folk performance popular during the Christmas season in Mexico and the United States along the Texas-Mexico border and New Mexico. Its characters include twelve dancers, a king, La Malinche (a young girl), and the *abuelo* or grandfather. The dance drama dates back to the early colonial period in Mexico and seems to be a syncretic product of European matachin dancing and Native American ritual dancing.

Judith S. Neulander

Jewish Oral Traditions

Oral traditions account for much of the contents of Homer, Hesiod, and the Hebrew Bible, three bodies of work that taken together represent the most enduring literary output of the archaic world prior to 500 BCE. Unlike Homer and Hesiod, however, the Hebrew Bible and the great folios of commentary that grew around it continue to inculcate, or to otherwise impart, a distinct body of beliefs, behaviors, and values that find ongoing expression in the oral traditions we recognize as Jewish (see Jaffee, this volume; for general ideas on teaching the Hebrew Bible, see Olshen and Feldman). The propensity of Jewish oral tradition to build upon these sources simplifies the task of recognizing Jewish items in global context and helps us determine what it is that makes a story or a proverb, a joke or a name, culturally Jewish.

Tradition and Transformation:
The Importance of Unrevised Sources

The key to productive study of Jewish oral tradition is to locate representative examples. These can be found in collections of oral materials that have not been repenned or rewritten in any way but are faithfully translated and carefully preserved as they were sung, told, or recited by the particular group one wishes to study.

Because the rules of artful discourse are subject to change and because they almost always depart from the rules of written communication, past traditions do not always speak to contemporary issues or current events, and many skilled oral productions will lose their communicative genius in written form (see Fine, this volume; Dubois, this volume). Therefore the overarching impulse on the part of tradition bearers is to "improve" traditional materials by transforming them to suit contemporary times, tastes, and means of transmission. This creative impulse speaks to the fact that tradition is not and has never been something static, the most stable aspect of any tradition being its ability to change in response to changing needs of different generations, different times, and different places. The impulse to keep traditions timely and relevant is characteristic of each generation of bearers. As a result, patterns of stability and change in an oral tradition give us access to the spirit and mentality of the different groups who have shaped the tradition over time and across space. But, unless we study oral traditions as they were expressed, used, and thought about by the specific groups we are interested in, we will wind up interpreting items revised in one age as typical of another age. Therefore teachers need to be aware that popular anthologies that have been revised or rewritten by modern philologists, storytellers, and other transformers will always reflect the spirit and mentality of the people and the age that shaped the rewrite or revision. Such revisions almost never give students access to the different peoples who at different times shaped the material differently. To study the oral traditions of other generations, students must have access to sources that are faithfully translated and in all other ways beautifully preserved — not beautifully revised.

Epistemology: The Birth of a Discipline

With the onset of the Industrial Revolution, European antiquarians began scrambling to collect rural folklore, in part because they thought it was the only kind of folklore they had and in part because they expected it to vanish as rural populations made their way to literate, urban, industrialized centers. The growing need to classify these growing collections of global tales called for two major indexes, both completed in the twentieth-century. The first, *The Types of the Folktale*, was put together by Antti Aarne and Stith Thompson, whose initials (AT) are used alongside the numbers Aarne and Thompson assigned to different tale types. *Tale type* is a term for a group of stories that configure into a set according to similarities in their plots. Similarities and differences that determine which tale type a story belongs to are found in the story's motifs, the smallest elements of a tale that are striking or unusual. For example, "clothing" is not a motif, but "clothes produced by magic" is. Similarly, "mother" is not a motif, but "wicked stepmother" is. The completion of Thompson's cross-referenced, six-volume *Motif-Index of Folk-Literature* followed that of the tale-type index, and both these major works are now published in the United States. While these indexes are cumbersome in many ways and their correct use requires specialized training and much experience, they remain useful because they locate traditional tales in global context; they refine our perception of variance and provide an invaluable restraint against the kind of oversimplifications that lead to incorrect categorization of cultural items and therefore to incorrect conclusions about the people who hold them in tradition.

Students will gain better access to the cultures they are studying through anthologies of unrevised, well-annotated tales, preferably categorized by tale types and motifs (or in some other cogent way) and showing who collected them from whom and when. Josepha Sherman's *Sampler of Jewish American Folklore* is an example of a well-organized text popular with beginning students. The book opens with a useful section on Jewish folklore and folklife, and then categorizes oral traditions by genre: wonder tales, proverbs and riddles, and

so on. In addition to providing unrevised samples, Sherman anno-
tates each item in endnotes, alerting teachers to some of the information that beginning students need to know. For example, we can easily identify Sherman's "Jewish Cinderella" as a Yiddish variant of
the global Cinderella (AT 510) according to the motifs and tale
type given in Sherman's notes. We also learn where this variant
came from, when it was collected, who collected it from whom, and
whether other Jewish communities carried it in tradition. Sherman
notes that a European proverb rather than a Hebrew proverb is retained in this European variant, and she identifies the Hebraization
of motifs as the vehicle for the tale's Jewish transformation (prince
into rabbi's son, fairy godmother into the prophet Elijah, etc.). Presented with this approach to identification and interpretation of
Jewish narratives and unburdened by specifically literary criticism,
students can begin to explore how proverbs are used in Jewish storytelling, along with the worldview and societal values reflected in this
Jewish variant.

Raphael Patai's *Gates to the Old City* is another skillfully annotated
and beautifully translated collection of tales, organized according to
sources in traditional Jewish literature: the Bible, the Apocrypha, the
Talmud, Midrash, Kabbalah, folktales, and Hasidic legends. Each
part is prefaced by informative commentary on the literary source
from which the tales are drawn. The section on Midrash, for example,
discusses the history and nature of the genre and lists a full chro-
nology of the Midrashim quoted from the second through the
fourteenth century. Patai's approach allows students to follow the
development of these distinct literary sources and to understand their
historical relation to one another.

Similarly well configured, the hardcover edition of *Mimekor Yisrael* (bin Gorion) is a highly diversified anthology taken from more
than 275 books, chapbooks, and pamphlets, as well as from mid-
rashic texts, folktale collections, popular histories, traveler's tales,
fables, and legends told by specific religious sects. Prepared by Dan
Ben-Amos, the book is fully annotated and has an appendix of tale
types and motifs, each indexed to the numbered tales in the collection. The tremendous scope of the hardcover edition makes *Mimekor*

Yisrael one of the most encompassing collections of classical Jewish folktales.

Gaining Access to a Culture through Oral Traditions

There is no prescribed path for studying one or all of the genres of any oral tradition. Over the course of the past century, however, a number of interesting paths have opened, and these can be followed singly or in combination, depending on how the teacher wishes to proceed and what the student wants to know. The following selection of approaches is not exhaustive, but it is comprehensive and informative enough to guide teachers and students to rewarding discoveries (see Zumwalt, this volume).

Comparative Study

A search for the origins and dispersal patterns of traditional tales led to the development of the major indexes we now use for comparative study. This approach compares and contrasts different traditions, or variants of the same tradition, for whatever their distinctions may reveal about different communities at different times and in different places. For example, the figure of the trickster, as noted by Paul Radin in his study of African and American Indian variants, is found in traditions around the globe. Both a creator and a destroyer, a duper who is duped, and an outrageous shape-shifter, the trickster is entirely innocent of values and is therefore guilty of complete submission to unbridled passions — yet it is through his disorderly conduct that world order is created and through his unprincipled actions that values come into being. According to this model, the Talmudic Ashmodai, a character found in Patai's *Gates to the Old City*, is a trickster par excellence. Taking time out from his studies in the Academy on High, Ashmodai begins an episode of drunkenness by quoting Scriptures on the virtues of temperance. When captured by King Solomon's men, he commits a series of antisocial and unjustified acts that precipitate corrections of social injustice in the Israelite community. Once at court, Ashmodai is ordered to help build Solomon's Temple, a venture that was historically supported by an overtaxed people who were never permitted to enter the facility. Vexed by Solomon, Ashmodai shape-shifts, tricks the king, and takes the throne, only to be recognized for his scandalous sexual behavior with the royal harem and even with Solomon's mother. What distinguishes these variants as ethnically Jewish is not simply the "Jewish" label placed on king and temple, for any non-Jewish (or even anti-Semitic) tale could be about a Jewish king and temple. Rather, Jewish specificity is reflected here in the Scripture-quoting format of the tale and in the personality of the trickster himself, for when Ashmodai is not wreaking havoc in the kingdom of Israel, he is studying Torah in the kingdom of God. It is toward such revelations that oral narratives are subjected to comparative study.

Social Function

Certain features of a tale — the presence of a millstone, the kind of transportation used — can occasionally tell us something about the way people lived in a given time and place, but tales are much more likely to serve a community's best interests than to be a community's mirror image. The telling of stories serves a community by creating a social event, by reinforcing group values, and by imparting them to the young. Oral traditions can also function as safety valves, relieving tensions caused by oppression and venting a society's animosities as well as expressing its aspirations. Proverbs help stabilize relationships, riddles sharpen wits, myths validate world and social order, and satires say things that are otherwise socially or politically unsafe to say. In examining how tales of Ashmodai functioned, for example, it becomes clear that they served as social criticism, contrasting Solomon's material enrichment of the Israelite monarchy with Ashmodai's spiritual enrichment of the Israelite community.

In later times, a similar role fell to a notorious Yiddish prankster who actually lived in eighteenth-century Ostropol. Hershele Ostropoler was a common man who lived by his wits and eventually found his niche in the dynastic court of Rabbi Boruch of Miedzebezh, grandson of the Baal Shem Tov. Able to lift Boruch's spirits when the rabbi was plagued by bouts of depression, Hershele's pranks and witticisms have since become legendary. Before long, his activities had become the focus of trickster tales that may or may not be based on fact. Like Ashmodai's antics, Hershele's antics often mocked local authority figures, in particular the rabbi (and other community sages), to the great delight of the common folk.

The figure of Gioha is less a trickster than a numbskull figure well known throughout the Mediterranean, the Middle East, and North Africa. As adopted into Judeo-Spanish tradition, Gioha remains the credulous fool, quick to literal interpretation of figurative advice. But he is also unexpectedly clever at overcoming those who try to harm him. In this regard, Gioha seems to buoy the hopes of an exiled people eager to transcend its misfortune and build a better future. In this and other connections, Reginetta Haboucha's *Types and Motifs of the Judeo-Spanish Folktales* provides a well-annotated resource for directing students to unrevised collections of Sephardic tales and for locating them in global context. By examining such factors as a tale's intended audience, the societal values the tale imparted, and its potential for releasing pressure or supporting hope, students will gain access to the cultures that shaped these stories as well as an appreciation of how the stories functioned in and for the communities they served.

Psychology and Cognitive Science

Historically, Freudian and Jungian interpretations of oral tradition have generated a full range of academic responses, from rejection to acceptance. In his controversial book, *Life Is like a Chicken Coop Ladder*, Alan Dundes examines a vast number of German proverbs and graffiti, children's rhymes, songs, riddles, and literary sources, to arrive at a Freudian interpretation of the German national character, and of German anti-Semitism in particular. Dundes has made an additional contribution to the study of anti-Semitic traditions by editing a casebook called *The Blood Libel Legend* and by coediting a casebook called *The Wandering Jew* with Galit Hasan-Rokem. In recent years, studies of human sense-making strategies have renewed interest in the seminal works of Giambattista Vico, Claude Lévi-Strauss, and Hayden White, all of whom pioneered in exploring the relation between cognitive categories and human expressivity. In this connection, the anthropologist Mary Douglas's *Purity and Danger: An Analysis of the Concepts of Pollution and Taboo* draws attention to important biblical thought categories for making ancient Hebrew sense of the world. Similarly, in my essay "Creating the Universe: A Study of Cosmos and Cognition," I examine the cosmic blueprint set forth in Genesis, as well as those found in other origin myths, to account for how and why distinct cultural groups bring distinct world orders out of universal chaos.

Structural Studies

Structural studies seek and interpret structural patterns in oral tradition. For example, in his classic essay "The Hero of Tradition," Lord Raglan lays bare a pattern of episodic experiences common to culture heroes, including the biblical figure of Moses. The messages encoded in formulaic patterns like "once upon a time" are explored in Jewish tradition by Ben-Amos in his article "Generic Distinctions in the Aggadah." Similarly, in *Folklore and the Hebrew Bible*, Susan Niditch analyzes the *mashal* category of analogic instruction and other literary patterns that appear in sacred text. The structural approach leads students straight to the nexus of creative heat in tradition bearing. It lays bare the artistry of narrative forms and deepens respect for those gifted artists who give perfect expression to the transcendent past while equally addressing the grounded present.

Folklore and Literature

The first generation of modern Jewish fiction writers belonged to the nineteenth-century Haskalah, an Enlightenment movement aimed at Europeanizing Jewish life and letters. As ardent admirers of the European culture complex, these writers often reflected many of its biases, among them a propensity to equate the debased condition of village life with Yiddish folklore, which was the villagers' richest

vehicle of cultural expression. As Dan Miron points out, Jewish literati maintained the elitist notion that Jewish folklore was itself the
shaping force of a grotesque ethnic specificity and that Yiddish was
not even a language but only a naturally deformed jargon. As a result,
Jewish prose fiction has been preoccupied with expressions of Jewish
ethnicity from its inception, obsessed from the moment of its birth
by a singular mission: to attract the reader's folkloric imagination,
but only to demean the very traditions that serve as bait.

   Although the folklore attacked by these literati constitutes the
most valid and reliable source for gaining access to Yiddish culture,
their literary attacks constitute secondary sources of that folklore,
representing the cultural characteristics of the literati themselves
more clearly than the cultural characteristics of the people they wrote
about. Because such pitfalls await all seekers of folkloristic data in
literary texts and because there are instances in which literary texts
can indeed serve as valuable primary sources, folklorists have developed three criteria to help identify accurate ethnographic reporting
in novels and short stories. These criteria are biographical accuracy,
internal accuracy, and corroborative accuracy. Biographical accuracy
requires that authors themselves be primary sources, so their descriptions of folklore and folklife will be based on firsthand knowledge.
Internal accuracy requires that authors not alter the tradition or its
cultural context to serve plot requirements or other literary goals.
Corroborative accuracy requires that an author's description be cor-
roborated by, or be consistent with, the historical record for the
people and the age being described.

   Discoveries made by using the above criteria may not always
agree with the popular view. For example, the tales of Shalom Rabinowitz (1859–1916), who wrote under the Yiddish pseudonym
Sholom Aleichem ("Peace be with you"), fail to meet the criteria set
by folklorists, because Rabinowitz's tales are about a life of poverty
and oppression that he never lived and that therefore does not appear
in his tales. His immense popularity stems from his highly skilled
ability to represent Yiddish folklife the way we deeply wish to remember it, not the way it really was. Theatrical productions built

on his works, like *Fiddler on the Roof*, make for similarly gratifying entertainment but fall short of being accurate ethnography.

Rabinowitz's colleague, Shalom Jacob Abramovich (1836–1917), using the pseudonym Mendele Mocher Seforim (Mendele the Book Peddler), often wrote from personal experience as a primary source on Yiddish folklife. Following tradition in Jewish folk literature, his novel *The Travels and Adventures of Benjamin the Third* begins with an allusion to sacred text: the Israelite exile popularly associated with the lost tribes of Israel (2 Kings 17.6). His novel is a parody of European travel writing, the most popular genre for discovering lost tribes and utopian lands since at least the tenth century CE. With a nod to Benjamin of Tudela, a Jewish traveler of the thirteenth century, and to Benjamin of Tudela's nineteenth-century counterpart, Joseph Israel Benjamin, Abramovich creates a third Benjamin. Benjamin III and his trusty sidekick are picaresque travelers. As determined as they are to discover the ten lost tribes, they remain unable to find—let alone cross—their own provincial borders, just as they are unable to transcend their own provinciality. Based on Abramovich's youth among vagabond beggars, the tale has its characters roam their way from village to village within the Yiddish Pale. In a parody of exotic travel fiction Abramovich zeroes in on mundane peasant life with deadly ethnographic accuracy. Significantly, Abramovich was not a product of the European academy; self-trained, he was therefore free of many of his colleagues' cultural biases. No one among the Haskala writers understood Yiddish colloquial power better than Abramovich, and no one but Abramovich recognized folklore as the most powerful expression of collective experience, vital to the continuity of Jewish identity. His broader intellectual vision and artistic skill account for the fact that he alone is frequently credited with revolutionizing both Yiddish and Hebrew literatures.

Twentieth-century authors of Jewish fiction, writing in English, are similarly impressed with the power of traditional folkloric themes to convey contemporary meanings to cosmopolitan audiences. But many of their works abandon ethnographic accuracy to meet aesthetic considerations. In the occult story "The Mirror," Isaac Bashevis

Singer forgoes traditional Jewish magic and demonology, inventing instead a distinctly Christian imp, along with a made-up magic incantation, to tell a dark tale of self-absorbed estrangement from the Yiddish community. Cynthia Ozick is similarly concerned with Jewish alienation in her story "The Pagan Rabbi." Recalling the identity crisis felt by Jews in their confrontation with ancient Greece, she weaves seductive images from Greek mythology onto the landscape of contemporary New York. By altering folk traditions and the cultural contexts in which they occur, both authors are able to create masterful literary images that comment on the modern community. But students who seek internal and corroborative consistency in these two stories will find that neither provides a valid, reliable example of either Yiddish folklore or Greek mythology; hence, neither can give us valid, reliable access to Yiddish or to ancient Greek traditions.

As we have seen in the example of Abramovich, novels and short stories can be valuable sources of Jewish folklore, but only when that folklore is described accurately and in appropriate cultural context. When the raw data of folklore are misrepresented, no matter how skilled the artist, the results will always be pseudoethnographic. The study of tradition in nontraditional literary contexts can be as productive as it is intriguing, provided that teachers encourage their students to use the three criteria applied by folklorists.

The Contemporary Community: Performance and Family Folklore

Oral tradition is not the private property of marginalized groups, nor is it primarily a thing of the past. Jewish humor, for example, prevails in modernity—on screen, on stage, and as performed in everyday life. Important studies have been done on the popular notion of a distinctly Jewish humor. In the article "The People of the Joke: On the Conceptualization of a Jewish Humor," Elliott Oring suggests that stereotypical views of the Jewish people create stereotypical interpretations of Jewish humor. Similarly, Ben-Amos challenges the conventional view that self-demeaning humor reflects Jewish self-hatred ("Myth"). *The Big Book of Jewish Humor*, edited by William

Novak and Moshe Waldoks, is a useful, well-annotated anthology of humorous genres.

In addition to literary texts, the oral performance of verbal art, as in the telling of jokes or anecdotes, oral histories, and personal experience narratives, can be studied as a source of traditional expressivity and contemporary cultural information. In *Number Our Days*, Barbara Myerhoff's interviews with elderly members of a Jewish community alert us to the power and value of extemporaneous oral performance. Stories that are sung, their texts and performances, are also rich sources of cultural information. Mark Slobin's collection and translation of Moshe Beregovski's *Old Jewish Folk Music* is an invaluable analysis of Yiddish traditions, while Slobin's incomparable *Tenement Songs: The Popular Music of Jewish Immigrants* (1880–1920) breaks ground in American Jewish studies. In recent times, the storytelling event as a skilled performance has also become the subject of enthusiastic study. Barbara Kirshenblatt-Gimblett explores cultural performance by individual artists, by the community in its calendrical festivals, and by family members in Jewish family context. In her essay "The Concept and Varieties of Narrative Performance in Eastern European Culture," for example, she shows how a proverb both creates and affects a social dynamic, mediating power struggles, restructuring relationships, and resolving tensions in communities and families. Steven Zeitlin's essay on Jewish family folklore, "The Wedding Dance," can help students locate Jewish family traditions in contemporary American context and provides students with a model for studying their own family folklore. Additionally, contemporary forms of printed and electronic communication can be fascinating sources of oral tradition, as evidenced in the 1994 issue of the *Jewish Folklore and Ethnology Review* entitled *Jews and the Media*.

Finding the Past in the Present

Oral traditions rise and fall with the ability of poets and scribes to keep them artful and relevant over time and across space. This phenomenon raises the question of whether ancient traditions like the Ashmodai figure still have currency and, if so, through what vehicles of transmission. Classrooms can be stimulated by studying traditional figures like Ashmodai in contemporary contexts. Woody Allen's film *Zelig* is a good choice for the Ashmodai exercise, since the film cites the media as an electronic tradition bearer and alerts students to the phenomenon of cultural exchange: the borrowing of Jewish traditions into the American mainstream, alongside the borrowing of mainstream Americana into Jewish tradition. Allen's use of the name Zelig — particularly in a setup of Anglo-American society — may represent just such a cultural exchange. That is, Allen's choice reflects the biblical pattern of giving connotative names, but it also plays on the Anglo-Saxon cognate cluster that conflates "silly" (*salig*), "blessed" (*selig*), and "holy" (*halig*) into the construct of the "holy fool," as exemplified in the Parsifal figure of European tradition. In the film, Leonard Zelig is a Jewish Milquetoast, completely alienated in twentieth-century Anglo-America. His pathological desire for safety leads him to shape-shift into perfect conformity with every community he comes across. Like the trickster of global tradition, the shape-shifting Zelig has no self-control, and his outrageous, amoral adventures provide a hilarious satire on Anglo-American society in the first half of the twentieth century. To seek patterns of stability and change in Zelig that would indicate a surviving variant of the Talmudic trickster, however, students need to look past the shared characteristics of all trickster cycles to those characteristics shared exclusively by Zelig and Ashmodai — specifically, for an obsession with a classical text, both in the format of the tale and in the personality of the Torah-reading trickster. By taking a folkloristic approach to ancient and contemporary variants of Jewish tradition, students will become better able to identify patterns in culture and to interpret these patterns for what they may reveal about the people who carry them in tradition. This approach can help students discern possible Talmudic patterns in Allen's documentary format, with its sidebar "commentators," and explore the fact that Zelig himself is obsessed with a classical text — not the Torah but Herman Melville's *Moby-Dick*, a book about the folly of obsession.

To the extent that sacred Hebrew text is itself a record of oral narratives, teaching Jewish oral tradition is more clearly a matter of taking new and different paths to the same type of material than of taking the same old path to new and different types of material. Opening new avenues of inquiry to a wider spectrum of traditional narratives will necessarily lead students on a far-reaching journey through a panoply of historical times and geographical spaces peopled by different groups of Jews. But almost without fail, the narrative forms we recognize as Jewish will lead them back to sacred text.

R. Parthasarathy

Indian Oral Traditions

The dearth of translations of Indian texts for study in the classroom severely restricts the scope of what can be taught.[1] The selection is limited to a handful of classics, notably from Sanskrit; translations from other Indian languages are meager. As a result, Indian texts generally tend to be excluded from courses in oral tradition. The problem is exacerbated by the fact that the texts are rooted in the Indian worldview, about which most students and teachers know very little.

Given the linguistic situation in India, it is not possible for any one writer to speak competently of the oral traditions in all the languages. Of the 105 languages spoken in the subcontinent, the constitution of India recognizes 18 (besides English) as official languages. Each of these languages has a rich oral tradition. In this essay, I deal with two languages: Sanskrit and Tamil. I attempt to explain the characteristics of Indian orality, including the greater power of the spoken over the written word; to discuss some textual and oral works suitable for study in the classroom; and to suggest some issues for discussion that may help students understand the nature of Indian verbal art.

Orality and the Power of the Spoken Word

The Vedas, the earliest literary texts of the Indo-Europeans, are the classic example of oral poetry. Composed from 1500 to 1000 BCE, they were orally transmitted by Brahmans learned in the Vedas (*srotriyas*) and were more or less unchanged for centuries. Oral transmission has preserved the Vedas to a remarkable degree; such preservation would have been unthinkable had they been copied and recopied by scribes, a process that would have left them open to the possibility of errors. To the Hindus, the Vedas are divine revelation spoken by God and heard by human beings. The spoken word has greater authority than the written: it is invested with sacred power. No such power is attributed to the written word, which is seen as an interloper. Indian society to this day remains essentially phonocentric rather than graphocentric. Unlike the Vedas, secular works such as the epics *Mahabharata* (The tale of the great war of the Bharatas), *Ramayana* (The wanderings of Rama), *The Tale of an Anklet*, and *Manimekalai* (Jeweled girdle) have been exposed to the "improvements" of bards and scribes. As a result, the texts of the epics that have come down to us are no longer available in their original form.

Textual and Oral Works

Epic poems originated in ballads (*akhyanas*) and in songs in praise of men (*gatha narasamsi*). They were recited by bards (*sutas*) who lived at the courts of kings, often accompanying the kings into battle. The bards composed songs praising the exploits of warriors. They constituted a caste of their own, and the songs were handed down by them from one generation to the other. Epics had their origin in bardic fraternities. Wandering rhapsodists (*kusilavas*) memorized the songs and performed them to the strains of the lute before the people. In the course of time, these songs were fashioned into epics by poets (*kavis*). And over the centuries, the epics gathered around them a whole range of materials that had little or no connection with the old heroic songs: legends of famous kings, myths about gods and sages, genealogies, folktales, and parables. I look at some epics with roots in the ancient oral tradition as well as at texts from the oral tradition today that derive from the epics.

The *Mahabharata*

The *Mahabharata* originated in the old heroic songs of the war of the Bharatas, and over a period of eight hundred years (from 400 BCE to 400 CE) it grew into an unwieldy epic of some 200,000 lines — about seven times as long as the *Iliad* and the *Odyssey* combined — in eighteen books and a supplement ascribed to the sage Vyasa. It is not one epic but an encyclopedia of the Indian epic tradition. The war of succession between the two branches of the Bharata family, the Pandavas and the Kauravas, takes up only about a fifth of the poem. The rest of the epic tells the history of ancient India through legends and tales and includes digressions into ethics, philosophy, and statecraft. One of the most famous tales, "Savitri," is narrated in book 3. Savitri is the ideal Hindu woman who in her devotion to her husband, Satyavat, wrestles with the god of death, Yama. With exemplary courage she is able to persuade Yama to restore her husband's life. The resemblance to the Greek story of Alcestis is obvious. To this day, Hindu women observe a rite in honor of Savitri to obtain happiness in marriage, and on that occasion the tale is recited. Equally famous are the tales "Nala and Damayanti" and "Rama and Sita." At the heart of the epic, in book 6, lies the great philosophical poem, the *Bhagavadgita* (The word of God). In it the god Krishna counsels the hero Arjuna on the eve of the great war to perform his duty with no thought of its outcome. Hindus revere the poem as scripture: its teachings have for them the unquestionable authority of a revelation.

The *Ramayana*

In composing the *Ramayana*, Valmiki put together earlier stories of Rama from the oral tradition and worked them into a frame tale (on the frame tale, see Irwin, this volume). The epic, as we have it today, comprises some fifty thousand lines in seven books and was composed by bards over a period of four hundred years (from 200 BCE to 200 CE). That books 1 and 7 are later additions is demonstrated by the number of interpolations. Books 1 and 7 are also the only ones in which Rama is presented as an incarnation of the god Vishnu. Valmiki's *Ramayana* is the earliest telling of the Rama story that has survived. It is the quintessential Indian epic, embodying the Hindu way of life with its emphasis on a strict observance of duty (dharma). Rama is the paragon of duty. To give but one example, when Rama's wife, Sita, is abducted by Ravana, king of Lanka, Rama and his brother Lakshmana march on Lanka, kill Ravana, and burn down the city. On his return to Ayodhya, Rama bows to the pressure of his subjects, who suspect that Sita, during her long absence, may have been violated by Ravana. Although Sita has not been violated, Rama does not accept her back. An enraged Sita then demonstrates her innocence by asking Mother Earth to open and receive her. The Earth does as Sita asks. Rama does not flinch from observing his duty as a king even if it means losing his wife forever.

The *Ramayana* enjoys an almost iconic status among Hindus. Though it is not a religious epic, it is still revered as a sacred text, recited as incantation and ritual, and performed at religious festivals. A 1987–88 Indian TV production of the *Ramayana* in fifty-two episodes took the country by storm to become the most popular TV serial ever in India. The serial also focused attention on the dominant, Hindu ideology. Such is the extraordinary hold that the *Ramayana* has on the Indian national consciousness. There are literally hundreds of tellings of the Rama story, not only in the languages of India but in those of Southeast Asia as well.[2]

Unlike the classical versions, the folk *Ramayana*s are presented in a wide range of performance styles: song, recitation, dance, and occasionally shadow puppets and painted scrolls. One of the tellings of the Rama story in the living tradition of Kerala in southwestern India is reported by Stuart Blackburn ("Creating"). It is performed as a shadow puppet play (*olapavakuthu*) over several nights at the festival of the goddess Bhagavati. The play is a ritual enactment of parts of Kampan's Tamil epic *Iramavataram*. The ritual itself is a form of propitiation of the goddess with a view to invoking her protection against harm. Each verse is chanted aloud in Tamil and is followed by a rambling commentary that is often spiced with legendary tales. Frequently the epic characters talk among themselves, drowning out the events of the Rama story. For the most part, the puppet play is based on Kampan's poem, but there are episodes, such as Rama's confession of guilt for killing Valin, that are absent in the epic. The puppet play, being a folk genre, often calls into question the presuppositions of Kampan's epic world: Rama is not an object of uncritical devotion; his faults are noted. The play makes fun of the poem's expectations as a devotional text, especially in the Surpanakha and Valin episodes. There are no sacred cows in the world of the folk play. By standing the epic on its head, the puppet play offers an unconventional interpretation of the Rama story. There is obviously more than one way of telling a story.

The Tale of an Anklet

The Tale of an Anklet, composed in the fifth century CE and attributed to Ilanko Atikal, offers a textbook example of a living oral tradition. For generations, bards (*panans*) have recited or sung the Kovalan story throughout the Tamil country in southeastern India. This story was transcribed from the oral tradition by a learned poet (*pulavan*). Thereafter, both the oral and written tellings circulated freely, each drawing on the other. The poem of 5,730 lines is divided into three books named after the capitals (Pukar, Maturai, and Vanci) of the three Tamil kingdoms (Cola, Pantiya, and Ceral, respectively) that constitute its setting. The protagonist is a woman named Kannaki. This last feature alone is significant enough for one to suspect that *The Tale of an Anklet* stands in a subversive relation to the *Ramayana*. By making a woman the protagonist, Ilanko is rewriting the epic tradition by undermining its essentially androcentric bias. As a female protagonist, Kannaki disrupts the epic structure. In her grief, she becomes a woman out of control and therefore dangerous. Viewed in this light, "The Book of Vanci" is probably an elaborate rite of propitiation to appease the wrath of Kannaki as the goddess Pattini and to invoke her blessing.

Numerous tellings of the Kovalan story arose in the centuries following Ilanko's poem (some are recounted in Noble). The earliest telling that has survived is a folk ballad, *Kovalan katai* (The story of Kovalan), attributed to Pukalenti (12th to 13th cent. CE) and first published in 1873. The ballad, together with the publication of the Tamil text of *The Tale of an Anklet* in 1892, revived interest in the story in the twentieth century. By "re-visioning" Ilanko's work, Pukalenti composed it from a new perspective that could also be regarded as subversive.

One interesting telling is "Chandra's Vengeance" (Frere 187–202). The princess Chandra is abandoned at birth by her father, the king of Maturai, when he is told by a Brahman that she will one day burn and destroy his country. Chandra is found by a merchant, who raises her as his own daughter. Later, she marries his son, Koila. Not long after, a nautch girl, Moulee, tricks Koila into marrying her, even though he protests that he already has a wife. When Moulee's mother insists that he pay for his support, Koila returns to Chandra to ask her for one of her anklets. Together they travel to Maturai to sell Chandra's anklet. The town jeweler has lost one of the two anklets that Queen Coplinghee has given him for cleaning. Seeing an anklet in Koila's hand, the jeweler accuses Koila before the king of the theft of the queen's anklet and has Koila put to death. Chandra avenges her husband's death by burning down the city. The king and queen perish in the fire, as do Moulee and her mother. The sequence of events narrated in "Chandra's Vengeance" corresponds to that in the first two books of *The Tale of an Anklet*. But the differences between the tale and the epic are striking. In the epic, the royal goldsmith steals the queen's anklet and thus betrays her trust. His cupidity brings ruin on the kingdom. The jeweler in the folktale does not steal Queen Coplinghee's anklet; two eagles carry it away from his porch to avenge the death of their young ones at the hands of the jeweler's son. The introduction of birds into the narrative is common in folktales. When Koila dies, Chandra tears her hair out. Fire at once bursts from her hair and destroys the city. This scene is even more dramatic in *The Tale of an Anklet*. In her rage, Kannaki wrenches her left breast from her body and hurls it at the city. It turns into a ball of fire that devours Maturai.

It is significant that in the folktale the anklet remains whole and unbroken, an allusion perhaps to Chandra's virginity. In the folk tellings, Kannaki is invariably a *virgo intacta*. For the Tamils, chastity goes beyond mere sexual abstinence; it represents sacred power. Further, they identify chastity with female spirituality. Kannaki embodies this best in the Tamil tradition. Her chastity empowers her to dispense justice. Kannaki is a resonant cultural symbol that has pulled together the different strands — religious, social, and political — in the Tamil cultural experience.

The epic's Jaina bias is replaced in the folktale by popular Hinduism. Kannaki, for instance, is depicted as an incarnation of the goddess Kali. The folktale reflects the ascendency of Hinduism and the decline of Jainism.

Manimekalai

Manimekalai is a continuation of the Kovalan story and is usually considered a sequel to *The Tale of an Anklet*. Composed in the sixth century CE, it is attributed to Cittalai Cattanar. It is the only surviving Buddhist epic in Tamil. Following Kovalan's death, the courtesan Matavi finds solace in renunciation: she becomes a Buddhist nun and takes the holy vows. In the prime of her life, Manimekalai, her daughter by Kovalan, follows her example. Book 3 of *The Tale of an Anklet* tells of their renunciation. Cattanar takes up the story from there. Embedded in the story are five cautionary tales that help strengthen the epic's presentation of the Buddhist view of life. In its call to renounce sexual desire as the first step on the road to enlightenment, the poem follows the teachings of the Buddha. In both of her roles — courtesan and nun — Manimekalai resists incorporation into the social order. She prefers to orbit in splendid isolation as a world renouncer. With the disappearance of Buddhism from the Tamil country after the eleventh century CE and the increasing presence of Hinduism, *Manimekalai* was all but forgotten. It did not become a part of the Tamil oral tradition thereafter, and it had no audience to speak of. It survived miraculously because of its association with *The Tale of an Anklet*.

In the literary history of India, oral traditions have thus existed simultaneously with written traditions, often as the voice of the underprivileged who expressed themselves not in elegant Sanskrit but in the rough-hewn vernaculars (*bhasas*) to produce an unrivaled body of devotional (*bhakti*) poetry over a period of some fifteen hundred years. And oral traditions continue to inform present-day Indian literature; witness, for instance, the extraordinary flowering of Dalit ("downtrodden") literature in Marathi by India's former untouchables.

Topics for Discussion

1. Any one of the above texts can serve as an introduction to the study of Indian verbal art in mythic and cultural contexts. Discussions may focus on specific topics such as a comparative study of the epic traditions of India and the West. The *Mahabharata* and the *Iliad*, for example, have much in common: the action is centered on events in the courts of kings and culminates in a great war; the protagonists, Yudhishthira and Achilles, are male and semidivine, Yudhishthira's father being Dharma, the god of justice, and Achilles's mother being the Nereid Thetis; the function of both epics was originally "magical and ritual" (Lord, *Singer of Tales* 67). The hexameter in the *Iliad* once had an apotropaic effect; the meter was the vehicle of Apollo's oracle at Delphi (Vries 9). The differences between the two epics are equally instructive. Unlike the *Iliad*, which is a pre-Christian Greek epic, the *Mahabharata* is essentially a Hindu epic. Revered as sacred poetry, it is considered the fifth Veda. The Indian epics are sacred texts that exemplify and promote the four great aims of human beings (*purusarthas*) — duty, wealth, desire, and liberation — through the characters as the characters evolve in the course of the story. The poet, protagonist, and audience participate equally in the regeneration of the human spirit. The poet is never primarily an entertainer but es-

sentially a spiritual guide who offers enlightenment beyond local social and political knowledge. This vision of the poet's role ultimately
shapes the generic characteristics recognizable in every Indian epic.
The epic attempts to narrate regeneration dramatically, through a sequence of onset, conflict, reversal, and denouement. Events are carefully selected as emblems of spiritual dilemmas. The action is circular
in that the protagonists find their way back to themselves after a series of humiliations and ascend to an enlightenment beyond time.

The Indian and Greek worldviews are fundamentally different.
Faced with the inevitability of death, the Indian mind turns to meta-
physical reflection, while the Greek mind engages itself with life
more fully and urgently. This difference is reflected in the Indian and
Greek epics. The protagonists in the Indian epics are urged to renounce the world as unreal and to seek enlightenment; the protagonists in the Greek epics cherish life and enjoy it to the utmost, for
with death comes the afterlife of epic renown (*kleos*). Whereas Homer
lies embalmed in a book and is the special preserve of scholars, the
daily life of the Hindus continues to resonate with the uplifting stories from their epics. We do not know if the *Odyssey* was at any time
a sacred text for the Greeks. Revered as sacred poetry, the *Ramayana*
is recited as incantation and ritual even today. Rama is considered an
incarnation of the god Vishnu. Students may be encouraged to view
Rama and Odysseus from this perspective and discuss them as em-
bodiments of the two cultures.

2. The *Ramayana* has been pressed into the service of politics
since the twelfth century, when invasions by the Turks threatened the
integrity of Hindu India. Hindu kings found in the Rama story a
representation of their struggle against the invading foreigners.
Hereafter, in both the written and oral tellings of the Rama story, the
Turks were regularly demonized. Even the discourse of contemporary Indian politics bristles with the idiom of the epic. The term *Ra-
marajya*, "the reign of Rama," is often used to evoke a Hindu golden
age. On December 6, 1992, for example, militant Hindus demol-
ished a sixteenth-century mosque built on the site of a temple in Ayodhya that they believed to be the birthplace of Rama. Riots broke

out between Hindus and Muslims all over northern India. Ironically, Gandhi himself died a martyr to the cause of Hindu-Muslim unity with the name of Rama on his lips.

Consider a recent European parallel. During their conflict with the Muslims of Bosnia and Herzegovina, Serbs received undiminished stimulation from the song cycles that narrated acts of heroism connected with the Battle of Kosovo in 1389, in which the Serbs were defeated by the Turks (see Alexander, this volume). Among the Christian nations of the Balkan peninsula, the Turk is the other. The Indian and Serbian examples forcefully demonstrate the truism that in times of national crises, the past is often invoked to legitimize a present course of action. Students will discover how folk traditions continually question and comment on the ideas and attitudes of the establishment. Students might also discuss the uses to which nations have put their oral traditions to evoke images of a utopian past as a panacea to set right the troubles of the present.

3. Unlike the *Mahabharata* and the *Ramayana*, *The Tale of an Anklet* has a female protagonist — Kannaki. It displaces the semi-divine warrior and the heroic ethos that surrounds him with a mortal woman who is transformed into a divinity. As a female protagonist, how does Kannaki disrupt the epic structure? Students might consider the source of Kannaki's empowerment and its implications for the epic as a genre. What explanation does the epic offer for her apotheosis?

4. Indian tradition offers powerful images of renunciation, from the Buddha to Gandhi. The life of an individual is divided into four stages: student, householder, hermit, and renouncer. Even more so than Hinduism, Buddhism encourages asceticism at the expense of family life. Liberation from the endless cycle of birth, death, and rebirth is perceived to be more accessible to those who renounce the world than to those who do not. Buddhism also emphasizes a human being's innate ability to obtain salvation on his or her own. Unlike Hinduism, Buddhism makes no gender distinctions. Students can profitably discuss the importance of Manimekalai's renunciation in the context of the Indian worldview and show how that worldview

acknowledges a woman's right to a spiritual life even if it means giving up a family life altogether.

Notes

1. English translations of the works mentioned in this essay are *The Bhagavad-Gita* (trans. Barbara Stoler Miller), *The Forest Book of the Ramayana of Kampan* (trans. George L. Hart and Hank Heifetz), *The Mahabharata* (trans. J. A. B. van Buitenen), *Manimekalai* (trans. Alain Daniélou), *The Ramayana* (trans. Robert P. Goldman et al.), *The Rig Veda* (trans. Wendy Doniger O'Flaherty), *The Tale of an Anklet* (trans. R. Parthasarathy), and *Tulsidas* (trans. W. D. P. Hill). See M. Mack for excerpts from four of the translations listed above; for excerpted translations of the *Mahabharata* and *Ramayana*, see also Caws and Prendergast; J. Smith.
2. Some tellings of the Rama story are recounted in H. Smith and in Brockington. Kampan's *Iramavataram* (The descent of Rama; 12th cent.), in Tamil, and Tulsidas's *Ramcaritmanas* (The holy lake of the acts of Rama; 16th cent.), in Hindi, are among the best known.

Mark Bender

Oral Performance and Orally Related Literature in China

China has rich traditions of oral performance and orally related literatures reflecting the country's long history and diverse, multiethnic composition. Texts of songs collected from the common people of the Yellow River region of northern China and then polished by Confucian scholars as the *Book of Songs* date to at least the fifth century BCE. Selections from that work are still taught to school children today in the People's Republic of China and Taiwan. Another collection of songs, some of which seem to be shamanic chants, exists from around the second or third century BCE and is of southern Chinese origin, coming from the area of the Yangtze River. These *Songs of Ch'u*, conventionally attributed to the legendary poet Qu Yuan (Ch'u Yuan), depict a culture very different from the northern China of the day. Thus, even when considering the earliest oral-based Chinese texts, readers are confronted with an often unexpected diversity.

Geographical environment, historical background, ethnic composition, local economies, material culture, and belief systems today vary widely among the peoples of China. However, there is a unity

250

in this diversity due to the pervasive influences of Confucianism, the Chinese writing system, the tradition of a massive, centralized bureaucracy, and the recent epoch of Chinese Marxism.

The majority ethnic group in China, the Han people, is actually a conglomerate of regional cultures, distinguishable in part by dialect, cuisine, customs, and oral performance traditions. Among the more prominent of these subgroups of the Han are those that speak Cantonese (Guangdong Province and the Guangxi Zhuang Autonomous Region), Wu (Yangtze River delta), Xiang (Hunan Province), northern and southwestern Mandarin dialects, Hakka (southern China), and Min (Fujian Province and Taiwan). Besides the Han majority, the government of the People's Republic of China recognizes fifty-five ethnic minority groups that together make up less than nine percent of the population. These very diverse peoples (see Ramsey) include the Mongols (Inner Mongolia); Uygur and Tu (northwest China); Hui (throughout China); Zhuang, Miao (known outside China as Hmong), Yao, Tujia, Dai, Yi, Bai, Hani, and Tibetans (south and southwest); and the Manchu, Daur, Oroqen, and Hezhen (northeast).

History and Form

Although the early history of oral performance and orally related narrative and drama in China is sketchy, one significant influence on the development of these traditions was the oral and written means used to propagate Buddhism, a religion that arrived in China from India as early as the first century CE and became widespread by the time of the Tang dynasty (618–907 CE). Among these means of propagation was a form of prosimetric narrative (combining verse and prose) called "transformation texts," a number of which have been found in the ancient caves of Dunhuang in northwest China.

Over time, the prosimetric convention became popular in hundreds of local styles of secular oral and written narrative in East Asia, many of which eventually flourished in the bustling urban entertainment districts of the later imperial period in China. The lengthy stories in one such form (called *tanci*, literally "plucked lyrics") were written, edited by, and circulated among elite women in the eighteenth and nineteenth centuries in the lower Yangtze region. A number of these works of prosimetric fiction tell of women donning men's clothing to take up roles in government and society normally reserved for males. Despite competition from the modern mass media, certain oral prosimetric styles such as the Suzhou and Yangzhou chantefable traditions (which are also called tanci but are of a different sort than that above), Peking drum singing, and Shandong clapper songs still have devoted local audiences. Indeed, a great percentage of the over two hundred local styles of professional or semi-professional oral performance in China is to some degree prosimetric in form.

A major development of orally related literature in China was the appearance by the sixteenth century AD of prose vernacular narratives written using conventions that simulated performances of professional oral storytellers of the urban marketplace and teahouse. These conventions include expressions that may have been similar to those used in the oral storytelling of the day, such as the direct address of readers in the manner of a storyteller, chapters ending in invitations to "find out what happens next," and the frequent incorporation of songs and verses. The best known of the shorter performance-related works are the narratives collected and edited by Feng Menglong in the Ming dynasty (1368–1644 AD). Novel-length works such as *Outlaws of the Marsh* (Shapiro); *The Journey to the West* (Yu), which includes many passages of verse; and the erotic narrative *The Golden Lotus* (Egerton; often published in translation under its romanized title, *Jin ping mei*) were among such texts written, often by several hands, between the fourteenth and eighteenth centuries. Though many of these works are now central in the present canon of traditional Chinese literature, before the early twentieth century they were regarded by Confucian scholars as a much lower order of writing than classical poetry, which was composed to conventional tunes and was intended to be sung or recited orally.

A rich operatic-dramatic tradition dates to the Mongol occupation of China in the thirteenth century. Southern forms such as Kunqu opera predate by centuries the well-known Peking (Beijing) opera, which developed as a combination of northern and southern musical and dramatic traditions only in the early nineteenth century. Recently, local forms of masked drama known as *nuotang* opera have been "discovered" among several ethnic groups in rural areas throughout south and southwest China. Mixed with elements of shamanism, these forms may have very ancient links with similar traditions in Korea and Japan. The elaborate festival dramas of Tibet combine shamanic elements with Tibetan Buddhism. During the Cultural Revolution (1966–76), when many traditional styles of folk song and storytelling were either co-opted as vehicles of propaganda or suppressed, a new "revolutionary opera" (*yangban xi*), combining Western dramatic techniques with traditional Chinese opera, enjoyed a forced reign of popularity. In recent years, such operas and their arias (e.g., "The Red Lantern") have seen a limited, nostalgic revival (for an overview of dramatic traditions, see Dolby, *History*).

Folk songs, folktales, and other forms of oral art common in rural areas are associated with all parts of China (see L. Miller). Antiphonal singing, especially of love songs, is an ancient and very widespread phenomenon in China and many parts of East and Southeast Asia. The largest antiphonal song festivals, in which groups of unmarried young men and women trade love songs with each other at parties that may last days, are central to the oral expressive culture of several of the ethnic minority groups in southwest China.

Oral epic traditions are performed by singers in many ethnic minority groups in China. The story of King Gesar of Ling (known as Gessar Khan among the Mongols), one of the world's longest narrative poems, is still performed widely in Tibet and neighboring areas.[1] Similar heroic epics were once popular among the Mongols and Kazakhs of north China. Southwestern peoples, including the Zhuang, Yi, Dai, Miao, Yao, and Hani, have rich traditions of creation epics and other long narrative poems, some sung antiphonally by several singers.

Historically, there has been a great deal of mutual influence among many of these diverse narrative and dramatic forms in terms of style, motifs, content, and, where applicable, music. For instance, professional storytelling, orally related vernacular fiction, and unofficial histories share a highly intertwined relation and development. Opera has influenced, and been influenced by, many styles of professional storytelling and other narrative genres, both written and oral. Although many of the traditions of the minority nationalities are relatively unknown to persons outside a particular group, instances of mutual influences and congruencies are not uncommonly found by scholars. Creation myths of many southern nationalities, for example, share the same or similar creators as certain Han myths. Some styles of minority oral performance have been popularized in the mass media, often in adapted or refined form. One example is a style of antiphonal folk song sung by peasants of the Zhuang nationality in Guangxi. The popular film *Third Sister Liu* (*Liu sanjie*), produced in 1961, concerns a young woman of that ethnic minority group who defeats evil landlords in a marathon antiphonal singing contest.

Translations and Background Information

Although the orally related narrative traditions, folktales, folk songs, and opera of China are quite well represented in foreign language translations, less is available, so far, on the urban professional storytelling traditions. With a few exceptions, good examples of ethnic minority traditions in English translation are still occasional, and those that exist are often translated from intermediate Chinese versions.

Among the orally related texts are Y. W. Ma and Joseph Lau's *Traditional Chinese Stories* and Cyril Birch's *Stories from a Ming Collection: The Art of the Chinese Storyteller.* Sidney Shapiro's *Outlaws of the Marsh* is a readable translation of a novel-length account of over a hundred colorful bandit heroes active during the twelfth century (see also Birch, *Anthology*). Anthony C. Yu's translation of *The Journey to the West* narrates the fantastic legendary journey of a Chinese monk who brings the Buddhist scriptures back with him from India. *The Columbia Anthology of Traditional Chinese Literature* (Mair) has numerous translations of orally related texts, including several of the Tang dynasty transformation texts mentioned above (see also Mair, *Tang Transformation Texts*). Several papers in *Popular Culture in Late*

Imperial China (Johnson, Nathan, and Rawski) provide background for certain performance traditions in the late Qing dynasty (1644–1911). The women's *tanci* traditions await translation.

Wolfram Eberhard's *Folktales of China*, though somewhat dated, contains tales from many regions and ethnic groups throughout the land. *Mythology and Folklore of the Hui: A Muslim Chinese People* (Li and Luckert) is devoted to myths and stories of this widespread ethnic group and religious minority. *The Tale of the Nisan Shamaness* (Nowak and Durrant) is a version of a famous Manchu folk epic that describes the journey of a heroic shamaness to the underworld. Foreign Languages Press and New World Press in China have published a number of collections of folktales and narrative poems from various ethnic groups in China. Among the best known is the narrative poem *Ashima* (Yang) about a heroic young woman of the Sani people (a subgroup of the Yi) in Yunnan province. A collection entitled *South of the Clouds: Tales from Yunnan* (L. Miller) includes folktales from a number of ethnic minority groups in the province.

William Dolby's *A History of Chinese Drama* provides an excellent historical overview of Chinese operatic traditions. Bell Yung's work on Cantonese opera as performance is a valuable source for understanding the social context and artistry of opera in a local region of China. Dolby's *Eight Chinese Plays* features short works from eight different operatic traditions. Stephen West and Wilt Idema's *The Moon and the Zither: The Story of the Western Wing* is a translation of a famous love story adapted into operatic form from earlier prosimetric traditions and performed in many styles of Chinese oral art. *Harvest Festival Dramas of Tibet* (Duncan) provides texts and an introduction to aspects of the Tibetan dramatic tradition.

The journal *CHINOPERL Papers* is possibly the best source for popular urban oral performance traditions in China. Nearly every issue has contextually oriented articles and translations showing performance styles from various regional cultures and ethnic groups. One general text covering the period from 1949 to the early 1980s is Bonnie McDougall's collection, *Popular Chinese Literature and Performing Arts in the People's Republic of China*. Journals that often include papers on orally performed arts in China are *Asian Folklore*

Studies and *CHIME*. *Renditions*, published in Hong Kong, often features English versions of styles of Chinese opera. Another journal, *Oral Tradition*, has also featured articles on urban oral performance styles and orally related literature in China.

Strategies for the Classroom

In the classroom, teachers should immediately stress the diversity of the performance traditions of China (and related written ones) and provide examples to illustrate this point. While the diversity theme should always be kept in mind, points of convergence may be noticed among many of the regional and ethnic traditions. The mixture of song and speech in narrative, the appearance of certain narrative and folk motifs, and the widespread occurrence of antiphonal singing are prime examples of such convergences.

When teachers present particular traditions, context and text should be combined. On one level, context means general historical, regional, ethnic, and social background of the culture that produced a text or tradition. On another level, it designates the information (to the extent that information is available) on performers; audiences; the situation of performance; repertoire; conventions; and the social meanings given to performance by local community, region, and nation. Subjects for discussion can include the varying aesthetics of performance, performance and politics before and after 1949, issues of social status, ethnicity, gender, and age in past and present-day China, the influences of elite and popular culture on performance in China, the historical marginality of professional performers, and the effects of modern technology and lifestyles on the traditional performing arts.

Ideally, the text (at least for the oral forms) would be presented by an actual performer or through audiovisual means supplemented by a written translation.[2] Without such resources, texts can be read — preferably aloud — and discussed in class. A more challenging project would be the actual performance of a text in translation (or in the original in a language class). In many instances, stories, songs, or selections from operas can be adapted for classroom use — and with little guilt, since in Chinese written vernacular and oral traditions there is not a strong tradition of fixed texts, at least not when the texts are secular. Indeed, Yung notes in a discussion of Cantonese opera that though creativity in performance is not free, being bounded by a tradition shared by both performer and community, the "outcome" of the "game" of performance is "left to the player's own skill and ingenuity in the circumstances of the moment" (ix). Thus, teachers and students should not be afraid to rise to the challenge of approaching China's diverse performance traditions by re-performing them in the living classroom.

Notes

1. On the Gesar epic, see David-Neel and Lama Yongden; also Penick and Dakpo. For other oral epics, see Bender.
2. Commercially available sources are few for most styles of Chinese oral performance, though several Chinese operas and examples of traditional music can be obtained through agencies such as China Books and Periodicals, Inc., 2929 24th Street, San Francisco, CA 94110.

Shelley Fenno Quinn

Oral and Vocal Traditions of Japan

Vestiges of Oral Composition in Early Documents

Japanese oral traditions are integral to understanding both the diversity of Japanese culture and a number of its continuities. On the one hand, orality and aurality have traditionally been viewed in Japan as the wellspring of religious and artistic expression — integral to an evolving sense of what it is to be Japanese. On the other hand, the oldest myths and legends of Japan, material that is assumed to have been orally transmitted from ancient times, come down to us in scripts that are either in classical Chinese or in characters taken from Chinese and used for their phonetic values in writing Japanese. It was not until the ninth century that simplified phonetic scripts for writing vernacular Japanese came into general use, and thus much of what we know of these preliterate oral discourses reaches us through the filter of a continental writing technology or adaptations thereof.

This tension between oral Japanese and literary Chinese is a continuity that runs through Japanese literary history but is especially

258

pronounced in literature composed before the development of vernacular scripts. For instance, the tension is reflected in what is thought to be Japan's oldest extant book, the *Kojiki* (Record of ancient matters, c. 712; see Philippi). The *Kojiki* is in three books (*maki*) and was compiled by imperial edict. It records creation myths, genealogies, songs, folk etymologies, and legends surrounding the imperial clan and other influential clans from ancient times to 628 AD. In the Chinese preface, the Japanese compiler, Ō no Yasumaro, explains that the book's contents consist of the transmissions of a certain Hieda no Are, who "possessed such great native intelligence that he could repeat orally whatever met his eye, and whatever struck his ears was indelibly impressed in his heart" (Philippi 41–42; it is not clear from the original Japanese whether Hieda no Are was male or female). Whether Hieda no Are was transmitting oral narratives, reciting written texts from memory, or both is unclear, although most scholars concur that, along with orally transmitted material, written chronicles that are no longer extant constituted the source material for the *Kojiki*.

The *Kojiki* employs a combination of Chinese characters, some used for their meaning and some for their phonetic value. For the recording of genealogical matter typically found at the opening of narratives, Yasumaro tended to favor writing with characters that carried the Chinese meaning. However, anecdotes and songs in the second and third books were more frequently recorded either in a hybrid style that employed Chinese characters for morphemes but partially altered Chinese syntax to suit the very different syntactic structure of Japanese or in a purely phonetic script called *man'yōgana*, in which Chinese characters were used not for their semantic value but for phonetic recording of Japanese syllables. The phonetic script occurs most consistently in the recording of *uta* (songs or poems) throughout the *Kojiki*.

The other major compendium of legends, genealogies, and quasi-historical accounts from the early classical age is entitled *Nihon shoki*, also known as *Nihongi* (*Nihongi: Chronicles of Japan*, 720; see Aston). This is a much lengthier work in thirty books, compiled under imperial patronage. The compilers of the *Nihon shoki* opted to record all prose sections in Chinese. However, like the *uta* of the *Kojiki*, *uta* in the *Nihon shoki* are recorded in phonetic characters. That the *Nihon shoki* includes versions of a number of the same poems appearing in the *Kojiki* suggests that both documents drew on orally transmitted material.

These earliest written documents, the *Kojiki* and *Nihon shoki*, are thus rather complex amalgams in which vestiges of oral composition coexist with and are influenced by Chinese models of literary composition. In both these corpora, the song selections are situated at climactic moments in the narratives. Many of these entries appear to have been originally folk songs from various regions of Japan; they were subsequently assigned places in the narratives as compositions of particular individuals. Although both corpora are the politicized and literary products of a circle of court aristocrats concerned with solidifying the legitimacy of the imperial clan, they also offer a glimpse of a rich array of lore descending from a preliterate age.

The eighth century saw the compilation of the first and the largest collection of Japanese *uta*. Entitled *Man'yōshū* (Collection of ten thousand leaves; see Levy), the compilation consists of 4,516 poems in twenty books. More than half are anonymous, although approximately 400 are attributed to individual poets. The *Man'yōshū* is primarily recorded in the phonetic *man'yōgana* symbols in an effort to preserve the prosody of the original Japanese. The verse form that occurs with greatest frequency in this collection is the thirty-one-syllable *uta* (today called *tanka*, "short song"). The *tanka* was subsequently to become the representative genre of court poetry for centuries and the most prestigious type of literature. From the tenth to the fifteenth century, twenty-one anthologies primarily composed of *tanka* were commissioned by the imperial court, and private collections were also numerous.

The most famous of many canonical tracts on *tanka* composition is the "Japanese Preface" to the first imperial anthology, the *Kokin wakashū* (commissioned in 905; see McCullough, *Kokin*). The preface was composed by a court aristocrat and compiler of the anthology, Ki no Tsurayuki (c. 872–945). By the time of the *Kokinshū*, as it was popularly known, simplified phonetic scripts for writing Japanese were coming into use among the literate circles of court society, and it was therefore possible for the first time to record vernacular Japanese easily and efficiently. The preface reflects an accompanying awareness of poetic composition in native Japanese as a literary activity on a par with the composition of Chinese verse. At the same time, Tsurayuki is careful to preserve the traditional link between poetry and song, as in the following excerpt: "Hearing the warbler sing among the blossoms and the frog in his fresh waters — is there any living thing not given to song?" (Brower and Miner 3). An observation like this seems a deliberate effort by Tsurayuki to canonize the oral heritage of the *tanka* at a time when *tanka* composition was increasingly becoming a self-conscious act of literary creation. Although the composition of poetry took a literary turn with the court poets of Tsurayuki's generation, the aural dimension of recitation was always to remain an important element in the practice of poetry and in the way that poets and audiences appreciated the art.

Vocal Literature of Traditional Japan

Japan's medieval period (1185–1600) saw a proliferation of performative genres and the increased participation of artists and audiences from all classes of society. Military and religious narratives provided material for various religious and secular bards, who performed in diverse arenas, from the salons of the aristocratic and military elites to the roadside or the street corner. Many of these itinerant performers were affiliated with religious institutions, both Buddhist and Shinto, and their performances had not only elements of entertainment but also such functions as pacifying the restless spirits of the dead or proselytizing.

From 1180 to 1185, Japan was engulfed in the Genpei War, a struggle between two military clans, the Taira and the Minamoto, for political and economic dominance of the country. Stories of that struggle and the resulting fall of the Taira clan were the inspiration for a number of styles of recited narratives, or *katarimono*. The first style that deserves mention is *heikyoku*, "Heike pieces." These were recited narratives from the epic work entitled *Heike monogatari* (*The*

Tale of the Heike; see McCullough, *Tale*), the account of the Taira clan, who enjoyed political and military supremacy before their demise in the Genpei War. *Heike monogatari* has multiple variants, some of them composed to be read and others to be recited. It is a pastiche of historical chronicles and not so historical legends surrounding the major figures in the struggle.

Heikyoku were performed by guilds of blind priests (*biwa hōshi*) who recited the texts from memory while playing accompaniment on the lute (*biwa*). The textual variant that is considered to be the culmination of the recited strain is the Kakuichi text (1371), credited to a blind priest by that name. The *biwa hōshi* disseminated the Heike legend cycles among the general populace, effectively creating what Barbara Ruch has described as the first national literature (293–94).

Ruch aptly characterizes *heikyoku* and other intoned narratives as vocal literature, a term that she uses to distinguish them from "oral literature" (286–87). She argues that vocal literature is premised on the existence of a literary script that forms the basis of the recitation. Integral to vocal literature is the art of voice projection and the intoning of a prose or poetic text. Generally its practitioners were literate or, as the blind *biwa*-playing priests, worked in close collaboration with literate individuals.

Another exemplar of *katarimono* in the martial mode is the *kōwakamai* genre, ballad recitations to simple instrumentation on the shoulder drum (*tsuzumi*). Today *kōwakamai* has virtually died out, although it is still performed in one village on the island of Kyūshū. In its heyday in the sixteenth and seventeenth centuries, *kōwakamai* enjoyed unrivaled popularity with military patrons, who would hold performances not only in their residences but in their military encampments as well. The *kōwakamai* repertory also drew extensively from the legend cycles of the Genpei War; these cycles, like *heikyoku*, were narrated in the third person. Fifty *kōwakamai* texts have been preserved (Araki 150–95). Little is known about their authorship, but it is thought that the librettos show influences from both oral and written sources.

The combination of voice, text, and instrumentation is also integral to traditional forms of theater in Japan. Although in its earliest phases Noh drama may have been largely impromptu, as early as the fourteenth century librettos exist as an important element of performance. In his pedagogical transmissions on this art, the seminal actor, playwright, and theorist Zeami Motokiyo (1363?–1443?) calls chanted text and choreographed movement the elements most basic to a Noh performance.[1] To recited text are added instrumentation on drums and a flute and the visual components of dance and mimetic techniques. A Noh libretto is situated at the crossroads of lyrical and narrative expression, incorporating such poetic elements as the *tanka* into a primarily narrative type of exposition. Noh continues to be performed regularly today.

The puppet theater (*ningyō jōruri*) is another genre in which dramatic and visual elements derive much of their effect from the expressiveness of recitation. A puppet theater performance has four major components: the reciter, the player(s) of the banjolike instrument called the *shamisen*, the puppets, and the text. The language of the text is primarily narrative interspersed with dialogue, and one reciter delivers the lines for all roles. Records of puppet performances date back as far as the eighth century. The *jōruri* recitation style traces to the adoption of the *shamisen* late in the sixteenth century, although the *jōruri* vocal style descends from *katarimono* genres, such as *heikyoku* and *sekkyōbushi*, that prospered throughout the medieval period. The innovation of joining the puppets, *shamisen*, and recitation into one composite art dates from the seventeenth century. The puppet theater is often said to have taken a self-conscious literary turn with the plays of Chikamatsu Monzaemon (1653–1724). Among Chikamatsu's many contributions was the creation of a genre of plays that treated contemporary characters and events drawn from urban life. Up to that time, the repertoire had consisted exclusively of plays about figures of historical or legendary repute. The mainstream commercial puppet theater enjoyed the peak of its popularity in the eighteenth century but has retained a devoted following ever since (for English translations of puppet theater works, see Keene).

Rakugo: A Storyteller's Art

Popular contemporary themes provided the subject matter for a number of arts of storytelling that flourished in the Edo period

(1600–1868). This era saw the three urban centers of Edo (present-day Tokyo), Osaka, and Kyoto develop into commercial hubs. Theaters established in large part to serve the increasingly affluent members of the merchant class also prospered. Along with the puppet and *kabuki* theaters were *yose*, variety halls that were the homes of professional storytellers of several types. One genre of storytelling that developed in the Edo *yose* is *rakugo*, which is often glossed as "short humorous stories ending in a punch line." As a genre, *rakugo* may be distinguished from the *katarimono* narratives by the absence of musical accompaniment and a lessened emphasis on vocal musicality. *Rakugo* unfolds in comic dialogue, with all parts played by a single narrator who punctuates his story with gestures but remains seated throughout.

Today the *rakugo* repertoire is divided into two categories, the classical pieces (dating up to around 1900) and the newer pieces (see Morioka and Sasaki). The majority of the characters in classical *rakugo* are Edo townspeople, and the repertoire treats a very broad cast of characters, among them the quick-witted, the newly wealthy, gallant samurai, boozers, lovers, thieves, ghosts, and the absentminded. The language of a *rakugo* text is more fluid than that of *katarimono* narratives. The opening lines (*makura*) are traditionally rendered in a conversational register, and the dialogue is replete with verbal jousting and parody. It is not surprising that the art of *rakugo* continues to draw an enthusiastic following today.

———

Although this essay introduces only a sampling of the oral and vocal traditions of Japan, each sample has been chosen to reflect the historical and generic range of those traditions. For genre, I gave special attention to the *tanka*, the most canonical of a spectrum of poetic forms composed for lyric recitation. From a historical perspective, the *tanka* is the representative lyric of classical Japanese letters (710–1185) and widely associated by the Japanese today with the imperial court and culture of that time. I also touched on an issue that cannot be ignored in studying the relation of orality to literacy in Japanese traditions: the complexities arising from the adoption of the Chinese writing system to suit the needs of the genetically unrelated language of Japanese.

Next I stressed arts belonging to a broad, generic grouping known as *katarimono*, arts of narrative recitation. With the exception of the puppet theater, which dates from the seventeenth century, those arts introduced here originated in the medieval period (1185–1600). I also highlighted the issue of the interdependence of oral and literary modes in the performance art of Japan, because *katarimono* performances are typified by recitation of previously composed literary texts rather than by principles of oral composition. Finally, I discussed one exemplar from a third major classification of performance genres, *hanashimono*, "storytelling pieces," focusing on *rakugo*, an art representative of the prospering urban centers of the Edo period.

In this sampling I featured arts that, in their inception, are representative of different historical periods. Moreover, I concentrated on exemplars from different generic groupings. It should be mentioned that today all the arts discussed above have contemporary versions, and they enjoy varying levels of popularity.[2]

Notes

1. See the collection by Bethe and Brazell; see also the remarks in Quinn.
2. For further explanation of the issues broached here and other concerns, the reader is encouraged to consult Araki; Aston; Brower and Miner; McCullough, *Tale*; Philippi; Ruch.

Susan Slyomovics

Arabic Traditions

The many-layered nature of Arabic has traditionally divided Arabic language and literature into two streams: the formal, written, literary, classical language, called *fuṣḥā*, and the many spoken regional and national dialects. These dialects can themselves be subdivided; colloquial Egyptian Arabic, for example, encompasses Cairene Arabic, Ṣaʿīdī southern Egyptian Arabic, and so on. A long-standing bias elevates the literate, written classical tradition, while Arabic vernaculars are frequently and mistakenly characterized as corrupt variants of Islamic high culture, language, and religion.

This complex sociolinguistic situation in the Arab world affects the transmission, reception, and editing of oral literature, because this literature is most often performed in dialect and yet written in classical Arabic. When scholars write down oral texts in classical Arabic, they employ a range of strategies, from approximate transcription of the dialect to partial transformation into a "corrected" literary language to direct translation into classical (or modern standard) Arabic. Such folk literature texts often achieve currency thanks to the

266

legitimizing force of written usage. In contrast, scholars who transcribe oral vernacular traditions according to the International Phonetic Alphabet (IPA) use Roman transliteration, a system not easily accessible to the Arabic-language reader.

The linguistic relation between the formal, written language and the spoken is complex; so too are the connections between oral and written narrative. It is noteworthy that exceptions to the dichotomy of oral-dialect versus written-classical Arabic abound. Orally performed traditions such as Quranic recitations (Nelson), religious praise songs, sermons, political speeches, and even formal, prepared poetic declaiming are pronounced in classical Arabic. Nonetheless, Egyptian folklorist Hasan El-Shamy characterizes oral narratives as a cognitive system separate from any written ones when he discusses the production of Egyptian oral folktales (*Folktales* l-li; Slyomovics, "Death-song").

The Arabian Nights

This essay focuses on English-language research that provides both text and performance contexts from oral traditions such as *A Thousand and One Nights* (on frame tales, see Irwin, this volume), the genres of folktale and epic, and the heritage of Arab vernacular poetry. Although the interactions between the written and the oral are not our primary concern here, the history of *A Thousand and One Nights* — since its appearance in Europe in 1704, the best known work of Arabic literature in the West — reveals much about overlaps between authentic oral variants and written versions. Scholars have argued whether the written collection is made up of tales of oral provenance or, conversely, of tales never recited or performed but rather consciously molded by an editor-redactor to mimic oral storytelling style (Slyomovics, "Performing" 390–93). These issues of Arabic linguistic and literary variation and interaction affect the many available editions and influence the reader's choice of English translations. Other factors are a varied manuscript tradition, linguistic registers from classical Arabic to dialect, and even idiosyncratic editorial emendations, the most notorious instance being Sir Richard Burton's eroticizing alterations. Here are some recommended texts available in paperback. The two-volume translation by Husain Haddawy, *The Arabian Nights* and *The Arabian Nights II: Sindbad and Other Popular Stories*, based on a fourteenth-century Syrian manuscript, recounts 271 nights. *Thousand Nights and One Night*, the four-volume English translation of Joseph Charles Mardus's French text by Edward Powys Mathers, based on the later Egyptian Bulaq and second Calcutta editions, consists of the canonical thousand and one storytelling nights. N. J. Dawood's *"Aladdin" and Other Tales from the* Thousand and One Nights translates selected tales (see also Dawood, *Tales*). *Arabian Nights' Entertainment* (R. Mack), the earliest English-language translation (1706–12), based on Antoine Galland's French text (1704) and produced by an anonymous Grub Street translator, has enjoyed a wide readership from the early eighteenth century.

Epic Tradition

Other tale cycles that recount adventures of historical and legendary heroes and heroines are part of the Arab *sīra* or epic tradition: *Sīrat 'Antar ibn Shaddād* tells about Antara, the black warrior hero of pre-Islamic times; *Sīrat az-Zāhir Baybars* tells about the medieval Egyptian ruler az-Zāhir; *Sīrat Dhāt al-Himma* relates the wars of the heroine queen Dhāt al-Himma against the Byzantine Empire; *Sīrat al-Malik Sayf Ibn Dhī Yazan* relates the wars of a south Arabian king against the Abyssinians; *Sīrat az-Zīr Sālim* is about the bedouin Arab hero az-Zīr Sālim; and *Sīrat Banī Hilāl* is the epic of the Banū Hilāl tribe (for historical and bibliographical materials, see appropriate entries in *Encyclopedia*). These epics exist in both oral and written forms. Numerous handwritten manuscripts are located in libraries throughout Europe and the Arab world; printed editions can still be purchased cheaply in many Arab countries.

Of all the epics, *Sīrat Banī Hilāl* continues to be the most widely performed by poets, storytellers, and singers from Iraq in the east to Morocco in the west, in the Arabian peninsula, and in parts of Sudan and central Africa. Contemporary bards consider the Hilali epic the true history of the Arabs. 'Awaḍallah, an Egyptian epic poet who sings the Hilali tales in dialect, also proclaims the uniqueness and intelligibility of epic performance in all forms of Arabic: "Blessing the Prophet is beneficial before all / my speech is earnest, my art is Arab / northwards and to the east of my words, / my art only Arabs understand" (Slyomovics, *Merchant* 112). The Hilali epic is based on historical events—the migratory waves of the Banū Hilāl bedouins leaving the famine-ridden Arabian peninsula for the verdant shores of North Africa from the eighth to the eleventh century. History and legend have become so intertwined that we know only one certain fact about the transmission of this epic: the earliest oral versions still extant were written down by the famed medieval scholar Ibn Khaldūn, who collected Hilali tales from bedouin tribes in North Africa around the fifteenth century (Rosenthal 3:412–40).

The importance of contemporary Egyptian reciters and narrators in preserving the Hilali epic is reflected in the scholarly literature.[1] Performance texts of the oral Hilali epic tradition are available in Susan Slyomovics's *The Merchant of Art*; in Dwight Fletcher Reynolds's *Heroic Poets, Poetic Heroes*; and in Bridget Connelly's *Arab Folk Epic and Identity*. These are versified narratives by Egyptian poets sung over many nights to the accompaniment of the *rabāba* (spike fiddle) or the *tār* (drum). Excerpts from the opening section of the Egyptian Hilali cycle, the birth of the hero sequence, are translated by Reynolds and Slyomovics and appear in John Johnson, Thomas Hale, and Stephen Belcher's anthology of African oral epics. Versions by J. R. Patterson in the Shuwa Arabic dialect of Nigeria and by Sayyid Hurreiz in Sudanese Arabic demonstrate the Arab-African cross-fertilizations. For additional Arab epics in translation, M. C. Lyons has compiled brief prose versions of twelve epics, and Lena Jayyusi has translated and adapted the epic of *Sayf Ibn Dhī Yazan*.

Folktale

The long-standing idea that the literate, written culture is innately superior to the oral, often illiterate, heritage affects the collecting of folk literature. The folktale in the Arab world, like its European counterparts, has endured rewriting, simplification, and censorship as it moves from oral rendition to written text. Rarely do Arab folk-tales, whether they are collected in Arabic or Western languages, preserve an authentic oral form. Two exceptions are the Egyptian collection by Hasan El-Shamy (*Folktales*) and the Palestinian collection by Ibrahim Muhawi and Sharif Kanaana.[2] Both provide biographical information about the tellers, ethnographic description of the storytelling context, and comparative annotation linking the tales to international tale types and their Arabic variants. Finally, in an effort to organize and structure the huge domain of Arabic folktales, epics, and legends, El-Shamy's two-volume guide (*Folk Traditions*) classifies Arab oral literature according to the standard Stith Thompson system of motifs (*Motif-Index*).

Folk Poetry and Gender

A consideration of performed folk poetry introduces yet another layer to the perceived dichotomies of written and oral, literate and illiterate, classical and vernacular Arabic: the role of gender (see Weigle, this volume). Lila Abu-Lughod's work on bedouin women of Egypt proposes that the oral composition and recitation of love poetry by women is a defiant move by the powerless against the powerful. These women use a poetic language to subvert social demands for modesty and denial of women's sexuality. Abu-Lughod's fieldwork demonstrates that paradoxically the poetry through which women (and another powerless group, young men) express subversive views is also highly valued by the community. Two ethnographies about male poets in the Arabian peninsula, on Yemeni tribal poets (Caton) and Saudi vernacular poetry (Sowayan), confirm the value and power of orally performed poetry among its practitioners and listeners.

Folk poetry is a key cultural event in Arabian society because it is an integral part of political, social, and religious institutions. Poetry, and by extension folk narrative, is central because it is also a form of political rhetoric—a means to persuade, to mediate, to praise, and sometimes to subvert. At certain times and places in the

Arab world, folk narrators and singers, such as Egyptian epic poets, are a specially trained, hereditary class, valued yet apart. In other times and places, as among Egyptian bedouin women or in premodern Arabia, dynamic tradition created a nation of folk poets. The oral literature of the Arab world is a primary literature; one cannot hope to approach the richness of Arabic literature if one remains bound to the classical tradition alone.

Pedagogical Approaches

Texts from the Arabic-speaking world introduce American students to the study of a living, oral tradition of "troubadours" and performers from the Middle East and North Africa. To illustrate the qualities of oral epic poetry from a fully comparative perspective, course syllabi may employ, for example, the ancient Greek epics as well as the medieval (written) and modern (orally performed) epics from the Arab world. Conflicts, cross-influences, and contacts between the Islamic and European epic traditions are reflected both in French and Spanish medieval epic texts and in poetry from the Arab world. A case of special interest is the Bosnian Muslim poetry composed and performed in the former Yugoslavia.[3] This poetry has been intensively studied by Milman Parry and Albert Lord in connection with their theories of Homeric oral composition, but it could be systematically related to the Middle Eastern tradition as well. Epics are also versions of national myths that retain their power and help in understanding the background to modern ideologies and fictions of national identity. By connecting Arabic material on epic, romance, folktale, and performed poetry to the mainstream traditions of classical Greek and other national literatures, the cross-disciplinary approach to oral literature will remain at the heart of the comparative folk literature enterprise.

Notes

1. I confine myself to English-language scholarship; French-language studies have concentrated on the Maghrebi (North African) versions.

2. These tales represent accurate translations from their respective dialects; Muhawi and Kanaana also transliterated one Palestinian Arabic tale in Roman transcription.

3. See Alexander, this volume. See also Foley, *Traditional Oral Epic*, chs. 5, 8, 10; *Immanent Art*, chs. 3, 4; *Singer*, ch. 4.

Ronelle Alexander

South Slavic Traditions

The category of South Slavic oral tradition embraces songs, stories, proverbs, laments, charms, and so forth from the peoples of Bulgaria and the former Yugoslavia. Oral tradition is well known to all South Slavs, although the extent to which it is still being created and transmitted in a traditional context varies. Among Christians, a living oral tradition is more widely preserved by peoples of the Orthodox faith: Serbs, Montenegrins, Macedonians, and Bulgarians. This preservation is largely due to the social and cultural organization of Eastern Orthodox society, which is much more ritualistic and patriarchal than the more individualized western, Catholic societies.

Oral tradition is also well preserved among the many South Slavs of the Muslim faith, those whose ancestors converted to Islam during the Ottoman occupation. In 1971, the Yugoslav government gave this group the official designation of Muslim. Both the genesis and current usage of this term are more ethnic than religious. During the long Ottoman period, the religious designation was more political than theological: a Muslim was someone who accepted the ways of the ruling civilization, and a Christian was one who resisted them.

Oral tradition in the South Slavic area reflects this state of affairs well, especially in the best known form, the epic song (*epska pjesma*, sometimes also *junačka pjesma*, "heroic song"). Both Muslims and Christians sing in the same language and according to the same metrical constraints, and they utilize the same formulaic and thematic material. The differences between them are in the ethnic identity of hero and villain and in the length of the songs (Coote). Muslims, as members of the ruling social stratum, had more leisure time and space to compose and listen to the longer oral forms, whereas the subject Christian people had to utilize what small spaces and free moments they could find. Both peoples lived in a "heroic age," roughly from the mid-fourteenth to the early twentieth century; for some that age is being revived in the current Balkan wars. The various struggles connected with the Byzantine, Ottoman, and anti-Ottoman Western powers meant that heroism was (at least theoretically) the business of nearly every male and that the singing of songs about this heroism was a crucial element of the social fabric. Largely for this reason, the term *oral tradition* among the South Slavs usually means heroic epic song, which is much better documented, studied, and translated than are any of the other genres of South Slavic oral tradition.

The basic unity of the epic tradition is clear to those who read the song texts without emotional, cultural, or academic prejudice. But most readers are subject to one or more of these prejudices. Because of nation-building efforts that began in the early nineteenth century and continue today, Serbian Christian songs are seen by Serbs as a unique expression of Serbian national identity. This is especially true for Kosovo songs. These songs relate events and emotions surrounding the Battle of Kosovo in 1389, which the Serbs lost to the Turks. According to the song texts, the Serbian Prince Lazar was offered a choice between victory on earth and loss on earth coupled with victory in heaven. The Serbian defeat is therefore glorified in these songs, and in the Serbian consciousness, as a moral victory; references to the martyrdom of Christ are present throughout the songs (Koljević). The other well-known set of Christian epic songs relates the adventures of Marko Kraljević, a Christian prince who became a vassal of the Turkish sultan after 1389 (Popović). Marko is characterized not only by superhuman strength and a magical horse but also by his ability to negotiate his position between the two worlds of Serb and Turk, often through cunning and guile.

Vuk Karadžić

Although the epic tradition is still alive (albeit minimally so) in some parts of Serbia, there is a set of songs about Kosovo, Marko, and certain other heroes and events that are known by nearly every Serb in a highly fixed format. These are the songs collected by the great Serbian ethnographer, historian, and language reformer Vuk Stefanović Karadžić (1787–1864) and published in his canonical four-volume *Srpske narodne pjesme* (Serbian folk songs). The best known of these narratives, including all the Kosovo songs and the most important Marko songs, have been frequently translated into English since they first became known to the West in the mid-nineteenth century (see esp. Low; Pennington and Levi; Matthias and Vučković). Some translations are rendered in prose, but the majority are in verse. The extent to which each translator has tried to reproduce the highly characteristic Serbian ten-syllable line, which for Serbs is a strong carrier of the emotions associated with the idea of epic, is only one of the many ways in which these translations differ radically from one another.

The importance of this set of songs rests not only in the fact that Serbs consider them a primary and essential expression of Serbian identity but also in the uniqueness of the collector of the songs, Karadžić, whom Serbs without exception call simply Vuk; scholars both in Serbia and abroad have adopted this custom as well. Although literate, Vuk was a member of an oral society and understood fully the oral nature of the songs and their contextual importance. As far as we know, his transcriptions are faithful to the song as sung, and, in accepting transcriptions from others, he always insisted on verifying for himself that the song in question was actually sung that way among the folk. Vuk's prodigious energy and total devotion to his task have given us an extremely valuable record of a singing tradition that was still fully living at the time. One cannot say the same now, since Serbs are so conditioned to view Vuk's published (and fixed) versions of the songs as the correct ones.

Milman Parry and Albert Lord

The other major enterprise of collecting epic songs among the South Slavs was that undertaken by the North American scholars Milman Parry and Albert Lord in the 1930s. Both their methods and their goals were very different from those of Vuk. Whereas Vuk aimed to uncover the rich folk heritage of the Serbs and to use this heritage in helping them regain a sense of identity and national independence, Parry and Lord sought an empirical answer to the Homeric question: Could a single singer have composed a song of the length and complexity of the *Iliad* or the *Odyssey* without recourse to writing, and, if so, how was such a remarkable feat accomplished? Their answers, based on extensive fieldwork with many different singers, are presented in the ground-breaking volume *The Singer of Tales* (Lord). This book has done much to establish both the field of oral tradition and the concept of orality per se. The materials gathered by Parry and Lord now reside in the Milman Parry Collection of Oral Literature at Harvard University; some have appeared in published form in the series *Serbo-Croatian Heroic Songs* (vols. 1–4, 6, 8, 14). Except for the most recent volume, the songs are presented in prose translation; the original versions, of course, are published in verse. Each of the volumes includes helpful notes or essays explaining in more detail the Parry-Lord method of collection and its results.

Parry and Lord sought to learn whether the singer memorized his material or composed it anew in performance and whether he had in his mind a single original version in relation to which all other versions could be considered variants. Their research showed that each performance by a singer was "'the' song" and that in consequence there was no single authoritative text. Instead, the song existed in the singer's mind in an abstract form. In *The Singer of Tales*, Lord called this set of concepts a "multiform" and provided illustrations with material he and Parry had collected. The theoretical discussion in *The Singer of Tales* is thus best supplemented by the actual song texts that Parry and Lord collected as well as by the notes they have given us to them in *Serbo-Croatian Heroic Songs*.

In *The Singer of Tales* Lord gives the impression that all the best singers he and Parry worked with were Muslim. The description of the Ramazan festival, during which singers were engaged to sing all night for the duration of an entire month, has remained for many the prevailing impression of South Slavic singers. In actual fact, Muslim singers were useful to Parry and Lord chiefly because they sang the longest songs and therefore provided the best material for solving Parry and Lord's empirical questions about Homer. Parry and Lord also worked with Christian singers; indeed, it is due to this aspect of their work, as well as to the material gathered by Luka Marjanović and other collectors at the turn of the century (none of which, unfortunately, has been translated into English; for an idea of the extent of collection, see Kay), that we can see the unity of South Slavic epic song.

The perceived dichotomy between the work of Vuk and the Parry-Lord enterprise is due more to the reception of the work of each (both in the West and in the former Yugoslavia) than to the material itself. The songs collected by Vuk are viewed almost as literary, inviolate texts, certainly as part of a canon; they also are inextricably connected with the question of Serbian identity. The songs collected by Parry and Lord are viewed as the raw field data on which a theory was constructed, and some scholars (significantly, those lacking a knowledge of the original language) criticize the songs as falling short of the aesthetic standards associated with Western epic. Epic songs have been widely recorded also in Macedonia and Bulgaria, but none of these collections has been translated into English. One of their striking features is that women in these other regions sing epic as frequently as if not more than men.

Nonepic Genres

Other genres of South Slavic oral tradition that have been recorded and studied are folktales, proverbs, lyric songs, genealogies, laments, and charms. The folktales recorded by Vuk and by later collectors exemplify many of the basic tale types but also show a marked degree of oriental influence. Lyric songs, a category comprising calendrical, ritual, and non-context-sensitive songs, were collected in abundance both by Vuk and by Parry and Lord (Bartók and Lord). Laments and charms, by nature confined to the highly specific contexts of mourning and illness, were collected somewhat less systematically but have also been studied in some detail.[1]

Epic singing as described by Vuk and by Parry and Lord largely no longer exists, although it was alive until the Second World War. Its disappearance can be ascribed to the advent of widespread literacy and of mass communication, which destroyed most of the traditional audience for singing, and to the socialist government's conscious repackaging of folk art as something for the stage, which turned traditional singers of this best-known genre into rote performers. Other genres of oral tradition survived better and many can still be found, although with some difficulty, in the more rural areas. The level of difficulty has been rendered vastly greater, of course, by the wars and displacements of the 1990s.

Pedagogical Strategies

Most teachers wishing to include South Slavic oral tradition will focus on the epic song, partly because of its historical role in the nineteenth-century Romantic wave of folk song collecting and in the twentieth-century formation of the Parry-Lord theory and partly because of the relatively extensive amount of texts and commentary available in English translation. In addition to the historiographical issues discussed above, teachers will want to stress the relation of song to actual historical event (esp. the Kosovo songs), the similarities and differences between Christian and Muslim songs, and the difference between studying a formalized text of an epic song (such as those found in the Vuk collection) and comparing an epic performance recorded from a single singer with the acoustic recording of that performance. An excellent example of this kind of comparison is provided by "The Captivity of Djulić Ibrahim," in the first volume of *Serbo-Croatian Heroic Songs*: the multiple song texts, together with the extensive footnotes quoting from the conversation with the singer, are very valuable for studying the composition in performance of South Slavic epic. Recordings of these same performances are kept in the Parry collection; one hopes that excerpts may be made available to teachers once the digitalization of the recordings, now under way, is completed (for further information on South Slavic epic, see Foley, *Traditional Oral Epic* and *Immanent Art*).

Finally, it must be stressed that one of the most important elements in studying and teaching oral tradition is a focus on the traditional context in which it exists and is re-created. In this respect, the work of Joel Halpern and Barbara Kerewsky-Halpern in describing a traditional village environment is Serbia has been salutary (see also Halpern); the studies made by John Miles Foley and Kerewsky-Halpern of living oral tradition in this specific context thus take on more value. Teachers can use these sources both to present the general social context for oral tradition and to analyze one particular genre of traditional lore occurring in a particular context. In a region where cultures and nation-states are being forcibly ripped apart and where tradition is dying in a particularly violent manner, such studies are all the more valuable as a record of what has been lost throughout much of the land.

Note

1. On laments, see Kerewsky-Halpern; on charms, Foley, *Singer*, ch. 4; on folk songs, Lockwood; on heroic ballads, Noyes and Bacon.

John D. Niles

British American Balladry

"When is a ballad not a ballad?" Bertrand Bronson once asked (*Traditional Tunes* 1:9), knowing full well what would count as the right answer: When it has no tune. Although his riddle scarcely settles the matter of ballad definitions, it can serve as a point of departure for teachers who wish to enliven the study of oral traditions by bringing the subject of balladry off the printed page and into the fresh air.[1] With one sweep, Bronson brushed aside all Nortonized packets of timeless but tuneless ballad literature in favor of a range of resources that document what ballads sound like when sung aloud. Although museum texts will continue to provide an entry to the genre and will furnish some readers with a permanent home, there is little reason for teachers to rest content with printed texts, thereby depriving students of the chance to distinguish balladry, as a living genre, from works such as the *Odyssey* and *Beowulf* whose study may be critical for the understanding of oral traditions but whose relation to actual performance must remain in doubt.

Basic Sources

Bronson's four-volume anthology *The Traditional Tunes of the Child Ballads* (1959–72) will not soon be superseded as the basic resource for the study of traditional British American balladry. It more than supplements Francis James Child's five-volume collection *The English and Scottish Popular Ballads* (1882–98), which has proved to be one of the durable monuments of nineteenth-century literary scholarship. Bronson's work opens up essential dimensions for ballad study, because the great majority of his examples derives from the lips of singers, not from the manuscripts, books, and broadsides that were Child's chief sources. One can generally count on the accuracy of Bronson's examples as records of what was sung on a particular occasion, whereas with Child's collections one is often left guessing as to the extent to which editorial interventions have shaped the text. In addition, most of Bronson's examples come from the twentieth century and from North America rather than the British Isles, although England and Scotland are amply represented as well. His anthology thus encourages study not only of the music of the ballads but also of patterns of cultural change and diffusion that are not apparent from recourse to Child alone.[2]

Child's and Bronson's standard anthologies can be supplemented by comprehensive personal fieldwork collections like Peter Kennedy's *Folksongs of Britain and Ireland*, focused anthologies like Roy Palmer's *A Ballad History of England*, and major regional collections such as the multivolume Greig-Duncan collection from Aberdeenshire (gen. eds. Shuldham-Shaw and Lyle), the two ballad volumes included in the Frank C. Brown Collection of North Carolina Folklore (ed. Duke Univ. Lib.), and Vance Randolph's massive collection of folk song from the Ozarks, either in its 1980 full four volumes or as abridged with excellent annotations by Norm Cohen in 1982 (*Ozark Folksongs*). Useful teaching anthologies are also available in libraries, though no longer in print (e.g. Leach; Friedman, *Viking Book*; Bronson, *Singing Tradition*). Enough texts and tunes are thus at hand to occupy many an hour. Some essential things fall outside the scope of any anthology, however. Despite the wealth of textual and musical information that can be gained from anthologies, it is worth reviewing those areas where teachers need to turn to other sources if their approach to balladry is to be a nuanced one.

Definition of the Genre

Students who use most ballad anthologies will find little discussion of what it is they are studying. For the most part, editors of such anthologies give priority of place to the "Child ballad" — that is, to the English and Scottish popular ballad as canonized by Child — and yet Child never defined what he meant by either the adjective *popular* or the key noun *ballad*. Bronson spares himself spiny problems of definition by using Child's collection of 305 items as the basis of his own work. His solution has a practical appeal given the difficulty of ascertaining Child's criteria for inclusion and exclusion. Thelma James, reviewing Child's project and the changes it went through over time, found the idea of a Child ballad tautological: a Child ballad is something anthologized by Child in his 1882–98 collection, no more and no less.[3] Partly because of the difficulty of distinguishing among Child ballads, broadside ballads, literary ballads, ballads native to North America or Australia, and other subtypes of balladry, some scholars prefer to shift the ground of discussion away from "the ballad," which they fear may be only a reified scholarly entity since it does not correspond to singers' native generic classifications, to "traditional narrative song," a more supple and open-ended category though still not a native one. Even those scholars who accept the practical usefulness of Child's canon may wonder what assumptions underlie its arrangement of subtypes. Why are ballads of the supernatural put first? Why does Child include so many ballads that relate to history — to Scots border history, in particular — even when their claim to popular status is tenuous? Why does he leave so little room for comic songs and almost none for bawdy ones, when these are favorites in living tradition?[4] Good surveys such as Gordon Gerould's *The Ballad of Tradition* and David C. Fowler's *Literary History of the Popular Ballad*[5] do not necessarily address these questions. In view of these uncertainties, it is not surprising that current scholars tend to avoid unproductive debate about ballad definitions and origins. Mary Ellen Brown has recently suggested that the question of defining the ballad might best be subsumed under the question of ballad use: Who is appropriating the idea of a ballad, in what ways, for what purpose, and in what intellectual context?

Balladry as a Scholarly Discourse

A response to this last set of questions requires engagement with the history of ballad scholarship. Teachers will have to go to sources other than Child and Bronson if they wish to orient their students to the two-hundred-year-old scholarly discourse that, in effect, has created the ballad as a genre. In the late eighteenth century the term "ballad" was first used by scholars (not singers) to designate a short, stanzaic narrative poem or song, often in common meter, as distinguished from lyric poems or songs of other kinds. Since then, while a definition along those lines has generally been accepted, a proliferation of writings on the subject has disciplined many researchers to approach balladry in primitivist or romantic terms. Why was it so important to Cecil Sharp, for example — the Cambridge-educated dance master, lecturer, and educational reformer who was perhaps the most influential ballad collector of the twentieth century — to rid English folk song of urban working-class influence (Harker 172–97)? Why did numerous field-workers in the southern Appalachians, working in Sharp's shadow, perpetuate stereotypes of that region as a reflex of rural Elizabethan England, ignoring the region's connections to mainstream American culture (Whisnant)? If students are inclined to approach balladry as a rural genre that is the property of peasants, hillbillies, and the like, teachers can draw on research by such scholars as Dave Harker and David Whisnant to set forth an alternative view of the ballad as a form of popular culture that has evolved in close interaction with factors affecting industrial and post-industrial society as a whole.[6] Intersecting with the debate about primitivist stereotypes in ballad scholarship is the debate about how ballads are learned and performed: by rote or by the technique of fluid re-creation that has been shown to be typical of heroic songs recorded by singers of tales in the Balkans (Lord, *Singer of Tales*)? The literature on this subject is reviewed by Albert B. Friedman ("Oral-Formulaic Theory"), who takes issue with the thesis maintained by David Buchan, among others, that there was once a period when fluid re-creation was the norm. Debate along these lines is not likely to cease, particularly given the need to reconcile singers' habits of memorization with the indubitable fact that many ballads show a pattern of variation that is creative, not just degenerative (J. Niles, "Context").

The Importance of Context

Teachers who restrict their attention to the standard ballad anthologies will discover only minimal information about who sang a song, when, to whom, in what social setting, and with what response. How do traditional songs function in society? What work do they do as social transactions? During the last twenty-five years, as questions of context and performance have gained an increasingly dominant place in folkloric research, the dearth of information in early collections concerning the social uses of traditional song has come to seem critical. Still, some contextual information is available in folksong collections published during the earlier years of this century (e.g., by Alfred Williams in England or Arthur Palmer Hudson in the United States), and a good deal is included in collections published more recently (e.g., by Hugh Shields in Ireland or Anne Warner in the United States). Attention to a social milieu also implies some engagement with those individual singers who inhabit it. In 1973 Herschel Gower posted a Wanted sign to stimulate collectors to provide information about singers' lives and critical reflections, supplementing this call with a case study of the Scots ballad singer Jeannie Robertson ("Wanted"; "Jeannie Robertson"). This research has now culminated in a major book by James Porter and Gower on this monumental figure of twentieth-century folk song.

Other case studies of individual singers are Roger Abrahams's study of the Ozark singer Almeda Riddle (*Singer*), Robin Morton's portrait of the Irish singer John Maguire, and Edward Ives's three studies of local songwriters from the northeastern states and provinces (*Joe Scott*, *Larry Gorman*, *Lawrence Doyle*). In keeping with the shift of emphasis from folklore to lore folk, Thomas Burton has organized an anthology of southern Appalachian materials around the singers rather than the songs, Ian Russell has edited a useful set of essays on particular singers and song communities of the British Isles, and William McCarthy has set the ballads of Agnes Lyle, an important early nineteenth-century source, into her Scottish regional context. In a broad sense, attention to context also implies an appreciation of how a body of traditional figurative language, including metaphor, is activated in particular social circumstances. Approaching folk song as a means of interpersonal communication, Barre Toelken has written on the ballad as a process of song giving and song receiving governed by semiotic systems that are often adapted to an immediate occasion (*Morning Dew*). By following leads like these, teachers can approach balladry not only as a literary and musical form but also as a nuanced social act.

The Influence of Cheap Print

In the past, perhaps assuming that cheap print kills oral tradition rather than serving as one of its nutrients, scholars influenced by Child have tended to discount the extent to which the popular press has served to disseminate traditional balladry. To take one example: overwhelmed by the enormous popularity of a song like "Barbara Allen," scholars have needed reminding that one reason this song is sung so widely is that it has been reprinted so often on broadsides and other products of the popular press (Cray, "Barbara Allen"). The elitist bias that some early ballad scholars directed against the broadside press need not be perpetuated. Supplementing standard works by Victor Neuburg and by Leslie Shepard are studies by Rainer Wehse ("Ballad"), Dianne Dugaw (*Warrior Women*, "Anglo-American Folksong"), and Natascha Würtzbach that document the rise of the broadside trade and analyze its interface with singing traditions. If teachers have no easy access to archival collections of broadside ballads (see Wehse, *Schwanklied* for a list of resources), they can consult published facsimiles, for example, *The Euing Collection of Broadside Ballads* (ed. U of Glasgow Lib.) and John Holloway and Joan Black's *Later English Broadside Ballads*. These two collections contain many examples of popular black-letter broadsides (of the seventeenth century) and white-letter broadsides (of the eighteenth and nineteenth centuries), respectively.

Sound Recordings

For practical reasons, few printed anthologies include sample recordings of actual performances. At most, anthologies provide a schematic diagram of voiced song in the form of printed tunes.[7] Particularly since few students are blessed with musical literacy equal to their textual literacy, such scores are of limited practical use. Fortunately, a wealth of British American recorded folk song is available on record album, audiocassette, and compact disc (see Daskalopoulos, this volume, for further information). One helpful resource is *The Long Harvest*, a ten-album set of ballad variants that Ewan MacColl and Peggy Seeger recorded with their own stylish arrangements. A good complementary resource, the ten-album series titled *Folksongs of Britain* edited by Peter Kennedy and Alan Lomax, consists entirely of field recordings featuring little-known traditional singers. Some of these recordings can be counted on to provide the culture shock that ought to accompany anyone's entry to the unmediated world of traditional song. Over the years the Library of Congress has issued many albums featuring American folk song and folk music recorded in Washington, DC, and in the field. The double album *The Muckle Sangs*, edited by Hamish Henderson, offers a sampling of the archival resources of the School of Scottish Studies at the University of Edinburgh. Teachers trying to locate recorded examples of a precise song may lament the lack of a comprehensive indexed guide to sound recordings. One invaluable aid is Beverly Boggs and Daniel Patterson's index of recorded folk song and folk music in the holdings of the University of North Carolina, Chapel Hill, for the Chapel Hill collection is so inclusive as to serve as a rough guide to the field. Another resource now available to individual researchers as well as libraries (though few libraries will have it yet) is a very comprehensive electronic *Folksong Index* (together with a *Broadside Index*), compiled by Steve Roud.[8]

These are some directions that teachers can take. Other perspectives await exploration, as well, especially if teachers wish to go beyond study of the ballad, narrowly defined, to take into account traditional song in general. Teachers wishing to explore the representation of folk-song subjects in the visual arts can take a recent study by Archie Green as their starting point. Those interested in the folksong revival can make use of Ailie Munro's book on the revival in Scotland or David Dunaway's study of Pete Seeger, or they might be able to obtain a video version of the recent PBS program *Folkways: A Vision Shared*, featuring the legacy of Woody Guthrie and Huddie Ledbetter. Songs featured in this program are available on LP or CD (see also *Folkways: The Original Vision*). Whenever I introduce contemporary recordings to the classroom, I never fail to find students who are familiar with "folk rock" or "electric folk" transformations of traditional songs and who are quick to provide me with tapes of favorite performances. Finally, students in a course involving balladry can easily draw on themselves or their family or friends as informants, thus turning the classroom into a laboratory for the study of oral tradition. In this way, going beyond sound recordings, students can engage directly with ballad singing as a form of social interaction.

––––––

In sum, why are ballads important to people interested in teaching oral traditions? Although many answers to this question might be given, I would single out two.

First, study of balladry can yield important insights into the workings of oral tradition in society. As a popular genre, balladry has been with us since the late Middle Ages, emerging gradually out of a crossing of a number of other genres.[9] As individual songs have developed over time, sometimes over a period of centuries, they have evolved in a complex counterpoint of oral tradition and print and have been subject, in either form, to influences and pressures affecting society as a whole. Traversing the seas with successive waves of emigrants, Old World ballads have taken root in various forms in both North America and Australia, all the while adapting to radically new cultural environments. Old song types have given rise to new ones; for example, songs celebrating Robin Hood and other Old World outlaw heroes have served as models for new songs celebrating outlaws of the American West (Steckmesser). Wherever traditional balladry has flourished, it has functioned as a mirror of social tensions and concerns and, occasionally, as an instrument of cultural adaptation. Study of balladry can thus well illustrate the ways in which local cultures are shaped through use of the materials of tradition. One research assignment that I favor is to ask students to choose a single ballad and report on its patterns of variation. As they follow one song through its changes over time, students not only familiarize themselves with a vast range of resources that are available for the study of balladry, they also gain insight into social factors that have affected how people think as well as how people use traditional song as a medium for individual or group expression.

Second, the study of balladry is of special interest for what it can tell about the nature of vernacular creativity. Since few if any genres based centrally on oral tradition have been documented as fully as has the ballad, study of balladry affords unparalleled insights into the contribution of individual tradition bearers to the making of an oral culture. Another research assignment I favor is to ask students to make a case study of a particular singer. They are thus led to appreciate the role of the strong tradition bearer who powers an oral culture (J. Niles, "Role"). By examining one person's style, repertory, sources, and song community, they can gain insights into how individual talent affects the dynamics of oral tradition. They can explore how one person's repertory reflects a particular worldview and connects to larger group allegiances centering on region, class, religion, or some other entity. An abstract term such as "oral tradition" thereby gains a local habitation and specific contours.

Balladry can be studied from many other perspectives, of course: as a species of fine literature, as the darling of the popular press, as a repository of ancient folklore, as a set of records relating to history, as a weapon of social conflict, as a means of dramatizing psychological issues that are otherwise difficult to articulate, and as a still viable form for contemporary singers and songwriters, to name a few possibilities. Any teacher who wishes to introduce students to the full range of English literature would do well to teach popular balladry alongside elite poetry and fiction. Those with an interest in oral traditions can profit from study of its astoundingly complex patterns of variation. Anyone at all who delights in the products of the imagination ought to be able to enjoy a genre that projects bedrock human concerns — courtship, parental control, sibling rivalry, death and bereavement, supernatural interventions into ordinary life, and other perennial themes — into the form of a story told in song.

Notes

1. Because of constraints of space, this essay deals only with English-language balladry. On the Hispanic tradition of balladry, see Herrera-Sobek, this volume; Zemke, this volume.
2. Coffin provides a helpful guide to the Child ballad in North America. Laws, in his *American Balladry from British Broadsides*, surveys non-Child ballads that have crossed over to North America and provides a working typology for the broadside ballad. Laws has also written the definitive catalogue of traditional ballads of North American origin (*Native American Balladry*). Cartwright has made a fine case study of how one ballad has adapted to different conditions in Scotland and North America.
3. On Child's background, achievement, and biases, see further Harker 101–37; Bell, "No Borders."
4. Although these questions cannot be answered here at any length, it is worth noting that the emergence of the ballad as a scholarly genre coincides roughly with the vogue of the gothic mode in fiction, the enormous popularity of Sir Walter Scott's novels of Scots border history, and the rise of Victorian middle-class prudery. Child's favoritism for tragic ballads may relate to his desire to create, through the corpus of balladry, a kind of English-language national epic dignified enough to stand comparison with the great literary monuments of any land. To combat prudery, Cray has edited a major unexpurgated collection of American bawdy songs, *The Erotic Muse*, but make sure your library keeps it under lock and key; it has a way of disappearing.
5. In a contribution to the *Manual of the Writings in Middle English*, Fowler also offers a valuable, chronologically arranged survey of both medieval

and postmedieval sources for study of the Child ballad subgenre ("Ballads").

6. Again, no lengthy answers can be given to these questions here, but it is worth stressing that twentieth-century ballad studies, like modern folklore studies in general, have not often been exempt from nostalgia for a simple rural past, associated with communitarian values, as a refuge from the aggressive world of urban industrial capitalism. Those teachers who wish to review the course of early ballad scholarship will find much of interest in Hustvedt and in Wilgus. Dugaw's casebook of scholarly articles on the ballad (*Anglo-American Ballad*) provides judiciously selected examples illustrating the main currents of debate (see also Dugaw, "Folksong"). Richmond's annotated bibliography of ballad scholarship provides many additional references.

7. An exception is P. Kennedy. Folktracks Cassettes (P. Kennedy's label) has issued audio cassettes with musical examples that are featured in the first sixteen chapters of *Folksongs of Britain and Ireland*; see P. Kennedy for ordering information (15).

8. *Folksong Index* and *Broadside Index*, published by Hisarlik Press, are available on diskette from the Vaughan Williams Memorial Library, Cecil Sharp House, 2 Regents Park Road, London NW1 7AY. The Roud indexes include references to both sound recordings and printed texts.

9. I am thinking here particularly of the romance, the carol, the fabliau, the lay, the riddle, and the lyric poem, but by no means does this list exhaust the sources of balladry as a genre.

Steven Swann Jones

Teaching the Folktale Tradition

Like legends, epics, myths, and other forms of folk literature, the folktale genre is a product of oral tradition, evolving over years, passing from performer to performer, spanning cultures and continents, and outliving generations. Accordingly, instructors need a specialized understanding of the nature of oral literature to introduce their students to folktales. While numerous texts offer valuable strategies for approaching this topic, my purpose here is to provide a concise introduction to the main issues and pedagogical strategies relevant to the study of folktales.[1]

Overcoming the Bias against Folktales

The proper starting point for the study of folktales is cultivating an appreciation of their oral heritage. Since we encounter our students in the context of an education that values literacy, there exists a tendency to ignore or dismiss the products of oral communication as insubstantial and therefore inferior. This tendency is particularly true for folktales, which do not carry the social prestige of other genres of folk narrative, such as myth or legend. Folktales are generally thought of as frivolous entertainment and thus as unlikely subjects for serious study. This literary bias must be addressed and corrected before any significant understanding and appreciation of folktales can be achieved.

One useful strategy for cultivating an appreciation for the products of oral tradition is to present an overview with extensive examples, not just of the many folktales that have enchanted audiences for generations but of other oral genres as well. Citing dozens of popular folktales, legends, and myths and linking these artistic creations together through their oral roots and method of transmission begins the process of reestablishing their cultural importance and lays the foundation for a more detailed investigation. Students can then focus on the nature of oral creation and transmission of verbal art and explore the fascinating way in which the components and techniques of narration are borrowed, shared, and adapted by successive storytellers.

The Transmission of Folktales

The next issue that needs to be addressed is how folktales are created and transmitted through oral tradition. Folktales are particularly valuable for studying the process of oral transmission, because we can find multiple versions of essentially the same story (the shared plot outline of these different versions is termed a tale type by folklorists). One useful assignment is to have students find multiple versions from different cultures of a favorite fairy tale or other folktale and then assess the similarities and differences. From this comparative study, students can gain a concrete sense of how narratives live in oral tradition. It is important to find cross-cultural examples for a number of reasons. Versions within the same culture are frequently simply different editions of a single oral text and thus reflect the process of literary editing, not the process of oral transmission. Furthermore, the degree of stylistic variation and of thematic stability can be fully appreciated only from a range of examples from different cultures and languages (where available in translation, of course). Of particular usefulness in this endeavor is Antti Aarne and Stith Thompson's *The Types of the Folktale: A Classification and Bibliography*, which provides an extensive list of the major folktales ("Cinderella," "Snow White," "Jack and the Beanstalk," etc.) and identifies some bibliographical sources for finding versions of these tales.

In addition to understanding the nature of oral tradition, and especially the principles of oral transmission, students need to appreciate the context and techniques of oral performance. Having a traditional storyteller present a selection of narratives provides an invaluable opportunity for studying the phenomenon of oral literature firsthand. (To locate available storytellers, instructors could contact local libraries or state or regional agencies that support traditional arts, such as the Ohio Arts Council or the California Council for the Humanities. See Birch, this volume.) After listening to a storyteller, students can grasp the extent to which the audience helps to shape the performance and accordingly the material of the storyteller. They can also see the relation among the different stories in the repertoire of the chosen storyteller. Here again, folktales represent an especially valuable subject for studying oral tradition, inasmuch as many accomplished performers of folktales can be found throughout American subcultures, and thus provide a wonderful resource for the classroom.

The Classification of Folktales

Once students achieve a sense of the fundamental process of oral tradition and its performance context, the range of examples in the folktale tradition leads them inevitably to the issue of classification. Is there some basis on which the numerous examples may be categorized and organized? While some scholars question the legitimacy of superimposing theoretical categories on the free-ranging specimens of folklore, other scholars have found the distinctions among myth, legend, and folktale to be useful. However, most scholars recognize that within specific cultures and ethnic groups the appropriateness of these abstractions may vary. Some societies categorize their narratives according to other principles — narratives told during harvest versus those told during the rainy season, or narratives considered to be true versus those considered to be untrue. Furthermore, even when narrators themselves have a sense of the basic genres of myth, legend, and folktale, they will play with them and sometimes dress a narrative commonly associated with one genre, such as a legend about a monster slayer like Beowulf, in the guise of another genre, such as a folktale about an anonymous youth who happens to kill a monster much in the way that Beowulf slays Grendel.

Two principles need to be emphasized here. First, there are certain identifiable generic paradigms and characteristics, on both ethnographic and cross-cultural levels, that are manifested in the tales, and we need to acknowledge them. Most cultures have myths about deities that describe the cosmos, legends about exemplary historical figures that embody social values and ideals, and folktales about ordinary figures that depict our quotidian concerns and personal desires (Bascom, "Forms"). The basic form and function of these three major genres seem remarkably consistent among different storytellers and across a variety of cultures. Second, that narrators play with these generic conventions is evidence that they are aware of them. So, in the attempt to catalog the varieties of folk literature, a good starting point is to distinguish among stories about ordinary protagonists (folktales), stories about extraordinary protagonists (legends), and stories about immortal or primordial protagonists (myths). In this schema, the subgenres of folktale would include fairy tales (ordinary protagonists who encounter a magical realm where they are tested in order to prove their worth), fables (ordinary protagonists whose actions are designed to illustrate a clear moral and didactic lesson), romantic tales (ordinary protagonists who engage in common human experiences), and jokes (ordinary protagonists who exemplify our ability to laugh at ourselves). Finding examples of these different subgenres and comparing their characteristics can promote an appreciation of generic classifications and can lead to the more important issue of why these genres exist — how their form is a product of some underlying function (see further S. Jones, *Tale*; Lüthi; Thompson, *Folktale*; Holbek, *Interpretation*).

The Interpretation of Folktales

Studying the meaning of folktales is the most problematic and potentially the most rewarding aspect of this subject. The devaluing of oral narratives by students, especially of the folktale genre, which is commonly thought of as offering simply juvenile and trivial entertainment, interferes with students' ability to see how these narratives serve important functions for their audiences. The pedagogical challenge facing instructors is to reveal to students the underlying themes, the intellectual content of these tales—how the tales show us our inner feelings and fears, promote certain social values and ideologies, or offer spiritual guidance and nourishment. There is a wealth of scholarship analyzing the themes and messages implicitly conveyed by folktales, and while these studies may argue among themselves about which meanings are predominant, taken as a whole they document the existence of a rich world of ideas that lies beneath the surface of the intriguing images and captivating events of folktales. It is incumbent on students of this genre of oral narrative to begin to offer some explanation for its existence. One way for them to get a handle on the enormous diversity of interpretive approaches to folktales is to contrast the psychological lessons found in a folktale (e.g., Bettelheim's oedipal assessment of "Snow White" [199–215]), the social messages of the tale (e.g., Gilbert and Gubar's feminist reading of "Snow White" [ch.1]), and the cosmic insights of the tale (e.g., Girardot's spiritual interpretation of Snow White's ordeal). Seeing the range of meanings generated by the provocative motifs of folktales can stimulate an awareness of just how deep these products of hundreds of years and generations of storytellers can be.

The wealth of folktale examples and the breadth of their influence on our culture makes them an important and promising subject of study. But to understand and appreciate folktales properly, we must first recognize their oral traditional heritage and assess them in their performance context, as products of a specialized process of oral transmission with particular forms and inherited conventions bearing a rich harvest of semiotically encoded messages. Knowing the generic paradigms of oral literature and understanding how they have been passed down and what they are trying to teach can lead us to a better understanding of who we are and of whom we want to become. Both the tales and their study can be rewarding journeys of self-discovery if we are critically prepared before we set off.

In the Classroom

One of the great advantages of teaching folktales is their general appeal and accessibility for students. Since most students are already familiar with a substantial number of folktales and since new ones may be easily introduced, folktales are an extremely profitable vehicle for instruction. Students are generally eager to talk about these stories and the lessons and values they promote.

Accordingly, a Socratic method of classroom instruction is highly recommended. Instructors should begin with questions about the form and classification of a given text. These questions may then lead naturally into a discussion of what lessons the students feel the stories offer and what functions the stories serve for their audiences. The richness of the texts, the colorful and stimulating motifs (the spinning wheel in "Rapunzel," the magic mirror in "Snow White," the giant in "Jack and the Beanstalk," or the glass slipper in "Cinderella") can provide the impetus for more incisive analysis, as the instructor asks students why they think a particular detail is present in the story.

The theoretical principles reviewed above lead to the fundamental premise that folktales are integral and coherent works of art in which every detail is essential and relevant. Knowing that the parts of the folktale are not there arbitrarily but indeed serve a purpose fosters a classroom strategy where the students try to account for the specific elements that constitute an artistic and cultural phenomenon. The analysis becomes something of an intellectual challenge or mystery, as students offer possible explanations for the clues with which they have been presented. By asking the class to answer the question of why these stories take the shape they do, the instructor is pointing students in the appropriate critical direction but ultimately letting them solve the riddle themselves. Watching students work toward understanding the magic of folktales is a most gratifying experience for teachers.

Note

1. To get a sense of the international richness of this field, see Thompson, *One Hundred*; Abrahams, *African Folktales* and *Afro-American Folktales*; Muhawi and Kanaana; Erdoes and Ortiz; Dorson, *Folktales*.

Marta Weigle

Women's Expressive Forms

A woman is the first named author in the world's written literature. The daughter of Sargon the Great of Akkad, Enheduanna (c. 2285– 2250 BC) composed a corpus of poetry in Sumerian, including a cycle of poems to the goddess Inanna and a cycle honoring Sargon's achievements. Enheduanna enjoyed privilege as high priestess at Ur and Uruk in Sumer and is today known as an exceptional participant in generally male-dominated ritual-literary traditions. Her unprivileged, unexceptional sisters then and since remain for the most part anonymous and mute, denied official media and public occasions but unofficially no less capable and creative in more immediate, often private oral expression.

Until recently, it has been difficult to analyze and appreciate women's expressive forms simply because those forms were not considered except when related to the female domestic sphere and work, reproductive life cycle, or child rearing (de Caro ix–xiv). Most fieldworkers were men and, even if so inclined, were not necessarily permitted to interact with, let alone study, women in the groups they researched. Male rather than female versions of field-collected texts were more likely to be edited and interpreted for publication. On the whole, both the ethnographic and the historical records long remained basically androcentric; women's expression, oral or otherwise, was not considered a worthy focus for and measure of the creative, aesthetic uses of language in a full range of social situations and cultural contexts.

However, studying women's expressive forms is not simply a matter of complementing accepted definitions and gendered domains by recovering, recording, and interpreting examples of women in language, folklore, and mythology; it is also a matter of "revisioning" oral tradition by exploring instances of women and their uses of these symbol systems (e.g., Stoeltje, *Feminist Revisions*; Mills, "Theory"). Very often these reinterpretations and strategic adaptations of acknowledged genres, as well as women's elaboration of forms not ordinarily considered artful, enrich understandings of verbal art performance. Thus, for example, interpreting more myths about goddesses and heroines recounted on public ceremonial occasions is of less importance than reconsidering narrative processes developed over time through gossip or during other ordinary conversations among women or between them and men or children.

The following heuristic notes on women and humoring, women and speaking, and women and storying are keyed by the classical mythological figures of Arachne, Philomela, and Penelope. Each epigraphic text involves weaving, associated in classical Greece literally with women and metaphorically with poets and prophets, and the notion of *mêtis*, what Ann L. T. Bergren calls weaving's "intellectual counterpart"—transformative power that is "a strategy of deception, the plot itself, and the mental ability to devise one" (73). Both the craft and the cunning are articulated by the goddesses Metis (Wisdom or Invention) and her daughter Athena, patron of weaving and expert in all such "trickiness." Classical *mêtis* resembles the coding, "covert expressions of disturbing or subversive ideas," that Joan Newlon Radner claims to be characteristic of women's folk culture and "a common phenomenon in the lives of women, who have so often been dominated, silenced, and marginalized by men" (vii).

Humoring

In his *Metamorphoses* (c. AD 8), the Roman poet Ovid recounts how the very talented weaver Arachne's hubris leads her to challenge and angrily curse Athena, who appears in the guise of an old woman (see Weigle, *Spiders* 8–11). During their ensuing competition, Athena weaves scenes of mortals' attempts to usurp immortals' powers, while Arachne portrays a catalog of gods known for seducing or raping goddesses and mortal women. Enraged at finding no flaw in Arachne's work, Athena beats her until in despair Arachne hangs herself. The goddess then takes some pity and revives her rival as a tirelessly weaving spider. Weaving is the vehicle for passionate encounter.

The four cardinal humors — blood, phlegm, choler, and melancholy — figured significantly in classical and traditional Western medicine as fundamental aspects of an individual's health and disposition. Humor has come to be associated primarily with disposition: a mood or state of mind, the emotive, generally considered the women's domain. Catherine Lutz claims that cultural beliefs "identifying emotion primarily with irrationality, subjectivity, the chaotic and other negative characteristics, and . . . subsequently labelling women as the emotional gender, . . . reinforce the ideological subjugation of women" (288). Humor in the sense of the comic, however, has more often been considered a male province.

The association of women with the emotional in humoring may be seen in the comparative study of music, frequently viewed as an especially moving form of expressive culture. Lullabies are commonly attributed to women, but so too is provocative singing. Many cross-cultural studies note links between women's sexuality and expectations about their musical behavior, and "some describe performances which include licentious sexual behavior, ranging from 'flirting' to actual copulation during performances" (Koskoff 3).

Mourning and lament traditions are frequently the province of women, some of whom may be professional lamenters. In a rural northwest Greek village studied by Susan Auerbach, for instance, women lament with grief and complaint while men sing, dance, and play instruments with joy and celebration; men never lament, and those women who choose to sing and dance publicly risk loss of reputation. Musical sound itself is so evocative of grief or joy "that even listening to the radio is taboo for mourners" (27). The two sexes are also thought to cry differently, but nothing is said about differential laughter.

K. M. Tiwary's characterization of men's and women's speech in northern India concentrates on women's "tuneful weeping," used on a variety of occasions ranging from greeting, visiting, leave-taking, and quarreling to a complex of marriage and mortuary rituals. Learned in part through doll play in girlhood, tuneful weeping is recognized as an artistic form. A weeping partner is required, and such emotionally supportive relationships may be compared with joking relationships, the sort of licensed aggression in verbal dueling and teasing more often thought to characterize male than female socialization and same-sex humoring.

Comic humor, aggressive or not, is highly sensitive to historical circumstance, social context, and individual psychology. Examination of jokes and joke telling, for example, will show that gender is but one variable of many affecting the creation, appreciation, and morphology of comic behavior. In a popular study of women's strategic use of humor in mainstream American society, the literature scholar Regina Barreca has chapters entitled "Do Good Girls Laugh with Their Mouths Open? Why Making a Joke Is Like Making a Pass," "'It's Hard to Be Funny When You Have to Be Clean': Sexual Differences in Humor Appreciation / Differences in Sexual Humor Appreciation," and "She Who Laughs, Lasts: The Importance of Defining and Using Our Own Humor."

Women's experiences with humor, particularly among women only, and women humorists have received comparatively little scholarly attention. A notable exception is Rayna Green, who in a 1977 essay, "Magnolias Grow in Dirt: The Bawdy Lore of Southern Women," introduced her maternal grandmother's "bad mouth" and later made it central to reflections entitled "'It's Okay Once You Get It [a tampon] past the Teeth' and Other Feminist Paradigms for Folklore Studies." She suggests that ignoring her grandmother's repertoire of outrageous humorous acts and her "delight in upsetting our notions of proper behavior" means overlooking genres as important to women as the generally recognized ones like "word play, recitation of doggerel, the embellished story, or a gospel hymn" (qtd. in Hollis, Pershing, and Young 1–2).

Speaking

Ovid gives a version of Philomela's story, which is also outlined by Apollodorus in the *Library* (c. AD 120), a handbook of Greek mythology (Weigle, *Creation* 183–84, 36): Tereus hides his wife, Procne, and son, Itys, in the country so he may seduce and marry Procne's sister, Philomela, whose tongue he cuts out. Philomela informs her sister of the rape by weaving letters in a robe, and Procne kills her son, boils him, and serves him to his unwitting father. The sisters flee with Tereus in pursuit, and eventually all three are turned into birds. In the Greek version, Philomela becomes the tongueless, incoherently chattering swallow.

Speaking is not simply a matter of knowing the language; to be heard, speakers must also use that language or its dialects appropriately for the social situation at hand. Whether or not to use profanity, grammatically correct forms, or intimate address, for example, depends on the setting of and participants in a particular social occasion. Sometimes silence is the only permissible form of speech, as in the proverb "Children should be seen and not heard." Sometimes people's speech is stigmatized as lower-class, foreign-accented, or too loud, and they must make efforts to overcome such social handicaps in order to make themselves heard.

The first English-language book on women's folklore, Thomas Firminger Thiselton-Dyer's *Folk-lore of Women as Illustrated by Legendary and Traditional Tales, Folk-Rhymes, Proverbial Sayings, Superstitions, Etc.*, includes the chapter "Woman's Tongue," where a woman's tongue is characterized primarily in "proverbal wisdom" (63). Thiselton-Dyer, a British clergyman, begins his account by comparing two sets of paired proverbs: "A silent woman is always more admired than a noisy one" (English) and "A woman's tongue is her sword, and she does not let it rust" (Chinese); "For talk I'm best, for work my elder brother-in-law's wife" (Hindustani) and "A woman's strength is in her tongue" (English) (63). He then proceeds to caution, "But, granted the effective use made by this weapon, the teachers of old were of opinion that 'Silence is the best ornament of a woman'; or, as another version expresses it, 'Silence is a fine jewel for a woman, but it is little worn'" (64). Content analysis of other proverbs and proverb collections yields similar, often contradictory and derogatory perspectives on women's speech.

Proverbs are not simply stored wisdom but rhetorical devices used strategically in interaction. Thus, the familiar "A whistling girl and a crowing hen will come to no good end" is not just a saying possibly derived from old notions of women witches being able to whistle up a storm (Weigle, *Spiders* 296) but also an artistic way to silence or at least marginalize those who might contest accepted gender domains. Such domains extend to conversation itself, and the sociolinguist Deborah Tannen contends that women's and men's different conversational styles are a source of much misunderstanding. Claiming that "each person's life is lived as a series of conversations" (13), she shows how men in mainstream American society generally expect talk to involve hierarchical "negotiations in which people try to achieve and maintain the upper hand if they can" while protecting themselves from others' attempts to dominate them. Women, however, view conversation as "a network of connections . . . negotiations for closeness in which people try to seek and give confirmation and support, and to reach consensus" (24–25).

Gossip is one named form of conversation that has received much scholarly and popular attention. By 1811, it was recognized both negatively and positively in the English language as "Idle talk; trifling or groundless rumour; tittle-tattle. Also, in a more favourable sense: Easy, unrestrained talk or writing, esp. about persons or social incidents" (*OED*). Because gossip deals informally and privately in particulars, personalities, and personal relationships, it is often viewed as a form of resistance to dominant, official, and public culture, as the province of those unwilling or unable to address issues openly.

Men certainly gossip, but women are popularly believed to be gossips, a definition first noted in 1566: "A person, mostly a woman, of light and trifling character, esp. one who delights in idle talk; a news monger, a tattler" (*OED*). However, in Old English *godsibb* meant "god-related," the ritually established relationships between godparents, whereas Middle English usage of *godsibb* designated familiar acquaintances of either sex, especially a woman's female friends invited to attend her during childbirth. Samuel Johnson gives as his third dictionary definition of gossip: "One who runs about tattling like women at a lying-in" (qtd. in Spacks 26). By Victorian times ascendant male obstetricians forbade female gossips during labor because they were too "noisy." Although the talk during midwifery, especially if only women are assisting in the birth event, has not received sufficient notice (Weigle, *Creation* 163–76), the godsiblingship and artistry of gossip and all ordinary as well as salon conversation (e.g., Bodek; Orenstein; "Salons") should be considered important women's expressive forms.

Storying

Homer's *Odyssey* opens with Athena's contriving to bring Odysseus home to Ithaca after the Trojan War. She visits his son, Telemakhos, in a once-great house now invaded by rowdy suitors for the hand of Telemakhos's mother. Although freed by her husband's parting words that she could marry again when their son was bearded, the enigmatic Penelope has devised a ruse to delay remarriage until she finishes a shroud for Odysseus's father, Laertes. Weaving by day and secretly unraveling the work at night, she confronts trials at home parallel to those Odysseus encounters on his return journey. Triumphant "on her own terms, the Penelope who emerges by the end of the poem is a forceful figure who operates imaginatively within the constraints of her situation and succeeds in keeping her options open until she reaches safety in her husband's embrace" (Felson-Rubin vii).

Storying is part of virtually every aspect of social life. It ranges from gossip and personal-experience narratives to creation myths. Recognized genres of narrative — the magic tale, the ballad, the epic, the chronicle, the romance — have different kinds of heroes and heroines. In Western cultures, oral epics have provided significant narrative models for heroism.

There is no *penelopy* equivalent to *odyssey* in English usage, and a heroine is not usually thought integral to heroic traditions. Ironically, the classical Hero (although etymologically unrelated) was a priestess of Aphrodite who lived in a tower at Sestos on the European shore of the Hellespont, or Dardanelles. At a festival honoring Adonis, she met and fell passionately in love with Leander, a young man from Abydus on the Asian side. He performed heroic feats by swimming the mile or so of sea channel to rendezvous with his beloved, whose only action was faithfully to light the beacon for his swim and later to throw herself from crag or tower to join him in death (Weigle, *Spiders* 197).

Nevertheless, ancient Greek heroines are mentioned from the time of Homer to around the third century BC. Concisely defined, such a heroine is a "cult recipient who, according to her devotees, was at one time a mortal woman" (Larson 3). Heroine cults were widespread but "still in many cases secondary or parallel to cults of male figures" (4). They did not significantly influence later Western notions of heroism, which for the most part were based on patriarchal, usually male warrior, values.

Heroes are constructed by those who proclaim them, for example, by the singers of epic tales in many warrior traditions. Any society's folktales may serve as narrative models for heroism. Märchen, or magic tales, have long done so in European and European-derived traditions. Literary collections like the famous ones by the Brothers Grimm usually portray women as passive heroines who await transformation from others, not as active agents of their own destiny like their male counterparts. But when such narratives are collected from women, men, and children in field context and actual performance (e.g., Falassi; Taggart), they challenge restrictive, conventional definitions and interpretations based on literary texts. The active and the passive, the masculine and the feminine, are not so clear-cut and may be negotiated during the course of telling and evaluating a single tale, a series of tales on one occasion, or a number of tales over time.

Historically influential hero studies — Otto Rank's *The Myth of the Birth of the Hero* (1909), Lord Raglan's *The Hero: A Study in Tradition, Myth, and Drama* (1936), and Joseph Campbell's *Hero with a Thousand Faces* (1949) — use male exemplars for the typical biographical patterns they delineate. If women are mentioned at all, they are exceptional and, like Joan of Arc, often portrayed as not much different from the men discussed (Weigle, *Spiders* 198–202). Because such biographical-pattern hero studies — and these include psychological and psychoanalytic works and case studies — are so androcentric, life passages unique to women (menstruation, parturition, menopause) are overlooked entirely in the essentially normative analyses. In mainstream American society, men's personal (autobiographical, life-history, biographical) narratives seldom address gender dynamics, while women's personal narratives are, among other things, stories of how women negotiate their exceptional gender status both in their daily lives and over the course of a lifetime. Women's narratives assume that one can understand a life only if one takes into account gender roles and gender expectations. Whether a woman has accepted the norms or defied them, her life can never be written [or told] taking gender for granted (Personal Narratives Group 4–5).

Heroism is constantly redefined, as even simple surveys of people's present and past heroes and heroines and the reasons people choose them readily demonstrate. Whether real or fictional, divine or mortal, historical or living, female or male, active or passive, celebrity-like or personally known, the figures chosen speak directly to contemporary and traditional social and personal values. Even the survey response "no hero" or "no heroine" is instructive. Some may feel that acknowledging personal heroes and heroines is too revealing, too juvenile, too patriarchal, or too accepting of the myriad, momentary, media-constructed heroes and celebrities in contemporary culture. Heroism today may be dead or irrelevant, but it may also be articulate in new and unexpected material, musical, and verbal ways.

Like humoring and speaking, storying constitutes social life.

Women's expressive forms, because they are less often acclaimed as part of formal, public, high-culture occasions, redirect attention from the extraordinary, other-time, and otherworldly to the ordinary, present, everyday events and protagonists of this world. They compel a revaluation of the mundane and the considerable arts of daily living.

Carol L. Birch

Storytelling: Practice and Movement

Five years into a storytelling career begun in 1971, I recognized that a larger purpose of my work would be to contribute to the development of an aesthetic and critical language for the consideration of storytelling as a form of conscious, platform performance. Since that time, it seems as if storytelling is everywhere. The term almost becomes meaningless as it is bandied about to cover oral, print, and multimedia events. With its associations of warmth from firesides and from shared memories of belonging, the word is appealing in part because it breaks through the chill and isolation of contemporary lives. "Kodak—America's Storyteller!" the ads read. Reviews announce that this writer or filmmaker is destined to be one of America's greatest storytellers. Reporters in small towns and big cities regularly proclaim the news that people "still tell stories," you can hear one at a local festival, and so forth. Only the names and locations of the next storytelling event change in these reports. There are no reviews of the performances themselves, just promotional articles. There doesn't seem to be a generally known way to approach story occasions with a variety of settings, audiences, tellers, and material from both oral and print sources. People who know nothing about theater history and criticism are able to say when something is too avant-garde, but language for evaluating storytelling tends to be bound to the "other" disciplines. Even within the storytelling community, there is a lack of consensus on terms distinctive to the art. How-to techniques and homages to the cult of personality dominate the written material in storytelling journals.

Teaching Storytelling

Over the years my thinking about storytelling has changed, as have my goals for the college and university courses I taught from 1977 to the present. Initially I taught storytelling in California for evening adult education classes at UCLA and Long Beach College. I presently teach in Connecticut, in graduate programs offered at Wesleyan University and Southern Connecticut State University. This essay charts issues that have affected my search for a critical language.

Basic criteria for my students have never changed. I've always valued conviction and credibility. I've always asked in one way or another: Do I believe what this person is telling me? This question is not in conflict with the fictions of stories, the lies of tall-tale telling, or sly anecdotes intended to dupe listeners. Rather, it stands in opposition to a lack of credibility resulting from a variety of approaches, from overwrought to stultifyingly dull deliveries. The first years of teaching were like coaching workshops where there was a microfocus on delivery. The goal was for students to leave with one or two stories polished and with a direction for working on others. Over the years the focus has become less micro and more macro. Students still need to think concretely about the evocation of character and setting in stories they tell, but they also need to think philosophically. The goal is to give them not answers but questions they need to ask themselves when working with a story. When they leave, they should leave hungry for stories and storytelling, and with models to use in working generally and specifically on a story. Credibility now encompasses issues related to the dynamics of text, audience, and teller.

The class is taught through lecture-demonstrations by me and one or two guest storytellers. Students evaluate storytellers on audio-cassettes and attend a storytelling concert with six or more performers. Similarly, students read and report on books that approach storytelling differently, such as Barbara Myerhoff's anthropological approach in *Number Our Days*, Rollo May's psychological model in *The Cry for Myth*, Elizabeth Stone's combination of folklore and psychological models in *Black Sheep and Kissing Cousins: How Our Family Stories Shape Us*, and a book like *Children Tell Stories* by Martha Hamilton and Mitch Weiss, which demonstrates how to use storytelling as a tool in the classroom (for another useful teaching aid, see Sadler). Without exposure to a variety of personal, family, folkloric, and literary narratives, without exposure to a variety of dramatic and understated storytelling styles, and without exposure to those who speak from within and from outside the culture of their stories, students simply do not grasp the challenges and diversity of storytelling forms, styles, and traditions.[1]

Storytelling in Libraries

I studied storytelling while completing a master's degree in library service at Rutgers University in 1971. Telling stories to children has always been an important activity in public libraries. It began soon after library service to children was established in the United States at the turn of the century. Anne Carroll Moore, the first superintendent of work with children at the New York Public Library, was one of a handful of early librarians who initiated a tradition of storytelling in library programs for children that has endured throughout America to the present. She loved the storytelling style of Marie Shedlock, an English actress who came to America and performed as a storyteller in theaters. Moore wanted children's librarians trained to tell like Shedlock, whose style stood in marked contrast to the stylized delivery developed in the elocution movement popular at the time. This style of elocution is humorously portrayed in *The Music Man*, where zaftig women in togas recite Keats's "Ode on a Grecian

Urn" in artificially exaggerated poses. In trying to establish a library tradition of storytelling, the librarians rejected such false pretensions.

The storytelling tradition in libraries is child-centered. The best performers believe a child who has "experienced such art through the listening-years" is blessed, "for these are the years . . . when to be filled to the brimming means that the years ahead will never run dry" (Sawyer 18). They are deeply committed to leading children from spoken stories back to the riches of stories in books. The tradition values keeping the focus on the story. It is rooted in the belief that tellers should not interpose themselves between the story and the audience. Stories are seen as having power and meaning sufficient to themselves, and children are respected as having the sense and sensibilities to interpret those stories for themselves.

The freshness of a child's response to a story was recently brought home during a telling of "Ashpit," by Barbara McBride-Smith, a librarian and storyteller from Oklahoma. In this story an old granny sequentially tells two terrible sisters that to receive a burn-ing coal for starting a fire they must brush her hair, and they refuse to do so. To a six-year-old in the audience, "Ashpit" was not some formulaic story with the predictable conclusion that the third child would brush the old woman's hair and gain many treasures. Instead this little girl was aghast at the behavior of the older sisters, and she earnestly whispered to her seat mate, "I would have brushed her hair!"

In trying to promote excellence, the librarians who trained oth-ers developed a language that sought to counteract sloppy perfor-mance decisions such as talking down to children, treating notable texts cavalierly, making inept attempts at cleverness, and employing poor acting techniques. Unfortunately, the cumulative effect over the years was the perception that the process of searching for a useful way to talk about storytelling had solidified into commandments that took on a life of their own in whispered cautionary tales. When li-brarians told stories just to satisfy job requirements and approached the task with the focus on playing it safe, the liveliness and the very art of storytelling were diminished. Modeling a storytelling style on externally imposed job rules instead of internally moderated decisions that grow out of a mix of cultural awareness and personal experience can lead to a high degree of ineffectiveness. I've been teased as having been trained in the marine corps of storytelling; I was not. Nonetheless, this misperception of military conformity persists and has been difficult to dispel.

In the late 1960s and early 1970s, "revival" storytelling began to emerge. It flourished beyond libraries, classrooms, places of worship, and the natural cultural settings in which it had always thrived. To be sure, there still were storytellers from active oral traditions in American cultures, but an influx of actors, mimes, performance artists, dancers, writers, poets, comedians, folk musicians, ministers, inspirational speakers, and educators also made their way onto the platforms of storytelling. People drew on aesthetic standards from other fields like anthropology, folklore, literature, communication, music, theater, theology, and stand-up comedy. Revival storytelling struggled without a critical language for approaching and assessing story occasions with widely diverse audiences, tellers, and types of material. The how-to techniques generally grew out of the disciplines in which the practitioner was trained.

Let us attempt a definition of storytelling that might be useful in the following discussion of the storytelling continuum: a primarily oral-aural event, with visual components, between an intentional speaker and an acknowledged listener for the purposes of witnessing, affirming, or participating in the unfolding of a narrative that has a beginning, middle, and, if not an end, a pause, break, or resting place. This broad view seeks to encompass the variety of storytelling events — from gossip over coffee in a kitchen to stories told on a stage with sound amplification and dramatic lighting — that is, from the most informal and least public to the most formal and most public of occasions.

Dimensions of Storytelling

Storytelling events belong on a continuum, not in a hierarchy. Many people would probably agree that the telling does not get better, the communication is not necessarily improved, by virtue of being more public and formal. Nor does storytelling necessarily degenerate because it is more consciously developed or because it moves from an intimate place to a more public one. Any storytelling event may be dull or glorious. In each situation, factors come into play that affect the credibility and effectiveness of the speaker, as well as the suitability of the story for the teller, the audience, and the location. There are important and real shifts along the continuum. These shifts grow out of and simultaneously feed into the perceptions of roles and obligations of speakers and audiences alike. Most notably, differences in the degree of informality and formality affect the intentions and expectations of both speaker and listener.

To evaluate the variety of storytelling occasions, we need to be able to talk about what worked in one situation better than in another, and why. Certainly the three central components of storytelling are the narrative, the audience, and the teller. Yet those components are influenced by other considerations along the continuum of storytelling events:

Relationship between speaker and listener(s). How well the participants know the teller and how much they trust the teller affect the initial receptivity of the listeners and therefore influence the degree of intentional persuasiveness or empathy that the teller consciously or unconsciously promotes.

Extent of community feeling among listeners. People are also affected by whether they have a sense of fellowship with other audience members or feel isolated or estranged from them. For example, a storyteller usually has less initial work drawing people into deeper association with one another at an event where a familiar, cohesive group of people is assembled.

Location of event. People listen and interact differently in intimate and public places. Entering a home, bar, church, classroom, lecture hall, tent, or theater affects people in myriad ways. There may be conscious and unconscious changes in their level of comfort, demeanor, dress, expectations, and behavior. The location may affect the story by affecting the audience and the storyteller in obvious or subtle ways.

Physical distance between speaker and listener(s). When the storytelling occasion shifts from one listener to a small or large group, both the content and style of the delivery can be dramatically affected. What is said and how it is said often change as people move farther apart. Factors like sound disturbances or amplification and diminished or increased visual stimulation bring very real challenges and opportunities.

Cultural context of story. The relationship both the storyteller and the audience members have to the culture from which the story comes plays a role in any storytelling event. Stories usually address, in one way or another, what it means to be a human being within a specific cultural context, a context that ranges from the highest spiritual aspirations of a people to a people's most basic injunctions about living. Stories also resonate in a universal dimension. If the universality of a tale is broth, then the ethnic, religious, geographical, and historical details season the stew pot of story and flavor the tale. Storytellers within a culture understand which seasonings can be added freely and which require a more judicious touch. Similarly, listeners within the culture have developed tastes for their stories and appreciate the care taken in the seasoning. Allowing for intracultural dissent, both speaker and listener share basic understandings about the equitable distribution of goods and the cultural definitions of good, beauty, and wealth. Whenever the storyteller or listeners are outside a culture, there is a tendency to emphasize the universal at the expense of cultural specificity, honesty, and vigor. The tale can become so diluted as to become unrecognizable. It can also be so inappropriately prepared that, in essence, it becomes inedible to those it once fed.

Relationship of audience and teller to story. Innumerable adjustments in listening and speaking occur as a story moves further and further from personal experience toward orally created and transmitted cultural tales, print-based folktales, and finally individually authored stories.

Three Kinds of Storytellers

In 1990, at the Fife Conference held each summer at Utah State University, the folklorist Bert Wilson heard me struggling to identify for discussion points along a continuum of storytelling. He proposed three terms to clarify the degrees of formality and informality indicated in my lecture. He suggested that there are situational storytellers, conscious cultural storytellers, and professional storytellers.

Everyone is a situational storyteller. Everyone is prompted at home, at work, and at play to create narratives about the recent or distant past. "Oh, seeing you there reminds me of the time . . ." or "You remember what Grandma said . . ." or "You wouldn't believe what happened at work today. . . ." People regularly spin stories (predictions) about the future: "When we win the lottery, we'll. . . ." Situations like the moments before bed or when people congregate around a campfire encourage storytelling. In a fundamental way, telling stories takes up a great part of each day.

Similarly, many people embrace the role of conscious cultural storyteller. They pass on cultural and ethical standards when they begin stories with "We men . . . ," "We line workers . . . ," "We Mennonites . . . ," and so on. The culture with which they identify may be based on gender, family, work, play, geography, ethnicity, religion, economics, education, or other criteria. When cultural views are passed on within community groups, the public acts of witnessing and affirming reinforce them. Conjointly, rituals, either as enacted or visual symbolizations of the stories that have shaped these same groups, are inherently cultural story occasions.

Not everyone is comfortable being what Bert Wilson calls a professional storyteller. The skills for being effective in this context are basically the same as those that effective communicators utilize reflexively in the other contexts. Nonetheless, the heightened intentionality and distance from the audience make some people reluctant to tell their family story, give voice to their religious beliefs, or retell an oral or print-derived story from any platform outside their immediate circle.

I prefer *platform storyteller* to *professional storyteller*. This new term suggests a kind of storytelling that may not be so culturally bound; it suggests that the primary cultural identification of the teller may not be the same as that of the story. In contrast to *situational story-teller*, *platform storyteller* also suggests some degree of formality and distance between teller and listener that has to be bridged. Finally, the term is removed from an emotionally charged and politicized history of value judgments.

The same story can be told in each of these three contexts. For example, Donald Davis compares how his Aunt Esther and various members of his family killed chickens. In this story, his aunt's intelligence and skill at slaughtering cause him to reevaluate other things she had said that heretofore he completely ignored. The subtext of Davis's story poses the question, Is ignorance bliss? The story is wonderfully suited to relating to family or friends. As a minister, Davis could use it in his preaching. And he tells it regularly at storytelling festivals. The words may not change; but as the context changes, the story is shaped and reshaped by myriad alterations growing out of the degrees of formality and informality that define each context.

At any place along the continuum of spoken, narrative communication are the creative tensions of accuracy and artfulness. To paraphrase John Barth, technique in art is like technique in lovemaking; heartfelt ineptitude has its charms, as does heartless skill, and yet what we all long for is passionate virtuosity (Barth 24). Creative tensions are at play among the story, the storyteller, and the listener. Like teetering on a seesaw, maintaining balance is often achieved by risking imbalance. Most diligent storytellers struggle to communicate effectively — whether they are parents who want their cautionary tales heeded or Diane Wolkstein telling "Inanna" at Lincoln Center's Avery Fisher Hall. For all tellers the most fundamental aspect of storytelling is to communicate the story effectively. The story's the thing.

Yet effective communicators also realize the importance of considering the needs of their audience, because leading listeners through a story is as interactive as leading someone in a dance. Dance partners flee from those who grab them by the scruff of the neck and push them around the floor, but they respond eagerly to the partner whose dance style invites them to follow. Skilled dancers take into account the experience of their partners. Though the story's the thing, the interaction between teller and audience creates the storytelling event. To a large degree, storytelling actually occurs in the minds of the listeners. Part of its power comes from the fact that storytelling is story-triggering. People may resonate to different tales, but all are eventually touched and reminded of their own stories and thus of their own humanity.

Contemporary storytelling traditions have been created by the independent vitality of oral and print traditions as well as by the places where those traditions bump, collide, blend, merge, and diverge again. One problem with how-to techniques is that they treat storytelling as a product. Whether we are situational, conscious cultural, or platform storytellers, storytelling is a process. At its best, it is a finely honed and flexible process where the separate strands of tale, teller, and listener are woven meaningfully together. For the art to grow and thrive, it needs a clearer and more specific language that recognizes the history, complexity, and vitality of these strands.

Note

1. For further sources on the art and teaching of storytelling, see Baker and Greene; Carol Birch; Birch and Heckler; Livo and Rietz; MacDonald.

Texts with Roots in
Oral Tradition

Martin S. Jaffee

The Hebrew Scriptures

Imagine, if you will, a room containing twenty-two books. All of them are composed by anonymous authors, many of whom lived centuries apart. Most of the authors, moreover, are not individual creative writers. Their creativity consists of compiling into coherent compositions earlier literary traditions — some transmitted in writing and others by word of mouth, some of rather recent vintage and others centuries old. The books are issued on leather scrolls ranging in length from a few feet to many dozen. The longest of them can weigh many pounds. Some original manuscripts are believed to exist, but most of the books are known only through copies made from earlier copies.

These copies represent a major investment of labor by tanners who produce the writing surface of the scroll and scribes who laboriously copy the text. Sometimes, by error, whole lines are skipped or miscopied. If such scribal mistakes go undetected and uncorrected, later copyists will reproduce the error and transmit it as the genuine text. Or sometimes an old copy will have in its margins helpful explanations by an earlier owner. These can also find their way into the "author's text" as a later copyist sees fit, and will be copied in turn by later scribes as integral parts of the text. In any event, the National Archive, where the entire collection is stored as a national treasure, has been given the task of preserving the versions deemed authentic.

Nearly the only people who ever see these books are government leaders and officials of the Ministry of Culture. While most people of the country are able to read in at least a rudimentary way, these books in particular are legible only with difficulty. In the first place, they are written in an ancient version of the national language, a version that is spoken, if at all, only by antiquarian scholars. There is also the matter of the copies themselves. The scribal handwriting is a specialized script difficult to decipher. The literary tradition, moreover, has neither punctuation marks indicating the beginning and ends of sentences nor consistent spellings of words. The convention of dividing words with short spaces between them is not customary in all scribal circles. Sometimes a dot — or nothing at all — separates one word from its neighbor. Finally, the consonantal alphabet of the written language has no symbols for vowels. Indeed, in the literary world we are describing, this very sentence might look something like this:

ndd·n·th·ltrry·wrld·w·r·dscrbng·ths·vry·sntnc·mght·lk· smthng·lk·ths

But illegibility is not that serious a problem for most people, since few have looked inside any but the most famous of these scrolls.

In fact, with the exception of tourists who may have visited the National Archive, hardly anyone has seen more than a few of these scrolls in any one place. To be sure, while learning the rudiments of reading and writing, many folk have copied out small passages of one of the most important books. They are intimately familiar with those brief passages. But what they know of most of the library's contents comes to them from hearing portions of some of the books read aloud by trained declaimers on national holidays, commemorative festivals, and other public occasions. These declaimers, and the political and religious figures who have collected and preserved the scrolls, are able to distinguish the "official text" of the works from the common interpretations and additions to them. But most audiences make no such firm distinction between the official text and its versions or interpretations.

If you can imagine a room with such books, you have imagined the library of the Hebrew Scriptures prior to the second century of the Common Era (CE = AD). By this century important developments in Judaism and early Christianity had combined to transform the physical appearance of the Hebrew Scriptures. Christians, who knew these texts primarily in Greek translation, were the first to depart from the scroll form; they transformed the scrolls into codices — collections of bound manuscript pages similar to the books of the Middle Ages and modernity. At last all of Scripture could be stored on a table or shelf. But before then, in the first centuries after the composition of the Torah of Moses (c. 450 before the Common Era, BCE = BC), the Jews of the Land of Israel ("Palestina" in Roman nomenclature) knew their scriptures in the form we have described.

Schools, Traditions, Canons

The centuries between 450 BCE and the second century CE witnessed an era of immense cultural creativity among the religious-intellectual elites of the Jewish homeland. That creativity was encouraged and presided over by a succession of priestly administrative dynasties ruling from the national capitol in Jerusalem, whose Temple archive served as the repository for officially approved literary works. The principal literary laborers were various scribal schools comparable to civil service bureaucracies. These schools devoted themselves to gathering and preserving venerable literary traditions remembered as having originated with the great heroes of the Jewish past. Those who composed this heritage into books of law, history, and poetry regarded themselves as the descendants of their heroes, as their literary executors and spiritual heirs, so to speak.

Thus were formed within these scribal groups impressive literary works ascribed, for example, to the national founder, Moses; the nation's greatest king, David; its wisest sage, Solomon; and many other prophets and sages. By the second century CE, twenty-two such works had been organized by a particular scribal society, the rabbis, into a scriptural canon. These rabbinic sages, building on and amplifying earlier scribal traditions, placed their definitive stamp on scriptural books by dividing them into chapters, paragraphs, and verses. These divisions, rather different from those followed by Christian traditions since early times, are still found in the scriptural texts of contemporary Jewish communities.

By editing a scroll and giving it a place in a canonical collection, the rabbis solemnized two decisions. The first was that the scroll in its edited form could be used, with others in the canon, as a source of public teaching and proclamation. The second was that books excluded from the canon could not be read in such public instructional settings. Without the benefit of a rabbinic edition, the excluded scrolls fell out of use in Judaism. Many of them were preserved for centuries in Christian monasteries, translated into languages like Amharic, Slavonic, Greek, and Latin. Some, preserved in Catholic and Orthodox canons of the Old Testament, remain Scripture for Christianity. Still others died an absolute cultural death until they were accidentally unearthed a half century ago among the Dead Sea Scrolls.

But it is the tripartite rabbinic canon that defined the Hebrew Scriptures for later Judaism. The first part of this canon, called the Torah ("instruction"), consists of the five books known today by the later Latin names Genesis through Deuteronomy. They were copied onto a single enormous scroll. The whole was believed to have been dictated by God to Moses during an audience on Mount Sinai. The second part, called Nevi'im ("prophets"), contains separate scrolls of historical writings (Joshua through Kings) and oracular poetry. These oracles were believed to have been received by prophets under a kind of God-intoxicated inspiration and transmitted to their disciples for literary finishing. Books ascribed to Isaiah, Jeremiah, and Ezekiel are on separate scrolls; the twelve books of Hosea through Malakhi are on a single scroll. The third part, Ketuvim ("authoritative writings"), is the most diverse in terms of literary genre. In addition to historical writings (Ezra, Nehemiah, Chronicles), it includes exalted religious poetry ascribed to David and other prophets (Psalms), wise sayings and songs ascribed to Solomon (Proverbs, Ecclesiastes, and Song of Songs), and even thrillers and romances (Esther, Ruth). Together, this collection of scrolls came to be known in Judaism as the Tanakh, an acronym formed from the initials of Torah, Nevi'im, and Ketuvim.

Scripture versus the Single Text

Except for the familiar names of biblical books, what we have described as the physical form and social dissemination of the Hebrew Scriptures is something very different from what most modern people recognize as their Bible. In the first place, the Bible — whether in the form of the Tanakh or Old and New Testaments — is a book for moderns in a way it never could have been for ancients. Strictly speaking, it is an anthology. It contains literary divisions called "books" (e.g., "the Book of Isaiah"), but these are first encountered in the context of a physical object that has its own identity — the Bible (for ideas on teaching the Hebrew Bible as literature in translation, see Olshen and Feldman).

Ancient Jews, by contrast, had the concept of Scripture as holy writing and knew of books (in Greek, *biblia*) that were treated as holy texts. But they had neither the concept nor the artifact of a Bible as an anthology in which all Scripture was, so to speak, gathered in one place. For these Jews, the place in which Scripture was gathered was not a book at all but a sanctified space. The Temple in Jerusalem, while it stood, held the original copies from which those stored elsewhere might be made. After the Temple's destruction in 70 CE, synagogues (study and prayer halls) came to serve as sanctified settings for the storage of scriptural scrolls.

Consider this last point: precisely because the modern printed Bible is all in one place — a single book — it is also available for moderns in a way it had never been for ancients. We see it ubiquitous in homes, bookstores, hotel rooms, and other locations. For most Jews of antiquity, by contrast, a scroll could be viewed only from a distance during a public reading at a festive or solemn occasion. Bibles, in other words, are common household objects in ways that scriptural scrolls could not have been for ancient Jews.

This fact has an important implication for understanding how the Hebrew Scriptures were read. Think first of our own situation. Even if we hear the Bible quoted or read in public from time to time, our most intimate knowledge of it is gained from scrutiny of the clean, printed text (complete with cross-references) held conveniently in our hands in the comfort of our home. For us, the words on the page are the primary subject of attention. We establish their meaning contextually from the literary setting and proceed on that basis to distinguish better from worse interpretations. Some of these interpretations, to be sure, are supplied to us by the traditions of religious communities found now in convenient commentaries. But we can distinguish these from the text itself and evaluate them on their own merits.

All the contextual clues that help modern readers fix the meaning of scriptural texts were unavailable to most ancient readers of the Hebrew Scriptures. For all but the professional scribe or exceptionally learned layperson, the written text was not experienced in isolation from the oral text. No page supplied the primary setting in which to establish a stable meaning of a verse. There were, in fact, no verses at all, only evocative utterances in inspired communal settings.[1] The interpretive context of Scripture, therefore, was supplied by communal memory and tradition. It was built up sedimentally, transmitted in the multiple, repeated settings in which Scripture had been rendered orally by reciters or teachers. Scripture was only incidentally words on a surface. Rather, it was utterances met in oral addresses, often expounded in translation, with frequent interpolations of explanatory or hortatory asides. The actual Hebrew text on the scroll, the supplementary rendering in Aramaic or Greek, and the added contextualizations by the public teacher — all this together was Scripture.

Clearly, modern academic interpretations of biblical texts are reached on terms utterly foreign to ancient readers. It is not simply a matter of a different worldview and possession of the methodological tools of historical criticism, although these too are important. It is also a matter of the dramatic differences between the nature and use of books in ancient Judaism's manuscript culture and the reality of books in the age of print. William Graham's study of the orality of the world's scriptural traditions is a good start toward understanding the cultural shift involved here.

In ancient Judaism, precisely because the scriptural book was difficult to use and often inaccessible, scribes and rabbinic scriptural experts routinely committed the entire text of Scripture to memory. Gifted teachers could give sermonic discourses that effortlessly wove scriptural texts into the orator's own message. The meaning of Scripture was always actualized anew in the latest sermon, and such meanings could not be overturned by referring to the text on the page. These orally mediated meanings are the meanings that the less expert would bear with them as they brought remembered words of Scripture to bear on their own experience.

Pedagogical Implications

This observation has important implications for teaching the Hebrew Scriptures in the context of oral literature and tradition. Let me conclude by pointing out a few of them. The most important step in teaching the Hebrew Scriptures as oral literature is to unsettle students' image of the text as a monolith of poured concrete. An effective first step is to teach the table of contents of a number of different Bible editions. This discloses the dramatic differences in the sequence and selection of books that distinguish Judaism's Tanakh from the various Protestant, Catholic, and Orthodox Old Testament canons. It helps students see the individual books as pieces in a puzzle, a puzzle that various scriptural religions have sorted out in light of their respective interpretive traditions.

Such an exercise should be supplemented by textual readings that highlight biblical books as independent compositions that need not be harmonized with other canonical works. The composite character of most biblical works can also be stressed through reading strategies that highlight traditions and sources in the text that appear to be in tension with one another. Works of biblical scholarship following the schools of documentary analysis, form criticism, and tradition criticism can be helpful here. These show how biblical books can be analyzed into the various layers of editorial work that combined oral and written tradition into the compositions before us. Barry Bandstra's textbook and some of the essays collected by Robert Culley as well as by Douglas Knight and Gene Tucker will be helpful guides for these issues.

At all costs teachers should avoid harmonization of textual contradictions. Readings that suppress contradictions and inconsistencies are the puzzle solvers supplied by theological traditions. These assume the existence of a biblical author (from a master editor to the Creator of heaven and earth, depending on the theory) globally in charge of all aspects of each text. At issue in our classrooms, however, is not the unity of the biblical text but its multivocality. Our task is not to teach the text as "the author intended it" but, rather, to give it the kind of life it might have had in the setting of its public performance. From the perspective of teaching oral tradition the correct question is not, How could the writer or editor have permitted this contradiction to stand? It is, rather, If hearers noticed the contradictions, how might interpretive traditions circulating beyond the written text have been deployed in resolving them?

In sum, the teacher of the Hebrew Scriptures as oral tradition needs to teach within the biblical text and beyond it at the same time. This means paying attention to the fissures and cracks in the biblical texts and asking how the compiler's work is itself an element in the text's literary meaning. It also means recognizing that the meaning of the text is found in the interpretive traditions of ancient Judaism and early Christianity, the communities responsible for preserving these writings as Scripture. The essays in Martin Mulder's volume are very helpful here.

In my own teaching, therefore, I have often adduced texts of the New Testament canon (Matthew and Paul) or the early Patristic writers (Barnabas, Justin Martyr). These are marvelous examples of how, for early Christians, the meaning of Jewish scriptural works was inextricable from the oral preaching of the Christian mission. Similarly, I lay great stress on the Jewish traditions of interpretation that pre-

and postdate the emergence of the rabbinic canon. Particularly instructive are the interpretations found in the Dead Sea Scrolls (e.g., the Genesis Apocryphon, the Nahum Pesher), in the early rabbinic translations of Scripture (Targum), and in the early rabbinic commentaries (midrashim). These Jewish sources show how, in ancient Judaism itself, the needs and expectations of discrete communities yielded remarkably diverse understandings of the scriptural word.

The Hebrew Scriptures were a highly oral and aural reality in ancient Jewish and Christian communities. Nevertheless, for most of our students they constitute the paradigm of what is meant by "book." Accordingly, teaching these texts is an occasion for more than a lesson in ancient literary history or the history of Judaism. It is an opportunity to illustrate how the textual phenomena that attract our literate attention were noticed and mediated in a culture for which the visual experience of the text was secondary to its oral presentation.

Note

1. Helpful insights into the oral and aural presence of the scriptural text in its own culture may be found in Rabinowitz (26–48). See also Niditch, *Oral World*. For a brilliant attempt to render the Torah of Moses so as to highlight its original word power, one should consult E. Fox.

Werner H. Kelber

New Testament Texts: Rhetoric and Discourse

We are accustomed to living with the Bible as a product of our print culture. Regularized by print technology and tidily organized into chapters and verse divisions, it presents itself as our typographical icon. Yet long before biblical texts were assimilated to mechanized printing processes, they were handwritten, without titles, chapters, or verse divisions, lacking in spaces between words and devoid of punctuation marks. At that time, composing in a hearer-friendly manner and reading aloud were prerequisites for gaining a hearing for these texts. This essay seeks to recover the oral, rhetorical functioning of two New Testament genres: the letter and the narrative (for an extended study of the Gospels and oral tradition, see Kelber, *Gospel*).

The Pauline Letters: From Theology to Rhetoric

"With what a river of eloquence [Paul's words] flow, even he who snores must notice." With these words Augustine pays tribute to Paul as paragon of Christian oratory (126). Belatedly, many of us have come to agree with Augustine. There is a growing realization that Paul did not seek the truth abstracted from human interaction. His reasoning evolved dialogically in argumentation with others, and his adversarial style, far from being an index of his personality, was primarily a product of the rhetorical environment of late antiquity. Increasingly, we are learning to understand him as a master in discerning the persuasive potential of current issues and in constructing appropriate epistolary responses.

To many of our students, however, Paul is known as a thinker who conceptualized the gospel by converting it into a theological system. Making the assumption that Christianity originated in the simple message of Jesus, they see the apostle reshaping original simplicity into the formal categories of theology or, as some of the more sophisticated interpreters would suggest, into the categories of Hellenistic philosophy. Whether they think of him as hero or villain, they are inclined to view him as a systematic theologian.

What I explain to my students is that they have recreated Paul in the prevailing image of modern thought. By casting him into the role of a theologian, they have subsumed his discourse under the discipline of a particular kind of logic. And logic, whose prestige has steadily risen in the Western tradition, has taught us to abstract universals from concrete situations. Confronted with the intricate and often obscure letters of Paul, our logical impulse is to reduce complexity to principles of universality. Yet the Paul of the first century CE defies all efforts at systematization. We do no justice to his mode of thinking by cataloging his letters under the dogmatic rubrics of eschatology, christology, ecclesiology, or the more distinctly theological headings of law, faith, justification, and so forth. This modern drive toward logical, theological consistency is ill suited for, and indeed antithetical to, discerning the heart of Paul's letters.

Instead, I advise my students that Paul's letters should be appreciated as models of rhetoric. And rhetoric, contrary to logic, is predicated on a high degree of involvement with audiences and their specific life situations. Once sensitized to the rhetorical dimension, students are surprised to discover the inescapably ad hominem focus of Paul's letters. Functioning in the fashion of interpersonal discourse, Paul's letters are both well-informed about the particularities of socioreligious circumstances and responsive with a high degree of specificity (the letter to the Romans being a possible exception). Truth in Paul's rhetorically designed letters is not proved abstractly but argued in dialogue, and thought itself is conceived of as a product of intersubjective communication.

Each letter serves the purpose of planting conviction into the hearts of hearers. In the case of 1 Thessalonians, Abraham Malherbe has shown that Paul's rhetoric of pastoral care was calculated to ensure the continuing nurture of the community. In regard to Galatians, Hans Betz's demonstration of an apologetic rhetoric enacted in the setting of a law court has become a classic. Contrary to the prevailing assessment of Philippians as a composite, even artless, letter, Duane Watson has uncovered an integral rhetorical strategy that includes tonal and argumentative shifts carefully crafted to persuade the audience to adhere to Paul's exhortations as a way of meeting opposition. There are two superb rhetorical studies on 1 Corinthians. Antoinette Wire has scrutinized the effects Paul's rhetoric had on women prophets, and Margaret Mitchell has traced the rhetoric of reconciliation the apostle brought to bear on a fractured community. J. P. Sampley's study of 2 Corinthians 10–13, the most contentious part of the Corinthian correspondence, has brilliantly demonstrated the apostle's rhetorical cleverness in wooing the goodwill of his audience by undercutting the charges against him. For Philemon, F. F. Church has explicated an intricately constructed rhetoric Paul uses to incline Philemon toward a mutually satisfactory resolution of a difficult situation. The strategy of Romans, finally, has been explained as ambassadorial rhetoric that aimed at preparing the Roman Christians for Paul's journey to Rome as ambassador of the gospel (Jewett). Rhetorical studies of Paul's letters are still in their infancy, and scholarly opinions remain divided on questions large and small. But what the upsurge in rhetorical studies reveals is a significant change in our concept of the Pauline letters: their meaning is determined primarily not by propositional theology but by the effect they seek to have on hearers.

Two specific examples must suffice to demonstrate the workings of Paul's rhetoric. The opening address of Romans (1.1–15) contains language that is unprecedented when compared with that of the other Pauline letters. A striking feature is the frequency and variability of Paul's references to the Roman Christians (1.6–7). The plurality of addresses is reinforced with language of inclusiveness. He wants to make sure he is reaching *all* of them (1.5, 7, 8, 14). Noteworthy also is the discreet manner in which Paul states the purpose of his impending visit to Rome: "[T]hat we may be mutually encouraged by each other's faith, both yours and mine" (1.12). This has rightly been called a rhetoric of "great diplomatic finesse" designed to assert the value of his own visit while at the same time avoiding offense to the sensibilities of an already existing church (Jewett 14). In sum, Paul's language of pluralism, inclusiveness, and diplomacy in the opening of Romans has "a credentialing effect" (16). Rhetorically, it is language designed to construct his ethos as a person who merits the trust of a pluralistic but divided Roman community (Wuellner 157–60).

The central section of Galatians (3.1–4.31) is notorious for what is often perceived to be a lack of logical connectedness. But Betz has ingeniously argued that Paul, in the mode of a skilled defense lawyer, deliberately changes his approach to the audience. Insult (3.1), appeal to experience (3.2–5), appeal to Scripture (3.6–14), appeal to legal practice (3.15–18), digression (3.19–24), appeal to experience (3.25–29), appeal to legal practice (4.1–11), appeal to emotions (4.12–20), and appeal to Scripture (4.21–31) alternate in rapid succession. This is not lack of organization but a strategy specifically designed to hold the oral audience's attention. For what matters in a rhetorically composed letter is less the sequential coherence of its individual units than their impact on hearers.

What are the implications of rhetoric for our teaching of Paul's letters? Negatively, we must wean students away from searching for a Pauline theology or ethics abstracted from specific cases. In a sense, Paul invents himself anew for each occasion. As students learn to grasp the letters separately and on their own rhetorical terms, they become involved in a series of case studies. I have students read the letters in the chronological order of their composition, commencing with 1 and 2 Thessalonians and ending with Romans. Listening to the argumentative voice of each letter and recognizing how closely Paul is responding to communal issues, the readers become attuned to voices in dialogue. Discernment of the mode of Paul's arguments invites reflection on what is being said at the other end of the line, and growing awareness of the issues raised by Paul's addresses in turn illuminates the apostle's rhetoric. In alerting students to the part Paul's correspondents played in shaping his responses, I draw their attention to key terms that emerge with exceptional force in a letter. When Paul introduces "wisdom" as a principal term—unprecedented in his letters—we can be sure that the occurrence is case-specific (1 Cor. 1–4). The impression is enhanced when we observe him developing wisdom in argumentative fashion, discounting a certain use of it and emphatically arguing the identity of the crucified Christ as wisdom (1.23–24). From this students can infer the Corinthians' identification of Christ as wisdom of unqualified power. Moving back and forth in this way, from Paul's arguments to those of the addressees, the two arguments illuminating each other, students become participants in the rhetorical situations of the Pauline letters.

The Gospels: From History to Narrative to Discourse

All of us whose training has been in the interpretation of texts need reminding that heard proclamation was the rule in early Christian life and worship. Jesus himself was an itinerant preacher, surrounded by listening and debating audiences, and the Gospel narratives were still meant to be proclaimed vocally rather than read silently. In teaching the Gospels, I dissuade students from a crudely historical reading, whereby meaning is equated with the historicity of the narratives; gradually introduce them to a literary, narratological appreciation, whereby meaning lies embedded in the immanent narrativity; and finally shift their attention away from meaning as historical reference, and from meaning as literary content, toward the Gospels' communicative directives, which encourage readers' interactive responses. The pedagogical move is, therefore, from history to narrative to discourse.

I start with an explication of the differences among the four narratives. My pedagogical rationale is to dishabituate students from the conventional model of a "metagospel," a composite made up of elements from all four Gospels, Sunday school lessons, pictorial impressions, Hollywood fantasies, and so on. Using the *Synopsis of the Four Gospels* (Aland), I graphically demonstrate plural versions of individual sayings and stories, point out different contextualizations, identify omissions of and additions to common traditions, and the like. When sensitized to manifest variabilities and dissimilarities, most students are ready to acknowledge that the aggregate of variations amounts to four rather different narratives. Given the Gospels' divergence in compositional design and content, each individual Gospel deserves to be read and appreciated on its own terms.

Although my primary focus is on narrative, I have found it necessary to respond to the inevitable questions raised about the historical Jesus. The Gospel narrators, I explain, are called evangelists, and for good reason. Rather than function as a custodian of the past, each evangelist seeks to update his Gospel so it will speak to the present. The Gospel narratives therefore have every appearance of revisions that arose from and were composed for different early Christian communities. I make it very clear that the course on the canonical Gospels I teach is about the narrative interpretations of Jesus and not about the historical Jesus.

The larger portion of the course introduces students into the world of gospel narrativity with an eye toward unmasking the historical bias of modern readers. The issue of time serves as a convenient starting point. The Gospels describe a time span of approximately one year (the synoptics: Matthew, Mark, and Luke) and three years (John). We call this dimension narrative time. The narrators managed to compress narrative time of one to three years into a reading time of one to three hours. This exercise illustrates the difference between narrative time and reading time, neither of which has anything to do with historical time. A principal problem facing the narrator was thus the reconciliation of narrative time with reading time and not the faithful reproduction of historical time.

References to the emotional state of characters and interior discourses help to illuminate the fictional nature of narrative. How could an evangelist know that Jesus "was moved with compassion" as he healed the leper (Mark 1.41) or was "deeply moved" when he approached the tomb of Lazarus (John 11.38)? Who informed the narrator of the wording of Jesus's lonely prayer at Gethsemane (Luke 22.41–42)? Close attention to these "illicit entries into private minds" (Booth 18) encourages students to make the transit from historical to literary categories. I use the term "narrative omniscience" to describe a narrator who knows more than any single character and "inside view" to refer to the narrator's uncanny discernment of the most private feelings of characters. Both are fictional prerogatives that are conducive to narrative realism and enhance the psychological depth of characters.

As students grow accustomed to narrative devices, their perception of the Gospels as plotted narratives steadily increases. Jesus's three Passion-Resurrection predictions, for example, positioned at measured intervals in the synoptic Gospels, heighten suspense and turn attention increasingly to the cross. They serve, in other words, dramatic and not historical purposes. Centrally located in each synoptic Gospel is the transfiguration story (Mark 9.2–8; Matt. 17.1–8; Luke 9.28–36), which anticipates what may materialize at some future point. In narrative terms, it is a proleptic story, explicated as such by Jesus (Mark 9.9; Matt. 17.9) and misperceived by Peter (Mark 9.6). Matthew's selection of the first three miracle stories is carefully patterned to dramatize the gospel's interest in marginalized people: the sick, Gentiles, and women (8.1–15). These and a host of other narrative devices make it abundantly clear that the Gospels are to a degree plotted narratives.

Pedagogically, I gradually wean students from the *Synopsis of the Four Gospels*, which has allowed them to discern differences, and move to running texts, preferably without chapter and verse divisions, which facilitate consecutive readings (Lattimore). I unfold before them the strange and sometimes forbidding landscape of each

Gospel separately, resisting the interpretive influence of all other Gospels. Increasingly, students make their own discoveries of narrative links and dynamics, actively moving toward an appreciation of the narrative integrity of each Gospel.

In the course of engaging students in the different Gospel worlds, I seek to strike a balance between encouraging the search for unity and arousing sensitivity to gaps and disconnectedness. For while each Gospel constitutes an integral narrative, by no means do all narrative elements fit into an unbroken web of unity. We are dealing with episodic narrative, a familiar characteristic of oral tradition, rather than with fully plotted stories. It is important for the students to learn that the Gospels are ancient narratives that do not, compositionally and artistically, mirror the standards of a Charles Dickens, Marcel Proust, or Thomas Mann. But the characterization of ancient and episodic does not suggest defectiveness. Compositionally, the stories of Jesus's life and death are constituted primarily by a series of action scenes and speeches, or dialogues, that are impressive primarily in their effectiveness for hearers or readers and only secondarily in their narrative connectiveness. Characters come to life through their words and actions and less as a consequence of descriptive prose. The woman who anoints Jesus, for example, remains nameless, speechless, and undistinguished by a single descriptive feature (Luke 7.36–50). But she emerges as a distinctly memorable character by virtue of her dramatic conduct and by the way others respond to her. Action-packed and speech-filled, the Gospel narratives are more like many television dramatizations that strive to affect viewers.

Reading the Gospels with an ear toward their discourse unveils dynamics that are not apparent to an approach that focuses exclusively on narrative content. By way of example, Jesus delivers his inaugural speech concerning the kingdom in the absence of the Twelve (Mark 1.14–15). They cannot know what the hearers or readers of the Gospel were privileged to learn. At a later point, the Twelve, and the Gospel audiences, are initiated into the mystery of the kingdom by way of parabolic discourse (4.10–34). Clearly, the narrator favors the hearers or readers who are privy to both speeches. The open ending of Mark (16.1–8) serves as a classic instance of the Gospel's discourse, because it challenges hearers and readers to take up the narrative where it left off and make sense of it. Matthew's famous Sermon on the Mount opens with eight beatitudes addressed in the third person plural, distinguished from a ninth in the second person plural (5.3–12). The first beatitude intones the kingdom theme, the fourth the theme of righteousness, and the eighth combines both kingdom and righteousness. In placing and repeating words at strategic points, the narrator assists the audience in *hearing* its way through the sermon and discerning its leitmotifs. By contrast, the opening of Luke's Sermon on the Plain makes its appeal through the simple mnemonic device of four blessings followed by four comparable woes (6.20–26). The Jesus of John's Gospel typically uses language in a double sense. The conversation between Jesus and the Samaritan woman, for example, revolves around the term "living water," which she can grasp only in its literal sense (4.4–15). On the discourse level, however, hearers and readers are receiving subsequent information identifying the Spirit as the living water (7.37–39). What often remains unconnected or incomplete on the story level finds a resolution in the act of hearing.

———

For those who in our rapidly changing media culture are looking for interactive teaching methods, the rhetoric of letter and narrative in the New Testament offers a convenient tool. When students are aurally attuned to Paul's arguments and the effects they have on audiences, they cannot help but become involved in these rhetorical events. And when we alert students to the multiple oral and readerly signals issued in the Gospels, thus initiating them into their role as hearing readers, they become natural participants in these narratives. In this way the rediscovery of the oral, rhetorical functioning of Paul's letters and of the Gospels can be utilized as an ideal teaching device.

Richard P. Martin

Homer's *Iliad* and *Odyssey*

The two long epics attributed to Homer have been read as texts for nearly 2,500 years, in paperbacks, massive scholarly editions, vellum manuscripts, or papyrus scrolls. This much is known, even though we are still hopelessly ignorant of how, when, by whom, and why the poems were first written down. Nor is there a way to determine what relation the texts we read now bear to the poems that audiences in archaic Greece (ninth–sixth cents. BCE) once heard as songs of Homer. That the epics, however, were qualitatively different from literary productions can no longer be in doubt, and so we must interpret them anew, reconsidering and sometimes abandoning the strategies of critical readers over the past two and a half millennia (for general ideas on teaching Homer, see Myrsiades).

What Makes Homeric Poetry Oral

There are five interlocking sources for the belief that Homeric poetry as we have it is derived from a performance genre that did not rely on writing. They are worth reviewing briefly.

Internal evidence of the poems. Most noticeable, Homeric poetry describes the art of narrating stories about heroes and gods with words related to "song," never to writing or even recitation. Achilles in his tent sings the "glories of men" while waiting out the war (*Il.* 9.189). Odysseus, having arrived on Scheria on his way home after twenty years, listens to the singer Demodocus perform three quite different compositions for his audience; two resemble news flashes about the Trojan War, while the third is an extended joke about how the god Hephaestus caught his wife Aphrodite in an adulterous moment. Meanwhile, back on Ithaca, those in the house of Odysseus are entertained by Phemius, his personal singer, who is shown responding to the whim of his audience (the unruly suitors of Penelope) by singing of the disastrous homecomings of the Greeks (including, the suitors hope, Odysseus). Penelope can ask Phemius to change the topic (*Od.* 1.339–40), just as Odysseus can ask Demodocus for a specific performance (8.492). Whether or not the poetry of Homer was composed in this way, it at least wants to imagine its roots in live, oral performance accountable to a demanding audience.

Archaeological evidence from sites, artifacts, and inscriptions. Unlike previous generations, the readers of Homer in the past century have known that something like the Trojan War indeed took place in the region described in the poems, used weapons like those Homer described, and destroyed and displaced populations. The traditional ancient dating of the war in the twelfth century BCE fits the Homeric account of the last heroic generation and also fits the archaeological record (Wood). Yet the medium of alphabetic writing to set down either poetic or prose accounts of such a war was not available in Greece for at least two hundred years. (In 1952 it was discovered that Linear B, a sign system dating from the fourteenth century BCE, actually had been used for writing Greek; but only brief administrative texts, on small clay tablets, were preserved in this Mycenaean form of the language. See Chadwick.) Therefore, an oral historical tradition of some sort must have predated the Homeric texts.

Linguistic and metrical evidence. When linguists in the nineteenth century began to study ancient languages that were related to Greek, such as Sanskrit, it became clear that the language of Homeric poetry contained a range of forms, even variant forms of the same words, from inherited archaisms to new coinages. Homer's language was thus never the spoken Greek of any one time or region. Metrical studies have supported this conclusion: at times the Homeric dactylic hexameter requires that within a given word one supply a *w-* sound (digamma), which had dropped out of Greek in Ionia by about 700 BCE. For example, the word *oinos* ("wine") was originally *woinos* (related to the Latin *vinum*) and has to be kept in this older form to make a line scan metrically. At other times, it is impossible to keep the older pronunciation for the same words and still produce a metrically regular line (because the additional consonant makes a preceding syllable long when one needs a short syllable to fit the meter). Therefore Homeric language was multilayered and highly conservative, keeping forms that had been current in the fourteenth century BCE but dropped out of Greek by the sixth century BCE (Foley, *"Guslar"*) Most important, the Homeric dialect appears to have been shaped by and for poets: among other oddities, it contains forms that have no historical basis, on comparison with other related languages, but are metrically convenient.

Evidence of poetic diction. The linguistic arguments were extended by Milman Parry in his work on the repeated formulas of Homeric poetry (*Making*). He knew that such features as the profusion of common pronoun forms in Homer were determined by metrical usefulness. Thus Homer has several ways to say "of me"; the newer form *emou* and older *emeio* act as complements, since one has two syllables, the other three. In composing, the poet had a convenient choice provided by the retention of an archaism (something like English *o'er* and *e'er* vs. the two-syllable *over* and *ever*). Only metrically useful duplicate items are preserved, however, at this level (Foley, *"Guslar"*). Parry found the same economy at work when he meticulously investigated the well-known system of adjectives applied to the important personages of the poems. "Swift-footed Achilles" and "Odysseus of much cunning" are at other lines described as "shining Achilles" or "Odysseus of many devices." When this variation happens, there is no perceptible shift in the narrative's emphasis, but the phrases involved fit a different metrical shape. Parry proved that for each major heroic and divine figure in Homer there existed one (and almost always only one) epithet per grammatical case. Therefore Homeric poetry once again represents a traditional, multigenerational art form: no one poet would have devised this economical system. It was probably created for the rapid composition of verse while in live performance (as the poetry indeed consistently represents itself).

Comparative evidence. Parry and his collaborator, Albert Lord, found through their fieldwork in Yugoslavia in the early 1930s that similar extensive and convenient dictional systems were employed by demonstrably nonwriting performers of traditional heroic poetry. Since then, field-workers and scholars in dozens of other oral poetries have found the same tendencies (Foley, *Oral-Formulaic Theory*).

Homer and His Audiences

So much for the evidence that suggests that Homeric poetry is the continuator of a traditional oral performance art. How can teachers responsibly and honestly transmit and use this knowledge? What is the alternative to treating Homeric poetry as though it were composed under the same conditions as the *Aeneid*, *Paradise Lost*, or *The Divine Comedy*? That is to say, how will our interpretations of the *Iliad* and *Odyssey* be different if we take the possibility of an oral Homeric art form into account? The first step in answering such questions is to determine for ourselves what living oral poetries actually involve. Of course, this is not to say that any one contemporary tradition reproduces exactly the conditions of Homeric art and should therefore be held up as the sole model. At best, we can expect thought-provoking analogies to emerge from the serious study of comparative material. But, given the circumstantial evidence for the origins of Homeric art and thus the error of assuming that text-based criticism is enough for interpreting that art, we simply must look farther afield. When we do that, two crucial differences surface that are relevant to Homer's poems: first, the poet-audience relation is unlike that of the writer-reader relation; second, the act of speaking is given a higher value in cultures where oral poetry flourishes. I pursue the implications of this first distinction in terms of association and those of the second by way of presentation.

From the details provided by ethnographers and students of oral poetry, we can piece together a picture of typical audience behavior during a performance of heroic song. The most recent and compelling descriptions known to me come from Central Asian (Reichl), African (Okpewho, *African Oral Literature*), North Indian (Lutgendorf), and Egyptian traditions (Reynolds). First, and most important, audiences react on two levels, commenting on the action within the narrative and on the performance by the singer in front of them. As a new character is introduced, someone among the listeners will often shout out his identity before the poet names him; if an omen is described, the crowd will murmur its anticipation of what it portends; if a descriptive phrase is used of a person in the narrative, someone might inform his neighbors in the audience why the character got this tag; sometimes, in Central Asian performances, the poet will ask the audience what a character said on a given occasion, and his hearers will chant the speech. This sort of relationship might at first seem either chaotic or destructive of what we consider key narrative elements, such as suspense. But in fact poets who have been studied in live performance encourage such give-and-take; through the infinite flexibility of their traditional art forms, they then expand on the episodes that it appears the audience likes, or trim down those that are not going over well that evening. In sum, the performance is shaped jointly; it is equally the product of performer and audience. As the audience changes — even from one night to the next — so does the performance.

Did such changes happen with Homer's audiences? One sign that Greek poets at least knew of such interactivity comes in book 11 of the *Odyssey*, when Odysseus himself has assumed the entertainment role of a bard and narrates (but does not sing) to his Phaeacian hosts the story of his journey to the underworld. Arêtê, the powerful queen, and Nausicaa, her daughter, are prominent among his listeners: it thus appears that Odysseus chooses to begin his narration by telling about the famous women he met because he wants to please the women in his audience. Further, when he breaks off abruptly and announces it is time for bed (11.330), he is urged by the audience to continue and tell of the Greek heroes he met in the underworld. Because his decision to resume comes immediately after the royal listeners promise more gifts (11.336–51), it is reasonable to imagine that the trickster Odysseus has held the most interesting portion of his heroic tale in reserve precisely to create audience demand. Although the spellbinding effect that Odysseus has on his listeners (11.333–34) is probably the poet's idealization of his own powers, the practical detail about the performer's payment sounds realistic when we read of actual song sessions in other traditions.

But interactive behavior in audiences of traditional performances can only occur because the listeners know every convention of the art and shape their responses according to the associations they make by means of these devices. John Miles Foley has well described this phenomenon as "traditional referentiality" (see also Bradbury, this volume). The field of reference is, as he puts it, "coextensive not with any single line, passage, or text but rather with the tradition as a whole" (Foley, *Immanent Art* 57). Searching for familiar examples of this mode of verbal perception often leads one to musical analogies: the aesthetic capacities of knowledgeable audiences for jazz or, better (since it includes a verbal component), for rap improvisation, the audiences' ability to recognize and make the right association for riffs and samples, might help us understand how Homeric performance resonated. But how can modern readers turn themselves into a traditional Homeric audience, appreciating the associations, the traditional reference?

The answer is through creative philology. The organized study of Homer has gone on for as long as there have been texts of the poems. In the Hellenistic period (third–second cents. BCE) at the literary center of Alexandria, Egypt, the Greek scholarly editors who shaped what is now the standard Homeric text practiced the meticulous comparison of word, phrase, and passage in order to cull the "genuine" Homer from what they believed to be interpolated lines. Their philology was no different from that practiced by modern classicists attempting to explain the significance of a Homeric scene. One does not need a theory of oral composition to draw attention to the presence of repeated phrases, verses, or scenes in Homer and their usefulness in explication.[1]

But students of Homer who are attuned to the oral traditional aesthetic are now entitled — or, rather, required — to expand on this procedure in a significant way. To understand better the universe of discourse underlying the poems, they bring into consideration every sort of tradition-based evidence, including poetry from other ancient genres (lyric and dramatic); information from myth, folklore, and ritual; and even modern Greek traditions. Modern folk traditions have been shown recently to illuminate a number of hitherto problematic passages in Homer; a compelling example is the demonstration by Ioannis Kakridis that the Meleager parable told by Phoenix in the *Iliad* (9.529–602) is structured through the device of the ascending scale of affection prominent in modern Greek ballads: only the most beloved, whose plea always comes last in a series, can sway the protagonist. In addition, Margaret Alexiou has shown how Homeric laments for the dead resemble in form and diction the tradition of the same genre in Byzantine and modern Greek times. These are not cases of modern performances consciously borrowing from an ancient text; they represent, rather, parallel continuations of similar verbal forms in a highly traditional and long-lived culture. Thus what is inaccessible for us in Homer — the exact reference to a deep, audience-shared tradition — can still be extrapolated from these other points of reference. Another way of posing the method is to say that it is horizontal instead of vertical: in order to read an oral-derived Homer, we should not treat Greek poetry as a chronological continuum starting with Homer but instead view traditional Greek poetic productions (those that show regularly repeated dictional and narrative strategies) as a synchronic whole, aligned by generic categories.

Reading an Oral Homer: Some Examples

It is time to illustrate more concretely the types of gains to be made by interpreting the *Iliad* and *Odyssey* through the philological effort of reconstructing the poetic encyclopedia (or mental CD-ROM disk, if you like) that informs the traditional audience associational network. Here are three small examples.[2]

1. A problem that has vexed many critics of the *Odyssey* centers on lines 172–73 in book 8, which resemble almost exactly lines 91–92 in Hesiod's *Theogony*. The topic in both sets of lines is the respect accorded to a man who speaks well in public. Assuming that one poet simply copied the other's text, critics have argued over which lines were composed first. But if we turn away from this text-based model-and-copy approach in favor of an oral-poetic perspective, the problem can be resolved in terms of genres known to the audience. Hesiod conveys a traditional doctrine about the nature of kingship (one paralleled by the instruction-of-princes compositions in other Indo-European traditional literatures, such as those of India and medieval Ireland). Whereas Homer, in the passage in question, presents the as yet unrecognized Odysseus discoursing to a young man about gifts given by the gods, including speaking ability; the framework of instruction to princes seems absent. But even if Odysseus's interlocutor, Euryalus, who has mocked Odysseus, does not know he is a king, the audience realizes it and might hear in Odysseus's words the doctrine made explicit by Hesiod, with the added twist that Odysseus is by these words indirectly referring to his own status as king and rhetorician. This audience does not necessarily hear the *Odyssey* lines as anything like a quote — to use a literary concept — from Hesiod; rather, it can understand them more generally as the manifestation of a topic appropriate to the genre of instruction.[3] By the same token, the match in diction between the *Theogony* and *Odyssey* lines can represent simply the formulaic language traditional in this instruction genre, independently embedded in two poems. If we regard Odysseus's speech in book 8 as an interpolation by editors, a borrowing by Homer from Hesiod, or the invention of Homer (later borrowed by Hesiod), we lose the resonance and ironic tone that instead emerge from our appreciating the nexus of traditional associations at work (Martin, "Hesiod").

2. In the *Odyssey*, the problems of the so-called Telemacheia —

the first four books focused on the son of Odysseus — have led some earlier critics to view those books as an appendage inessential to the poem. In the literary model that views the epics as subject to inorganic textual accretions and redactions, questions of audience go unanswered. If we apply the perspective of oral aesthetics, however, the Telemachus episodes gain new significance. For the way they focus audience attention on the young man's point of view accords well with our evidence that the primary purpose for epic performances in at least the fifth century was the moral education of young men (see Richardson). The education of the son of Odysseus would thus be an image of the audience's own situation, imported into the poem — a phenomenon attested in living oral traditions (see Reynolds 198–206). In Homeric poetry, an illustration of the same process at work is the narrative already mentioned, the story of Meleager told by Phoenix to Achilles and obviously constructed around the situation of Phoenix's hearer. A traditional audience would interpret this narrative not so much in terms of dictional items as on a larger scale, that of paradigmatic figures and their associated traits.

3. The meaningfulness of repeated phraseology captured most of the attention in the debates over poetics that followed Parry's demonstration of the compositional utility of formulaic language. There are still die-hard defenders of writerly Homeric epics who claim that the perspective of oral traditional aesthetics is a denial of poetic beauty or of an author's freedom (see Vivante; Shive). Yet without an acknowledgment of traditional referentiality, debates over whether or not such phrases as "life-giving" (or "grain-bearing") earth (*Il.* 3.243) contain the "high poetical truth" attributed to it by John Ruskin (and denied by Matthew Arnold) degenerate into sterile exercises in subjectivity (Foley, *Immanent Art* 252). From an oral perspective, more progress can be made if one looks not only at the metrical usefulness of phrases but also at all the contextual regularities in their deployment, and not only within narrative portions (where Parry's initial studies of noun-epithet formulas naturally lead later investigations) but also within the frequent direct-speech sections of the poems. At the level of direct speech, we can see how the characterization of a figure relies on the audience's appreciation of

the associations underlying a rhetorical ploy repeated elsewhere in Homer. When Telemachus's mother tries to prevent Phemius from singing, the young man intervenes, saying, "Poets are not responsible; Zeus, somehow, is responsible / Who gives to bread-winning men, to each, what he wants. / There is no reason to fault the singing of the Danaan's bad fate" (*Od.* 1.347–49). Telemachus concludes by telling his mother to "go back to your quarters and do your own work . . . and tell the maids to do theirs; big talk (*múthos*) will be a care to men, to all of them, especially me. For the power in the house belongs to this one" (1.356–59). His words sound authoritative.

When we make oral traditional philological comparisons, however, we find more complexity. In book 11, the king, Alkinoos, uses nearly the same words to assert his power over the arrangement of Odysseus's trip home: "The send-off will be a care to men, to all of them, especially me. For the power among the people belongs to this one" (352–53). Given what we know about the Phaeacians, the queen is in fact more powerful (see, e.g., 6.310–12). This pragmatic fact appears as well in the most famous occurrence of this formulaic rhetorical pattern in the *Iliad*, when Hector tells Andromache, "Go home; war will be a care to men, especially me" (6.490–93). For it is clear from his earlier words that he will not succeed; he fully expects to die in his defense of Troy. In short, the philologist's investigation of repetition takes us this far, showing that two speakers whom the poetry represents as less than powerful use similar phrases to claim authority. The oralist simply adds that such repetition, like formulaic repetition generally, is an indication of traditionality; therefore, the audience, even if they never had heard the compositions we now identify as the *Odyssey* and the *Iliad*, would be familiar with the formulaic rhetorical ploy and so detect irony in Telemachus's words. Telemachus asserts that he can handle the situation on Ithaca precisely when it is about to prove too much for him (see Martin, "Telemachus").

These examples hardly begin to show the depths one can plumb when helped by oral theory. They are meant only to illustrate the various levels at which oral-influenced interpretation can prove fruitful. It is worth pointing out that students and teachers working with accurate English translations can often undertake this type of explication. (Ideally, they would use the translations now available online, with related text-search functions to locate similarities. These translations could also be represented in hypertext formats, so that clicking on one scene would bring up cognate passages.)[4] The oral approach calls for a shift in pedagogical strategy: instead of teaching the *Iliad* and *Odyssey* as the prelude to later written epics, we should teach them either alongside demonstrably oral poems or within an immersion course in Greek culture and poetry. After all, if the approach of oral poetics shows us again and again how these compositions depend on implicit contextualized meanings, it makes little sense to ask that the *Iliad* and *Odyssey* be read denuded of the meager but precious cultural information we still can garner. Hesiodic verse (*Theogony*; *Works and Days*), at the least, and preferably thematically selected portions of Greek lyric and tragic poetry as well, should surround the presentation of Homeric epic. Then students can obtain a real sense of what a sophisticated, intricate, and rich tradition means.

Homeric poetry, in the context I am suggesting for study, does not finally differ from other genres of ancient Greek literature in at least one respect: until the fourth century, at the earliest, all the verbal art of this culture — drama, lyric, rhetoric, history, even philosophy — values and foregrounds the act of speaking in a way that is difficult for us to appreciate fully, standing as we do in the shadow of these primeval forms that determined later European literary expression. This ancient focus on the speech act should form the ultimate framework for analysis of poetic acts in the culture. Without appreciating the culture's powerful ideological assurance that speech matters — that one must be, as Achilles was taught to be, a "speaker of speeches and doer of deeds" (*Il.* 9.443) — the obsession of Homeric poetry with mimesis, the representation of speeches, remains puzzling. Homeric poetry calls these "powerful utterances" *muthoi* (the word that gives us "myth" — but that is another story). Such speeches have their own internal poetics in Homer; moreover, comparative analysis shows us that the types of speeches designated *muthoi* in Homer are, in many living oral cultures, utilitarian, nonpoetic, yet formal genres of self-presentation: insults, commands, memorializations (Martin, *Language*). Studying how Homeric poetry represents the social interactions of heroes and gods cannot be divorced from a study of Homeric poetics; or, put another way, an anthropology must accompany our philology. Perhaps this is the most enduring lesson that we can take away from the *Iliad* and *Odyssey*, a lesson immensely enhanced by the perspective of oral traditional poetics. Poetry as a form of commemoration, assertion, performance, with all its shared conventions and traditions, has a central role to play, in our lives as in those of Homer's fictional beings.

Notes

The translations from the *Iliad* and *Odyssey* are mine.

1. For example, the study of Homeric "type-scenes" by modern scholars originated independently of Parry's work. See Edwards.
2. Many more could be discussed, for which I refer readers to Foley, *Traditional Oral Epic*; Lord, *Epic Singers*; Martin, *Language*; Nagler; and Nagy, *Best*.
3. That a Greek audience would have known such a genre is evident from several separate ancient compositions designated *hupothêkai* ("advice").
4. Searchable, online texts in English can be located on the World Wide Web at a number of sites featuring collections of literary classics; a Web search engine such as Yahoo or Lycos can help find them. Searchable Greek texts of the Homeric poems (and most of ancient Greek literature) are available for lease in CD-ROM form from the *Thesaurus Linguae Graecae* project at the University of California, Irvine.

Alexandra H. Olsen

Beowulf

The Old English period (449 CE–1066 CE) marks the beginnings of the transition in England from orality to literacy. The poetic works composed during this period are transitional, interweaving oral traditional and literary structure and reference. *Beowulf*, the most important work in Old English, is known to us only in written form, from the manuscript British Museum Cotton Vitellius A. xv (Malone), but it shows signs of the techniques of orally composed poetry. One frequently debated question concerns exactly where *Beowulf* lies on the oral-written continuum. Some scholars consider *Beowulf* a transcription of a scop's (oral poet's) song, several manuscript copies removed from the original; others, a literary text composed in writing with roots in oral tradition; and still others, a literate work with no roots in oral tradition (see O'Keeffe).

Method of Composition

The question of means of composition is pedagogically fundamental, affecting even the choice of translation. One widely used translation

351

is the prose rendering of E. T. Donaldson, found in the *Norton Anthology* (Abrams); it gives readers little sense of the language of the poem. A better choice is a verse translation, like the one by Stanley B. Greenfield (*Readable* Beowulf) or the one by Burton Raffel. The question also affects how we read and teach the poem. Some scholars view *Beowulf* as a work composed in writing for private manuscript reading and based on literate models. The perspective from oral tradition is diametrically opposed to such an approach. The preponderance of the evidence suggests that *Beowulf* is neither a work displaying primary literacy nor the direct record of a scop's song but instead a copy of a copy, an oral-derived work that may have been revised by scribes (on scribal revision, see Kiernan; O'Keeffe). When the Danes return from Grendel's mere the morning after Beowulf and Grendel have fought, the poet includes a passage about a scop composing a poem praising Beowulf and comparing him to Sigemund and Heremod (lines 867b–74a), characters present in both the Old Norse (*Saga of the Volsungs*) and Middle High German (*Nibelungenlied*) traditions. As scholars like Jeff Opland have noted, this passage presents a picture of the oral singer practicing his craft. It suggests that orally composed poetry underlies our extant text and was still of interest to the audience. As a result, understanding the context of oral tradition is crucial for understanding *Beowulf*.

Audience

The question of the composition of *Beowulf* is intertwined with another question, that of the intended audience. Some scholars assume that the audience was clerical, literate in both English and Latin, and acquainted with a spectrum of written works. In contrast, other scholars assume that the audience was the elite class of lay society — illiterate, dependent on oral transmission, and valuing narrative or eulogistic songs dealing with historical material. Literacy came to England with Augustine and his missionaries in 598 CE and at first was exclusively the possession of the clerical classes. After the Viking invasions, King Alfred the Great of Wessex (849–99) envisioned a world of vernacular literacy, commanding that Latin works necessary for all to know be translated into English. It is important to realize that neither the laity nor the clergy abandoned oral traditional ways of thinking and doing business at the first draft of literacy. Oral songs continued to be performed, even in monastic settings, if we accept the witness of Alcuin (735–804), who complains about vernacular songs sung in the refectory of Lindisfarne.

Beowulf seems to be directed at a lay audience that shared aristocratic values and is best interpreted as what Robert Payson Creed calls "a traditional Germanic 'chiefdom tale'" ("Sutton Hoo" 71). Set on the continent in the fifth century, *Beowulf* evokes the values of a warrior community and the shared history of the audience's ancestors. It would have served to bind the members of the community together by giving them a common identity and purpose.

It is important to reiterate that although oral-derived, *Beowulf* is known to us only from the manuscript. Generations of editorial emendation have produced a received text of *Beowulf* (replicated in translations) that differs from the manuscript in many ways. As more and more scholars delete many of these cumbersome emendations, practicing what Whitney F. Bolton has called "subtractive rectification" (Beowulf 88) of the edited text of *Beowulf*, it becomes clear that the manuscript version that underlies our critical editions is neither metrically neat nor textually consistent. If we read the text in the linear way that we would hear an oral performance, we are reading *Beowulf* in a way as much attuned to its oral traditional roots as is possible today.

Beowulf and Oral Tradition

The oral-derived nature of the poem is most apparent when we become aware of the oral traditional structure of the poem (Olsen, "Oral-Formulaic Research . . . I" and "Oral-Formulaic Research . . . II"; Foley, *Theory* and *Traditional Oral Epic*). Correspondingly, the stylistic and formal features of *Beowulf* are most easy to understand when we take into account its oral roots (Irving). These features include the plot (traditional Germanic heroic material) and elliptical allusions to legendary material, often so cryptic that we cannot recover the story from the poem alone. The tale recounted by Hrothgar's court poet (lines 1068–1159) serves as an example. In this episode of *Beowulf*, the battle partially told both by the poet and in a separate poem known as the "The Finnsburg Fragment," the actual presentation is relatively sketchy. While it is clear that Finn, a Frisian prince, has married Hildeburh, a Dane and sister to Hnæf, a warrior who has come to Finn's stronghold, the circumstances of the attack against Hnæf and his men remain inexplicit. But undoubtedly this brief allusion would have evoked all the narrative power of the entire story for an audience familiar with Germanic oral traditions, much in the same way that the phrase "Once upon a time" evokes the larger setting of a fairy tale (for further analysis of this episode, see Bonjour, *Digressions*).

Other symptoms of the poem's oral-derived nature include the additive style, the mixture of dialect forms with many archaisms, and the use of formulaic diction and themes. The additive style is suggested by the appositive nature of the poem, by the formulaic structure of the verse (see below), and by the free-standing proverbs throughout *Beowulf*, such as the advice to young warriors in lines 22–25.[1] None of these features is directly relevant to the most immediate context of *Beowulf*, but each helps to place the poem clearly in the Anglo-Saxon heroic tradition as a whole. The variety of dialects represented in the text, compounded by unstable spelling conventions, suggests a specialized poetic language (or register) that diverges from regular spoken or written language. Likewise, words such as *guma* ("man") that appear in Old English poetry (e.g., *Beo.* 878a) but never in prose suggest archaisms that are retained only in the traditional poetic idiom.

The evidence of oral tradition, however, is clearest on the level of diction, labeled formulaic by Milman Parry and his followers. The *formulas*, the building blocks of traditional phraseology, are metrically bound units usually larger than a single word and available to the author as part of the specialized language used to construct the poem. One example in *Beowulf* is the whole-line formula that introduces speeches: X spoke, Y's son. The author says, "Unferth spoke, Ecglaf's son," "Beowulf spoke, Ecgtheow's son," and "Wiglaf spoke,

Weohstan's son" (499, 529, 2862). Such formulas, however, are more than conventional metrical devices. The patronymic phrases, for instance, evoke not only lineage but also, as John Miles Foley states, "the entire mythic figure for which this nominal description metonymically stands" (*Immanent Art* 197). Some phrases are *formulaic systems*, half lines that express a given idea with some variation of particular words. For example, there exists a system "X under the clouds," where X is a variable element. The system yields half lines like "he grew up under the clouds," "he advanced under the clouds," and "water under the clouds" (8a, 714a, 1631a). Whatever the exact method of composition of *Beowulf*, it is clear that the poet employed oral traditional phraseology. When we are aware of the traditional method, we read the poem — even in translation — as part of the oral-derived poetic tradition common not only to the Anglo-Saxons but also to the other Germanic peoples of the northern European continent with whom the *Beowulf* audience shared its cultural heritage.

Oral traditional works also contain typical narrative scenes that scholars have called themes. Themes are recurrent scenic units like Exile (such as the "Lament of the Last Survivor" in *Beo.* 2247–66), the Beasts of Battle (the wolf, the raven, and the sea eagle who accompany armies and feed on carnage following battle, appearing in *Beo.* 3024b–27), and the Hero on the Beach (the hero in a liminal situation at the beginning or end of a journey, found in *Beo.* 301–07a, 1963–66).[2] The Beasts of Battle theme, identified by F. P. Magoun, is relatively common in the surviving corpus of Anglo-Saxon poetry and has associative meanings for audiences familiar with traditional Germanic narrative structures.[3] Foley observes how this theme functions associatively in *Beowulf* 3018–30a, a scene preceding rather than following battle (*Immanent Art* 228–31). After the messenger's report predicting doom for the Geats after the loss of Beowulf, the image of the raven, eagle, and wolf serves to "emphasize the nature of that bleakness" to "[betoken] defeat and physical mutilation of the dead even before the battle is joined" (230). Themes and formulas are both regularly employed by oral singers to develop songs, and both tend to survive in poetry long after the compositional function they served in the performance of primary oral narrative has shifted or diminished. As Alain Renoir points out, the traditional paradigms contextualize different poems, and their "impact upon our consciousness will be reinforced every time we read another poem in the group" (*Key* 94).

Pedagogical Strategy

Beowulf's roots in traditional oral narrative directly and importantly affect basic pedagogy, in that a teacher must discuss the mode of composition and its ramifications. Students should be reminded that the performance of such a traditional heroic piece as *Beowulf* did not simply entertain its audience but also shaped its members into a community through the articulation of shared cultural values and ideals that were embodied in their ancestors' heroic actions. For example, the honor associated with fighting alongside one's leader, even in the face of certain defeat, is reflected in Wiglaf's and Beowulf's joint combat against the dragon after the other warriors have fled. As for likely pedagogical contexts, the poem is valuable to study in both a survey course of British literature and in a course on oral tradition. It is appropriate as well in a multicultural class, because it gives us a glimpse of a heroic northern European society. Whatever the course, it is useful to assign Albert Lord's *The Singer of Tales* in order to present the nature of oral-formulaic literature and its widespread provenance. Students should also understand the artistry of the *Beowulf* poet. Scholarship by Foley (*Traditional Oral Epic* and *Immanent Art*) and Renoir (*Key*), used in conjunction with the theories of Lord and Parry, illustrates how meaning is created through specific realization of traditional forms.

Ideally, a teacher should provide students with an opportunity to hear selected passages from the original; given *Beowulf*'s roots, we do the poem a disservice when we approach it as we would a text composed in writing. Tapes are available (like that of Creed, whose performance of the poem is accompanied by Mary Remnant on a reconstruction of the Sutton Hoo harp) that give students an idea of the aural reality of the poem.[4] As part of this exercise, I customarily provide transcriptions of the passages from the original poem on the tape, asking students to pay careful attention to the trademark alliteration and to try to perform a few lines themselves to get a feel for giving as well as hearing an oral performance.

A parallel exercise involves introducing the concepts of formula and theme through handouts. I provide a digest of formulas and formulaic systems in the original, with references to the translation, so that students can appreciate the patterns involved and understand them as oral traditional units of expression. Once they understand that repetitive phraseology generates meaning not by uniqueness of expression but by its use of the "word-hoard" (*Beo.* 259b) of oral tradition, I turn to a discussion of themes, providing handouts of translations from *Beowulf* or from other Old English poems. For example, Beowulf's disarming before his battle with Grendel makes for an interesting comparison with arming scenes before the conflicts with Grendel's mother and the dragon. While all three scenes are instances of the traditional theme of a hero preparing himself for battle, each one uses the theme uniquely to inform completely different encounters with completely different results. (Each Beowulfian battle has its own particular shape and outcome.) Discussion of such themes is aimed at exploring how the traditional theme is adapted to its narrative context while retaining its traditional schema and how variations on a traditional theme resonate in a way unknown in modern literature (see Foley, *Immanent Art*). Consideration of these narrative units leads to the discussion of other cultural values, such as images of the hero, the lady, and the king, as well as how those values inform Beowulf's fights against the monsters.

If students wish to study *Beowulf* in the original, Howell D. Chickering Jr.'s dual-language edition is a helpful tool. In addition, computer-assisted materials like *The Beowulf Workstation* (see Conner, Deegan, and Lees) are available. An electronic *Beowulf* can be accessed on the Internet from Georgetown University's server *Labyrinth* (http://www.georgetown.edu/labyrinth). *Beginning Old English*, instructional software providing an introduction to Old English grammar with an exercise diskette by Constance B. Hieatt, Brian Shaw, and Duncan Macrae-Gibson, is another useful resource. Such electronic teaching aids permit students to complete exercises involving Old English at their own pace rather than in a classroom setting and may make learning the language and studying *Beowulf* in the original more appealing to a computer-literate generation.

———

We must recognize the oral traditional structure of *Beowulf* in order to do justice to the poem, and we must endeavor to teach the aesthetic implications of that structure to our classes, reconstructing an awareness of the poem in the context of distinctly Anglo-Saxon poetic traditions. By understanding the functions of oral traditional formulas, themes, and larger rhetorical patterns, we can move toward Renoir's goal that these structures "be taken into account not only by experienced scholars but also by readers trying their hand at literary interpretation for the first time" (*Key* 111). By explaining and even performing an oral traditional *Beowulf* in the classroom, the essence of this text can literally come alive for all involved. Our students will no longer have to approach *Beowulf* from the confining perspective of private readers; rather, they will be able to experience the poem as an audience that is to some extent familiar with implications of the oral traditional idiom.[5]

Notes

1. "So young men build / The future, wisely open-handed in peace, / Protected in war; so warriors earn / Their fame, and wealth is shaped with a sword" (trans. Raffel 1).
2. For discussion of the Exile theme, see Greenfield "Expression"; Rissanen; Renoir, *Key*. The Beasts of Battle theme is analyzed in Magoun; Bonjour, "*Beowulf*"; Renoir, *Key*; Metcalf. For discussion of the Hero on the Beach, see Crowne; Renoir, *Key*; Fry, "Hero"; Thormann; Olsen, "Guthlac."
3. Magoun gives twelve instances of this theme: *Battle of Brunanburg* 60–65a; *Beowulf* 3024b–27; *Elene* 27b–30, 110b–14a; *Exodus* 162–67; *Finnsburg* 5a–7a, 34–35a; *Genesis A* 1983b–85a; *Judith* 204b–12a, 294b–96a; *Battle of Maldon* 106–107; and *The Wanderer* 81b–83a.
4. Available on cassette from RadioArts, Inc., 833 West End Ave., No. 6D, New York, NY 10025. See also Daskalopoulos, this volume.
5. For additional ideas on teaching *Beowulf*, see Bessinger and Yeager.

Carl Lindahl

Chaucer

To students of oral traditions, Chaucer at first glance presents a baffling double image. The first Chaucer is supremely literary, a translator of Latin philosophy and French poetry who reads himself to sleep in silent solitude (*Parliament of Fowls*, lines 15–98).[1] For this man, books possess semisacred importance, holding the very key to remembrance (*Legend of Good Women*, line F26). This Chaucer seems to crave the immortality that only fixed, imperishable writing can confer. He adores the canonized poets of antiquity (*Troilus and Criseyde* 5.1792) and upbraids his scribe for miscopying his poetry (*Adam Scriveyn*). There seems to be little oral tradition in the concerns of this man.

The second Chaucer, teller of the *Canterbury Tales*, presents a different image altogether. He is an acute and impressionable listener, reporting the speech of a diverse pilgrim band that spans a social range from knight to peasant, and he retells with relish the pilgrims' pious legends and dirty jokes. This Chaucer is a fluid narrator, vitally aware of how expert tale-telling requires sensitivity to audience and situation and deeply conscious that oral artists create each tale anew for the context at hand. When the Friar — engaged in a war of words with his fellow pilgrim, the Summoner — takes his turn to tell a tale, he casts a summoner in the role of the dupe, for the first time on record. Many medieval tales identical in plot structure to the Friar's feature lawyers, judges, or other figures as dupes, but only Chaucer's Friar ridicules a summoner — and in so doing manages not only to amuse his audience but also to embarrass his foe. The second Chaucer thus manipulates written sources to ensure that his pilgrims will tell apt and effective tales. When, in the *Canterbury Tales*, the second Chaucer must tell a tale himself, he performs an "ale-house romance" spiced with the diction of lower-class poetry. Yet, even as he mocks his own poetic pretensions, Chaucer shows deep knowledge of popular poetry and suggests that he is somehow connected to its traditions. Reading Chaucer's Tale of Sir Thopas with the image of the first Chaucer in mind, students may well experience cognitive dissonance, as if they were hearing T. S. Eliot tell a tall tale in Mark Twain's voice.

The two Chaucers resolve into a single figure only when we have realized that literary and oral cultures of Chaucer's England possessed far more continuity and complementarity than literary scholars or folklorists were once willing to admit.[2]

Chaucer's Elite Oral Traditions

The first Chaucer represents an elite oral culture. Education in schools and at court required mastery of Latin as well as exposure to literature in French, the language of the aristocracy. Nevertheless, this elite world possessed substantial oral dimensions. The trivium, or elementary school curriculum, required students to recite poetry. Such elite rhetorics as Geoffrey of Vinsauf's *Poetria Nova* coached poets in oral delivery, prescribing the intonations and gestures appropriate for live performance. Training in dialectic required students to think orally as they engaged in continual dialogue with their teachers. Textbooks and lessons were not merely silently read, they were also orally performed.

Beyond the classroom, in courtly and merchant-class milieus, entertainment literature was also orally performed, often in dramatic settings. Thirteenth-century London merchants recited love poetry in annual competitions. After Chaucer's death, many of his associates held monthly dinner meetings during which they performed poetry. In 1386 — about the time Chaucer began the *Canterbury Tales* — several French knights of his acquaintance were imprisoned in Damascus; they passed the time communally composing a poetic debate in which each author framed an answer to the same question: whether to be loyal or faithless in love. Once released, the knights performed their composition at the papal palace in Avignon (Lindahl, "Festive Form" 569–70). Throughout Chaucer's age, poetry was an art crafted for oral performance and often composed with a specific audience in mind.

Once students recognize that even the refined literature of Chaucer's day was an oral pastime, they are better prepared to experience his art. Medieval elite orality so deeply affected Chaucer's poetry that many critics have argued that even in times and places far removed from its composition it must be read aloud to be properly read at all. Innumerable readers have recognized this precept. Three centuries after Chaucer's death, the circle of Wordsworth and Coleridge entertained themselves by reading the *Canterbury Tales* to one another (Spurgeon 2: 5, 14). Betsy Bowden has argued persuasively that Chaucer's poetry contains many ambiguities that can be resolved only by oral interpretation, and to underscore her point she collected oral readings from twentieth-century Chaucerians, which are issued in an audiocassette accompanying her book, *Chaucer Aloud*.

Thus, even in the most elite sense, Chaucer is undeniably an oral poet. Students in literature classes, a rather elite and artificial group, may at first experience Chaucer by simulating his original context and making his poems oral entertainments. I ask students to overcome the daunting orthography and variant spellings of Middle English by reading aloud while preparing for class, and in class we employ continuous oral readings. I read to them, they read to one another, and we play Betsy Bowden's tapes and other sound recordings to demonstrate the vividness of Chaucer's refined orality.

Chaucer's Folk Oral Traditions

Chaucer's second tradition—the storytelling of the *Canterbury Tales*—represents what folklorists most commonly associate with the term *oral*. He taps the narrative styles of "sundry folk" to present a persuasively oral story-swapping session seldom if ever equaled in world literature. Only in the twentieth century, with such masterpieces as Zora Neale Hurston's *Mules and Men*, has Chaucer been matched at translating oral narrative strategies into writing.

Chaucer's success in depicting storytelling was so great that some nineteenth-century critics treated the *Canterbury Tales* as a blow-by-blow account of an actual days-long entertainment. The critics fashioned elaborate itineraries to account for how many tales were told on a given day and where each was told along the road to Canterbury. This response is a remarkable tribute to Chaucer's art, as the poem embraces many obvious artificialities: no reader believes, for example, that a group of horseback pilgrims would exchange tales in elaborately patterned verse.

Nor does the oral effect of the poem rest primarily in the fact that the great majority of the *Canterbury Tales* possess analogues in folktales told orally in the Middle Ages—and, often, today. That the Reeve's Tale, for example, has been recently retold as a folktale in the Ozarks (Randolph, *"Who"* 29–30, 190) bears little relevance. Plot or subject alone does not make a folktale. Shakespeare's *Cymbeline* shares the plot of "Snow White" and Donald Barthelme's "Grandmother's House" retells "Little Red Ridinghood," yet no one claims that either literary work is a folktale.

What sets Chaucer apart from Shakespeare and Barthelme is that he puts his tales in lifelike contexts, showing how oral stories spring from specific situations, how tellers twist the plots and styles of their tales to affect an immediate audience. In the General Prologue, Chaucer introduces his storytellers—some twenty-nine pilgrims assembled by chance to travel together to Canterbury—and reveals aspects of their status and backgrounds that will come into play when the storytelling begins. He then introduces an innkeeper Host who proclaims himself master of ceremonies for a traveling storytelling contest to be conducted according to rules similar to those of festive games actually enacted in fourteenth-century England (Lindahl, "Festive Form"). When studies and records of Chaucer's social milieu are read together with his poetry, powerful similarities are revealed between medieval London society and the society of the *Canterbury Tales*.

It soon becomes clear that the pilgrims represent two basic social divisions — upper-class gentils and lowly churls — and perform according to two corresponding oral codes. Such refined narrators as the Knight and Squire employ the elite oral styles of the trivium — beginning with elaborate apologies for their lack of skill and spicing their tales with rhetorical devices familiar to schooled artists. The gentils may outrank the Host in real life, but they hale him as the uncontested master of their game. Such lower-class figures as the Miller and Cook, however, rebel against their Host. Holiday games afforded a rare opportunity for churls to talk back to gentils, and Chaucer's lowly characters are not about to surrender their holiday privileges to anyone.

While the upper-class pilgrims treat the storytelling as an individual competition, the churls craft their tales as weapons of class and occupational conflict. Aside from oral testimony recorded imperfectly in trial transcripts and chronicles, there is no record of Chaucer's contemporaries' everyday speech; thus the accuracy of Chaucer's depiction of oral performance can never be conclusively established. However, we can be certain about some aspects of the churls' performances. As they argue during breaks between tales, the Miller, Reeve, and Cook employ expletives and proverbs seldom found elsewhere in Middle English poetry but often attested in the oral testimony of slander cases. These churls use proverbs, *blasons populaires*, and dialect found in records of oral performances from subsequent centuries, though not in medieval writings. Most enticingly, the churls shape their tales into elaborate indirect insults strikingly similar in form and function to those in tales performed orally in corresponding situations today. Such common twentieth-century insult games as the dozens (see Abrahams, "Playing") offer telling analogues to the verbal and social dynamics at work, for example, in the narrative duel between Robin the Miller and Oswald the Reeve.

Robin enters the contest as a lower-class rebel seizing his holiday privileges: talking back to the Host, claiming to know a tale as noble as the Knight's, and using it to insult Oswald indirectly. Oswald responds defensively, saying in effect, You're insulting me and I don't like it! Robin denies the charge, but his apology is so insinuating that it makes Oswald even angrier. In Chaucer's game, as in the dozens, showing anger is a sign of weakness; Robin bests Oswald in this oral skirmish and then goes on to tell a tale that can be said to ridicule all his adversaries: the Knight, the Host, and Oswald.

I recommend that students dramatize the repartee of the pilgrim churls, with each student being assigned a pilgrim. Having finished the General Prologue, they will be familiar with Chaucer's upper-class diction, and the folk orality of the churls will strike them for what it is: a different language altogether. Performing the pilgrims' wordplay, students will encounter the second great oral tradition of Chaucer's time, and the churls' orality may strike them as more complex, more subtle, and more artful than the elite orality of the Knight. Just as the meaning of a folktale is inseparable from its function in its immediate context, Chaucer resists interpretation until teachers and students — through contextualizing research and interactive performance — have recovered something of the vitality of the two great oral traditions on which he drew.

Notes

1. Citations in this essay are from *The Riverside Chaucer*. For general ideas on teaching Chaucer, see Gibaldi.
2. For thorough discussions of the folktale styles of Chaucer's lower-class pilgrims and of parallels between the *Canterbury Tales* and medieval festive performances, see Lindahl, *Earnest Games*. For a recent overview of oral approaches to the *Canterbury Tales*, see Parks, "Oral Tradition."

Leslie Stratyner

The Middle English Romance
and the Alliterative Tradition

It is no surprise that many of the hallmarks of traditional oral poetry
are present in the Middle English romances and poetry of the alliterative revival, from the repetition of phrases and scenes to the formation of the often stereotypical characters who populate them. As
Mark Amodio points out, "The central affective, metonymic character of the oral tradition (something which insured its continued survival before the introduction of writing) does not vanish once the
text becomes encoded in manuscripts" (*Oral Poetics* 19).

Thus scholars generally agree that the Middle English romances
and the poetry of the alliterative revival have strong roots in oral
tradition (Bradbury; Janet Coleman).[1] The alliterative revival traces
its origins back to Anglo-Saxon alliterative oral and oral-derived poetry, and thus it is no surprise that even fourteenth-century poets
utilize the kinds of themes and formulaic phraseology employed by
their poetic predecessors. The survival of the alliterative line, most
probably through oral transmission in the aftermath of the Norman

invasion, is a testament to the essentially conservative nature of orally derived verse.

Yet the beginning of the English medieval romance (which has significant ties to the alliterative revival) was not in England but, rather, in France, in the twelfth century, and the original ideas associated with the romance, such as the quest, courtly love, and attention to manners and courtesy, survived after its import into Britain. Developing out of French feudalism, the romance in the medieval sense of the word was a narrative describing the adventures of a hero progressing toward a goal (see Vitz, this volume).

That, of course, is the definition of romance in the broadest sense. The English medieval romance, however, is typically divided by subject matter into four subcategories, often termed "the matter of France," "the matter of Rome," "the matter of Britain," and "the matter of England." The first three of these terms were coined by Jean Bodel (a late twelfth-century writer of romance); the last is often employed by modern scholars to describe romances based on English and Anglo-Norman tales (as opposed to stories ostensibly of Celtic origin). The matter-of-France romances (such as *Firumbras* and *Outel and Roland* [O'Sullivan]) are all based on stories involving the exploits of Charlemagne and his knights, while stories of the matter of Rome (including *Sir Orfeo* and *The Seege of Troye* [Barnicle]) use legends and tales from the ancient world as their base. Arthurian legend and folktales of Celtic origin are the subject matter of romances of the matter of Britain (Malory's *Le Mort D'Arthur*, the *Alliterative Morte Arthure*, and *Sir Gawain and the Green Knight* are all in this vein).[2] Stories of the matter of England concern English heroes and are usually situated in England. These stories testify as well to the significant Germanic influence on the development of the Middle English romance; one of the oldest extant English romances, *King Horn* (early thirteenth cent.), is set during the Viking raids before the conquest.

A key question in beginning any assessment of poetry produced in an even vestigially oral tradition is the method of transmission. There is an enormous amount of textual variation in the Middle English romances, and thus the transmission process of the romances has been a matter of constant debate. Did minstrels produce the differences in the texts? Were the scribes responsible? If the romances were memorized, who memorized them? As Murray McGillivray points out, we have no way to tell, but he does claim through an analysis of "memorial error" (errors in the text that are introduced due to faulty memorization) that minstrels and not scribes memorized the poems (27).[3]

Ready examples of this phenomenon can be found in *Sir Orfeo*, which exists in three separate manuscripts. One of these (the Auchinleck) antedates the other two (the Ashmole and Harley) by more than a hundred years. While the Ashmole and Harley manuscripts both differ from the Auchinleck, it is the Harley that diverges most significantly in its "corruption." The omissions and contractions of text increase steadily as the poem progresses. In the end, the poet of the *Sir Orfeo* found in the Harley manuscript has utilized 509 lines to tell the same story that the poet of the *Sir Orfeo* found in the Auchinleck manuscript tells in 602. A. J. Bliss explains this disjunction by specifically citing memorial transmission: "Probably the text was written down by a minstrel from memory. This would explain the steadily increasing omissions, the transpositions, and the greatly advanced corruption of the readings" (xvi).

Yet it is important to note that though the Harley text may be contracted, it does not differ significantly from the Auchinleck and Ashmole manuscripts in narrative detail, even when later in the poem its poet uses less than half as many lines as the Auchinleck poet to describe an identical incident. A poem like *Sir Orfeo* illustrates that although the romances seem to be heavily reliant on texts, their transmission (as Bradbury has also shown) may owe as much to memorial as scribal tradition. We may conclude, then, that although the Middle English romances and the poetry of the alliterative revival cannot be described as orally composed, they clearly can be termed "oral-derived" (Foley, *Traditional Oral Epic* 5).

Teaching Situations

Poems such as *Sir Gawain and the Green Knight*, *Le Mort D'Arthur*, *Havelok the Dane*, and the *Alliterative Morte Arthure* (a trustworthy translation is included in B. Stone) are certainly flexible enough and available enough to be incorporated into any number of courses, from general surveys to more focused surveys to upper-division seminars on medieval literature or epic and heroic narrative. But how does one approach teaching such works to students whose experience of verbal art is almost always exclusively textual, especially if the course is introductory and not centered on works rooted in oral tradition? Often students are confused and perplexed enough by any literature far removed from them in place and time. When we add the extra dimension of explaining and incorporating the different kind of mind-sets associated with oral and oral-derived works, we may fear that the students will not stay involved.

In practice, however, the incorporation of a focus on oral tradition can and does promote a high level of student response and interest. Much of what students encounter in the classroom involves a teaching experience that is restricted either geographically or temporally or both. A primary or secondary focus on the features associated with oral-derived texts will allow students to make connections that go beyond the limitations imposed by place and time. Some specific examples follow.

Epic Literature and Oral Tradition Classes

Since much of worldwide epic literature is oral or oral-derived, the Middle English romances and poems from the alliterative revival (despite seeming differences in genre, style, and subject matter) mesh very neatly with epic works that range from modern Africa to ancient Greece. A unit on the alliterative revival or the Middle English romances fits comfortably and logically in a comparatively configured course including everything from *Gilgamesh* to *The Song of Roland* (see Goldin's trans.). A particularly effective nexus of discussion is a poet's own description of his process of composition and of how the poem was transmitted to him. In *Sir Gawain and the Green Knight*, for example, we have the oft-quoted lines from the second stanza, where the poet himself makes mention of oral transmission:

If you will listen to my lay but a little while,
As I heard it in hall, I shall hasten to tell
anew.
As it was fashioned featly
In tale of derring-do,
And linked in measures meetly
By letters tried and true.

(Borroff 1, lines 30–36)

Though he speaks of the story's being fashioned in letters, the poet clearly asks his audience to listen to him tell a story that he heard first in court. If the *Gawain* poet is taught opposite *Beowulf*, a comparison can be made between this Middle English poet's assessment and the Anglo-Saxon bard's description of oral composition (*Beo.* 867b-71a). If Homer is included as well, the students can be asked to consider Odysseus's sparing of the bard Phemius and Phemius's speech to Odysseus concerning Phemius's poetic gift (*Od.* 22.344–53).

In this connection the students can be drawn into a discussion of how audience and audience response help create the poet's art. What is the difference (with respect to both poet and production) between composition in isolation for an unknown and future audience and composition before a known and present audience? What kind of audience response characterizes both scenarios? How might that audience response affect the poet and the poetry? Even in oral-derived works like the Middle English romances, evidence of that dynamic is still vital.

In tandem with this kind of discussion, a preliminary introduction to the thematic aspects of orally derived literature is also in order. Further progress can be made by examining some of the linguistic building blocks of oral traditional literature. A persistent feature of oral tradition that may be pointed out to students reading Malory, for example, is his use of alliterative clusters (T. McCarthy 69). Such clusters can be found as well in the *Alliterative Morte Arthure*.[4] The formula, the fundamental phraseological unit in many oral narrative traditions, is ubiquitous in Middle English romance and alliterative poetry from *King Horn* and *Havelok the Dane* to *Sir Gawain and the Green Knight*.[5]

General Surveys of Western and Non-Western Literature

Though certainly the poems of the alliterative revival and the Middle English romances cannot in today's terminology be deemed multicultural, they can be effectively taught with multicultural works. In fact, with oral tradition as the basis for discussion, students can be guided into a realization not only of the differences among varied cultures and their modes of poetic expression but also, and even more, of their startling similarities.

There are significant thematic unities that bind oral and oral-derived literatures, whether Western or non-Western. For example, the thematic pattern of battle in the *Alliterative Morte Arthure*, including such elements as challenge or message, arming for battle, arraying of troops, exhortations, dying prayers, and victory and aftermath, is a feature found in other oral and oral-derived poetry. The arming of the hero is a good topic for discussion and for comparative study. In a survey of Western literature, any number of examples can be elicited, from *Beowulf* to the *Iliad* to *Sir Gawain and the Green Knight*. Yet the hero twins of *Popol Vuh*, the Quiché Mayan epic, arm themselves as well before they engage in a contest with the lords of Xibalba. Another typically oral traditional thematic element such as renarration or resinging, in which a story is told first by the narrator and then by characters in the story, can be found in oral and oral-derived works from *Beowulf* to *Havelok the Dane* and *Sir Orfeo* (Bradbury).

An understanding of these and other typical features enhances any multicultural course that includes oral or oral-derived literature. Diverse societies shape their art in oral traditions, and an appreciation of similarities stemming from parallel origins and means of transmission adds a dimension to multicultural awareness.

Survey Courses in British Literature

A focal point for students enmeshed in a discussion of oral tradition is its conservative and traditionalist nature (Ong, *Orality* 41–42).

Many alliterative poems and romances are concerned with establishing and preserving the history of Britain. A course on the literature of Britain would also likely have as a focus the distinctly national flavor of some of the Middle English romances and the poetry of the alliterative revival as well. Lawman's *Brut* (Rosamund Allen), for example, falls squarely within the romances classified under the matter of Britain. So, too, *Le Mort D'Arthur* and the *Alliterative Morte Arthure*. Some romances subsumed under the matter of England (e.g., *Havelok the Dane* and *King Horn*) also highlight the Germanic legacy (*Horn, Havelok the Dane*, and *Sir Orfeo* are included in Sands).

––––––

The oral-derived status of the Middle English romances and the poems of the alliterative revival deserve continuing discussion as poetry produced in a culture with prominent ties to oral tradition. Though all these poems have been composed by literate authors in letters "tried and true," we cannot ignore their ties to oral tradition; we must also listen to the tales they tell (see also Aertsen and MacDonald; Barron; Meale).

Notes

1. For a review of scholarship on oral tradition's influence on Middle English poetry, see Parks, "Oral-Formulaic Theory"; for ideas on how oral tradition is reflected in the works of Chaucer, see Lindahl, this volume; for a general overview of medieval drama that includes oral aspects, see Emmerson. On oral tradition and Old English poetry, see O'Keeffe, this volume; Olsen, this volume.
2. For general ideas on teaching the alliterative *Sir Gawain and the Green Knight*, see Miller and Chance; on the Arthurian tradition, see Fries and Watson.
3. McGillivray covers a number of theories on the transmission of the romances, including A. C. Baugh's adaptation of the Parry-Lord ideas of formula and theme as applied to the romances, and William Quinn and Audley Hall's theory of the minstrel's use of improvised rhyme. Parks also discusses "possible avenues by which a poem might flow from 'original creator' to audience" ("Oral-Formulaic Theory" 678).
4. Ritzke-Rutherford defines the cluster as "a group of words, usually loosely related metrically and semantically, which is regularly employed

to express a given essential idea without being restricted to a certain form or sequence, or to a certain number of lines" (73).

5. Parry's definition of formula is "a group of words which is regularly employed under the same metrical conditions to express a given essential idea" ("Studies" 80). See also Parks, "Oral-Formulaic Theory."

Evelyn Birge Vitz

Old French Literature

A Medieval French Scenario

A jongleur, or professional entertainer — we baptize him Gautier — is traveling toward a count's castle in northeastern France around 1210, on the day before Pentecost. In his haversack Gautier carries a vielle, a small, bowed, fiddlelike instrument that he plays at his shoulder. Gautier's speciality is the chanson de geste: with his vielle he sings the deeds of great warriors of the past (mostly of the Carolingian era — the eighth and ninth centuries). Gautier learned his songs from his uncle Pierre, also a jongleur. Neither man knew where the songs came from; both had heard them from other singers. Gautier also knows how to make up songs and to adapt them for different audiences and situations by reworking the formulas with which the songs are composed. (Formulas are prefabricated chunks of words used to describe men, women, horses, swords, arguments, battles, death scenes, and the like. See Bradbury, this volume; Zumwalt, this volume.) Gautier also knows some songs of more recent vintage. The jongleur from whom he learned his latest acquisition claimed it was written by a *clergeon*, a young student in Paris, but it sounded much like the other songs.

Gautier has a distinctive style and personal formulas that he has developed. His manner is less solemn than his uncle's (Pierre particularly loved to lament Roland's death at Roncevaux, in a story we know as *The Song of Roland* [Brault]). But though Gautier sings in a gay and cheerful manner, he always emphasizes religious themes, beginning and ending each of his songs with prayer. Gautier often performs along pilgrimage routes and at shrines — he has even been, singing all the way, to visit Saint James ("Santiago") at Compostela in Spain and has been in courts, at religious celebrations such as the upcoming Feast of the Holy Spirit.

Walking along, he falls in with other jongleurs on their way to the castle: this is to be a great gathering, with dozens of entertainers and festivities lasting for days. Gautier meets a slender Breton called Bréri the Young who accompanies himself on a small gilded harp as he sings *lais* (short poetic stories set to music; see Hanning and Ferrante). Bréri tells the tragic tale of Tristan and Iseut. There are many versions of this tale,[1] but Bréri's can make a stone weep. Another jongleur, Guillaume of Champagne, mostly tells romances — stories of King Arthur and his knights, composed in verse (Cline). Guillaume also knows a good many chansons de geste, and he performs both the songs and the romances to vielle accompaniment. With him is Aélis, a talented jongleuresse: they will do the chantefable, or song-story, of *Aucassin et Nicolette* together, Aélis playing the part of Nicolette (Mason).

Of these jongleurs only one can read and write. This former monk (or so he claims) knows his letters, even some Latin. He carries around with him, to the amazement of his fellows, a little book in which he says he keeps stories to "refresh his memory." The other jongleurs refresh theirs simply by performing their songs and tales often.

This particular castle draws them because its lord, Henri, is a lover of fine entertainment. Himself a trouvère, an "inventor" or maker of beautiful lyric poetry, he sings only love songs, in honor of an unnamed *dame*, and occasionally of the Blessed Virgin (see Abbott; Goldin, *Lyrics*; Rosenberg and Tischler). The count is said to know how to read. (He didn't need to learn to write; that is what scribes are for.) He owns some books, which he keeps in a special cupboard. Whether he can actually read or not, he is unquestionably learned. He surrounds himself with knowledgeable men called clerks (men trained in church schools, who often serve as archivists and notaries); his court is frequented by bishops as well. The count also has his own *menestrel*, or "minstrel," his private entertainer whom he keeps with him always. The *menestrel* sings to him and tells him stories every day.[2] The count appreciates art of the noblest and most refined sort, so the jongleurs with performing bears and those who tell vulgar stories with crude gestures (such as fabliaux; see Robert Harrison) stay away. For the feast the count is bringing in a jongleur who can recite a romance about the War of Thebes, made long ago, it is said, for the king of England (Coley).

The count's mother, Maud, will be there. She is devout—and she can certainly read. On an earlier visit to the castle, Gautier once observed her behavior, which seemed strange to him: she sat at a window and softly read aloud to herself from the life of a saint (Cazelles; Head). It is said that in her youth she used to read aloud from love romances to her intimates. The count is a widower, but his daughter will be present. She also sings, in a high, clear voice, *chansons de toile*, traditional women's weaving songs (Abbott; Rosenberg and Tischler; Zink). Also present will be the count's uncle, Hervé, a great brute of a man but a fine knight. Good news!—he loves to hear the songs in honor of Guillaume d'Orange, a similarly large and ugly man—he lost half his nose in battle to a Saracen!—but a mighty warrior and a saint. Gautier knows most of the many songs, at once comic and pious, devoted to Guillaume d'Orange and his beautiful and courageous wife, Guibourc.

A few hours later, after dinner in the great hall of the castle, Gautier's turn comes. He tunes his vielle and rises to sing, before the noisy but enthusiastic gathering, the song of Guillaume's *Conquest of Orange*: "Oyez, seigneurs!": "Listen, my lords, and may God give you grace!" (Ferrante 141).

General Implications of the Scenario

What does this scenario suggest about oral traditions in Old French literature?

1. Medieval France did not have a purely oral culture, by any means. Christians who went to church saw and heard the Bible and the liturgy read and chanted. Both ecclesiastic and secular authorities had recourse to written documents. Few people lived in full ignorance of writing and the written tradition (see Clanchy, *Memory*; Stock, *Implications*; Vitz, "Rethinking" and *Orality*).

2. In the early thirteenth century (and well beyond), few laypeople could read. Generally, great lords, women, and members of the bourgeoisie learned to read earlier than male aristocrats. Much of the reading was done for devotional, administrative, or commercial purposes rather than for pleasure (Clanchy, "Looking").

3. It cannot be said that in French medieval culture "oral" meant unsophisticated — simple, ignorant, folkloric, or the like — and that "written" meant subtle and learned.[3] Many noble nonliterates of the twelfth and thirteenth centuries were highly sophisticated men and women with refined tastes. And some literates — some clerks, in particular — produced and enjoyed simple, even crude, works.

4. Works that we today know and experience as texts — we read them privately, to ourselves, and silently — were in the Middle Ages almost invariably heard (Chaytor; Crosby; Saenger) and generally performed, in a fairly strong sense of that word: they were often recited from memory; many were sung, often to musical accompaniment (Page); sometimes they were partially acted out as well (Hult; Vitz, "Romans" and *Orality*). Most reading was done aloud and commonly to a group. Even people who could read for themselves liked to hear — and see — works performed aloud (Joyce Coleman). Thus, rather than read medieval works silently to ourselves over and over in order to get to know them well, we would generally do better to read them once or twice aloud to appreciate the quality of voice and the use of voices and sound effects; and we would do well to think in terms of appropriate gestures. When we are reading or teaching from a translation, we will find it worthwhile to use one (e.g., Cline)

that stays close to the original lexically, syntactically, and formally rather than one that smoothes out and rationalizes the Old French into modern prose. It is not just the plot or message that concerns us but the entire feel of the work.

5. Medieval works played many important social functions (Duggan, "Social Functions"). They were there to entertain — to give delight and solace; to make people laugh and cry. They also bound the members of the culture (or subculture) together by transmitting key social and religious values; they inspired; they informed. Some works reflected the particular tastes and values of the patrons who supported them, and of the poets and performers themselves. We cannot merely study medieval texts in and of themselves, analyzing the words and internal structures or constructing complex hermeneutical systems for interpreting them. Rather, we must devote thought to the social and cultural role played by individual works and by entire genres, and to the kinds of influence they were intended to have on their audiences.

6. Medieval France, a heterogeneous culture, knew many kinds of oral tradition. Along with the epic, which has strong Germanic roots, we find an abundance of material of Celtic origin, such as *lais* and the story of Tristan and Iseut; the story of Arthur, too, has Celtic roots. Lyrics may show Arabic influence as well as indirect influences from liturgical song and local traditions (P. Dronke). There were indigenous forms of women's love songs, weaving songs, and laments. Performers typically specialized in certain kinds of works. From the twelfth century on, increased frequency of travel, because of fairs, pilgrimages, and the Crusades, brought jongleurs, nobles, and bourgeois alike into contact with an increasingly wide variety of oral forms.

7. There were different levels of entertainment and entertainers, in an established hierarchy from the *grand chant courtois* (the noble love lyric, often sung by great lords and ladies themselves) down to shows by acrobats, magicians, and the like (Faral; Page; Vitz, *Orality*).

8. We find complex blends and interactions between oral and written traditions. Works that were originally written could be

learned by heart and recited or sung by illiterate jongleurs. Traditionally oral genres (like the chanson de geste and the weaving song) might also be composed by literates, such as clerks; these works could then be copied and compiled into manuscripts by scribes. If it were not for these scribes and the patrons who supported their work, we would know little or nothing about the oral traditions of the medieval period. But that a work was ultimately written down does not mean it was originally composed in written form or by a person who was in any way literate. Insofar as possible, we must distinguish between composition, performance, and transmission.

9. Both oral and written traditions had prestige in the medieval period; each carried its own authority: the former that of lived experience, of the eyewitness, the latter that of the book (Zumthor, *Oral Poetry* and *Toward a Medieval Poetics*). Storytellers sometimes claim that they "read it in a book" but that doesn't mean we must believe them. Similarly, writers may declare that they "heard the story told"; they too may be making this claim simply to win audience favor. We should understand all such statements not as reflective of biographical realities but, rather, as flowing from a rhetorical need, found in poets and performers everywhere, to delight and satisfy an audience.

10. Those of us who study, teach, and love the great stories and songs of medieval France might see our role as part archaeologist, part drama-historian. Like archaeologists, we need to try to imagine—to dig up and reconstruct—how the texts that we read today functioned and came alive in medieval culture. Like historians of drama, we need to think of these works as performed, in the many and varied senses of that word.

Pedagogical Implications of the Scenario

Issues of Genre

Certain medieval genres are strongly marked by oral or by written traditions. The chanson de geste is, as we have seen, strongly rooted in orality. By contrast, the saint's life might be the translation of a Latin work and might quote from other literary lives, the liturgy, or the Bible; it might be read or sung from a book in a religious service;

it might reflect knowledge of classical rhetoric. But no medieval genre is absolutely oral or absolutely written and literary. To take the lyric, songs have been sung in every culture since time immemorial; the lyric is not a written tradition. But literary motifs and themes, and the influence of learned authors and models, also exist in the lyric. Moreover, writers sometimes imitate oral style, as with traditional women's weaving songs that were apparently sometimes composed by professional male writers. Thus the lyric contains oral and written possibilities, and the same is true of other genres. There are oral saints' lives, such as the entertaining hagiographical epics devoted to Saint Guillaume d'Orange. Some chansons de geste, like the *Song of Roland* in the Oxford version that we normally read today (Brault),[4] may have had some literary polish laid over an oral original; and clerks composed some French epics, especially from the thirteenth century on. Many works, and genres as a whole, show the pull of both oral and written traditions. This is particularly true of early romances, where we find clerks trying to sound like minstrels and minstrels trying to sound like clerks — and we are not always sure which is which. Probably the most strikingly oral of surviving romance-type narratives is Béroul's *Tristan* (Lacy); among the unquestionably writerly early romances is Benoît de Sainte-Maure's *Romance of Troy* (*Roman de Troie*). Many romances, such as those of Chrétien de Troyes (Cline; Vitz, *Orality*), lie somewhere in between.

Issues of Historical Development

Over the course of the Middle Ages, the written tradition grows increasingly dominant: more texts are copied, more works written; more libraries exist; increasingly fewer poets and authors are nonliterate; more laypeople know how to read and write — and more people have at least pretensions to literacy;[5] more works are read (in one mode or other), fewer recited or sung from memory. The thirteenth century is a watershed, representing a growing break from a culture in which oral traditional mentalities and practices have largely dominated the vernacular world. By the fourteenth century, the oral tradition is waning. It is emblematic that poetry and music part company; after Guillaume de Machaut (1300–77) the lyric is no longer truly song but becomes a written tradition.

But we should not rush to ring the death knell for French oral tradition. True, the chanson de geste is moribund (or preparing to be transmogrified into the literary epic of the Renaissance: *Roland* will become *Orlando*). True, in almost every genre professional writers have supplanted the trouvères, jongleurs, and *menestrels* of an earlier era. But there is a strong oral backwater in many parts of France, as elsewhere in Europe, a tradition that we now call popular or folkloric, and many works from it eventually become part of "children's literature." More significant, perhaps, is the fact that to the end of the medieval period and well beyond, groups commonly gather to hear works sung or read aloud to them; such is apparently the performance norm. Private readers are few and mostly read not for literary pleasure but for instruction or religious edification (Joyce Coleman); to read alone is frowned on as antisocial. Finally, late medieval theater represents, to some degree, the continuation of oral tradition in its open appeal to powerful emotions; in its communal character and its invitation to audience participation; and in its lively blend of narrative, lyric, and dramatic elements.

———

Those who study the emergence of literary tradition keep their eyes peeled for references to such motifs and themes as the pen, the parchment, the folio, the codex; the school and the classical and scholarly learning acquired there; the pleasures and torments of the solitary writer and reader. Conversely, those of us with a strong interest in oral traditions must be alert to echoes of tale and song; alert to words and discourses molded by ancient traditions and carried through time and space by the human voice, transmitted in memory rather than impersonally by quill or codex; alert to the particular moment, the occasion that will not recur; alert to the performer, listener, and spectator, and to the interactions among them; alert to community in the real sense of that term. Perhaps such considerations can help us respond intelligently to the many words that have come down to us from the Middle Ages and arrive at a proper understanding of the complex tensions and positive relations between the oral and written traditions in this formative and fascinating period of Western culture.

Notes

1. Two of the surviving versions are those of Béroul (see Lacy) and Thomas of Britain (see Gregory).
2. One of many charming fictional works in which we see this practice — also historically attested — is *The Romance of the Rose; or, Guillaume de Dole*, by Jean Renart. See Terry and Durling.
3. On this issue in general, see Finnegan, *Oral Poetry*; for the medieval scene, see Zumthor, *Oral Poetry* and *Toward a Medieval Poetics*.
4. There are many versions of this great song: see Gouiran and Lafont; Short et al. for different manuscripts.
5. The actual number of people who could read and write, even from what we would call the middle and upper classes, remained very low, even well into the Renaissance. See, e.g., Cressy.

Joseph Harris

The Icelandic Sagas

The ultimately oral derivation of many "sagas" should not disguise
the fact that there are few or no closely comparable genres in the oral
literatures — the "epics," "ballads," "tales," "legends," and so on — of
the world. The English word *saga*, despite its contemporary extension of meanings, is a borrowing from the land of the quintessential
sagas, Iceland, its root reflecting the verb for "say, tell," *segja*; and a
number of scenes of oral "saga telling" in the texts themselves can
be taken as images of their own roots (cf. Kellogg). The sagas are,
however, not direct recordings of oral performances and cannot be
treated as transcripts of saga-telling sessions. They are, on the contrary, sometimes compared to historical novels (J. Harris). That
comparison is a justifiable heuristic device to suggest briefly to a contemporary lay audience what kind of thing a "saga" might be, and it
brings out some unsuspected features of the relation between the
family saga and the thirteenth-century Icelandic culture that spon-
sored it. Ultimately, of course, the saga — or, better, any given saga
genre — can only be itself, and such metaphorical and "analytic" con-

ceptions of genre have to give way to the description and "ethnic" understanding of text types (Ben-Amos, "Analytic Categories").

Whatever sagas are, they are one chapter in the must-read book of medieval literature, verbal artifacts so appealing to the modern reader and material so relevant to contemporary needs that they should on no account be missed in a liberal education. The best of the family sagas should rank among the monuments of world-class literature; but every saga text, regardless of literary quality, opens up a fascinating vision of life in a society that is both like and radically unlike standard European models in both medieval and modern times. Even without extensive reference in the classroom to orality and literacy, the sagas have a great deal to contribute in a variety of college and high-school contexts. Still, a rich subject becomes richer if problems of the saga's oral background are considered, and before returning to the pedagogy of the saga literature in general, I suggest some aspects of that background and how it intersects with saga texts themselves.

Genres of the Saga Literature

References to "the sagas" are most often to the forty-odd Icelandic family sagas, but by a more liberal usage the term can designate the hundreds of native Icelandic narrative works in prose or prose with inset verses. Still more generally, the "saga literature" is the whole corpus of medieval narrative prose of Icelandic or Norwegian origin, whether native or adapted from continental models (Schier). The possibilities for misunderstanding are excellent, so a few technical terms are in order. The core of the saga literature comprises: the famous family sagas or sagas of Icelanders (*Íslendinga sögur*),[1] together with the closely related realistic short stories of Icelanders (*þættir*, sing. *þáttr*); mythic-heroic or legendary sagas (*fornaldarsögur*); historical sagas of Scandinavian kings (*konunga sögur*); and what I will call contemporary sagas (with the major subgroups *Sturlunga saga*, sagas of the Icelandic church and bishops, and sagas of the later kings). Peripheral genres include, among others: a large corpus of European romances in prose adaptation (*riddarasögur*), a huge and

ill-defined body of late romantic narratives that combine features of
the native mythic-heroic genre with the ethics and language of
the borrowed romances (*lygisögur*), a formidable body of sagas on
non-Icelandic saints, and pseudohistorical narratives from foreign
sources. It is the four core genres that are of greatest interest in the
North American classroom: the literary peaks are to be found there,
and the challenge of an oral derivation is intrinsic to them. But the
contemporary sagas differ from the other core groups in having been
written relatively close in time and space to the events they portray,
particularly Icelandic political struggles of the twelfth and thirteenth
centuries (a period also characterized by the prominent Sturlung
family). The contemporary sagas have a great deal to offer the historian, but their lush local detail is difficult to penetrate, and the effort
less rewarding to the student of literature.

The first three core genres — the sagas and short stories of Icelanders, mythic-heroic sagas, and kings' sagas — are "historical," even
where they are patently legendary, in that they can be described
roughly as purporting to portray a world separated from their
thirteenth-century audiences by two hundred years or more, for they
deal chiefly with events of the Saga Age (c. 870–1030) in Iceland or
with more remote times and places. The histories of (mainly Norwegian) kings, who are of course also removed in space insofar as their
audiences were Icelandic, are continuous and blend into our contemporary category. But little of the historical saga material, outside
Snorri Sturluson's great synthesis *Heimskringla*, is likely to be taught
in translation, and the genre's problems of source, development, and
specific relation to orality are too intricate for comment here (see
Whaley). Henceforth I mean by "sagas" principally the family sagas
and short stories and the mythic-heroic sagas.

The Oral Background

The contemporary sagas are partly based on what we would now call
oral history, memorial accounts of participants in and witnesses to
events; in some historical work, such as Ari Thorgilsson's *Book of the
Icelanders* (c. 1130), there were carefully monitored chains of oral

witnesses. But for the realistic, locally grounded family sagas, scholars have long debated, as the central problem of the genre, how the
gap to the Writing Age will have been bridged. (Though Christianity
came to Iceland in 999 or 1000, the first recorded writing there was
the writing down of oral laws in the winter of 1117–18. Preserved
manuscripts of religious works begin about 1170, and writing spread
relatively early to genealogies. Other secular genres, like the sagas,
are thought to have been written chiefly in the thirteenth century.)
The free-prose (*Freiprosa*) school held, in general, that notable events
of the Saga Age were early crystallized as oral sagas and handed down
more or less intact to scribes of the Writing Age; the theory was
bound up with historicity and supported by references to "sagas" in
eminently believable contexts and by anecdotes such as the story of
a young Icelander who recites the saga of the youth of King Harald
the Tyrant before the king himself (Simpson, *Northmen* 6–7). By
contrast the book-prose (*Buchprosa*) school emphasized written documents, violations of history, and literary invention during the Writing Age. A nuanced account of the long and subtle debate is offered
by Theodore M. Andersson (*Problem*), but today a synthesis seems to
have been reached somewhere between the oral and literary extremes
though closer, perhaps, to the Icelandic school's emphasis on literary
creation. Long sagas comparable to the extant *Njáls saga*, *Egils saga*,
or *Grettis saga* (*Grettir's Saga*) are generally thought now to be dependent on writing; yet oral anecdotes, the materials of saga and short
story, were performed in a wide range of degrees of formality (see
Bauman, "Performance and Honor"). Many have welcomed Carol
Clover's suggestion that the elements of the later sagas existed in oral
times as "immanent saga," a construct in the minds of audiences that
was never realized in full until a writing culture elicited the whole,
and several critics characterize the style of extant sagas, in relation to
a primary oral style or to actual performance, as a re-creation of oral
style parallel to the re-creation of events of a golden Saga Age in the
midst of the turbulent thirteenth century (see Richard Allen).

The mythic-heroic sagas, having practically no grounding in real
events, have a somewhat different genealogy but can provide a valuable snapshot of the oral genre at a relatively early point (cf. Foote).

One of the contemporary sagas (*The Saga of þorgils and Hafliði*, written between 1160 and about 1250) reports on a wedding held at Reykjahólar in 1119; among other entertainments, such as wrestling and dancing, there was saga telling by two named individuals. The first, Hrólf of Skalmarnes, whom the contemporary-saga historian had earlier characterized as "a saga-teller and a good poet," told "a saga about Hröngvi∂ the viking and about Óláf Warriors'-King and about the break-in in the funeral mound of Thráin the berserk and about Hrómund Gripsson, and many poems in it" (my trans.). Not only are these typical events of mythic-heroic sagas, but also versions of the very saga described here still exist in late medieval forms, and the story's evolution can to some extent be reconstructed. Both the oral and the written lives of these legendary sagas must have been bound up with the poems in them; the oral protoform of the mythic-heroic group apparently was a prosimetrical mixture that associates those sagas closely with another form of oral literature in early Iceland, Eddic poetry. Despite its formulaic diction, Eddic poetry is generally thought to have had a textuality that more nearly resembled the relative rigidity of skaldic verse than the fluidity of, for example, the South Slavic epic (see Alexander, this volume). The prose element in prosimetrical compositions, however, will have been freely recomposed, and new verse invented. Later in the Writing Age similar sagas are thought to have been composed for reading aloud; as the traditional element weakens, the genre grades into the native romances (the late romantic narratives mentioned above).

The second sagaman at the wedding was Ingimund the Priest, mentioned earlier in the saga as "a good poet" and "a man of learning who was much concerned with sagas and both entertained with poems and composed them." "He had himself made good poems and received rewards for them in foreign parts." On this occasion he "told the saga of Orm, skald of Barrey, including many verses and with a good lay [*flokk*], which Ingimund had composed [*ortan*], at the end of the saga" (my trans.). This time the genre of the oral performance of 1119 is not so secure. The hero of the saga, Orm, was a historical poet whose most productive period is tentatively set late in the tenth century; his saga has perished, but it too was apparently heavy with verses, at least one of which the narrator attributes to the prosimetrical performer Ingimund. If, as seems likely, the poems of *Orms saga* were more skaldic than Eddic in style, Orm's lost poetic biography may have been an oral predecessor of the subgroup of family sagas known as "sagas of the poets," perhaps closest to the extant biographies of Kormak and of Hallfred.

Sagas and Orality in the Classroom

An exciting development in the study of oral literature is the postulate of distinct "mentalities" correlated with oral and literate cultures. According to Walter Ong, "writing is a technology that restructures thought" ("Writing"); and for Jack Goody the correlation between writing technology and mentality fills a gap in anthropological theory left by the demise of evolutionary models (*Domestication*). Though some social scientists deplore this "Great Divide" hypothesis (e.g., Finnegan, *Literacy* 12), a student working with translations can occasionally identify traces of oral and literate mentalities in operation in Old Norse. For example, a fuller reading of the wedding in 1119 will reveal an obscure but profound difference of opinion in the audience. Can this difference be interpreted as contrasting degrees of belief in oral sagas, a clash of traditional "syncretic truth" (Steblin-Kaminskij 24) with notions of fiction and documentary verification in the incipient literate culture? A clearer instance is offered by the two versions of Atli's treacherous invitation to the Burgundians in the *Poetic Edda*. In the older poem, *Atlakviða*, Gudrun warned her brothers by twisting a single wolf's hair around the golden arm ring she sent with her husband's messenger. This natural sign or index is, of course, culturally structured, but it yields almost immediately to interpretation: "I think she offered us a warning . . . / Our way is wolfish if we ride on this journey" (U. Dronke 4). The younger poem, *Atlamál*, though a product of an old and essentially oral poetics (*pace* U. Dronke 111–12), shows acquaintance with a form of writing; Gudrun's warning is incised in runes, which have, however, been changed by the messenger. Here it is not the heroes but the wife Kostbera who puzzles over a "purloined letter"; apparently the text never fully gives up its secret, but in sleep her troubled mind divines the writer's original meaning. The *Atlamál* poet—like another witness to early literacy, Plato—clearly distrusts writing, and the poem overdetermines the woman's warning by adding dreams of disaster with their traditional male misinterpretations. In deconstruction, writing (or language) is inadequate to expression; here the physicality of writing also makes it further alienable from intention. The older poem, reflecting the consensual unity of an oral world, has no misunderstanding, even though the brothers do ignore the warning and commit themselves to the journey; here "slippage" inheres not in the sign system but in Gudrun's understanding of heroic psychology, for her warning made the journey inevitable.

The sagas refer occasionally to runes — Egill's daughter will carve his elegy for his sons on a rune stave, Grettir's enemies send a rune-inscribed log against Grettir in his island stronghold, and so on — but otherwise they portray a purely oral world. A student may expect an oral mentality in simple contrast to the Writing Age reflected in the contemporary sagas, but such differences as are observable may well be due to the historical imagination of the writers and are difficult to distinguish from other cultural forces, such as religion and (Norwegian) imperialism. Visible language had been well known in the North for hundreds of years through runes. Sometimes both runic monuments and skaldic poetry couple language, as a material thing, with fame in contexts of conscious authorship, for example, in the verse inscription at Nöbbele, Sweden ("Hróðsteinn and Eilíf, Áki and Hákon, those lads raised this eye-catching monumental stone after their father, after Kali dead; thus must the noble man be mentioned as long as the stone lives and the letters of the runes" [after Jansson 137]), and in Egill Skalla-Grímsson's *Lay of Arinbjörn* ("Now is easily seen where, before a host of men, in the view of many, I shall set up the steeply-climbed praise of the mighty kin of noblemen. . . . I was awake early, I carried words together. With the morning work of the slave of language [the tongue] I heaped up a cairn of praise which will long stand unbreakable in the enclosure of poetry" [263, 267]). Early skaldic poetry is unimpeachably oral, but in many ways — its authority, textuality, and intertextuality — it is literary *avant la lettre*. Unlike skaldic poetry, sagas are quite accessible to our literature students, who can be encouraged to analyze the oral world in the sagas—the structure of speech events, the relations of speech acts, the ethnography of talk, and so on—but simplistic realizations of a Great Divide between oral and literary can be expected to be rare.

The sagas are eminently teachable, however we choose to integrate them into the modern curriculum; here the saying "traduttore, traditore" has its lowest truth value, and even those who chafe at the impossibility of teaching *Beowulf* or Eddic poetry without the original language may experience exhilaration at the way the many excellent translations succeed in rendering transparent the purity of this literature of action.[2] Not that there are no problems for a contemporary student, but the difficulties themselves yield worthwhile instruction. Many features of the (oral) world of the sagas need special explication—the names, genealogies, family and social relationships, motivations such as honor, and so on. (A friend suggests that students *chant* the strange Icelandic names to exorcise their terror and on the principle that tongue grip facilitates memory.) The famous chaste style of the sagas is largely composed of formulas and unselfconscious idealizations of natural speech. These features seem to be inherited, in the Europeanizing culture of the twelfth and thirteenth centuries, from the narrower "Little Tradition" of the oral Saga Age (Wax 15), and what from our point of view is saga's stylistic laconism requires an active reader. One successful teacher of sagas in translation advises building up a knowledge of the saga world by starting with short stories, working up from *Ívars þáttr* (which in its three pages anticipates the kernel of *Laxdæla saga*) to the increasingly complex masterpieces *The Story of Auðun*, *The Story of Hreiðar the Fool* (both found in *Hrafnkel's Saga and Other Stories*), *Hrafnkels saga*, and *Njáls saga*. Less tightly woven but still engrossing texts such as *Gísla saga* (*Saga of Gisli*), *Grettis saga* (*Grettir's Saga*), and *Færeyingja saga* (*Saga of the Faroe Islanders*) can follow, and, if time permits, flawed but fascinating sagas such as the stories of Kormak or of the Foster Brothers (*Sagas of Kormák and the Sworn Brothers*). Few teachers will have the opportunity to conduct a course exclusively on sagas, but *Völsunga saga* (*Saga of the Volsungs*) is an accessible representative of the mythic-heroic sagas that fits well into courses in folklore and mythology, while short stories, family sagas (taken as historical novels), and romances would repay treatment in the context of genre-based courses. Current fashions, however, favor thematic courses, and the sagas can supply one's need for: strong women, brotherhood, and gender transgressions; language as a martial art; the monstrous and the other; law and society; and, of course, the ever-popular revenge, violence, and reconciliation—to name a few exemplary themes. The saga's bounty is delimited and defined by its folk heritage, but attentive students—applying perhaps a little intuition from the "oral residue" (Walter Ong's term) in their own culture—can penetrate the saga's oral world to the enrichment of their own.[3]

Notes

1. For an overview, structural analysis, and criticism of twenty-four classic sagas, see Andersson, *Icelandic Family Saga*.
2. A bibliography of translations of many sagas and stories mentioned in this essay can be found in Fry, *Sagas*; Acker. Especially to be recommended for language, scholarship, and availability is the Penguin series. Among the volumes in that series are *Hrafnkel's Saga*, *Egil's Saga*, *Laxdæla Saga*, and *Njal's Saga*. For other translations, see *The Book of the Icelanders*, *Heimskringla* by Snorri Sturluson, *The Saga of Þorgils and Hafliði*, *Grettir's Saga*, *The Saga of Gisli*, *The Saga of the Faroe Islanders*, *The Sagas of Kormák and the Sworn Brothers*, *The Saga of Hallfred*, and *The Saga of the Volsungs*.
3. In addition to reference works such as the thirteen-volume *Dictionary of the Middle Ages* and *Medieval Scandinavia: An Encyclopedia*, teachers of sagas may wish to consult the following: Andersson, *Icelandic Family Saga*; Clover and Lindow; Kristjánsson; Lönnroth; S. Mitchell; Schach; Tucker.

Bonnie D. Irwin

The Frame Tale East and West

Oral storytelling takes place in any number of situations: a teacher uses stories to illuminate moral lessons; a storyteller captivates her audience late into the night by fashioning enchanting worlds; competing narrators vie for audience approval, each telling a story more amusing or risqué than the last. The frame tale depicts these storytelling events in all their variety and in the process carries many of the keys to oral performance onto the printed page. The genre thus occupies a unique place in the relation between orality and literacy and can be a valuable component of both literature and folklore courses.

Background, Definitions, and Distinctions

The frame tale can be traced back three millennia in India (Blackburn, "Domesticating" 527), where it is believed to have originated. It differs from a simple anthology in several ways. Foremost among these is its narrative form. The frame tale is a fictional narrative composed for the purpose of presenting other tales. Such collections are

usually written in prose, but as Geoffrey Chaucer and Juan Ruiz skillfully demonstrate, they may also take the form of an extended verse
narrative. The varied use of *frame*, *framing*, and terms such as *novella*
and *boxing tale* in reference to this genre can lead to confusion over
its elements. It is therefore useful to employ the term *frame tale* to
refer to the entire collection and *framing tale* to designate the outer-
most tale that depicts storytelling events and provides a context for
their inclusion. The stories within the frame — which command more
space and attention than the framing narrative — are generally referred to as *interpolated* or *intercalated*. Though there is debate over
whether the frame tale as a whole could have flourished in the oral
tradition (Belcher; Irwin), there is no doubt that many of the interpolated tales did so (and in some cases still do), and thus frame tales
have long been used by folklorists and literary scholars as a source of
ancient and medieval folktales.

The most famous early frame tale is the Sanskrit *Panchatantra*
(Ryder), a collection of didactic fables compiled, as legend has it, for
the edification of a king's three foolish sons more than two thousand
years ago. By the ninth century, the genre appeared in the Near East
and continued as a popular vehicle into the Middle Ages, leaving us,
among many other works, the Arabic *Thousand and One Nights*,[1]
which tells the story of Shahrazad spinning tales throughout the
nights to protect herself from her tyrannical husband. Medieval European examples date from the twelfth century with Petrus de Al-
fonsí's *Disciplina clericalis*, a collection of advice tales told by a father
to his son, but the frame tale reached the height of its popularity in
Europe in the fourteenth century with the composition of Juan Ruiz's *Libro de buen amor* (1330 and 1343), which depicts through tale
and song an archpriest's romantic misadventures; Juan Manuel's
Conde Lucanor (1335), fifty tales of advice from counselor to count;
Giovanni Boccaccio's *Decameron* (begun c. 1350), in which a group
of young men and women tell romantic and comic tales out in the
countryside to escape the physical and emotional ravages of the
plague; Geoffrey Chaucer's *The Canterbury Tales* (begun c. 1386),
largely but not entirely composed of comic and ribald tales told by a

socially diverse group of pilgrims on their way to Canterbury (see Lindahl, this volume), and John Gower's *Confessio Amantis* (1390), in which Genius, priest of Venus, tells tales to console a distraught lover. Most notable among the few later European compositions is Marguerite de Navarre's *Heptaméron* (published posthumously in 1558), which depicts five men and five women telling tales as they take refuge from a flood in an abbey. The foregoing list is necessarily incomplete but includes the most prominent texts available in student-friendly editions.[2]

A frame tale differs categorically from a novel or epic that uses extensive framing, such as *Don Quijote*. *Don Quijote* without all the interior stories would be less of a masterpiece, but the tale of the errant knight would still be entertaining and meaningful. In contrast, a framing tale is a rather brief story that depends almost entirely on the interpolated tales for its significance. Boccaccio's framing tale of men and women trying to forget the plague by telling one another stories would be rather ineffectual without the stories themselves. Despite this fact, the framing tale exerts considerable control over an audience's reception and interpretation of the interpolated tales. The ideology of a particular author or the social context from which a frame tale springs also has an influence on the interpretation of characters and narrators. The medieval Muslim subjugation of women, for example, contributes a degree of irony to all the tales Shahrazad tells as well as to her motives for telling them. A similar tale placed in the mouth of one of Chaucer's pilgrims would suggest a far different interpretation, not only because the tale would be told on a pilgrimage but also because it would be told by a pilgrim of a particular social class. When a tale appears in different frames, it effectively becomes different tales, insofar as its purpose and sense change.

Frame tales are characterized by their almost infinite adaptability. By substituting interpolated tales, adding a narrator, or ascribing a tale to a different narrator, compilers or storytellers can introduce subtle or considerable changes to suit their audience. A framing tale can contain any number of interpolated tales, according to the storyteller's whim and the performance or presentation context. This flexibility allowed frame tales to transmit traditional stories across linguistic and cultural boundaries as well as along the continuum from orality to literacy in the Middle Ages.

Frame tales vary considerably in their length and complexity. Some, such as *The Thousand and One Nights,* have a single character who serves as narrator for the interpolated tales. Others, like *The Canterbury Tales,* have several narrators. Most have a rather loose structure, to which almost any entertaining tale will conform; some, particularly the more didactic framing contexts, have a tighter structure that determines the type of story that must be interpolated at any given point. A frame tale may also comprise many layers; that is, an interpolated tale may itself be a frame tale. Such layering creates ample opportunities for dramatic irony. Each layer frames the experience of its audience and thus guides the reception of each framed tale. The more narrators and layers involved, the more complex the structural dynamic and the more difficult the task of the external audiences, including modern undergraduates, who try to interpret the various designs and intentions.

Teaching Situations

Instructors may incorporate frame tales as reading assignments in different kinds of courses. Because frame tales are repositories for traditional stories, they may be included in an oral tradition or folklore course as oral-derived texts. In the single-language literature course, frame tales are good representatives of medieval tastes and styles. Because the frame tale originated in the East and was later successful in the West, it can also be included in a variety of multicultural or world literature survey courses.

Oral Tradition and Folklore Classes

Reading a frame tale in conjunction with examples from modern oral traditions can provide students with a context for learning to recognize and interpret oral or oral-derived texts. Hallmarks of orality, such as traditional linguistic forms and structures, reiteration of themes and typical scenes, and traditional characterizations (e.g., lack of personal names and psychological character development), are characteristic of many frame tales. Therefore, many of the techniques outlined elsewhere in this volume may be applied with relative ease to the frame tale.

Moreover, because frame tales *depict* the oral traditions from which they are derived, a class may study performance aspects in these texts. For example, Boccaccio's and Chaucer's narrators compete, each trying to tell the most entertaining story. One can incorporate this feature of the frame tale into a discussion of the agonistic dimension of oral tradition (Ong, *Orality* 43–45). In *The Thousand and One Nights* Shahrazad's narrating only at night furnishes an example of cultures in which it is considered bad luck to tell stories during the day, when both narrator and audience should be engaged in more productive activities. In the *Panchatantra*, stories are used as teaching devices, a fact that may be incorporated into a larger discussion of the dual roles of education and entertainment in traditional narrative.

The storyteller-audience dynamic portrayed in the frame tale is illuminating. Even though we cannot treat verbal art like a folklorist's field notes, the genre shows to what extent medieval societies valued storytelling and those who did it well. Because the characters in a frame tale are sometimes narrating for their lives against seemingly impossible odds, the empathetic quality of their narration, another element of orality (Havelock, *Preface* 145–46; Ong, *Orality* 45–46), is significant. Despite the myriad themes within the interpolated tales, frame tales essentially celebrate storytelling, and in this function they serve the class on oral tradition well.

Single-Language Literature Classes

Because frame tales play an especially important role in the Arabic, Italian, Spanish, and English literary traditions, students in these fields may be asked to compare frame tales and other medieval genres. Students are often startled by the extent of racism, sexism, and other stereotyping they observe in these tales, extreme even by medieval standards. At the same time, the tales often contain strong moral lessons, and the layering of narrators allows individual authors and storytellers to distance themselves from anything offensive. For example, in the *Decameron* Boccaccio exploits the structural device of the frame tale to mock elements of his society while at the same time deflecting responsibility for the criticism onto his narrators.

Keeping in mind the oral provenance of these works may help explain certain unanswered questions, particularly those associated with completeness, that have arisen in studying the frame tale as medieval literature. Why are there not 1001 nights in *The Thousand and One Nights*? Why didn't Chaucer "finish" *The Canterbury Tales*? Why does the *Libro de buen amor* lack a clearly defined plot and main character? All these issues may be addressed from the perspective of oral tradition. When one has an entire immanent tradition to consider (Foley, *Immanent Art*), literary notions of the completeness of any one version are no longer relevant; the contemporary listening audience already knew the stories and would fill in the blanks.

One can also use the frame tale in the single-language course to demonstrate the intersections between orality and literacy in the Middle Ages. In medieval courses that include an oral or oral-derived epic poem as well as texts that emerge primarily from literacy, a frame tale provides an interesting intermediary example, demonstrating how oral and literate stories were incorporated into a context that was received equally well by both listeners and readers.

Multicultural and World Literature Classes

Just as the frame tale forms part of the bridge between oral and literate art, it also transcends East-West boundaries. Boccaccio and Chaucer incorporate in their collections tales that appear in such earlier Eastern works as the *Panchatantra* or *The Thousand and One Nights*. From the Middle Ages to the present day, Western readers have been using Eastern frame tales as a window into another world, often not realizing how distorted the view can be.

The best text for incorporating the frame tale into a multicultural class is, without doubt, *The Thousand and One Nights*. It still lives in the oral tradition and has influenced countless other works of literature, both written and oral. Many students are somewhat familiar with it, but their perceptions have been shaped by inaccurate translations that promote orientalism, or Eurocentric views of the East. *The Thousand and One Nights* is available in English in several paperback translations, the most authoritative of which is by Husain Haddawy. At first, students may be disappointed that this text does not include the tales of Sindbad and Aladdin, but a fruitful discussion may arise out of the fact, explained in the introduction to this text, that neither of these famous tales was actually part of the earliest versions. In fact, it appears that the first European translator, Antoine Galland, added Aladdin from notes taken from an oral source (Mahdi). Even without knowledge of Arabic, students can use various texts to gauge the extent to which editions have been altered and how European tastes and literate expectations have determined the nature of the translations.

Teaching Strategies

After the Renaissance, readers lost interest in the frame tale as a form. So it is no surprise that modern students find reading an entire frame tale from start to finish a tedious enterprise, even though they judge individual tales to be quite entertaining. A generally discouraged practice — teaching an excerpt — is thus sometimes necessary. This strategy is not at odds with the medieval reception of these tales. Certainly some medieval readers also selected only their few favorite tales to read. And using excerpts can serve the interests of the student-centered classroom. Different stories may be assigned to different individuals or groups for analysis that leads to a comparative discussion. Groups may perform their stories for one another, competing for the appreciation of the in-class audience, or even compose their own stories, either orally or in writing, to fit a certain frame.

By sharing assignments of reading, analyzing, and composing across the class, individual students do not feel overwhelmed by the material, and the whole class can gain a substantial degree of familiarity with a large portion of the frame tale. The inclusion of performance and composition assignments brings the dynamics of the oral tradition to the students in a way that merely reading and discussing the tales cannot.

In an exercise that demonstrates transmission and reception, a teacher assigns a group of students to orally compose and tell a tale, then asks another group to produce a written version of the same tale and recite it to a third group, which in turn may compose yet another version. The class can then compare their experiences with the experiences of the narrators and audiences in the frame tales they read and come to a fuller understanding of storyteller-audience dynamics in the oral tradition.

Using excerpts from more than one frame tale clearly allows for more comprehensive discussions of the genre. Students are often disconcerted as well as fascinated by the levels of narration, and many have difficulty — especially with *The Thousand and One Nights*, which has as many as five layers in some sections — determining who is telling what to whom and for what purpose. Leading questions enable the students to analyze the layers of narration. Does the tale chosen by the narrator demonstrate the desired lesson? Do the students know other stories that might do the job more effectively? How does storytelling rank as an instructional tool?

The interpolated tales are entertaining traditional tales but not the fairy tales with which students may be more familiar. Given Disney's recent foray into the frame tale in the film *Aladdin*, a class might also profitably consider the idea of audience. For example, how would students translate Arabic or medieval European cultural keys into contemporary American equivalents to render a tale more palatable for their peers? As in any other literature course, inviting students to consider themselves as audience leads to a greater awareness of audience in general. The frame tale transfers the resonance of oral tradition to a literary form that, through guided reading and effective composition assignments, will shock, enchant, and otherwise entertain students, just as the original tales — and tale — delighted medieval audiences.

Notes

1. The earliest extant manuscript is from the fourteenth century. On Arabic oral traditions, see Slyomovics, this volume.
2. For convenient paperback editions of some of these works, see Boccaccio; Caws and Prendergast; Chaucer, *Tales*; Haddawy, *Nights*; M. Mack; Navarre; Ruiz; Ryder.

Part IV

Courses, Readings, and Resources

Lynn C. Lewis and Lori Peterson

The National Curriculum and the Teaching of Oral Traditions

In the summer and fall of 1995, we conducted a national survey targeting colleges and universities whose catalogs described courses related in some way to oral tradition. This survey revealed a wide range of ways in which the study of oral traditions has been incorporated into the classroom. Academic departments in various disciplines from across the country provided descriptions of courses and seminars, detailed syllabi, reading lists, and assignments. (Many instructors included out-of-print sources in course packets photocopied for class use.) Institutions not directly affiliated with colleges and universities, such as the American Folklife Center of the Library of Congress, the Smithsonian Center for Folklife Programs and Cultural Studies, the Philadelphia Folklore Project, and the Museum of New Mexico, have also aided this project by providing descriptions of available resources (see Daskalopoulos, this volume).

The majority of the seventy-five course descriptions received—whether from departments of English, various foreign languages, folklore, anthropology, religious studies, or history—stress the importance of social context and performance in the transmission of oral traditions, offering alternatives to strictly literary approaches to interpretation. Many of these courses also encourage an awareness of the various methodologies and types of analysis employed in the study of verbal arts. Survey results reveal how the teaching of oral traditions has blurred the boundaries that typically separate academic disciplines. This merging of fields is borne out by the interdisciplinary content of the readings and assignments as well as by the cross-listing of courses, many being offered simultaneously by two, occasionally even three, academic departments.

The multiple possibilities in teaching are also evidenced in the host of different ways courses have approached the study of oral traditions. Many courses examine a wide range of cultural traditions and genres, others focus on the traditions of specific regions or cultures, and still others concentrate on specific genres such as ballads or folktales. A smaller number address important, specifically theoretical concerns involved with the relations between orality and literacy. Unfortunately, constraints of time and space make an exhaustive report within the scope of this essay an impossibility. To be sure, there are many related courses of which we are unaware, since we could include only those for which we were sent information. Even among the materials we did receive, there are many syllabi and course descriptions we wish we could treat here in more depth.[1]

The brief sketch that follows attempts, instead, to provide a representative sampling of how the study of oral traditions has been incorporated into college and university curricula across the country. Very few of the courses described below are devoted exclusively to the study of oral traditions, but all illustrate in some way how these traditions can be taught, whether through the overall design of a course, through special emphasis on a day or week, or through the choice of specific texts. An overview of courses devoted to theoretical concerns of orality and literacy is provided first. Discussion of a range of folklore courses follows, starting with general and introductory offerings and moving on to courses that examine the relations between folklore and literature. Next, more specialized subject areas are addressed in alphabetical order: African traditions, American traditions, biblical studies, British traditions, classical studies, speech and storytelling, and women's traditions. Specialized topics for which we received only a limited amount of information, or which deny easy classification, have been discussed in the final section of the essay, "Other Courses." These include courses devoted to the ballad, Korean traditions, Japanese folklore, Arabic folklore, Scandinavian folk narrative, Jewish folklore, children's folklore and literature, and culture and cognition.

In what follows, quotations are drawn from course syllabi, college and university catalogs, and instructors' comments.

Theories of Orality and Literacy

The course Theory of Oral Literature, offered through the English department at the University of California, Berkeley, includes reading and discussion of a number of influential theorists during the first portion of the semester, including Alan Dundes (*Sacred Narrative*), Ruth Finnegan (*Oral Poetry*), John Miles Foley (*Theory of Oral Composition*), Jack Goody (*Interface*), Eric A. Havelock (*Muse*), Albert B. Lord (*Singer of Tales*), Walter Ong (*Orality*), and Paul Zumthor (*Oral Poetry*). Primary texts providing focal points for discussion, including *Beowulf* and texts chosen according to students' interests, become increasingly important as the semester progresses (for a course description and list of texts, see pp. 445–46). The course is described as "an inquiry into the human habit of storytelling, the dynamics of oral tradition, and the power of oral narrative (together with other forms of verbal expression) to shape the contours of the world and encode the essentials of culture" (for a survey of methodologies, see Zumwalt, this volume).

The University of Wisconsin's course Orality and Textuality in the Middle Ages addresses the practical issues, such as editing and transcription, involved in oral tradition scholarship as well as theoretical concerns associated with oral-formulaic theory and orality-literacy studies. Ong's *Orality and Literacy*, Dennis Tedlock's *The Spoken Word and the Work of Interpretation*, and Michael Riffaterre's *Text Production* provide theoretical background, while primary texts include *Beowulf, The Song of Roland, The Nibelungenlied,* and the Middle English Harley lyrics (for a course description and list of texts, see p. 448). The course description explains that the focus on the Middle Ages was chosen because "most texts are or were voice or ear texts that have come down to us as eye or hand texts so that we are always forced to enter the first realm in terms of the second."

A course entitled Orality, Literacy, and the History of Religious Traditions, offered by the Jackson School of International Studies at the University of Washington, Seattle, examines the possible applications of scholarship in cultural anthropology and literary theory to the comparative study of religion in an attempt to understand memory, speech, and writing as structuring elements in the transmission of religion. The first four weeks are devoted to study of theoretical perspectives as set forth by such scholars as Ong (*Orality*), Finnegan (*Literacy*), Goody (*Logic*), and Talal Asad. The remainder of the semester explores the problems and applications of comparative religion, such as the oral dimension of Scripture (readings in William A. Graham's *Beyond the Written Word*), orality and linguistic science in Vedic tradition (readings in Fritz Staal's *The Fidelity of Oral Tradition and the Origins of Science*), and memory and textuality in medieval learning (readings in Mary Carruthers's *The Book of Memory*).

The University of Missouri's course, Oral Tradition, offered at three different levels (general undergraduate, advanced undergraduate / masters, and doctoral seminar), concentrates on answering the question, What differences do a work's roots in oral tradition make to its interpretation as verbal art? Approaches and readings on the theoretical side address the topics of ethnography of speaking (Bauman, *Verbal Art*; selections from Bauman and Sherzer), ethnopoetics (Hymes, *"In Vain"*), oral-formulaic theory (Lord, *Singer of Tales*; Foley, *Theory of Oral Composition*), and traditional referentiality (Foley, *Immanent Art* and *Singer*). The works studied change from one semester to another but always juxtapose living traditions and oral-derived traditional texts from the ancient and medieval periods. In recent years the works have included South Slavic epics and magical charms (Medjedović's *The Wedding of Smailagić Meho* and materials collected during fieldwork by the instructor), Native American narrative poetry (Tedlock, *Finding the Center*), African epic (J. Johnson, *The Epic of Son-Jara*), Homer's *Iliad* and *Odyssey*, the Anglo-Saxon *Beowulf*, the Old French *Song of Roland*, the medieval Spanish *Poem of the Cid*, and the Finnish *Kalevala* (for a full syllabus, see pp. 455–58). Among the topics addressed are the structure of phraseology, narrative scene, and story pattern; the role of performance; the persistence of oral traditional features into texts; and the edition and translation of oral traditions.

General and Introductory Folklore Courses

Because of the fundamental importance of oral traditions in the study of folklore, a large number of colleges and universities offering introductory folklore responded to our survey; the result was a collection of materials rich in ideas that can be applied in a wide range of courses. A number of these courses are organized around folklore genres. Through the departments of English, history, and anthropology, for example, Utah State University offers the course Legends, Myths, and Folktales. In the study of these forms of folk narrative, strong emphasis is placed on how oral communication affects composition in various traditions, including urban legends in the United States, Mayan myths, both biblical and prebiblical versions of the flood myth, and Palestinian Arab folktales. One of this course's objectives is to learn how to use folk stories to gain insights in other fields, especially literature and history. The course also encourages students to become familiar with different kinds of oral narratives and their significance, to experience collecting and analyzing oral narratives, to recognize some of the social functions of traditional storytelling, and to become familiar with theories about oral narratives. Legends are studied using Jan Brunvand's anthologies (e.g., *The Choking Doberman*), various myths are read from a course folder that includes parts of Genesis and the *Atrahasis Epic*, and folktales are approached using Stith Thompson's methods along with Ibrahim Muhawi and Sharif Kanaana's volume of Palestinian Arab folktales. A film depicting the first half of the *Popol Vuh* (*Popol Vuh: The Creation Myth*) is shown in conjunction with the study of the creation myth of the ancient Mayans (*Popol Vuh*).

Folklore, a general course offered through the University of South Florida's anthropology department, devotes the first half of the term to folklore genres and the second to specific nationalities. It allows one week early in the term for discussing oral tradition and performance, a unit supplemented by readings from Alan Dundes's *The Study of Folklore* (especially the chapter "The Search for Origins"). Students are also encouraged to take advantage of local events that illustrate living traditions in folklore. Students in Northern Arizona University's course Folklore, which is offered through the English department, learn the importance of social contexts by listening to field-recorded folk poetry and recitation as well as by viewing films illustrating such performances. Saint Xavier University's Folklore, a general course offered through the English and anthropology departments, intersperses discussion of folklore genres with discussion of performance, devoting one week to the social context and cultural significance of folk speech, proverbs, riddles, and folk poetry and another week to the oral performance and oral style of folk narratives. Axel Olrik's "Epic Laws of Folk Narrative" is used to foreground the study of narrative, and David Evans's "Structure and Meaning in the Folk Blues" supplements discussion of oral traditions in folk music. This course, like a large number of folklore courses included in our survey, addresses the importance of context and performance by requiring collection and analysis of folklore items.

Many introductory folklore courses attempt to provide a survey of oral traditions from a wide variety of nationalities. Southern Illinois University's course Anthropology of Folklore, for example, involves comparative study of the role of folklore in various cultures of the world, with special emphasis on differences between nonliterate and literate groups. Folktales and Mythology, taught through the English department of the same university, explores methodologies and theories set forth by such scholars as Vladimir Propp and Thompson to increase understanding of myths and folktales from the cultures of Greece and Rome, the Middle East, northern Europe, the British Isles, the Far East, and the Americas. Readings are selected from anthologies by Donna Rosenberg (*World Mythology*) and Thompson (*One Hundred Favorite Folktales*) (for a course description and list of readings, see p. 449). Syracuse University's course Folklore is also arranged according to geographical regions and gives particular attention to the influence of colonial powers on traditions from India, Africa, and Chile (for a full syllabus, see pp. 453–54). An introductory unit early in the term is titled Folklore as Performance and includes discussion of Barre Toelken's *The Dynamics of Folklore* (esp. chapters 3 and 4). A group project designed for this course draws attention to the role of the audience in oral traditions, asking students to examine several versions of a given tale and "address variation for particular audiences from particular tellers." Tulane University's anthropology department offers Myth and Life, a sampling of Native North American, Native South American, and African traditions, with attention to the social organization, cosmology and religion, folktales, and myths of each tradition.

Oral Literature: An Introduction to Folklore and Mythology, Harvard University's introductory folklore course, addresses issues of art, performance, interpretation, transmission, and social context in oral literatures through case studies of epics, lyrics, dramas, märchen, legends, myths, and ballads. After an introduction on orality, literacy, and folklore, the course presents a unit devoted to theoretical issues related to performers and audiences of oral epics, centering the discussion on Lord's *The Singer of Tales* and selected songs from South Slavic tradition (*Song of Baghdad* and *The Captivity of Djulić Ibrahim*). The following unit concentrates on the European ballad (British ballads selected from Whiting's *Traditional British Ballads*; Danish and other European ballads compiled in a course packet) and the controversies over ballad composition as addressed in James H. Jones's "Commonplace and Memorization in the Oral Tradition of the English and Scottish Popular Ballads" and Albert Friedman's "The Formulaic Improvisation Theory of Ballad Tradition." Subsequent units treat similar issues in the genres of legend (readings from Bascom's "Forms of Folklore" and Brunvand's *Vanishing Hitchhiker*), folktale (special focus on "Cinderella," with readings from Olrik's "Epic Laws of Folk Narrative" and Dundes's "Structural Typology"), myth (the Venezuelan *Watunna*, ed. Civriaux, and the Icelandic *Saga of the Volsungs*, with additional readings from Dundes's *Sacred Narrative*), and folk drama (focus on mummers' and Robin Hood plays). (For a description of an introductory folklore class with a more narrow focus, see the University of Toledo's course under "American Traditions" in this essay.)

Folklore and Literature

Among the number of courses that have been designed to explore relations between oral performances and texts is Louisiana State University's Folklore and Literature, which devotes three class periods to examination of the problems of presenting folklore and oral traditions to readers. This unit concludes with a writing assignment asking readers to explore "what problems would be involved in capturing for a reader the qualities of oral folk performances" in Zora Neale Hurston's *Mules and Men*. Likewise, the Folklore and Literature course at Loyola University, New Orleans, investigates the folkloric genres and the oral traditional means of expression that inform the work of Eudora Welty, Angela Carter, William Faulkner, and Leslie Marmon Silko. Primary texts by these and other authors are supplemented with readings from Ruth Finnegan's *Oral Poetry*. The course further explores the relations between written and oral culture through two in-depth case studies, in which students examine the ethnographic methods employed by Hurston (*Mules and Men*) and William Butler Yeats (*Celtic Twilight*) in their literary representations of folklore. (For a description of a course examining issues of folklore and literature specifically in Native American traditions, see the University of Arizona's course under "American Traditions" in this essay.)

African Traditions

The Folklore and Mythology Program at the University of California, Los Angeles, offers the course African Myth and Ritual, which examines the web of relations among myth, society, and the mythologist (see Cosentino, this volume). Concerned with the multiple sources for myth and the impact of the interpreter's ideas on our apprehension of its meaning, units in this course cover myths of the hero, myths of the trickster, and myth and ritual. Also taught at UCLA, Oral Traditions in Africa surveys the art of storytelling in sub-Saharan Africa. Course work—including readings in Paul Radin's *African Folktales*, Roger Abrahams's *African Folktales*, and Amos Tutuola's *The Palm Wine Drinkard*—focuses on oral performance, classification, and appreciation of various oral narrative traditions as well as on the beginning of written literature (for a full syllabus, see pp. 451–53). The University of Florida's course African Folktales is devoted to folktales, proverbs, riddles, and beliefs about human behavior that have been passed on by word of mouth. By the third week of class, after an introductory unit establishing geographical and cultural contexts (including the showing of three films: *Africa: A New Look*, *West Africa: Two Lifestyles*, and *Country to Town*), the course examines African religious concepts. Subsequent units treat the topics of language and community, addressing a number of genres sequentially. The course concludes with a unit on human behavior. Abrahams's *African Folktales* serves as the primary text. The University of Florida's course Yoruba Oral Literature provides an overview of genres that use the spoken word in Yoruba culture as well as of the training of verbal artists and their place in society. Students are introduced to Yoruba verbal art through viewing videotapes of actual performances and reading basic texts in bilingual editions. In addition to covering customs and language, modes of delivery, performance, and literary features of Yoruba verbal arts, the course devotes separate units, one to two weeks each, to four specific oral traditions: *oriki*, praise poetry; *ifa*, divination poetry; *ijala*, hunters' poetry; and *rara iyawo*, nuptial chants and women's poetry (for a full syllabus, see pp. 454–55).

African Narrative Tradition, offered through Harvard University's Folklore and Mythology concentration, introduces students to African narrative in contemporary as well as traditional contexts through study of folktales collected by Abrahams, novels by Tutuola, scholarship on the contexts and performance of African narratives by Donald Cosentino (*Defiant Maids and Stubborn Farmers*) and Harold

Scheub (*The African Storyteller*), and the theories of orality by Walter Ong. Oral performance techniques in African theater, cinema, and popular culture are also considered through reading of scholarship by Athol Fugard (*Statements*), T. O. McLoughlin ("Reading Zimbabwean Comic Strips"), and Mbye Cham ("Structural and Thematic Parallels in Oral Narrative and Film") and through viewing of the film *Saaraba*. Special emphasis is given to the nature of orality as it exists prior to and alongside literacy and to the function of symbols and metaphors in oral prose narrative and poetic forms. Harvard also offers a course focusing specifically on the oral narrative performances of Swahili women storytellers. Discussion of the nature of storytelling in contemporary and traditional contexts begins with a unit on Swahili history, supplemented with readings in *The World of the Swahili* (Middleton) and *Africa and the Disciplines* (Bates, Mudimbe, and O'Barr). Corresponding written assignments ask students to discuss the difficulties of constructing Swahili history and the fluctuating identity of Swahili people. The following units address storytelling patterns, the nature of orality in Swahili culture, the function of metaphors and models in Swahili narratives, and performance and cultural contexts, with readings from Cosentino's *Defiant Maids and Stubborn Farmers* and Mtoro bin Mwinyi Bakari's *The Customs of the Swahili People*. Important compilations used throughout the course include Edward Steere's *Swahili Tales* and Sarah Mirza and Margaret Strobel's *Three Swahili Women*.

American Traditions

The sampling of course materials received during our survey can reflect the diversity in American culture only very selectively (units on traditions in American culture also appear in the courses British and American Folklore [p. 416], Jewish Folklore [p. 420], and Literature of the Young Child [pp. 420–21]). Courses addressing a wide range of cultural traditions in the United States are discussed first and are followed by the specialized topics of African American traditions and Native American traditions (see Prahlad; Toelken; McDowell — all in this volume).

In order to take full advantage of local resources, the University of Toledo focuses its introductory folklore course on American traditions in northwest Ohio. Social context is emphasized in the students' fieldwork projects, and one class period early in the term is devoted to discussion of text versus performance. Louisiana State University's course American Folklore deals with the colonial period, immigrant groups, and African American and Native American traditions. Prior to these units is an introduction that assigns readings from Richard Dorson's *American Folklore* and *America in Legend* to supplement discussion of folklore in its historical context. Subsequent readings are drawn from Brunvand's *The Vanishing Hitchhiker*, Toni Morrison's *Song of Solomon*, Mary Helen Ponce's *Hoyt Street*, Simon Bronner's *Piled Higher and Deeper*, and Patricia Turner's *I Heard It through the Grapevine*.

The University of Toledo's course The Ballad and the Blues surveys "two of the most important forms of oral folklore in the United States." The first half of the course concerns the development of the British and American folk ballad and its relation to modern American culture, with selected readings from Alan Lomax's *The Folk Songs of North America in the English Language* and Albert Friedman's *The Viking Book of Folk Ballads of the English-Speaking World*. The second half of the course deals with blues music, using Robert Palmer's *Deep Blues* and Houston A. Baker's *Blues, Ideology, and Afro-American Literature* as texts.

Florida State University offers a course devoted to oral traditions of African American women (for a course description and list of texts, see pp. 447–48). Topics of study are the role of the woman as performer and preserver of traditional verbal art forms, her connection to the blues tradition, and her traditional culture and expressive behavior. This course also explores the ways in which experiences are made meaningful through narratives, the dynamics and impact of traditional domesticity, social roles and power, female sexuality, and "marked moments in African American women's life cycles." Indiana University's course African American Folklore / Folklife / Folk Music studies African American culture in terms of history and social change. Folklore, folk music, and oral history are considered as means of illuminating black culture and history (see Prahlad, this volume).

The University of Arizona's course Oral Tradition (for a course description and list of texts, see p. 446) focuses on oral rather than written language and attempts to determine the role of Native American oral tradition in the context of American literature. Through comparison of oral and written traditions, the course explores the "rich existence" of language in the absence of writing and examines the complexities of the nature and function of Native American oral traditions in written literature. Texts include N. Scott Momaday's *The Way to Rainy Mountain* (on general pedagogical approaches to this novel, see Roemer), Richard Erdoes and Alfonso Ortiz's anthology *American Indian Myths and Legends*, Peter Farb's *Word Play*, and John Bierhorst's *The Sacred Path*. Arizona State University offers a similar course entitled American Indian Literatures, which examines selected oral traditions of American Indians and the influences of those traditions on contemporary Native American literary works.

Saint Joseph College opens its course Native American Literature (for a full syllabus, see pp. 449–51) with discussion of the centrality of storytelling in Native American tribes, traditional songs and chants, and the relation of myth and ceremony. Understanding of the performance medium is enhanced through a series of videos, taped readings, and slide presentations. In the film *Running at the Edge of the Rainbow*, for example, Leslie Marmon Silko identifies the oral traditions in Laguna culture—formal storytelling as well as gossip—and discusses her writing and its relation to the oral tradition of her people.

Biblical Studies

The English department at Auburn University, Montgomery, offers the course The Bible as Literature: The Gospels, which is devoted to "historical-critical analyses" and asks questions about historical context, method of composition, and meaning for the original audience (see Jaffee, this volume; Kelber, this volume). Specific books from the Old or New Testament (varying each time the course is taught) constitute the focus. Amherst College's course Folklore and the Hebrew Bible incorporates biblical scholarship by Hermann Gunkel (*The Legends of Genesis*) and Susan Niditch (*Folklore and the Hebrew Bible*) alongside scholarship on oral traditions by Toelken (*The Dynamics of Folklore*), Dan Ben-Amos ("Toward a Definition of Folklore in Context"), and Olrik ("Epic Laws of Folk Narrative") into a unit devoted to discussion of composition, performance, and transmission in oral and written cultures. The second unit centers on Lord's theories regarding distinctions between orally composed work and written work and explores how later scholars such as Bruce Rosenberg ("The Complexity of Oral Tradition") and Finnegan have been influenced by, and deviated from, Lord's ideas. The first written assignment requires students to make a case for the oral composition of the plagues account in Exodus and to consider whether or not a written work can be "traditional" in style and form and how the dimension of performance might influence approaches to biblical texts (for a full syllabus, see pp. 458–62).

British Traditions

The course Nineteenth-Century British Vernacular Literature at the University of Texas, Austin, so titled to encompass traditions that draw from folklore as well as from popular culture, is offered through the departments of anthropology and English and places strong emphasis on the social contexts of oral literatures (on British traditions of an earlier period, see Lindahl, this volume; Stratyner, this volume). The class description explains that the term *literature* "does not really capture the topic's ramifications" because the material was most often encountered by "nineteenth-century British men, women, and children in performance rather than in print, was experienced in company rather than in solitude." A similar course taught at the same institution is Folklore of the British Isles. Defining folklore genres such as games, jokes, and verbal epithets as "traditional, stylized, artful performances," the course first addresses traditional tales of early Gaelic-speaking Ireland, then proceeds to Anglophone folk songs popular in England, lowland Scotland, and Anglo-Ireland. Another section deals explicitly with performance through the study of dramatic activities, such as mummers' plays. The final section involves the study of "working-class poetry" that was shared through recitation with both neighbors and fellow workers. At every stage, the course stresses "the material's significance in its natural contexts of everyday use."

The University of California, Berkeley, sent information on its course Folklore and Mythology of the British Isles, which serves as an introduction to folklore research and draws examples chiefly from the oral traditional literatures of England, Scotland, Ireland, and Wales. One week of class is devoted to a study of "singing and storytelling in cultural context." Students view slides of Scottish ballad singers and read selections, such as John Niles's "Context and Loss in Scottish Ballad Tradition," from a course packet addressing the importance of recording social context during ethnographic fieldwork. Similar topics are covered in Berkeley's course British and American Folklore: The Mythopoeic Impulse. Primary texts, revealing features of myth in a wide range of genres, include Geoffrey of Monmouth's *History of the Kings of Britain*, Malory's *King Arthur and His Knights*, Iona and Peter Opie's *Classic Fairy Tales*, and Brunvand's *Vanishing Hitchhiker*. Dundes's *Sacred Narrative* and Linda Dégh's *American Folklore and the Mass Media* are recommended as supplements to help students understand the cultural roles performed by myths and "emergent narrative forms that show mythlike features." The course also extends the study of myth to show its use in the mass media.

Classical Studies

Theories of oral tradition have been incorporated into a number of courses offered through classical studies departments, such as Brown University's Early Greek Literature (see Martin, this volume). This course includes a full unit on formula and oral poetry, with extensive reading on ancient Greek oral-formulaic diction drawn from Milman Parry's *The Making of Homeric Verse*, Lord's "Homer as Oral Poet," Eric Havelock's *Preface to Plato*, Joseph Russo's "Homer against His

Tradition," and David Gunn's "Narrative Inconsistency and the Oral Dictated Text in the Homeric Epic." The course Homer's *Iliad*, taught at Vanderbilt University, is designed primarily as a reading course, but it also devotes class time to discussing the characteristics of oral poetry. Readings from Parry's work supplement primary texts. Students of the course The Epic, taught at the University of California, Berkeley, study Homer's *Odyssey*, Virgil's *Aeneid*, Ovid's *Metamorphoses*, and other works, examining the "stylistic particularity" of each and discussing the historical contexts of specific passages. The course Seminar in Archaic Epic at the University of Missouri, Columbia, focuses on the contribution of oral tradition to Homeric art, with selected readings from the *Iliad*, *Odyssey*, and Homeric hymns. Special attention is devoted to formulaic and thematic structure, issues associated with performance, textual transmission, comparative epic (especially South Slavic), and traditional referentiality.

Speech and Storytelling

The English department at Sheldon Jackson College in Alaska lists the course Speech and Liberal Arts, which encourages students to develop verbal communication skills through the study of storytelling conventions in various cultures (see Birch, this volume). Traditions of the Irish shanachie, African griot, and Tlingit elder are among those studied. Students are required both to write a paper exploring an aspect of storytelling conventions and to compose and present a story orally. In The Oral Tradition, the University of North Alabama's speech department provides an overview of various oral traditions, from classical epic to contemporary presentations. Having familiarized themselves with performance techniques in a wide range of genres, students are required to make several classroom presentations, which can be "literary selections, storytelling, or impromptu oral presentations." Dominican College offers a Certificate in Storytelling program, which teaches performance skills and offers core courses in storytelling, voice, critique clinic, and analyzing stories. Supplementary electives to help students contextualize skills through understanding of storytelling in various cultures include the study of Celtic folklore, urban legends, and world mythology.

Women's Traditions

Among courses focusing on oral traditions specific to women is Louisiana State University's Women and Folklore, which examines how oral traditions are affected by gender (see the descriptions for the courses Swahili Women Storytellers [p. 412] and African American Women [p. 413]; see also Weigle, this volume). One unit addresses how men and women differ as performers of and audiences for oral traditions. Another examines how women negotiate power and social control through folklore performance skills. Readings from *Women's Folklore, Women's Culture* (Jordan and Kalčik), *Feminist Messages: Coding in Women's Folk Culture* (Radner), and Maxine Hong Kingston's memoirs, *The Woman Warrior* (on general pedagogical approaches to this book, see Lim) inform discussion of these issues. The course Women and Oral Tradition, taught at the University of New Mexico, encourages consideration of the contexts of various distinctly feminine traditions in the past and present in a number of ways. During the first section, students compile ethnographies of important aspects of their own experience and examine how geography, race, class, and ethnicity affect women's traditions through comparison with classmates' ethnographies; historical factors are taken into account through comparison of students' experience of oral traditions with that of their mothers. In another unit, portrayals of women's mythology and language in current newspapers are examined in the light of mythology and language in oral or folk tradition, historical or contemporary. Barbara Babcock's edition of Elsie Clews Parsons's essays *Pueblo Mothers and Children*, Deborah Cameron's *The Feminist Critique of Language*, and Marta Weigle's *Spiders and Spinsters: Women and Mythology* are among the assigned readings.

Other Courses

A course at Rice University devoted exclusively to the ballad and folklore allows for extensive discussion of the oral traditional idiom employed in ballad composition and transmission. Students read from Bertrand Bronson's *The Ballad as Song*, David Buchan's *The Ballad and the Folk*, and Albert Friedman's "Oral-Formulaic Theory" (see Niles, this volume). African American spirituals, blues, toasts, and rap are also studied as oral traditions. Discussions of style, form, social function, and the role of memory are foregrounded through readings in Ong's *Orality and Literacy*.

The course Korean Folklore at the University of California, Los Angeles, emphasizes the varied traditional expressions of Korea: in rituals (shamanistic and Confucian-influenced), folk narratives (myths, legends, and folktales), folk performances (primarily mask-dance drama), and folk music (*p'ungmul*). Not only does this course compare other east Asian and more disparate cultures to the traditions of Korea but it also examines the transplantation of indigenous traditions to the United States and their adaptation to the new cultural landscape. With the focus on emerging Korean American ethnic groups, students engage in their own fieldwork projects and are encouraged to take advantage of Korean and Korean American populations in Los Angeles. Readings are drawn from In-Sob Zong's *Folk Tales from Korea*; Laurel Kendall and Griffin Dix's *Religion and Ritual in Korean Society*; Roger Janelli and Kim Dawn-Hee Janelli's *Ancestor Worship and Korean Society*; and Kendall, Mark Peterson, and Martina Deuchler's *Korean Women*.

In the University of Florida's course Japanese Folklore, the class studies folktales and festivals. Ethnographies and films are used to establish a basic understanding of the native religious belief systems of Shinto and Buddhism (see Quinn, this volume). The course explores topics such as ritual and the unconscious, the structure of myth, the nature of speech, and the formation of personality, all aimed at enabling students to interpret the verbal arts of Japan in context (for a course description and list of texts, see p. 447). Selections from Royall Tyler's *Japanese Tales*, Kunio Yanagita's *Legends of Toono* and *About Our Ancestors*, and *International Perspectives on Yanagita Kunio and Japanese Folklore Studies* (ed. Koschmann, Oiwa, and Yamashita) serve as focal points for discussion. Also taught at the University of Florida, Arabic Folklore examines verbal arts, games, dances, and music of Arabic culture (see Slyomovics, this volume).

Among the texts read are Inea Bushnaq's anthology, *Arab Folktales*; Hasan El-Shamy's *Folktales of Egypt*; and Saad Abdullah Sowayan's *Nabati Poetry: The Oral Poetry of Arabia*. Documentaries and slides are also used to increase understanding of the folk culture of the Arab world from historical, sociological, philosophical, and artistic perspectives.

The course Scandinavian Folk Narrative, taught at the University of California, Los Angeles, provides an introduction to the fairy tales and legends of Scandinavian tradition, examining how various interpretive methodologies associated with such scholars as Vladimir Propp (*Morphology*) and Bengt Holbek ("Language") help us understand why and how these stories have been told. With discussion centering on narratives found in John Lindow's *Swedish Legends and Folktales* and Jacqueline Simpson's *Scandinavian Folktales*, the course also explores the relations between legend and folktale in the Scandinavian tradition (see Harris, this volume).

Jewish Folklore, taught at the University of Texas, Austin, examines how historical and social circumstances have affected traditional creative expressions (see Neulander, this volume). The course focuses on Jewish oral traditions in selected periods: the Middle Ages, nineteenth-century Eastern Europe, and the United States during the various stages of Jewish immigration. Anthologies compiled by Micha Joseph bin Gorion [Berdichevsky] (*Mimekor Yisrael: Selected Classical Jewish Folktales*) and Joachim Neugroschel (*Great Tales of Jewish Occult and Fantasy*) are supplemented by Joshua Trachtenberg's *Jewish Magic and Superstition* and Barbara Myerhoff's *Number Our Days*, which is used during a unit on Jewish ritual in America.

Oral traditions of children — such as rhymes, games, and stories — are addressed in Indiana University's course Children's Folklore. These traditional folklife forms, as well as music associated with the culture of childhood, are studied for the role they play in peer-group activity and in the social and cognitive development of the child. Similarly, the University of Florida, Gainesville, offers Literature of the Young Child, which traces the history of American children's literature and the roots of that literature in oral traditions, from tales circulating in medieval England to stories told in colonial

America and finally to the literature of the present day. Emphasis is placed on the sociological and psychological effects of various sources that reflect and promote specific societal values (for general approaches to teaching children's literature, see Sadler).

Rice University's course Communication, Cognition, and Culture traces the evolution of information technologies and their influence on civilization, exploring the passage from oral to written, from manuscript to print, and from print to electronic communication. Through readings in Ong's *Orality and Literacy*, Elizabeth L. Eisenstein's *The Printing Revolution in Early Modern Europe*, Lucien Febvre and Henri-Jean Martin's *The Coming of the Book*, and Werner Kelber's "Language, Memory, and Sense Perception," students examine the ways in which these media influence the organization of human culture, technological progress, and individual experience (for a full syllabus, see pp. 462–64).

——

The materials we have received and described reflect a variety of teaching styles and a wide range of aims among academic disciplines and departments. This diversity attests to the breadth of scholarship inspired by numerous approaches — among them, performance theory, ethnopoetics, and oral-formulaic theory — to the understanding of oral traditions. Instructors who have incorporated the study of oral traditions into classrooms across the country, unified by their awareness of the interconnectedness of orality and literacy in traditional texts, the significance of traditional forms and themes, and the crucial importance of social context in the performance of oral narratives, have illustrated in this survey not only possible models of but also the infinite potential for innovation in addressing various traditions and meeting the needs of different student constituencies. In academic institutions, which by necessity rely predominantly on texts, instructors have found numerous ways of compensating to some degree for a textual medium that is often inadequate in reflecting the complexity of performance and referentiality in orally composed and oral-derived traditional works. Their methods speak importantly to the understanding of cultural traditions.

Note

1. Our strategy in conducting the survey was to write department chairs and heads, asking for descriptions and syllabi for particular courses listed in the college or university catalogs and for any other related courses. Later on, we sent copies of (sometimes lightly edited) versions of these materials to individual instructors or department chairs or heads for correction and approval. We wish to take this opportunity to thank all those departments and teachers who responded to our requests.

Beverly J. Stoeltje and Nancy Worthington

Multiculturalism and Oral Traditions

Difference and sameness. Strange and familiar. Identification and differentiation. Us and them. Ancient as culture itself, such paired terms characterize human consciousness and account for much of human history. Yet the twentieth century has dramatically shrunk the space between paired opposites, enhancing social life in some settings and leaving carnage in others. The melting-pot theory of society, which erased cultural differences, has proved inadequate in this milieu, and a new model known as multiculturalism has filled the space. The postmodern and postcolonial conditions underlying the new model have engendered bewildering challenges and abundant choices. They make possible the live performance of Andean music in Prague and the appearance of South Africa's Ladysmith Black Mambazo in Chicago, but they have also brought into relief questions of identity and pointed to the deep significance of culture.

Based on the recognition of diversity, multiculturalism insists that cultural differences as well as human rights must be recognized. The key to this new model is collective identity and the goal is

423

recognition. In his essay on the politics of recognition, Charles Taylor explains that the issue is no longer one of survival only but one that centers on the appreciation of the equal value and the worth of each distinct culture. The demand for this level of awareness has been made explicit by the spread of the idea that we are formed by recognition and by the understanding that recognition is related to image (64–65).[1] Expanding on and responding to Taylor, Kwame Anthony Appiah introduces the concept of narrative into the process of recognition, arguing that people want to be able to tell a story of their lives that reflects a narrative unity consistent with the standards of their own culture (160–61). The implication of his argument is that recognition must extend to the narrative traditions of specific cultures, encompassing aesthetic standards, intellectual functions, and the life experiences represented in them.

Oral narrative, an inclusive category spanning stories from the short joke to the long epic, is central to the oral tradition of any culture, but proverbs, songs, rumor, poetry, insults, cheers, curses, and other such verbal forms, transmitted informally and without an author, are also defined by the term "oral tradition." Through careful study of these nonnarrative forms, students can encounter the history, experience, and aesthetics as well as the fears, anxieties, and prejudices of a specific culture through its own artistic constructions and interpretations.

Because they are informal, such nonnarrative forms of communication are seldom scrutinized, and therefore some students regard them as private forms or as entertainment and argue that they are beyond the scope of analysis. Yet we are certainly aware that attitudes and emotions of all kinds are freely voiced in these genres. If, therefore, we wish to pursue the subject of multiculturalism in an educational curriculum, we must include in our study the informal channels and symbolic forms of communication. If we define our subject as variations in human collective identity and their representations (both internal and external), and if our goal is students' comprehension of identity and representation, then all oral traditions can serve as a rich resource. Tapping into this widely defined resource transforms strangeness into familiarity and deconstructs stereotypes, reducing the fear of that which is different or unknown. Such ends are accomplished by introducing students to social processes and verbal genres that serve as a foundation for shared identity.

Cultural Context and Critical Skills

Students will need to be encouraged to explore oral traditional forms as the beliefs, perceptions, and interpretations of a culture, developed out of social experience over time, and not as texts to be examined as true or false or to be measured against the standards of the dominant culture. Understanding the forms of oral tradition in the context of the culture that creates them is the goal. To achieve it, students must develop critical skills that permit them to recognize the oral traditions of their own culture; these traditions may be accepted or practiced by some people and not by others, but selected ones are known to a majority. An example familiar to most American undergraduates is the creation myth in Genesis. Explaining that all cultures tell a story to account for the creation of the universe and its inhabitants, that these are commonly known to scholars as myth, and that the stories in the Bible circulated in oral tradition before someone wrote them down helps students develop a multicultural approach to oral tradition (see Jaffee, this volume; Kelber, this volume). A useful text for this purpose is Marta Weigle's *Spiders and Spinsters*, a resource book on women and myth that contains excerpted texts from Native American and ancient Greek myth (see also Weigle, this volume).

Treating the whole spectrum of oral tradition can invoke fascination among students, especially when they discover that their adolescent horror stories are anthologized and analyzed as legends (the choking Doberman, Pop Rocks candy deaths, the promiscuous cheerleader, and so forth; see G. Fine for a study of sex and money in contemporary legends). When these stories involve racism, sexism, or class discrimination, students may become engaged in heated arguments or slip into a deep silence. It is useful, therefore, for instructors to make every effort to contextualize oral traditions in social and political time, to insist that members of the class listen to one another's stories even though one person may try to deny the validity of another's story, and to demonstrate parallels in the stories of several different social groups, pointing to their formulaic nature and the social problems addressed in them. With careful application it will be possible for the students to cultivate the ability to distinguish between cultural difference and stereotype and to enhance the ability to reflect rather than react.

Concepts and Processes: the Interpretation of Experience

All self-identified groups who share common experience create oral traditions: narrative, music and song, festival and sport. These genres function to process experience, shaping it to fit into the existing belief system or cognitive framework. Roger Abrahams has argued that the performance of folklore impersonalizes a problem that is recurrent in a society, establishing a link between the individual and the larger group and suggesting a guide for future action ("Personal Power" 19). These forms, then, reveal how a particular culture or group processes its perceived problems and historical experience. Whether the given culture is defined as ethnic, religious, occupational, political, or social, experience relevant to the group will be transformed into familiar genres and performed according to aesthetic principles familiar to the group. The dynamic of this process is complex, but the fundamentals may be summarized as follows: experience combines with belief in a genre of oral tradition to be shared with others through a performance that will interpret the experience.

Identity: Shared or Differential

Identity is a concept essential for students' understanding of multiculturalism. Most self-identified social groups utilize principles of difference and similarity and the genres of oral tradition to differentiate between "us" and "them." Although the principles of identity that underlie the term *culture* can be based on any characteristic shared by a group, within cultures people divide into smaller social units and utilize these same principles. Examples of smaller units are fraternities and sororities, gangs, the military, political parties, and Deadheads.

Because jokes, songs, stories, and insults can be performed on the basis of either shared or differential identity, it is important to caution against an assumption of rigid boundaries, namely, that oral traditions circulate only within a group. The significance of oral traditions is most readily grasped if we seek to identify the communicative purposes they serve in social relationships, whether they create hostility, transcend differences, or disguise messages in codes (Bauman, "Differential Identity"; Appadurai, Korom, and Mills; Radner).

The path of development for oral traditions follows the path of social relationships, with the meaning of a story dependent on the cultural and political context in which it is told. For example, legends tell stories of strange and bizarre events that are believed by someone to have really happened, usually to a friend of a friend (see esp. Brunvand, *Vanishing Hitchhiker*). In such stories, anxieties are expressed about those who are different from us and who thus pose a threat. A recent example is the story known as "The Mall Slasher," which had such currency that it merited a full-length article in the *Chicago Tribune* (Kendall). In this legend a nonwhite male who was hidden under a woman's car at a shopping mall slashed her ankles when she returned; when she fell to the ground, he sexually assaulted her.

This legend exhibits the basic set of characteristics associated with legends: it situates the action locally (it is reported to have happened "right here in our very own town"), lending immediacy to the story, and it sweeps through the country rapidly. People repeat the story to their associates, reporting that it happened to a friend of a friend. Resting on deep-seated prejudice and reflecting racial tensions reverberating through the larger society, such a story enlists passionate believers. Barre Toelken has analyzed this ubiquitous form in terms of the "psychology of ethnic folklore"; he explains that majority groups symbolize anxieties about minority groups by perceiving those groups as sexual threats to innocent males and females, that majority groups always see virtue on "our side" and aggression on the "their side" (*Dynamics* 273; citation here is to the original 1979 edition of *Dynamics*).

The minority group that is perceived as a sexual threat represents a form of the scapegoat phenomenon. Another widespread legend that functions similarly is the ancient narrative known as the blood libel legend, an anti-Semitic tale that circulated among Christians in Europe for centuries before World War II. Based on the false belief that Jews sacrifice Christian children in their rituals and drink the blood, the tale claims that some specific Jewish family in the local area has kidnapped a Christian child for use as a human sacrifice.[2] Ironically, as Bill Ellis has demonstrated, this same accusation was lodged by the Romans against the Christians in pre-Christian Rome. In both contexts this legend exemplifies how people translate into oral narrative legends their fears about others who practice a different religion.

Oral forms do not discriminate between stereotypes and cultural differences. Clichés, values, prejudices, shock, history, anxieties, and general cultural knowledge are all transmitted through oral traditions. However, such forms do function additionally as commentary on social relations and evidence of political conditions; although they may contain either truths or lies, or both, their study reveals to us how people think and feel. An excellent pedagogical device for illustrating these problems is *Fires in the Mirror*, the television performance and accompanying text by the performance artist Anna Deavere Smith. After interviewing African Americans and Hasidic Jews from Crown Heights in Brooklyn on the riot and conflict between them, she performed their responses in character, playing both African American and Hasid, female and male.[3]

Any rumor or legend that circulates rapidly and reflects social problems may contain a kernel of truth, if only in that an actual event triggered the story (as the accident that set off the riot in Crown Heights). But the power of fear, filtered through social stress and shaped into formulaic narrative, can transform any small trace of truth into a full-blown expression of racism or, at times, move it into the realm of the supernatural, depending on the prevailing system of belief. Consequently, all oral genres must be approached as symbolic communication. A precautionary note must be made, however; special effort may be required to explain the symbolic function to many students, some of whom are inclined to interpret anything they hear socially as literal truth. It is useful, therefore, to point out the formulaic elements that signal the genre of legend: the local setting that moves as the story travels; the report that the story happened to a friend of a friend; and the element of social stress, as manifested by fear of others. In general, an oral text must be deconstructed just as thoroughly as a written one.

Because oral traditions serve as an index to the complexities of social identity, they can provide a link connecting popular opinions with relevant social, historical, and political conditions. When change is under way or a crisis threatens, oral traditions provide an important channel for the rapid transmission of information, true or false. This capacity has significance for the understanding of multiculturalism, in high schools and universities as well as in the larger society. To study oral traditions productively, however, students must be aware that they are not limited to any one political position in the functions they serve. In one group oral traditions may express resistance to domination, while in another they may actually be enlisted by the forces of racism or sexism.

The Symbolic Apparatus: Constructing Identity and Symbols

Sports, beauty pageants, rock concerts, Santa Claus — these and more serve as the means by which students experience social identity and oral traditions. Almost every high school and college sponsors sporting events and adopts the symbolic apparatus that provides an identity for those who belong: a name and totem or mascot (Bears, Longhorns, Wolves), colors (worn as uniforms), songs and cheers ("Fight, Fight, On to Victory"), jokes that portray the inferiority of the other team, and stories that demonize "them" and heroize "us." Similarly, sororities and fraternities, the military, urban gangs, nations, and rock fans utilize the same apparatus — with variations, of course.

Music is another resource students use extensively for constructing identity. Talking with students about their musical tastes can help them understand the dynamic of identification and differentiation and the extent to which choice can be involved in identity.

Musical taste helps some students locate roommates or select friends or choose lovers, enabling them to align themselves and their partners according to the principle of same and different. The social functions of music can be explored as a parallel to the same functions served by oral traditions in specific cultures.

Among the most powerful characteristics of oral traditions is their capacity to diffuse beyond their point of origin, adapting to circumstances as they travel. Familiar to most of the Western world, the image and associated beliefs and legends of Santa Claus embody this symbolic process. Steven Swann Jones has tracked this figure's evolution, showing that Santa Claus originated as a Greek bishop in the fourth century who performed miraculous deeds for the poor and thereby generated a large body of legends about gifts. After his death the bishop was canonized by the church as Saint Nicholas, and his image as a saint then spread throughout Europe, becoming associated with December, children, good behavior, and gifts ("Fertile Imagery"). Saint Nicholas crossed the Atlantic with the Dutch to the United States, where he acquired a jolly fat belly, reindeer from Lapland, and the new name of Santa Claus. Although his day of celebration fused with that of Jesus's birthday, he himself became independent of any religious association. As a culturally vital symbol, Santa continues to generate oral traditions, not the least of which is the fundamental question of belief in his existence. For many American children the discovery that Santa's existence is fictitious performs a socially significant function, marking the end of the age of innocence.

Ethnic Identity: Epics and Ballads

Two closely related genres of oral tradition have long represented a narrative response to conflict: the epic and the ballad. Both genres narrate events located in border areas, and in both the narrator casts the story in poetic form and usually sings it with musical accompaniment, employing familiar formulaic phrases. The epic and the ballad represent the perspective of us versus them in a conflict that usually features a hero who has defeated or escaped from the enemy,

exhibiting extraordinary courage and ability that subsequent generations can admire and emulate. These narrative songs remain in the
repertoire of the group for as long as the conflict is relevant or as
long as the empire, nation, or family remains in power. For some
scholars and teachers, *epic* applies to long narratives that represent a
quasi-historical conflict believed to have served a nationalistic purpose, whereas *ballad* applies to family, ethnic, or regional conflicts.
Classic examples of the heroic epic and a related form, the saga, are
found throughout Europe and in Africa, the Middle East, Asia, and
the Americas (see Parthasarathy, this volume; Slyomovics, this
volume).

Of course, *epic* and *ballad* are English terms; in other languages
these genres will have different names, with differing intracultural
taxonomies. The Mexican American ballad (the *corrido*) often deals
with border conflict between Mexicans and Anglos (see Herrera-
Sobek, this volume; Bauman and Braid, this volume). The *corrido* of
Gregorio Cortez, for example, sings the praises of a Mexican folk
hero in turn-of-the-century Texas who long eluded the Texas Rangers
only to be betrayed by a fellow Mexican at the border. Américo Paredes's book *With His Pistol in His Hand* provides an account of this
incident against the background of its historical period, in which racism against Mexicans was intense. Paredes demonstrates the centrality of shared experience in the interpretation of events and their
characterization in oral tradition by tracing the different variants of
the legend and the song told by Anglos, Mexicans, and the press.
For the Mexicans, the story illustrates Anglo inferiority, because the
Anglos' Spanish was too poor to make the distinction between mare
and horse (the misapprehension that consequently resulted in two
deaths) and because the Anglos' most touted lawmen, the Rangers,
were outsmarted by a single Mexican.[4]

Oral Traditions and Social Identity over Time: African Americans

As social relations undergo modifications, the modifications will
be reflected in oral traditions. This continually evolving process is

especially evident in the oral traditions of African American culture, making it possible to link historical experience with verbal forms (see Pavlic; Prahlad, this volume). The first Africans in the United States adapted their African oral traditions to plantation life in the South. Particularly prominent were narratives known as trickster tales, the most familiar centering on Brer Rabbit. Scholars have linked these tales to the trickster tradition in Africa, especially to Anansi the spider, from Ghana (see Prahlad, this volume; Cosentino, this volume). The tale types of Brer Rabbit and Anansi share a number of the same motifs, including the superiority of wit and cunning over force: the unscrupulous trickster, a small animal or spider, dupes the stronger animal out of something of value. Another variant of the trickster tale features characters from plantation life, John (the African American slave) and Old Marster or Massa (the white slave owner). In these stories John outwits Massa, whose naïveté, greed, or slow wit permits the cleverer John to gain wealth, food, or other material benefits. Whatever the details, these tales recount the relationship between a defiant slave and the master he outwits. Zora Neale Hurston, a folklore scholar as well as writer, has described John as "hitting a straight lick with a crooked stick," "winning the jackpot with no other stake but a laugh," and knowing things like "Heaven arms with love and laughter those it does not wish to be destroyed" ("High John" 543, 544).[5]

In his insightful study of the black folk hero, the contemporary folklorist John Roberts discusses the dynamic of the trickster as a model of action for enslaved Africans that aided them in securing the material necessities for survival in the context of repression (35, 185). However, as social relations evolved, and conditions dramatically changed around the turn of the century, during the period of emancipation and segregation, the trickster tales became outmoded. Along with gaining their individual freedom, African Americans became newly responsible for meeting their own material needs through direct participation in wage labor. Roberts points out that under these conditions many of the adaptive strategies of the trickster became ineffectual, such as those involving manipulative tactics to avoid work, which was now directly linked to survival.

The bad man evolved from the trickster, John, to become the new hero of oral tradition, representing a revised model of resistance adapted to the existing forms of oppression. The violence associated with the bad man character has drawn scorn from white folklorists, but Roberts argues that the violence stems from white disregard for historical circumstances, specifically, from whites' use of the law to oppress African Americans after emancipation. He interprets the bad man, then, as an example of the heroic outlaw tradition that Eric Hobsbawm identifies with social bandits such as Robin Hood. The outlaw seeks to modify the social order, like the much-toasted Stackolee character, who stood up to newly imposed laws that were designed to oppress African Americans. This resistance did not occur with the sanction of the legal system, of course, but it existed in the margins of the social system. Stackolee, a gambler who was loved and admired, at least by some, is the subject of numerous toasts. These long or short narrative verse forms, performed on the streets or wherever men gather, feature the exploits of a bad man. Those knowledgeable about Stackolee believed that he possessed great supernatural powers and that his murder of Billy Lyons was not an arbitrary act of violence but a response to the circumstances that developed in the game between them, climaxing in the loss of Stackolee's Stetson hat to Lyons. One verse of a toast praises Stackolee as a good man: "Stack-O-lee was a good man, / One everybody did love. / Everybody swore by Stack. / Just like the lovin' stars above. / Oh, that Stack-O-lee Stack-O-lee" (Roberts 208).[6]

With integration and the discrimination that accompanied it in the second half of the twentieth century, the strategies as well as the typical characters and plots of oral tradition are adapting once again to parallel social changes. In response to the dominance of corporate influences in current social life, narratives often focus on relations between African Americans and whites through entities such as businesses, organizations, and agencies. Because of the exercise of power by the dominant culture through a corporate model, political or business entities have become the targets of fear, suspicion, and speculation in the contemporary African American oral tradition. Tricksters and bad men who act with wit and courage are no longer the central characters; rather, the hero is the average American citizen-consumer. Patricia Turner's study of contemporary legend and rumor analyzes beliefs and narratives like the one associated with the Church's Fried Chicken franchise. This legend holds that the fast-food chain is really owned by the Ku Klux Klan, and that the chain's chicken has been chemically treated to cause sterility in African American males (the accusation reenforced by the company's preference for inner-city sites). Like the Troop sporting goods company that was the target of similar stories, which diminished its sales, Church's suffered significant financial losses. Troop finally declared bankruptcy, and Church's sold out to Popeye's. As Turner notes, such rumors and legends are especially telling in their revelation of racial anxiety. She found that these and the large body of conspiracy rumors she collected were widely known among African Americans but not at all familiar to whites.

Turner also shows how anxieties about systemic racial injustice are revealed in conspiracy rumors about officially sanctioned racism. She unearthed widespread belief among African Americans that the FBI or J. Edgar Hoover himself was directly responsible for Martin Luther King's death; she found that the CIA was frequently mentioned in association with conspiracies against African Americans. The kernels of truth Turner identifies are the official government policies that regarded the black body as a commodity at the disposal of whites, as evidenced by the Public Health Service's Tuskegee Institute experiment.[7]

———

Rumors and legends illustrate the general model of oral tradition, in which social experience combines with existing beliefs and genres to interpret contemporary occurrences. Moreover, rumors and legends demonstrate how minority fears of the majority are manifested as a reversal of those legends that exhibit majority fears of the minority. Thus oral tradition maintains an intimate link to social experience; the various genres convey knowledge of group identity and aesthetics, perspectives on relations among different cultural groups, and an understanding of the process by which experience is interpreted and transformed into performance for others. These characteristics argue persuasively that the study of multiculturalism benefits from serious consideration of these communicative forms, just as any study of oral traditions naturally benefits from a multicultural perspective.

Notes

1. Taylor builds on the work of Frantz Fanon in his concentration on image. See also O'Barr for a discussion of advertising images that reflect domination and subordination; Stoeltje for a study of the adaptation of images of women as the American frontier was settled ("Helpmate").
2. See Dundes, *Blood Libel* for a collection of articles tracing the blood libel legend over several centuries and through print as well as oral sources.
3. The Hasidim are an ultraorthodox sect of Jews. Many live in Crown Heights, a neighborhood heavily populated by African Americans. A speeding car in a Hasidic funeral procession hit and killed an African American child, causing a riot in the neighborhood.
4. The theme of persecution, heroism, and flight is common to the oral traditions of many other cultures who have suffered oppression.
5. Hurston includes texts of trickster tales, told by the characters of the town of Eatonville, in her *Mules and Men*. In *Afro-American Folktales*, Abrahams devotes a section entitled "Getting around Old Master (Most of the Time)" to trickster tales.
6. Texts of toasts featuring Stackolee and other bad man heroes are included in Roberts's study of the black folk hero; see also Abrahams, *Afro-American*.
7. This forty-year program (begun in 1932) studied African American men infected with syphilis who were not provided any available treatment (P. Turner 111). President Clinton apologized on behalf of the American people for this heinous experiment.

William Bernard McCarthy

Using Oral Tradition
in a Composition Classroom

Ever since the first Foxfire books came out in the late sixties,[1] teachers have been using local traditions as the writing focus for courses in composition. I teach a remedial course called Basic Writing Skills to first-year students at a small Penn State campus in a largely rural part of the state. The students, both recent high school graduates and returning adults, are often first-generation college students, usually convinced that they hate English and always convinced that they cannot write. We focus on learning how to take charge of making texts that are adequate to the purpose and leave no reasonable question unconsidered. The students select some available tradition, traditional genre, folkway, person, or institution that they will research and write about, preparing a portfolio to document their research and present their findings and writings. The research must allow for an oral component, since oral transcription is a key element of the process. The general format grows out of my own experience editing oral tapes for publication. Because the assignment is for an undergraduate composition class, the format incorporates elements of current composition practice not only from the Foxfire approach but also from the portfolio approach (self-selection and multiple genres; Graves and Sunstein) and from the work of Robert Scholes (textual manipulation and textual competence), Ken Macrorie (indirect pedagogical techniques and the I-Search paper), and Peter Elbow (collaboration and process), to give just a few examples. Though I focus here on the basic studies classroom, there is nothing inherently remedial in the format itself; the format is adaptable to a wide variety of writing classrooms, at any grade or competency level.

Praxis

In a fifteen-week semester students complete two portfolios. Since the first portfolio project is in part a warm-up for the second, I recommend that the first project be simple and close to home: the reminiscences of a congenial family member, perhaps, or a friend's repertoire of jokes or children's rhymes. An alternative, perhaps more efficient, first project would be a unit based on a genre the students share, such as urban legends, jokes, or family narratives. Elizabeth Radin Simons offers syllabi and practical advice for a variety of such units, including effective suggestions about how to use discussion to draw out issues for the students to be aware of and reflect on, such as stability and change, gender, and function. Such a unit could be completed fairly quickly, allowing students more time to devote to the second, more ambitious portfolio. In any case, field collecting for the second project usually overlaps with the writing up of the first project.

Occasionally, a student's first project is so rich with opportunities for gathering data and writing that I suggest the student keep that focus for the whole semester, and we work out an appropriate set of assignments. In such cases I make sure that the student writes out a fuller and more complete prospectus or proposal at the time the other students are doing proposals for their new projects.

A typical portfolio usually contains the following items:

Prospectus: a statement of what tradition will be studied, who
will serve as informant, when and where collecting will take
place, the value of the data, and related information

Transcript: a story, oral history, or other performance; about 500
words for the first project, longer for the second

Essay describing a collecting event (an early study for the final
essay)

Field log or journal, including a summary of any taped material
not transcribed, as well as

data sheet(s) on the performer(s)

tape(s) of the performance(s) and interview(s), with a
tape log

photos or other documentary materials

Journalistic essay or other piece of writing growing out of the
project and incorporating material from the transcript

The range of possible projects is very wide. Legends, jokes, and
group songs (camp, jump-rope, fraternity songs) are fairly easy materials to find. So are hunting stories, stories of pregnancy and childbirth, and stories and traditions associated with holidays, birthdays,
and rites of passage. Students have done worthwhile projects on reminiscences of youth by their elderly relatives, on war experiences, and
on family businesses. Some have access to folk-song and folktale traditions. Indeed, the full range of American and immigrant folklore is
out there waiting for students to tap. Nor is it necessary that the
project focus on a specifically oral tradition, as long as there is a
strong oral component. One student did an exemplary project about
an uncle who was a traditional white-oak basket maker, and another
has documented a farm with fine vernacular buildings and a long and
colorful history in the same family. To open students to possibilities,
I use George H. Schoemaker's *The Emergence of Folklore in Everyday
Life*, an inexpensive guide compiled and published by students of the
Indiana University folklore program. The book discusses more than
fifteen different social groups or genres—with examples, collecting
strategies, and writing suggestions—from which students have de-

veloped successful projects. Documenting traditions that they themselves have identified and selected gives students a sense of authenticity as writers and of ownership of what they have written.

Transcriptions

Central to this approach are the transcriptions, in which students make texts out of oral materials (see Fine, this volume; DuBois, this volume). Not alert even to superficial lexical differences between talking and writing—to say nothing of the more profound rhetorical differences discussed, for example, by Susan Miller—students are inclined to think of writing as simply talking on paper. I know of no process that foregrounds the differences so well as the process of making a text out of oral material. Students cannot help attending to distinctively oral vocabulary, sentence structure, rhetorical strategies, and parataxis as opposed to hypotaxis (cf. Summerfield and Summerfield, ch. 9; Lord, *Singer of Tales*, chs. 3–4) as they wrestle with the difficulties of transferring these elements to paper clearly and effectively.

For basic writers there are a number of further benefits. Transcribing requires decisions about sentence and paragraph boundaries, punctuation, grammar, spelling, levels of diction (colloquialisms and expletives, for example), clarity, and readership. When is one best served by a fairly exact transcription that retains all the *er*s and *uh*s and self-corrections, and when is a smoother-looking transcription needed? Should minor grammatical matters be adjusted to the norm for standard written English? And what, in the final analysis, is the relation between punctuation and the spoken language: *Can* you hear periods and commas? (Most of the time, yes.) I have students start by being painstaking and exact in transcribing every vocalization. But when they use this transcription in a journalistic essay, they find that they want to make adjustments for clarity or to present their subjects in a fair and attractive light. And when the student finally reaches that completed transcription—a substantial piece of writing several pages long, neat, in an acceptable format, with professional-looking margins and a real title, a text for which the student has had primary responsibility—the process of authentication as a writer is well on the way.

Related Tasks

This set of assignments also gives students the opportunity to use writing in a variety of ways other than transcribing, from jotting down events and impressions and recording facts to expressing values and experiences in a fully organized essay for a popular audience.

The essay describing a collecting event is one of the first writing assignments in the course. It serves as a warm-up exercise. But I also use it to show how to begin a piece of writing with narrative ("Satisfied, I dropped the receiver back onto the hook. Uncle George said he would talk to me. . . ." or "Dropping my camera, tape recorder, ballpoint pen, and pad of paper into my bookbag, I headed out the door. . . ."). Since this is a descriptive assignment, it provides a good opportunity to stress reliance on nouns and verbs in writing as opposed to overreliance on adjectives—on showing what things are doing rather than on telling how they appear ("Green curtains filtered the sunlight" rather than "Her curtains were pretty and green").

Field notes help students achieve the fluidity and reflectivity that can come from journal writing. A teacher could expand this part of the assignment into a full journal of the project. In any case students should be encouraged to think in terms of upcoming assignments and include in their field notes or journals an abundance of materials that might prove useful. They need to make entries after reviewing a day's fieldwork as well as during the fieldwork. While I expect essays and data sheets to be public documents and therefore correct orthographically and grammatically, journals and notes are private texts, practical or reflective, with the writers themselves as first audience, and may acceptably reflect any nonstandard orthographic or grammatical habits the particular writer may have (cf. Summerfield and Summerfield, ch. 1).

Data sheets record information about the informant and the collecting event, in both tabular and narrative form. We start with the format in the Library of Congress's pamphlet *Folklife and Fieldwork* (27–32), by Peter Bartis, available free from the library's American Folklife Center. Generally, however, the student feels the need to choose and adapt from this format to reflect the particular project and the available data. Since the emphasis is on accuracy in recording, this piece of writing requires careful spelling, especially of proper names; clarity; and correct grammar in any narrative sections.

The prospectus for the first project is usually fairly perfunctory, designed as it is to jump-start the student's thinking while enabling the instructor to guide or even redirect. The prospectus for the second project, however, turns out to be one of the most important pieces of writing in the course. Noting that a good piece of writing must stand on its own feet and explain itself adequately, I require the students to lay out their projects fully in terms that would be understandable to someone unfamiliar with our class, our campus, and our region — what I call an over-the-shoulder reader. Likewise, students must make clear the projected value of their project, whether to themselves or to others. In other words, students must think about motivation, audience (both intended and accidental), completeness of coverage, and adequacy of explanation.

The capstone assignment for the first project is a journalistic essay. Students are to think of a particular newspaper or a particular magazine that might be interested in the subject, and tailor the piece accordingly. The piece might focus on a tradition bearer, on a product (or products) of that tradition, or on a traditional process. That is, it might focus on Grandma herself, on the stories she tells or the quilts she makes, or on how to frame up a quilt, lay out a pattern, and quilt it. Whichever approach is chosen, the article is to include material from the transcription and may well incorporate elements from the earlier fieldwork description.

For the capstone assignment in the second project, I let students decide for themselves what they want to write, urging them to think in practical terms. Many students produce albums or booklets for their families. But many find wider audiences to serve. For instance, mining-town baseball was important in our region, and some major players from the early part of this century (most notably Honus

Wagner) came out of that tradition. But there is little in the local historical collections about mining-town baseball. Two students who came from former mining communities have begun to address that lack. Another historical example: in 1978 a group of young men from Brockway, Pennsylvania, built boats and took them from Toby Creek down the Clarion, Allegheny, Ohio, and Mississippi Rivers to New Orleans. Artifacts from their journey—including one of their homemade boats—were preserved in the Brockway Historical Society Museum, but without any documentation. A student who knew those latter-day Huck Finns did interviews and produced an account to be kept in the museum. Another student's hundred-year-old grandfather had been an avid trapper in the early years of this century: the student wrote up an account of his grandfather's trapping methods, with an eye to submission to a regional wildlife publication.

In a basic writing course it is especially important that assignments build on one another, with particular pedagogical goals to be achieved at each stage. But these pedagogical goals can often be achieved more effectively if they are achieved indirectly—in passing, as it were—while the students' primary focus is on some more concrete task. So while the students are focusing on transcribing—on getting down on paper what is on the tape—they are, in passing, reviewing sentence completeness and basic punctuation. They likewise learn the difference between composing and editing, that even when something is already composed, it can require a good deal of editing. Then, while they focus on completing a data sheet about an interviewee, they are learning, in passing, about careful spelling and about accurate, economical sentences. The description of a collecting event provides an occasion to learn about introductions and organization as well as about reliance on nouns and verbs instead of on adjectives. Questions of audience come up in the prospectus for the second project and in the two capstone assignments. By the time they come to these capstone assignments, in which they have to derive for themselves and their audience a significance based on their data, they are worried not about finding something to say but, rather, about choosing from all the many possible things they could say about their subject. Thus at every stage the learning emerges out of a felt need and a focus on the task at hand.

Extensions

In our university the processes particular to writing longer and fuller papers constitute the subject of Rhetoric and Composition, the course that succeeds Basic Writing Skills. But teachers who wish to adapt the approach I have outlined to more advanced writing courses will have no trouble building in a library-research component. The student's field research can be one element in a project of larger scope that also incorporates primary or secondary materials from books, periodicals, local newspapers, archives, museums, or historical societies. Or the emphasis of the project can remain on the field research, with library, archive, or historical-society research providing background, comparative data, or a theoretical focus. Works by Schoemaker and by Simons, as well as many essays in the present volume, can suggest avenues of research.[2] The folklore volume of the annual *MLA Bibliography* (vol. 5) provides the most comprehensive current indexing of published materials.

The skills developed in a writing course such as I have described provide a practical foundation for other college courses and indeed for many employment situations as well. Data sheets are required for laboratory and research courses and for sales records. Journals are an evaluation tool recognized by professors and by the IRS. Interviewing is essential in communication and business courses as well as in professional communications and business. The skills honed in making an effective proposal are transferable to making an effective report, whether for a class or for a board of directors. And I would hope that the sharing, collaboration, and peer evaluation that goes on at every stage of the project would convince students that we do not accomplish great work by working alone.

Finally, as students open their writing to one another, they come to a much keener appreciation of the aesthetic aspect of writing. Sharing delight in the evocation of a small-town diner, a cranky old man's workshop, a close encounter with a bear, or a storyteller's quirky sense of humor (to take four examples from a recent semester), they come to realize that good writing is pleasurable in itself—a pleasure to produce, a pleasure to read.

Notes

I wish to thank Penn State colleagues Patrick McLaughlin and Claudia Limbert for advice and suggestions.

1. These volumes were the fruit of a high school project on collection of Appalachian folk customs, music, and verbal arts. See *Foxfire*.
2. See especially part 2 of this volume, "Critical Approaches." Other useful sources are Brunvand, *Choking Doberman*; Brunvand and Bowman; Graves and Sunstein; Purves, Quattrini, and Sullivan.

Lynn C. Lewis and Lori Peterson

Course Descriptions and Syllabi

Descriptions of Selected Courses

This section of course descriptions and the section that follows it, "Complete Syllabi of Selected Courses," have been assembled according to the criteria outlined at the beginning of our essay "The National Curriculum and the Teaching of Oral Traditions" in this volume. Course descriptions are from the respondents to our survey.

Theory of Oral Literature
University of California, Berkeley
English 250 and 251
Comparative Literature 212

Course Description
An inquiry into the human habit of storytelling, the dynamics of oral tradition, and the power of oral narrative (together with other forms of verbal expression) to shape the contours of the world and encode the essentials of culture. During the first part of the course we discuss and

evaluate the work of influential theorists. Increasingly, as the semester goes on, specific literary works (chosen according to students' interests and specialties) provide the focal points for discussion.

Texts

Alan Dundes, ed., *Sacred Narrative: Readings in the Theory of Myth*; Ruth Finnegan, *Oral Poetry: Its Nature, Significance, and Social Context*; John Miles Foley, *The Theory of Oral Composition: History and Methodology*; Jack Goody, *The Interface between the Written and the Oral*; Stanley B. Greenfield, trans., *A Readable Beowulf*; Eric A. Havelock, *The Muse Learns to Write: Reflections on Orality and Literacy from Antiquity to the Present*; Albert B. Lord, *The Singer of Tales*; Lord, *Epic Singers and Oral Tradition*; Walter J. Ong, *Orality and Literacy: The Technologizing of the Word*; Paul Zumthor, *Oral Poetry: An Introduction* (trans. K. Murphy-Judy)

Oral Tradition
University of Arizona
English 350 and 596M

Course Description
This is a course in the study of language. We investigate some of the ways in which people think about and use language. Our focus is on oral instead of written language and on the oral tradition of the Native American in particular. The Native American, who has lived for untold generations in an oral tradition — that is, in the absence of writing — has nonetheless a very rich existence in the element of language. We try to define the nature of that richness and to ascertain the place of Native American oral tradition in the context of American literature. In the process we compare the oral and written traditions on several levels. Our principal objective is to reach a fundamental understanding of the oral tradition, its nature, function, and place in the complexity of language.

Texts for English 350 (in the order in which the books are to be read)
Peter Farb, *Word Play*; John Bierhorst, *The Sacred Path*; Richard Erdoes and Alfonso Ortiz, eds., *American Indian Myths and Legends*; N. Scott Momaday, *The Way to Rainy Mountain*; Theodora Kroeber, *The Inland Whale*; Arthur L. Kopit, *Indians*

Texts for English 596M (in addition to the books required for English 350)
John Bierhorst, *The Mythology of South America*; LaVonne Ruoff, *American Indian Literatures*

Japanese Folklore
University of Florida
Department of African and Asian Languages and Literatures
JPT 4502

Course Objectives
To gain an understanding of the development of the discipline of *minzo-kugaku* (folklore, ethnography) in Japan and of the importance of folk ritual observance in cultural identity; to study native religious belief systems of Shinto and Buddhism as they are reflected in the folk practice and folklore of Japan; to study the psychology of the Japanese through the thematic typology of Japanese folklore; to enable the student to interpret the traditional tales, myths, songs, and verbal riddles of Japan in terms of thematic typology and native belief system.

Texts
Kunio Yanagita, *About Our Ancestors: The Japanese Family System*; Yanagita, *Legends of Toono*; J. Victor Koschmann, Keibo Oiwa, and Shinji Yamashita, eds., *International Perspectives on Yanagita Kunio and Japanese Folklore Studies*; Hayao Kawai, *The Japanese Psyche: Major Motifs in the Fairy Tales of Japan*; Royall Tyler, ed. and trans., *Japanese Tales*

Writing Projects
The first paper is an analysis of a cultural practice viewed in the light of Yanagita's *About Our Ancestors* and the secondary literature we have read on Yanagita. The second is a critique of an article analyzing the thematic content of Japanese folktales. Students should use tales found in Kawai, Tyler, or in other anthologies to establish the reference point for their critiques. Articles presenting cultural practices such as festivals and analyzing the thematic content of folktales may be found in the following journals: *Asian Folklore Studies*; *Transactions of the Asiatic Society of Japan*; *Memoirs of the Research Department of the Toyo Bunko*.

Folklore: African American Women and Folklore
Florida State University
English Department
Literature 4322

Course Description
This course explores a broad range of topics relating to African American women's traditional culture, arts, and expressive behavior, as well as attitudes toward and beliefs about them. Topics will include the historic

stereotyping of African American women; the ways in which African American women make their experiences meaningful through legends and personal experience narratives; the place of African American women as performers and preservers of traditional verbal art forms; African American women and the blues tradition; traditional domesticity and African American women; marked moments in African American women's life cycles; and the social powers and dangers of female sexuality in the context of African American women.

Texts
Linda Brent, *Incidents in the Life of a Slave Girl*; Kathryn Morgan, *Children of Strangers*; Zora Neale Hurston, *Mules and Men*; Daphne Harrison, *Black Pearls*; Gloria Naylor, *Linden Hills*; Ntozake Shange, *Sassafras, Cypress, and Indigo*; Bessie Jones, *For the Ancestors*; Patricia Hill Collins, *Black Feminist Thought*

Orality and Textuality in the Middle Ages
University of Wisconsin, Madison
Department of English, Graduate Division
English 754

Course Description
An intensive study of the problematics of "texts" that are produced by the voice or hand and received by the ear or eye. We focus on the Middle Ages because most texts are or were voice or ear texts that have come down to us as eye or hand texts so that we are always forced to enter the first realm in terms of the second. Topics in the seminar will be orality, oral-formulaic theory, textuality, literacy, writing, editing, theoretical aspects, and practical problems for historical and critical scholarship. We will read both critical and theoretical works (a few of which are listed below) and primary texts, but our concentration will be on methods of interpretation and inquiry rather than on "readings."

Texts
Primary: *Beowulf*; *The Song of Roland*; *The Nibelungenlied*; the Middle English Harley lyrics; and others. Theoretical: Walter Ong, *Orality and Literacy*; Dennis Tedlock, *The Spoken Word and the Work of Interpretation*; Michael Riffaterre, *Text Production*. Students will be expected to work on at least one text in an original (textualized) form or language. Modern texts and problematics will be added to the syllabus according to the interests of individuals.

Folktales and Mythology
Southern Illinois University, Carbondale
English 332

Course Description
This course is designed to introduce the student to the fundamental myths and folktales of the world and to provide a basic understanding of the science of mythology and folklore. Readings include myths from Greece and Rome, the Middle East, northern Europe, the British Isles, the Far East, Africa, and the Americas and the folktales of Grimm, Perrault, Andersen, Wilde, and *A Thousand and One Nights*. The course also considers theoretical issues as presented by such scholars as Freud, Frazer, Jung, Lévy-Bruhl, Eliade, Lévi-Strauss, Frye, Campbell, Propp, and Starobinski.

Texts
Donna Rosenberg, ed., *World Mythology: An Anthology of the Great Myths and Epics*; Stith Thompson, ed., *One Hundred Favorite Folktales*; Martin Hallett and Barbara Karasek, eds., *Folk and Fairy Tales*

Complete Syllabi of Selected Courses

Native American Literature
Saint Joseph College
English 238

Course Description
This course focuses on an ethnic voice not often heard in the canon of mainstream American literature, that of the continent's aboriginal inhabitants — the American Indians. Through a reading and discussion of both ancient oral texts and contemporary fictional works, it is hoped that the student will gain a deeper understanding of the richness and diversity of Native American cultures and critically reconsider a number of culturally ingrained assumptions about progress, "savagery" versus civilization, and the "winning" of the West.

Texts (in the order that we will read them)
Alice Marriott and Carol Rachlin, eds., selections from *American Indian Mythology* (1972); Charles Eastman, *From the Deep Woods to Civilization* (1916); D'Arcy McNickle, *The Surrounded* (1936); Leslie Marmon Silko, *Ceremony* (1977); Michael Dorris, *A Yellow Raft in Blue Water* (1987). These texts will

be supplemented by a number of photocopied short stories, essays, and poems as well as by a variety of audiovisual resources.

Schedule

Class	Topic, Reading, Assignment
1	Course introduction; the white man's Indian; oral versus written culture; the centrality of storytelling in Native American tribes
2	The power of the word (traditional songs and chants)
3	The relation of myth and ceremony. Reading: "How the World was Made" (Cheyenne, Modoc), "How the Sun Came" (Cherokee) in *American Indian Mythology*
4	Video: *Emergence* (1981). This animated short tells the story of the events leading to the entrance of the Dineh, the Navajo people, onto the surface of this earth through a number of underworlds. The traditional chants heard in this piece are versions of origin myths sung as part of Navajo healing rituals.
5	Myths of sustenance and survival: corn and buffalo (*American Indian Mythology*, pt. 2)
6	Video: *Hopi: Songs of the Fourth World* (1983). This piece presents many facets of present-day life among the Hopi, whose ancient spiritual traditions remain deeply integrated in daily existence.
7–8	Questions of assimilation, identity, and adaptation. Reading: Eastman, *From the Deep Woods to Civilization*
9–10	Slide presentation: "The Ghost Dance Tragedy at Wounded Knee" (1977). These slides illustrate the conditions that led to the Sioux interpretation of the Ghost Dance religion and its relation to the massacre at Wounded Knee Creek, South Dakota, on 29 December 1890, when members of the Seventh Cavalry killed more than three hundred Indian men, women, and children.
11	Video: *Our Sacred Land* (1984). This film, by the independent Lakota filmmaker Chris Spotted Eagle, shows how strongly sacred places continue to be valued by native people. Its focus is the Black Hills of South Dakota, which the Sioux regard as the spiritual center of the universe.
12	The federal government and Native American life: tracing the effects of the General Allotment Act (1887) and government boarding schools. Reading: McNickle, "Train Time" (from *The Hawk Is Hungry*); Louise Erdrich, "Indian Boarding School: The Runaways"
13	Video: *In the White Man's Image* (1992). This piece, part of the PBS series *The American Experience*, discusses the establishment of government boarding schools for Indians in the late nineteenth

century and their adverse impact on native culture, identity, and pride.

14　Reading: E. Pauline Johnson, "As It Was in the Beginning"

15–19　Reading: McNickle, *The Surrounded*

20–21　The contemporary quest for cultural identity. Video: *Running at the Edge of the Rainbow: Laguna Stories and Poems* (1978). Silko discusses her writing and its relation to the oral tradition of her people. She observes that the telling and retelling of ordinary tales can hold the community together and provide a way for understanding the perennial nature of human actions. Reading: Silko, "Yellow Woman"

22–25　Reading: Silko, *Ceremony*

Ways of Survival, Part 1

26　Reading: Alfonso Ortiz and Richard Erdoes, eds., "Coyote Laughs and Cries: Trickster Tales," from *American Indian Myths and Legends*

27　Reading: Vine Deloria, "Indian Humor"

28–31　Video: *Harold of Orange* (1983). This film confronts with ironic humor the issue of the interconnection between reservation communities and the powerful bureaucracies on which they must often rely, presenting both a group of young Indian "tricksters" and a well-intentioned, though woefully paternalistic, white institution. Harold Sinseer (played by Oneida Indian comedian Charlie Hill) is the leader of the Warriors of Orange. Using wit and humor as their weapons, he and his group disarm a white foundation, a symbol of the dominant society's reserve of power and capital.

Ways of Survival, Part 2

32–37　Reading: Michael Dorris, *A Yellow Raft in Blue Water*

38　Course summation

Oral Traditions in Africa
University of California, Los Angeles
Folklore 155/English M111G

Course Description
This course surveys the art of storytelling in sub-Saharan Africa. Course work focuses on oral performance, classification, and appreciation of various oral narrative traditions, the epic, and the beginning of written literature.

Texts

Paul Radin, *African Folktales*; Roger Abrahams, *African Folktales*; Amos Tutuola, *The Palm Wine Drinkard*

Schedule

Class	Topic, Reading

1   Introduction

2   Reading an oral narrative. Abrahams, introd., 1–29; "Monkey Steals a Drum," 45–56 (Yoruba); Radin, no. 66, "The Town Where None May Go to Sleep" (Hausa)

3   Narrative: talking in images. Radin no. 49, "How an Unborn Child . . ." (Bena Mukuni); no. 67, "The City Where Men Are Mended" (Hausa); no. 79, "Kenkebe" (Xhosa)

4   The art of performance: tales and lives. Abrahams, "A Competition of Lies," 89–103 (Mende)

5   Myths of the golden age. Radin, no. 19, "Mantis Creates an Eland" (Khoisan)

6   Performance: the singer of tales. In-class viewing: *Bitter Melons* (Khoisan)

7   The age of creation. Radin, no. 4, "How Abosom, the Lesser God . . ." (Asante); no. 5, "Why the Sun and Moon Live in the Sky" (Efik-Ibibio); no. 7, "The Brothers Sun and Moon . . ." (Kamba); no. 16, "How Kintu Was Tested . . ." (Ganda); no. 17, "The Son of Kimanueze . . ." (Mbundu)

8   The trickster. Abrahams, "Tales of Trickster . . ." (151–227)

9   Ananse: the Akan trickster. In-class viewing: *Anansi the Spider* (Asante); Radin, no. 21, "How Spider Read Sky God's Thoughts"; no. 32, "How It Came About that We Shall Always See Okra . . ."; no. 33, "How It Came About that the Hinder Part of Kwaku . . ."; no. 40, "How Kwaku Got Aso in Marriage"

10   Natural wo/man. Radin, no. 41, "The Young Man Who Was Carried Off by a Lion" (San); no. 69, "The Child and the Eagle" (Ila); no. 63, "The Enchanted Fowl" (Lango)

11   Rites of passage 1. Radin, no. 45, "Konyak and His Father" (Masai); no. 65, "The Handsome Ogre Girl" (Kamba); no. 72, "Ngomba's Basket" (Kongo); suggested reading: Arnold van Gennep, *The Rites of Passage*

12   Rites of passage 2. Radin, no. 62, "The Wonder-Worker of the Plains" (Ronga); no. 68, "M'wambia and the N'jenge" (Kikuyu); no. 61, "Untombinde, the Tall Maiden" (Zulu); no. 64, "The Adventures of Mrile" (Chaga)

13 A flawed world. Abrahams, "The Child in the Reeds," pp. 324–31 (Sotho); Radin, no. 76, "The Old Woman Who Stole Milk" (Zulu); no. 77, "The Wife Who Ate the Wrong Porridge" (Bena Mukuni); Epilogue (Ila)

14 The tale in society: the case of Malagasy. In-class viewing: *Angano . . . Angano*

15 Africa in the Diaspora: Storytelling in Belize and Jamaica

16 The Epic. Abrahams, "The Mwindo Epic," 238–92 (Nyanga)

17 The Mwindo Epic: the adventure continues . . .

18 Old Heroes in New Media. Tutuola, *The Palm Wine Drinkard* (Yoruba)

19 Oral traditions and writing

Folklore
Syracuse University
Anthropology 376

Course Description
This course looks at issues of identity, community, and resistance through the lens of those cultural documents usually termed folklore. After defining *folklore* and examining its relation to community and identity, I introduce collection methods and the types of analysis used in folklore studies. We then use folklore to gain an understanding of identity and community among South Asians, African Americans, and various American groups. The use of folklore as a means of opposing repressive regimes, such as colonial powers, partriarchy, the rich, or the state, is a theme throughout the course. A variety of genres of folklore are examined, including songs, tales, games, proverbs, folk dramas, and trance.

Text
Barre Toelken, *The Dynamics of Folklore*

Schedule

Class   Topic
  1 Folklore and the folk
  2 Folklore, community, and identity
  3 Achieving a sense of self through folklore
  4 The family as a folk community
  5 Collecting folklore — lecture and computer lab
  6 Folklore as performance

Yoruba Oral Literature
University of Florida
Department of African and Asian Languages and Literatures

Course Description
This course provides an overview of the various genres of Yoruba oral literature. It stresses the importance of the spoken word in Yoruba cul-

ture, the training of Yoruba verbal artists and their place in society, and prospects for the future. The course also examines some characteristic features of Yoruba oral texts. Videotapes of actual performance in addition to basic texts in bilingual editions introduce students to Yoruba verbal art.

Texts

Abraham, *Dictionary of Modern Yoruba*; N. A. Fadipe, *The Sociology of the Yoruba*; Abimbola, ed., *Yoruba Oral Tradition*; Abimbola, *Sixteen Great Poems of Ifa*; Bade Ajuwon, *Funeral Dirges of Yoruba Hunters*; Olatunji, *Features of Yoruba Oral Poetry*

Schedule

Week	Topic
1	Introduction: the Yoruba country, customs, and language
2	Orality in Yoruba culture
3	An overview of various oral genres: modes of delivery
4	The oral artist: his/her training and role in the society
5	Film: performances
6	Oriki or "praise" poetry in Yoruba culture
7–8	Divination poetry: Ifa
9	The hunter's poetry: Ijala
10	Nuptial chants and women's poetry: Rara Iyawo
11	"Minor" genres: riddles, proverbs, incantations
12–13	Literary features of Yoruba oral literature
14	The future of Yoruba oral literature: films

Oral Tradition
University of Missouri, Columbia
English 387

Course Description
This course seeks to answer the question, "What implications do a work's roots in oral tradition have for its interpretation?" We are interested in living oral traditions, in literary texts that derive from oral traditions, and in performances and texts at all points along the spectrum between these poles. Our itinerary includes South Slavic, African, African American, and Native American works alongside the Judeo-Christian Bible, Homer's *Iliad* and *Odyssey*, the Old English *Beowulf*, the Old French *Song of Roland*, and the Finnish *Kalevala*. Each semester the selection of

traditions changes. Likewise, instead of adopting any single approach as the canonical methodology, we investigate a number of different interpretive options: performance theory and the ethnography of speaking, ethnopoetics, oral-formulaic theory, and traditional referentiality. Thus we also read analytical studies by scholars such as Richard Bauman, Joel Sherzer, Dell Hymes, Dennis Tedlock, Albert Lord, and John Foley. Students undertake a semester-long study of an oral tradition (or oral-derived traditional work) as an individual project.

Text
Albert B. Lord, *The Singer of Tales*; Walter J. Ong, *Orality and Literacy*; John Miles Foley, *The Theory of Oral Composition*; *Gilgamesh* (trans. Sandars); *Odyssey* (trans. Fitzgerald); *Beowulf* (trans. Raffel); *Finding the Center* (trans. Tedlock); *Kalevala* (trans. Kirby and Branch); *The Wedding of Smailagić Meho* (trans. Lord)

Schedule (a recent example)

Week	Topic
1–3	Introduction; various theories and approaches
4–5	The South Slavic tradition
6	A Native American tradition: Zuni
7	*Gilgamesh* and the Sumerian tradition
8–9	The *Kalevala* and the Finnish tradition
10–12	The *Odyssey* and the ancient Greek tradition
13–14	*Beowulf* and the Anglo-Saxon tradition

Seminar in Oral Tradition
University of Missouri, Columbia
English 487

Course Description
This seminar studies the phenomenon of oral tradition, that is, the communicative medium that precedes writing and texts and that continues alongside writing and texts in many cultural settings. To focus our discussions, we concentrate on a single guiding question: "What difference does it make to its interpretation that a given work of verbal art either comes directly or stems from an oral tradition?" Methods used to approach this challenging question draw from many fields and include (but are not limited to) oral theory, traditional referentiality, the ethnography of speaking, receptionalism, and ethnopoetics. No prior acquaintance with any of these approaches is required or expected, since each is ex-

plored fully as part of the seminar's activities. Among living oral traditions, we consider African, African American, Native American, and South Slavic genres; among the oral-derived works examined are the Bible, the Homeric poems, *Beowulf*, and the Old French *Song of Roland*. The goal of the seminar is to encourage a deeper understanding of the variety of verbal art in an international context and particularly to glimpse the spectrum of expressive forms on the cusp of oral tradition and literary tradition.

Texts

Beowulf (trans. Raffel); *The Odyssey* (trans. Fitzgerald); *Finding the Center* (trans. Tedlock); South Slavic packet (trans. Foley); *The Epic of Son-Jara* (trans. Johnson); Brother Peter tales (trans. Morrissey and Canales); R. Bauman, *Verbal Art as Performance*; J. Foley, *The Theory of Oral Composition*; J. Foley, *Traditional Oral Epic*; D. Hymes, *"In Vain I Tried to Tell You"*; W. Ong, *Orality and Literacy*

Schedule (a recent example)

Week	Topic, Reading
1	Introduction to the seminar: prospects and theoretical approaches

Breaking the Code: The Literate Bias

| 2 | Ong, *Orality and Literacy* |

Oral-Formulaic Theory and Traditional Referentiality

3	Foley, *The Theory of Oral Composition*
4	Foley, *Traditional Oral Epic*
5	Former Yugoslavia: South Slavic packet
6	Ancient Greece: *Odyssey*
7	Anglo-Saxon England: *Beowulf*

Performance

8	Bauman, *Verbal Art as Performance*
9	Africa: *The Epic of Son-Jara*
10	African American: selected genres

Ethnopoetics

| 11 | Tedlock, *Finding the Center* |
| 12 | Hymes, *"In Vain I Tried to Tell You"* |

13　Guatemala: Brother Peter tales

14　Gospels—guest lecturer

15　Summary and project reports

Folklore and the Hebrew Bible
Amherst College
Religion 38

Course Description

This course is an introduction to the cross-discipline of folklore and an application of that field to the study of Israelite literature. We explore the ways in which professional students of traditional literature describe and classify folk material, approach questions of composition and transmission, and deal with complex issues of context, meaning, and message. We then apply the cross-disciplinary and cross-cultural methodologies of folklore to readings in the Hebrew Scriptures. Selections include narratives, proverbs, riddles, and ritual and legal texts. Topics of special interest include the relations between oral and written literatures, the defining of "myth," feminism and folklore, and the ways in which the biblical writers, nineteenth-century collectors such as the Brothers Grimm, and modern popularizers such as Walt Disney recast pieces of lore, in the process helping to shape or misshape us and our future.

Schedule

Class	Topic, Reading
1	Introduction
2–3	Folklore and Hermann Gunkel. Readings: F. L. Utley, "Folk Literature: An Operational Definition," in Dundes, *The Study of Folklore*, 7–24; Dan Ben-Amos, "Toward a Definition of Folklore in Context," in Paredes and Bauman, *Toward New Perspectives in Folklore*, 3–15; Alan Dundes, *Interpreting Folklore*, 1–32; B. Toelken, *The Dynamics of Folklore*, 3–12, 23–43; Axel Olrik, "Epic Laws of Folk Narrative," in Dundes, *The Study of Folklore*, 127–41; H. Gunkel, *The Legends of Genesis*, 37–122; S. Niditch, *Folklore and the Hebrew Bible*, 1–4. The above are classic older pieces and some contemporary works. Questions and concerns for our classes are 1) what folklore is, the discipline and the material studied, questions of content and form; 2) who the folk are, questions of author and audience; 3) the legacy of Hermann Gunkel, a Bible scholar of the early twentieth century who recognized the value of folklore as it was understood in his time.

4–6   Oral versus written: composition, performance, and transmission. Readings: A. B. Lord, *The Singer of Tales*; Bruce Rosenberg, "The Complexity of Oral Tradition," in *Oral Tradition* 2 (1987), 73–90; Ruth Finnegan, "Oral Literature and Writing in the South Pacific," in *Pacific Quarterly Moana*, 7.2 (1982), 22–36; S. Niditch, *Folklore and the Hebrew Bible*, 4–12, and "The Composition of Isaiah 1" (read Isaiah 1); D. Gunn, "Narrative Patterns" and "Traditional Narrative Composition" and the Old Testament passages with which Gunn deals. Questions: For Lord, what distinguishes the orally composed work from the written work? What are his contributions to the study of style and form in traditional literature and how might these contributions carry over to the study of the traditional literature of the Bible? How does Finnegan's approach differ and with what significance?

7   Written assignment for class 9: In a three-page essay make a judicious case for the oral composition of the plagues account in Exodus 7.1–12.40. Questions: How might the "performance factor" influence the ways in which we approach the traditional literature of the Bible? Is the line between oral and written works always clear? Can a written work nevertheless be traditional in style and form?

8–9   Collecting, classifying, and comparing types and motifs: the legacy of the historic-geographic school. Readings: S. Thompson, "The Star Husband Tale," in Dundes, *The Study of Folklore*, 414–74, a classic example of the methodology and interests of Thompson's school of scholarship; S. Niditch, *Folklore and the Hebrew Bible*, 12–18; Gen. 37–50, Exod. 1–4 (tales of Joseph and Moses). D. Irvin, "The Joseph and Moses Stories," in Hayes and Miller, *Israelite and Judaean History*, 180–209; S. Niditch and R. Doran, "The Success Story of the Wise Courtier." Questions: What are the goals of Thompson's research? How successful are the above examples by Old Testament scholars to employ the indices? Must one share the historic-geographic or Finnish school's assumptions to make good use of the indices?

Women and Folklore: Case Studies in Exploring
Versions of Traditional Narratives

10–11   Women's stories and stories about women. Readings: Gen. 18.1–15, 16.1–16, 21.1–21, 27.1–45, 38 (tales of the matriarchs); Gen. 34 (the rape of Dinah); Judg. 4, 5.24–30 (the tale of Jael); Judg. 11.29–39 (the tale of Jephthah's daughter); Grimm no. 31, "The Girl without Hands," in Zipes, *The Complete Fairy Tales of the Brothers Grimm*; Jack Zipes, "Recent Psychoanalytical Approaches with Some Questions about the Abuse of Children,"

110–34 in his *Brothers Grimm*; S. Niditch, *Folklore and the Hebrew Bible*, 29–31. Showing of Disney's *Snow White*.

12–13   What a difference the collector-teller makes: traditional narrative as people shaper. Readings: Ruth B. Bottigheimer, "'From Gold to Guilt': The Force Which Reshaped Grimms' Tales," in *The Brothers Grimm and Folklore*, ed. McGlathery, 192–204; Jack Zipes, "Dreams of a Better Bourgeois Life," in *The Brothers Grimm and Folklore*, ed. McGlathery, 205–19; Grimm no. 53 in Zipes, *The Complete Fairy Tales*; Kay Stone, "Three Transformations of Snow White," in *The Brothers Grimm and Folklore*, ed. McGlathery, 52–65; In-class surprises from "Fairytale Theatre." Showing of Disney's *Beauty and the Beast*. A discussion of Grimm no. 88, "Beauty and the Beast" (any version) and Disney's film version. Showing of Disney's *Cinderella*.

14   Cinderella trajectories with help from Stone and Yolen. Readings: Jane Yolen, "America's Cinderella," in *Cinderella: A Casebook*, ed. Dundes, 294–306; Kay Stone, "Things Walt Disney Never Told Us," in *Women and Folklore*, ed. Farrer, 42–50; Grimm no. 21, in Zipes, *The Complete Fairy Tales*; "Katie Woodencloak," "Cap o' Rushes," "Rushen Coatie," "The Dirty Shepherdess."

15   A biblical trajectory: three versions of the same story. Readings: S. Niditch, *Underdogs*, chapter 2, and the biblical texts mentioned there; the Book of Esther. Apply what we have learned. Locate motifs and types. What is special about the telling of this seemingly familiar tale? A feminist approach to Esther.

Russian Formalism: Methods of Dealing with Content and Structure

16   A brief lecture on biblical form-criticism: on wholes and parts and the formation of literary tradition. Readings: Gene Tucker, *A Guide to Form-Criticism*; V. Propp, *The Morphology of the Folktale*; A. Dundes, "Structural Typology in North American Indian Folktales," in Dundes, *The Study of Folklore*, 206–15; S. Niditch, *Folklore*, 18–20; Jack Sasson, *Ruth*, 196–252; Ruth; 1 Sam 17.1–54; Gen 3.1–24; Judg. 3.12–30; Exod. 14.1–30.

17   For class: Attempt a Proppian-style analysis of one of the Grimm tales in your anthology and of one of the biblical tales assigned for today. Does this sort of structuralist analysis give you insight into the tales? Do any of the biblical tales fit Propp's outline of functions? Is Dundes's more simplified variety of patterning more helpful? How biblical narratives do not fit Propp's scheme may be as helpful as how they do, as we seek to learn more about the workings of various sorts of narrative. Does the Bible contain any "wondertales"? Discuss the boundary shared by form-criticism and Russian formalism.

18–19 From Propp to Lévi-Strauss: deep structures, myth, and folklore in concert. Readings: S. Niditch, *Folklore*, 22–23; William Doty, *Mythography*, 192–213; C. Lévi-Strauss, "The Structural Study of Myth," in Sebeok, *Myth: A Symposium*, 81–106; Edmond Leach, *Claude Lévi-Strauss*; Gen. 1–11; S. Niditch, *Chaos to Cosmos*, 1–56. Lévi-Strauss, we should recall, is not concerned merely with texts but also with ethnography; that is, as an anthropologist he tried to understand the roles that narratives play in human lives and cultures. He is interested in the patterns of texts that reveal deep, underlying, and recurring patterns of thought. Written assignment for class 20: Attempt a Lévi-Straussian analysis of one of the folktales in your anthology and of one of the following biblical tales: Gen. 27 (the stealing of the birthright); Gen. 22.1–14 (the binding of Isaac); Gen. 38 (the story of Tamar); Gen. 32.22–32 (Jacob's wrestling with the angel). Be prepared to share your findings in class. Is all narrative grist for the structuralist mill?

20–21 Proverbs and riddles: classic approaches and structuralist-influenced studies. Readings: A. Dundes, "On the Structure of the Proverb," in Dundes, *Analytic Essays in Folklore*, 103–20, "Toward a Structural Definition of Riddles," in *Analytic Essays in Folklore*, 95–102, and "Proverbs and the Ethnography of Speaking Folklore," in *Analytic Essays*, 35–49; Barbara Kirshenblatt-Gimblett, "Toward a Theory of Proverb Meaning," in Mieder and Dundes, *The Wisdom of Many*, 111–20; S. Niditch, *Folklore*, 67–87. Written assignment for class 21: After reading some essays about proverbs and riddles, attempt a four-page analysis of either Samson's riddle (Judg. 14.34) in the context of the larger narrative or of one proverb in Prov. 11. What pieces make for the whole? How do they combine to convey messages and what sort of messages? Be sure to make use not only of various structuralist approaches but of the motif indices as well. What transforms elements of content into particular, definable literary forms? Also relevant to your analysis is Lord's emphasis on "formula patterns" and performance.

22–24 Psychoanalytical approaches to folklore: psychic contexts. Freudian- and Jungian-influenced works in both psychology and folklore are numerous. This semester we read examples of Alan Dundes's Freudian approach to folktales and portions of Joseph Campbell's *Hero with a Thousand Faces*, a work influenced by Jungian and Freudian approaches. We then test the usefulness of these studies for an analysis of the tale of Joseph. Readings: William Doty, *Mythography*, 131–66; A. Dundes, *Interpreting Folklore*, 33–61, and "Interpreting Little Red Riding Hood Psychoanalytically," in *The Brothers Grimm and Folklore*, ed. Mc-

Glathery, 16–51; J. Campbell, *Hero*, 3–246 and 315–64 (skim); Gen. 37–50; Prov. 1–9.

25–26   Anthropological and sociological approaches to folklore: community and cultural contexts. Readings on symbolism in a sociocultural context: Victor Turner, "Themes in the Symbolism of Ndembu Hunting Ritual," in Middleton, *Myth and Cosmos*, 249–70; Louis C. Faron, "Symbolic Values and the Integration of Society among the Mapuche of Chile," in Middleton, *Myth and Cosmos*, 167–84; Mary Douglas, "Animals in Tele Religious Thought," in Middleton, *Myth and Cosmos*, 231–47; Barbara Kirshenblatt-Gimblett, "Culture Shock and Narrative Creativity," in Dorson, *Folklore and the Modern World*, 109–22. On folklore as performance event see Kirshenblatt-Gimblett, "A Parable in Context," in Ben-Amos and Goldstein, *Folklore*, 105–30; S. Niditch, *Folklore*, 49–65. Written assignment for class 28: Choose one: 1) An anthropological-sociological analysis of either ritual: Lev. 16.1–28 (ceremony for the expiation of sin) or Num. 5.11–31 (ceremony for the suspected adulteress). Questions: What is the content and structure of the ritual? What roles might the ritual play in a living community? Examine the symbolism in the ritual to uncover essential cultural and community concerns reflected in and affected by the ritual. Discuss the boundary shaped by ritual drama and folk performance. 2) Prophecy as performance in a sociocultural context: a close analysis of 1 Kings 20.26–43.

27–28   Myth: a definable genre? Reading: William Doty, *Mythography*, 1–40. Is myth a special category of folklore? How is it to be defined? Is the Old Testament rich in myth? Here we arrive at another boundary where text, texture, and context meet.

29   A final class for summing up

Communication, Cognition, and Culture
Rice University
Religious Studies 302

Course Description
This course traces the evolution of information technologies and their influence on civilization. It explores the passage from oral to written, from manuscript to print, and from print to electronic communication, whose global network instantaneously transmits words, numbers, ideas, and images to all corners of the earth. We examine the influence of these media of communication on the organization of human culture, technological progress, and the experiences of individuals and the place of these media as crossroads at which humanistic, social, and scientific

ideas meet. This lecture-discussion course includes a team project as a major component. Teams consist of at least four and at most six students. Each group has one of the faculty members as its mentor. The topics are the role of memory in media history; communication and work; interfaces of the world: cultural implications of media changes; communications, nationalism, and imperialism; media changes and the transformation of factual knowledge; censorship and social control; communications and warfare; the shifting role of self and community; image and visualization in the history of communications; media changes and the transformation-subversion of authority; media and communications in the construction of the idea of self. A student may try to form a group and propose a topic not on the list. Such a proposal must be approved by at least one of the faculty members in this course.

Texts

Walter J. Ong, *Orality and Literacy: The Technologizing of the Word*; Lucien Febvre and Henri-Jean Martin, *The Coming of the Book: The Impact of Printing, 1450–1800*; Elizabeth L. Eisenstein, *The Printing Revolution in Early Modern Europe*; Stanley Joel Reiser, *Medicine and the Reign of Technology*; Susan Sontag, *On Photography*; Albert Lord, *The Singer of Tales*; Eric Havelock, *Preface to Plato*; Mary Carruthers, *The Book of Memory*; Werner Kelber, "Modalities of Communication, Cognition, and Physiology of Perception: Orality, Rhetoric, and Scribality" (*Semeia* 65 [1994]: 193–212) and "Language, Memory, and Sense Perception in the Religious and Technological Culture of Antiquity and the Middle Ages" (*Oral Tradition* 10 [1995]: 409–50); Gale Stokes, "Cognition, Consciousness, and Nationalism" (*Ethnic Studies* 10 [1993]: 27–42).

Schedule

Class	Topic, Reading
1	Introduction

Oral and Manuscript Culture

2	Primary orality. Ong, 1–77.
3	Oral composition and performance of the Homeric epics. Lord.
4	Plato caught between orality and literacy. Havelock.
5	Rhetoric as exemplified by Paul. Kelber, "Modalities."
6	Manuscript culture: the technologies of the scriptorium, and concepts of reading and writing. Ong, 78–179.
7	Manuscripts, memory, and the sensorium. Carruthers.
8	Scholasticism and nominalism: the chirographic impact on

philosophical-technological thought. Kelber, "Language, Memory."

9   The Bible in the history of media. Kelber, "The Bible in the Book Tradition" (in press).

Print Culture

10   Print technology, 1450–1850. Febvre and Martin, 29–76, 248–61; Eisenstein, 3–41.

11   Printing and humanism. Febvre and Martin, 262–87; Eisenstein, 42–147.

12   Printing and the Reformation. Febvre and Martin, 287–319; Eisenstein, 148–86.

13   Printing and science. Eisenstein, 187–254.

14   Printing and the vernacular. Febvre and Martin, 319–32, 255–78; Eisenstein, passim.

15–16   Midterm recess.

17   Printing, memory, and the sensorium. Ong, 117–38.

18   Expanding literacy, audience, and nationalism. Febvre and Martin, 143–66; Stokes.

19   Science, technology, and communication in the nineteenth century.

Multimedia and Electronic Culture

20   The story and the sound. Reiser, chapters 1, 2.

21   The power of the picture. Reiser, chapters 3, 4; Sontag (entire).

22   Numbers, graphs, and reality. Reiser, chapters 5, 6, 8, 9.

23   Media and the structure of organizations. Reiser, chapters 7, 10.

24–25   The emergence of the global information infrastructure. WWW sites (TBA).

26   Information technology and organizational development. WWW sites.

27   Virtual communities. WWW sites.

28   The saturated self. WWW sites.

29   Group presentations and discussion.

30   Group presentations and discussion. Course evaluations.

Anastasios Daskalopoulos

Selected Audiovisual and Internet Resources

My main purpose in making a selected list of audiovisual resources easily available to the instructor for classroom presentation is not to present a universal compilation of materials covering as many traditions as possible but to reflect the national survey conducted in the fall and winter of 1995 and the submissions that were received (see Lewis and Peterson, "National Curriculum," this volume). Category 1 lists the names and addresses of organizations that specialize in audiovisual material associated with oral traditions and folklore, with the major focus on verbal art. In category 2, ancillary areas such as customs, music, art, and dance are sampled for the purpose of providing context. Category 3 suggests specific audiovisual materials by subject area. The various catalogs presently available offer a wide range of material at a relatively small cost. Category 4 presents some resources located on the World Wide Web.

Category 1

All the language and subject areas presented in this volume are covered in one or more of the following catalogs. Category 1 concerns itself foremost with verbal art and performance. Instructors are referred to categories 3 and 4 if they do not find suitable audiovisual material in a specific language area.

Smithsonian Folkways Recordings: A World of Sound. Administered by the Smithsonian Institution's Office of Folklife Programs, this extensive catalog (over 2,100 listings) provides audiocassette and CD recordings of many oral traditions worldwide and provides audio resources for all the subject areas in this volume. The cassettes derive from master tapes recorded between 1900 and 1995 and provide rare examples of primary oral performances as well as readings from well-known literary texts. The *Folkways* catalog also features performances by noted scholars of oral-derived texts from the ancient world (the *Iliad* and *Odyssey*) and the medieval period (Old English poetry).

> Smithsonian / Folkways Recordings
> Office of Folklife Programs
> 955 l'Enfant Plaza, Suite 2600
> Smithsonian Institution
> Washington, DC 20560
> 202 287-7298
> fax: 202 287-3699

Folk Recordings: Selected from the Archive of Folk Culture. This resource lists, in either audiocassette, CD, or LP format, recordings of folk songs made in the United States from the Anglo-American and African American traditions. It also includes an extensive collection of Native American music and chants.

> Motion Picture, Broadcasting, and Recorded Sound Division
> Library of Congress
> Washington, DC 20540

American Folklife Center: Publications in Print. This directory of Library of Congress publications (many of them free) contains lists of folklore recordings.

> Library of Congress
> American Folklife Center
> Washington, DC 20540-8100

An Inventory of Finding and Reference Aids Prepared by the Archive of Folk Culture is a large bibliography providing references for many traditions around the world. It is divided into two sections, "Bibliographies, Directories, and Other Reference Aids," which covers oral traditions ranging alphabetically from Alaskan to Zuni, and "Finding Aids and Other Descriptions of the Archive of Folk Culture," a directory of field recordings and transcriptions of a depth similar to that of the first section.

> Library of Congress
> Archive of Folk Culture
> Washington, DC 20540-8100

The Folk Resources in the Library of Congress Motion Picture, Broadcasting, and Sound Division has a large collection of traditional performances on video and film available online at http://lcweb.loc.gov/folklife/fr_mbrs.html.

The Center for Southern Folklore has compiled two useful resources: *American Folklore Films and Videotapes: An Index* (Memphis: Center, 1976) and *American Folklore Films and Videotapes: A Catalog* (New York: Bowker, 1982).

Category 2

These archives do not focus on the performing verbal arts but reflect such ancillary elements of folk culture as customs, music, art, and dance. The resources listed here are intended only as selective supplements.

The Archive of Folk Culture, a division of the Library of Congress American Folklife Center, provides resources on a wide array of cultural activities of many ethnic groups, primarily from the United States.

> American Folklife Center
> Library of Congress
> Washington, DC 20540-8100
> 202 707-5510
> fax: 202 707-2076

Smithsonian Institution Center for Folklife Programs. This organization has collected films, videos, and other educational materials and has organized exhibitions about many aspects of various ethnic and folk cultures in the United States.

Center for Folklife Programs and Cultural Studies
Smithsonian Institution
MRC 914
Washington, DC 20560
202 287-3262

The folklife archives and centers in the Library of Congress, and other programs dedicated to the study of folk culture, can also be reached from the home page of the Center for Studies in Oral Tradition at the University of Missouri, Columbia: http://www.missouri.edu/~csottime.

Category 3

This list of additional audiovisual material, arranged by the subject areas found in this volume, supplements material described in the survey of the national curriculum. Other titles can be found in *Bowker's Complete Video Directory 1995* (New Providence: Bowker). ISBN numbers, places, and order numbers have been listed where available.

General
Catalogue de films d'interêt archéologique, éthnographique, ou historique. Paris: UNESCO, 1970.
Films on Traditional Music and Dance. Paris: UNESCO, 1970.
International Index to Music Periodicals. Alexandria, VA: Chadwyck-Healey, 1997. http://music.chadwyck.com

Native American (North)
The Faithkeeper. New York: Mystic Fire Videos, 1991. ISBN 1-56176-208-3.
Native American Folktales. 4 vols. Boulder, CO: Dane Hansen Productions, 1994. ISBN 1-57031-046-7.
Words and Places: Native Literature from the American Southwest. Producer Larry Evers. Tucson: Univ. of Arizona, 1978.

Native American (South)
Jaguar: A Yanomamo Twin Cycle Myth As Told by Danamasiwa. Watertown, MA: Educational Resources, Inc., 1976.
Chilean Indian Legend. Greenwich, CT: Arts America, Inc. ISBN 0-942475-26-7.

African Oral Narrative Traditions
African Masks: Dance of the Spirits. Iowa City: Univ. of Iowa Audiovisual Center, 1976.

Griottes of the Sakel: Female Keepers of the Songhay Oral Tradition in Niger. University Park, PA: Penn State Audiovisual Services, 1991.
Redefining Our Oral Traditions: From Storytelling to Mass Media. Ann Arbor: Univ. of Michigan, 1991.
Saaraba. San Francisco: California Newsreel, 1991.

American
Blood Memory: The Legend of Beany Short. New York: Cicada Films, 1992.
The Dreamkeepers: Oral Tradition, the Printed Word, and Democracy. Englewood, CO: Univ. of the Rockies, 1991.
The Eagle Stirreth Her Nest, by C. L. Franklin. Chicago: Chess/MCA, Chess LP 19, 1984.
JVC / Smithsonian Folkways Video Anthology of Music and Dance of the Americas. Montpelier, VT: Multicultural Media, 1995.

General Hispanic
El Rey de Bandolin. Watertown, MA: Documentary Educational Resources, 1985.
Legends of Mexico and Puerto Rico (in Spanish). Guilford, CT: Audio Forum. Order No. V72278.
Romancero, by Paloma Diaz Mas. Barcelona: Crítica, 1994.
Romancero Panhispánico: Antología Sonora. 5 vols. By José Manuel Fraile. Saga Records AD 5–10/9004. Junta de Castilla y León / Consejería de Cultura y Bienestar Social (Centro de Cultura Tradicional, Diputación de Salamanca, Plaza de Colón, 4, 37001 Salamanca, Spain), 1991.
Cancioneiro Popular Português (Breve Antologia), by Michel Giacometti. Lisbon: Círculo de Leitores CL 60640, 1981.

Jewish
A Life of Song: A Portrait of Ruth Rubin. New York: Ergo Media, Inc., 1986.

Indian
The Mahabharata. New York: Parabola Video Library, 1989.

Chinese
Love Songs of the Miao. New York: Filmaker's Library, 1992.

Japanese
Noh, the Classical Theatre of Japan. East Lansing: Michigan State Univ., IMC Marketing Division, 1980.

Teaching the Folktale Tradition
African Story Telling. East Lansing: Michigan State Univ., IMC Marketing Division.

British

Dragonquest. Santa Fe: Dragonquest, 1988.

The Long Harvest: Some Traditional Ballads in Their English, Scots, and North American Variants. Sung by Ewan MacColl and Peggy Seeger. 10 vols. London: Argo ZDA 66-75, 1967–68.

Lyrics from the Old English: A Reading by Burton Raffel and Robert Creed. Smithsonian/Folkways 9858, 1964.

Old English Poetry. New York: Filmaker's Library, 1993.

Ancient Greek

The Iliad of Homer. Read by Stephen Daitz. Guilford, CT: J. Norton, 1990.

The Iliad — Beyond Heroism. Los Angeles: Univ. of Southern California, Davidson Conference Center.

The Odyssey of Homer. Read by Stephen Daitz. Guilford, CT: J. Norton, 1995.

Women's Expressive Forms

Women's Art and Mythology. Chico, CA: Instructional Media Center, 1977.

Women's Spirituality, Women's Empowerment: Myths, Stories, Realities. Seattle: Perspectives and Reality, 1993.

This list offers only a small sample of what can be gleaned from an online bibliographical service such as OCLC FirstSearch. The instructor can locate many other audiovisual materials through this computer resource by typing "su:oral tradition" or "su:folklore" followed by the subject and then limiting the search to "media" or "recordings." Films and videotapes may also be located through the *Film and Video Finder* (National Information Center of Educational Media, 3 vols. Medford, NJ: Plexus Publishing, 1989). Instructors can order CD-ROMs from Films for the Humanities and Sciences, PO Box 2053, Princeton, NJ 08543-2053.

Category 4

Many oral traditional and folklore resources are to be found on the World Wide Web. The Media History Project has on its home page an "Oral & Scribal Culture" link (http://www.mediahistory.com/oral.html) that contains a list of electronic resources of a great variety of mythology, language, and culture areas such as Native American, European, African, and Asian traditions, each with its own link to related fields. The user should remember that the subjects located on the World Wide Web vary in usefulness, reliability, or even legitimacy, so caution is advised. The home page of the Center for Studies in Oral Tradition lists links to oral tradition and folklore resources as well (http://www.missouri.edu/~csottime).

Notes on Contributors

Ronelle Alexander, professor of Slavic languages and literatures at the University of California, Berkeley, teaches courses in Slavic and general folklore, as well as South Slavic languages, literatures, and linguistics. She is the author of four books and over forty articles in South Slavic linguistics, poetics, and folklore and is currently working with unpublished materials from the Parry Collection at Harvard. She is interested in all aspects of oral tradition as a living force in communities.

Mark C. Amodio, associate professor in the Department of English at Vassar College, has published a collection of essays and numerous articles on aspects of oral tradition in Old and Middle English, including oral poetics, tradition, and criticism. His research and teaching interests involve Old and Middle English literature, oral theory, contemporary critical theory, and cultural criticism. His current projects are writing a book on medieval English oral poetics and organizing a volume of essays on new directions in oral theory.

Richard Bauman, Distinguished Professor of folklore and professor of communication and culture and anthropology at Indiana University, Bloomington, is the author of *Verbal Art as Performance*; *Story,*

Performance, and Event; and *Folklore, Cultural Performance, and Popular Entertainments*. He is a former president of both the Semiotic Society of America and the Society for Linguistic Anthropology and a former editor of the *Journal of American Folklore*.

Mark Bender, assistant professor in the East Asian Studies program at Ohio State University, has written articles on oral performance in China and done translations of Chinese ethnic minority folklore. His current projects involve translations of several ethnic minority epics from southwest China, a reader of Chinese folklore and popular oral performance, and a book on professional storytelling in the region of Suzhou in southeast China. He has lived in China for seven years and is interested in oral and oral-derived literary traditions of minority cultures in China.

Carol Birch has performed as a storyteller across the United States, Europe, and Australia. Her repertoire includes tales from different genres, drawing on folklore, short stories, and poetry. Among her publications is *Who Says? Essays on Pivotal Issues in Contemporary Storytelling* (with Melissa Heckler). She has also contributed to *The Storytelling Encyclopedia*, *The Storyteller's Guide*, *Joining In*, and *Ready to Tell Tales*.

Nancy Mason Bradbury, associate professor in the Department of English at Smith College, teaches Chaucer, Women Writers of the Middle Ages, Epic and Romance, and other literature courses. She coedits an anthology for college students, *Audiences and Intentions*, now in its third edition, and her articles have appeared in *Studies in English Literature*, *Studies in Philology*, and *Chaucer Review*, as well as in scholarly collections. Her book *Writing Aloud: Storytelling in Late Medieval England* (U of Illinois P) is in press.

Donald Braid teaches in the Department of English at Butler University. His research and teaching interests include questions of belief, identity, and meaning in oral performance, especially as these concepts relate to narrative theory and practice. He is currently studying the use of narratives and ballads among the Travelling People of Scotland and exploring the roles played by oral narratives in the work of physical scientists. His essay "Personal Narrative and Experiential Meaning" appeared in the *Journal of American Folklore*.

Donald J. Cosentino, professor of English and chair of the Folklore Program at the University of California, Los Angeles, is coeditor of *African Arts* magazine and the author of *Defiant Maids and Stubborn*

Farmers, The Sacred Arts of Haitian Vodou, and *Vodou Things,* in addition to numerous scholarly and popular articles. His main research and teaching areas are African and Caribbean folklore, mythology, and literature. He has done fieldwork in Nigeria, Sierra Leone, and Haiti and curated the traveling exhibition *The Sacred Arts of Haitian Vodou.*

Anastasios Daskalopoulos, a graduate student in classical studies and an editorial assistant at the Center for Studies in Oral Tradition at the University of Missouri, Columbia, is writing his dissertation on orality and the technology of literacy in archaic Greece. Homeric studies, oral tradition, and modern Greek oral poetry are his main research areas. He has contributed articles to the forthcoming *Encyclopedia of Folklore and Literature* and currently is working on a project on Greek guerrilla folk songs of World War II.

Thomas DuBois, associate professor in the Department of Scandinavian Languages and Literatures at the University of Washington, Seattle, has written *Finnish Folk Poetry and the* Kalevala as well as various articles on ethnopoetics, Finnish folklore, and Saami folklore. He researches Nordic and American folklore, linguistic approaches to folklore study, and ethnoaesthetics. He is currently working on monograph projects on Nordic pre-Christian religions, Finnish folklore, and North European lyric, the last with assistance from the John Simon Guggenheim Memorial Foundation.

Elizabeth C. Fine, associate professor in the Center for Interdisciplinary Studies and the Department of Communication Studies at Virginia Tech, is the author of *The Folklore Text: From Performance to Print* (Indiana UP, 1984, 1994); the coeditor, with Jean Haskell Speer, of *Performance, Culture, and Identity* (Praeger, 1992); and the editor of *Politics and Culture,* the 1994 *Journal of the Appalachian Studies Association.* She is the 1993 recipient of the Lilla A. Heston Award for Outstanding Scholarship in Interpretation and Performance Studies.

John Miles Foley is Byler Chair in the Humanities, Curators' Professor of Classical Studies and English, and director of the Center for Studies in Oral Tradition at the University of Missouri, Columbia, as well as founding editor of the journal *Oral Tradition.* In addition to *Immanent Art, Traditional Oral Epic, The Singer of Tales in Performance,* and *The Theory of Oral Composition: History and Methodology,* he has written numerous articles in the fields of oral tradition, ancient Greek, Old English, and South Slavic.

Lee Haring is professor of English at Brooklyn College. His main research and teaching areas are folklore theory and literary criticism.

His publications are *Verbal Arts in Madagascar*; *Ibonia, Epic of Madagascar*; *Collecting Folklore in Mauritius*, *Malagasy Tale Index*; and articles on folklore. His current project is the study of creolization as evidenced in folktales of the southwest Indian Ocean.

Joseph Harris, professor of English and folklore at Harvard University, is currently working on a bibliography of the Eddas, a study of prosimetrics in Old Norse and in world literature, and other scholarship involving heroic poetry and heroic legend. His teaching and research centers on Old English and Old Norse language, culture, folklore, and mythology. Among his publications are "A Nativist Approach to *Beowulf*: The Case of Germanic Elegy," "Love and Death in the Männerbund," and "Beowulf's Last Words."

María Herrera-Sobek holds the Luis Leal Endowed Chair in Chicano Studies at the University of California, Santa Barbara. She is interested mainly in Chicano and Chicana literature and cultural studies and in Latin American literature. Among her books are *The Bracero Experience: Elitelore versus Folklore*, *The Mexican Corrido: A Feminist Analysis*, and *Northward Bound: The Mexican Immigrant Experience in Ballad and Song*. She is currently working on projects concerning Chicano and Chicana *pastorelas*, or shepherds' plays, and critical theory and is doing fieldwork on oral history.

Bonnie D. Irwin, associate professor of English at Eastern Illinois University, Charleston, is currently working on a book-length manuscript about the *Seven Sages of Rome* and the *Book of Sindbad*. She has written articles on the frame tale, including "What's in a Frame? The Medieval Textualization of Traditional Storytelling," in *Oral Tradition*, and has contributed entries on the *1001 Nights* and *Seven Sages* to the *Encyclopedia of Folklore and Literature*. Trained in English, Spanish, Arabic, and Latin, she teaches a wide range of medieval and comparative literature and folklore.

Martin Jaffee is professor of Jewish studies and comparative religion at the University of Washington. Among his essays on Jewish oral traditions are "How Much Orality in Oral Torah?," "Writing and Rabbinic Oral Tradition," and "A Rabbinic Ontology of the Written and Spoken Word." He has done research on the role of oral teaching in the disciple communities of early rabbinic Judaism and teaches courses on the entire range of early Jewish literature from the Bible to the rabbinics. He is working on a monograph about early Judaism and the oral Torah.

Steven Swann Jones is a professor of English at California State University, Los Angeles. He is the author of *The Fairy Tale: The Magic Mirror of Imagination, Folklore and Literature in the United States: An Annotated Bibliography of Studies of Folklore in American Literature*, and *The New Comparative Method: Structural and Symbolic Analyses of the Allomotifs of Snow White*. He is past president of the California Folklore Society.

Werner H. Kelber is the Isla Carroll and Percy E. Turner Professor of Biblical Studies at Rice University. His widely acclaimed work *The Oral and the Written Gospel* (Philadelphia: Fortress, 1983; paperback, Indiana UP, 1997) examines orality, literacy, and the interaction between the two at strategic points in the early Christian tradition. His research interests include rhetoric, hermeneutics, visualization, communication, and cognition. He has also written articles about language, memory, and technology from antiquity to the Middle Ages.

Lynn C. Lewis is completing her doctoral dissertation, "Towards an Ethnography of Voice in Amerafrican Verbal Arts," from the Department of English at the University of Missouri, Columbia, and currently teaches literature, oral traditions, and composition at Tennessee State University, Nashville. She is the author of "The Enlightened Continent Recognized and Reclaimed," in *Middle Atlantic Writers Association Journal*, and poems in *Frost at Midnight* and in *Outstanding Poets of 1994*.

Carl Lindahl, professor of English and folklore at the University of Houston, is author of *Earnest Games: Folkloric Patterns in the* Canterbury Tales and the founder and series editor of the World Folktale Library. He researches and teaches medieval folklore, folk narrative, and twentieth-century American folktales. He is currently working on an encyclopedia of medieval folklore, a study of medieval British romances and folktales, and a history of the folk narrative traditions of the Appalachians.

Richard P. Martin, professor of classics at Princeton University, has written *Healing, Sacrifice, and Battle* and *The Language of Heroes: Speech and Performance in the* Iliad, as well as many articles on Greek poetry, myth, and folklore. He is currently working on "The Trickster's Son: The Generation of the Odyssey," a translation of Sophocles's *Trachiniae*, and a collection of materials on classical and world myth. His research interests are ancient and modern Greek poetic traditions, Irish literature, and comparative literature.

William Bernard McCarthy, professor of English at Penn State University, Dubois, is the author of *The Ballad Matrix*, a study of the nineteenth-century Scottish traditional singer Agnes Lyle, and *Jack in Two Worlds*, a book on the Jack stories recorded primarily in Appalachia. He teaches composition, oral theory, and ballad and folktale traditions and is currently editing an anthology of North American folktales.

John H. McDowell, professor and former chair of the Folklore Institute at Indiana University, Bloomington, focuses his research on the oral poetry and song, viewed in cultural and historical context, of Latin American peoples. His books are *"So Wise Were Our Elders": Mythic Narratives of the Kamsá, Sayings of the Ancestors: The Spiritual Life of the Sibundoy Indians*, and *Children's Riddling*. He has also written on issues of semiotics, folklore, and traditional Andean music. He is currently researching poetry and violence on the Costa Chica of Mexico.

Judith S. Neulander has a PhD from the Folklore Institute at Indiana University, Bloomington, with a specialty in Jewish civilization and culture. She lectures frequently, publishes widely, curates exhibits of traditional arts, and creates Indiana folklore segments for a local PBS program. She teaches courses in folklore and religious studies at Indiana University, Bloomington, and at several campuses of Indiana University-Purdue University.

John D. Niles, professor of English at the University of California, Berkeley, is the author of Beowulf: *The Poem and Its Tradition*, editor of *Old English Literature in Context*, and coeditor of *A Beowulf Handbook* and *Anglo-Saxonism and the Construction of Social Identity*. He has also written numerous articles on balladry and on medieval English, medieval French, and ancient Greek poetry. His current project is a book that addresses both Old English literature and contemporary singing and storytelling traditions.

Katherine O'Brien O'Keeffe is professor of English and fellow of the Medieval Institute at the University of Notre Dame. The main focus of her teaching and research is the literature and culture of early England. She has written *Visible Song: Transitional Literacy in Old English Verse* and has edited *Reading Old English Texts*. Her current projects include a book on the textual dimensions of the subject in Anglo-Saxon England and a volume on England before 1300 (with L. Georgianna) for the *Oxford History of English Literature*.

Alexandra H. Olsen, professor of English at the University of Denver, teaches and does research in Old and Middle English, Old Norse, hagiography, and the history of the English language. Her publications in the fields of Old English and oral tradition include *Speech, Song, and Poetic Craft: The Artistry of the Cynewulf Canon*. She is coeditor of *New Readings on Women in Old English Literature* and *Poetry and Prose from the Old English*.

R. Parthasarathy, director of the Program in Asian Studies at Skidmore College, is a poet, translator, and critic. He is the author of *Rough Passage* (1977) and has edited *Ten Twentieth-Century Indian Poets* (1976). His verse translation of the Tamil national epic, *The Tale of an Anklet* (1993), received numerous awards, including the 1995 Sahitya Akademi Translation Prize, given by the National Academy of Letters in India. His current projects are a translation of the Buddhist epic *Manimekalai* and an anthology of poems from Old Tamil. His research and teaching interests are Tamil and Sanskrit literatures, comparative poetics, epic traditions, and translation studies.

Lori Peterson received her master's degree from the University of Arkansas and is currently a doctoral candidate in the Department of English and editorial assistant at the Center for Studies in Oral Tradition at the University of Missouri, Columbia. Her main fields of study are Old English, medieval literature, and folklore.

Sw. Anand Prahlad, associate professor in the Department of English at the University of Missouri, Columbia, is the author of *African-American Proverbs in Context* and *"Hear My Story" and Other Poems*. His writings have appeared in such venues as *Proverbium, Southern Folklore, Journal of the Missouri Folklore Society, International Folklore Review, Western Journal of Black Studies,* and *Chariton Review*. His research areas are proverbs, folklore and literature of the African diaspora, sociolinguistics and performance studies, folklore and popular culture, and creative writing.

Shelley Fenno Quinn, associate professor in the Department of East Asian Languages and Literatures at Ohio State University, Columbus, specializes in Japanese traditional performance genres and performance theory. She has had published articles on Noh and has trained for seven years in Noh acting. Her forthcoming book on Noh is *Developing Zeami: From Mimesis to Poesis*.

Susan Slyomovics, the Geneviève McMillan–Reba Stewart Professor of the Study of Women in the Developing World and professor of anthropology at the Massachusetts Institute of Technology, is the author of a book on Egyptian folklore, *The Merchant of Art: An Egyptian*

Hilali Epic Poet in Performance, and a book on Palestinian folklore, *The Object of Memory: Arab and Jew Narrate the Palestinian Village*.

Beverly J. Stoeltje, associate professor in the Folklore Institute at Indiana University, Bloomington, does research in Ghana and in the United States and uses both literary and anthropological theory. She has coedited *Beauty Queens on the Global Stage: Gender, Contests, and Power* and has had published articles on Asante queen mothers, festival, and American rodeo. Her interests also include popular culture, nationalism, the ritual genres, ethnographic field methods, and feminist theory.

Leslie Straytner, assistant professor in the Humanities Division at Mississippi University for Women, is interested in epic literature, Anglo-Saxon literature, and popular culture. Her articles have appeared in journals such as *Oral Tradition* and the *Yeats Eliot Review*. She is working on a project provisionally entitled "Beyond Archetype: Feminism and the Possibility of Female Volition in *Beowulf.*"

Barre Toelken, professor of English and history and director of the American studies graduate program and the folklore program at Utah State University, is a folklore and Native American traditional literatures specialist and the author of *Morning Dew and Roses: Nuance, Metaphor, and Meaning in Folksongs*; *Ghosts and the Japanese*: *Cultural Experience in Japanese Death Legends*; and *The Dynamics of Folklore*. He is also past president of the American Folklore Society and has served on many national and state folklore panels and societies.

Evelyn Birge Vitz is professor of French at New York University. Her present teaching and research interests include oral and written traditions, hagiography and religious literature, and medieval romance. Her books include *The Crossroads of Intentions: A Study of Symbolic Expression in the Poetry of François Villon*, *Medieval Narrative and Modern Narratology: Subjects and Objects of Desire*, and *Orality and Performance in Early French Romance* (forthcoming). She is currently writing a book on the influence of the liturgy on medieval vernacular literature.

Marta Weigle, University Regents Professor and chair in the Department of Anthropology at the University of New Mexico, specializes in mythology, women and oral tradition, and studies of the Southwest. She is the author of *Spiders and Spinsters: Women and Mythology* and *Creation and Procreation: Feminist Reflections on Mythologies of Cosmogony and Parturition*; the coauthor, with Peter White, of *The Lore of New Mexico*; the coeditor, with Barbara A. Babcock, of *The Great Southwest* *of the Fred Harvey Company and the Santa Fe Railway*; and the coeditor, with Donna Pierce, of *Spanish New Mexico*.

Nancy Worthington, a doctoral candidate in mass communication at Indiana University, Bloomington, teaches media studies. She is the author of "Classifying Kenyan Women: Press Representation of Gender in Nairobi's *Daily Nation*" in *Women's Studies in Communication*. She is currently writing her dissertation on twenty years of female portrayal in Kenya's post-independence press.

John Zemke, assistant professor of Spanish in the Department of Romance Languages at the University of Missouri, Columbia, has written articles on poetics and orality in Shem Tov de Carrión's *Proverbios morales* and an annotated bibliography of criticism addressing Shem Tov de Carrión (Juan de la Cuesta, 1997). His teaching and research specialties are medieval Spanish literature, the *romancero*, Old Spanish, and Judeo-Spanish. He is completing an edition of R. Moses Almosino's *Regimiento de la vida* (Salonica, 1564).

Rosemary Lévy Zumwalt, professor of anthropology at Davidson College, is the author of *Wealth and Rebellion: Elsie Clews Parsons, Anthropologist and Folklorist* and *American Folklore Scholarship: A Dialogue of Dissent*. She has also coedited *Folklore Interpreted: Essays in Honor of Alan Dundes* and *Sephardic Folklore: Exile and Homecoming*. She teaches courses on folklore, mythology, women's narratives, ethnography, and Native American studies and is coauthoring, with Isaac Jack Lévy, a book on Sephardic folk religion.

Works Cited

Aarne, Antti, and Stith Thompson. *The Types of the Folktale: A Classification and Bibliography*. Folklore Fellows Communications 184. Helsinki: Suomalainen Tiedeakatemia, Academia Scientiarum Fennica, 1973. Bloomington: Indiana UP, 1987.

Abbott, Claude Colleer, ed. and trans. *Early Mediaeval French Lyrics*. London: Constable, 1932. London: Folcraft Lib., 1975.

Abrahams, Roger D., ed. *African Folktales: Traditional Stories of the Black World*. New York: Pantheon, 1983.

———. *Afro-American Folktales: Stories from Black Traditions in the New World*. New York: Pantheon, 1985.

———. *Deep Down in the Jungle*. Chicago: Aldine, 1963.

———. "Folk Drama." Dorson, *Folklore and Folklife* 351–62.

———. *The Man-of-Words in the West Indies: Performance and the Emergence of Creole Culture*. Baltimore: Johns Hopkins UP, 1983.

———. "Personal Power and Social Restraint in the Definition of Folklore." Paredes and Bauman 16–30.

———. "Playing the Dozens." *Journal of American Folklore* 75 (1962): 209–20.

———. "Shouting Match at the Border: The Folklore of Display Events." *"And Other Neighborly Names": Social Process and Cultural Image in Texas Folklore*. Ed. Richard Bauman and Abrahams. Austin: U of Texas P, 1981. 303–21.

————, ed. *A Singer and Her Songs: Almeda Riddle's Book of Ballads*. Baton Rouge: Louisiana State UP, 1970.

Abrahams, Roger D., and Alan Dundes. "Riddles." Dorson, *Folklore and Folklife* 129–43.

Abrams, M. H., ed. *The Norton Anthology of English Literature*. Vol 1. New York: Norton, 1993.

Abu-Lughod, Lila. *Veiled Sentiments: Honor and Poetry in an Egyptian Society*. Berkeley: U of California P, 1986.

Achebe, Chinua. *Things Fall Apart*. London: Heinemann, 1958.

Acker, Paul. "Norse Sagas Translated into English: A Supplement." *Scandinavian Studies* 65 (1993): 66–102.

Aertsen, Henk, and Alasdair A. MacDonald, eds. *Companion to Middle English Romance*. Amsterdam: VU UP, 1990.

Africa: A New Look. Videocassette. New York: Intl. Film Foundation, 1981.

Aland, Kurt, ed. *Synopsis of the Four Gospels*. 10th ed. Stuttgart: German Bible Soc., 1993.

Alexiou, Margaret. *The Ritual Lament in Greek Tradition*. Cambridge: Cambridge UP, 1974.

Allen, Richard F. *Fire and Iron: Critical Approaches to* Njáls saga. Pittsburgh: U of Pittsburgh P, 1971.

Allen, Rosamund, trans. *Lawman: Brut*. London: Dent; New York: St. Martin's, 1992.

Allen, Woody, dir. *Zelig*. Orion, 1983.

Amodio, Mark C. "Affective Criticism, Oral Poetics, and Beowulf's Fight with the Dragon." *Oral Tradition* 10 (1995): 54–90.

————. "Introduction: Oral Poetics in Post-Conquest England." Amodio, *Oral* 1–28.

————, ed. *Oral Poetics in Middle English Poetry*. Albert Bates Lord Studies in Oral Tradition 13. New York: Garland, 1994.

Andersen, Flemming G. *Commonplace and Creativity*. Odense, Den.: Odense UP, 1985.

Andersson, Theodore M. *The Icelandic Family Saga: An Analytic Reading*. Cambridge: Harvard UP, 1967.

————. *The Problem of Icelandic Saga Origins*. New Haven: Yale UP, 1964.

Angano, Angano. Videocassette. California Newsreel, 1989.

An Anthology of African American Poetry for Young People. 1958. Audiocassette. Washington: Smithsonian Folkways, 1992.

Appadurai, Arjun, Frank J. Korom, Margaret A. Mills, eds. *Gender, Genre, and Power in South Asian Expressive Traditions*. Philadelphia: U of Pennsylvania P, 1991.

Appiah, K. Anthony. "Identity, Authenticity, Survival: Multicultural Societies and Social Reproduction." Gutman 149–63.

Araki, James T. *The Ballad Drama of Medieval Japan*. Rutland: Tuttle, 1964.

Armistead, Samuel G. *The Spanish Tradition in Louisiana*. Ed. Thomas Lathrop. Newark: de la Cuesta, 1992.

Armstrong, Nancy, and Leonard Tennenhouse. *The Imaginary Puritan: Liter-*

ature, Intellectual Labor, and the Origins of Personal Life. Berkeley: U of California P, 1992.

Armstrong, Robert Plant. *The Affecting Presence: An Essay in Humanistic Anthropology*. Urbana: U of Illinois P, 1971.

———. *The Powers of Presence: Consciousness, Myth, and the Affecting Presence*. Philadelphia: U of Pennsylvania P, 1981.

Arora, Shirley L. *Proverbial Comparisons and Related Expressions in Spanish*. Berkeley: U of California P, 1977.

———. "Proverbs in Mexican American Tradition." *Aztlán* 12. 1–2 (1982): 43–69.

Asad, Talal. *Genealogies of Religion: Discipline and Reasons of Power in Christianity and Islam*. Baltimore: Johns Hopkins UP, 1993.

Aston, W. G., trans. *Nihongi: Chronicles of Japan from the Earliest Times to A.D. 697*. Rutland: Tuttle, 1972.

Auerbach, Susan. "From Singing to Lamenting: Women's Musical Role in a Greek Village." Koskoff 25–43.

Augustine. *On Christian Doctrine*. Trans. D. W. Robertson. Lib. of Liberal Arts 80. New York: Macmillan, 1958.

Babcock, Barbara A. "The Story in the Story: Metanarration in Folk Narrative." Bauman, *Verbal Art* 61–80.

Baker, Augusta, and Ellin Greene. *Storytelling: Art and Technique*. 2nd ed. New York: Bowker, 1987.

Baker, Houston A., Jr. *Blues, Ideology, and Afro-American Literature: A Vernacular Theory*. Chicago: U of Chicago P, 1984.

Bandstra, Barry L. *Reading the Old Testament: An Introduction to the Hebrew Bible*. Belmont: Wadsworth, 1995.

Barnicle, M. E., ed. *The Seege of Troye*. Early English Text Soc. 172. London: Oxford UP, 1927.

Barreca, Regina. *They Used to Call Me Snow White . . . but I Drifted: Women's Strategic Use of Humor*. New York: Viking, 1991.

Barron, W. R. J. *English Medieval Romance*. London: Longman, 1987.

Barth, John. *Chimera*. New York: Random, 1972.

Barthes, Roland. *Image—Music—Text*. Trans. Stephen Heath. New York: Hill, 1977.

Bartis, Peter. *Folklife and Fieldwork*. Washington: Amer. Folklife Center, Lib. of Congress, 1990.

Bartók, Béla, and Albert B. Lord. *Serbo-Croatian Folk Songs*. New York: Columbia UP, 1951.

Bascom, William R. *African Tales in the New World*. Bloomington: Indiana UP, 1992.

———. "The Forms of Folklore: Prose Narratives." *Journal of American Folklore* 77 (1965): 3–20. Rpt. in Dundes, *Sacred Narrative* 5–29.

———. "Four Functions of Folklore." *Journal of American Folklore* 67 (1954): 333–49. Rpt. in Dundes, *Study* 279–98.

———. "The Talking Skull That Refused to Talk." *Research in African*

Literatures 8 (1977): 266–91. Rpt. in Bascom. *Contributions to Folkloristics.* Meerut, India: Folklore Inst., 1981. 185–211.

Basso, Ellen. *The Last Cannibals: A South American Oral History.* Austin: U of Texas P, 1995.

———. *A Musical View of the Universe: Kalapalo Myth and Ritual Performance.* Philadelphia: U of Pennsylvania P, 1985.

———, ed. *Native Latin American Cultures through Their Discourse.* Bloomington: Folklore Inst., Indiana U, 1990.

Basso, Keith H. "'Stalking with Stories': Names, Places, and Moral Narratives among the Western Apache." Bruner 19–55.

Bastien, Joseph. *Mountain of the Condor: Metaphor and Ritual in an Andean Ayllu.* Amer. Ethnological Soc. Monographs 64. Minneapolis: West, 1978.

Bates, Robert H., V. Y. Mudimbe, and Jean F. O'Barr. *Africa and the Disciplines: The Contributions of Research in Africa to the Social Sciences and Humanities.* Chicago: U of Chicago P, 1993.

Bateson, Gregory. *Steps to an Ecology of Mind.* New York: Chandler, 1972.

Bauman, Richard. "Contextualization, Tradition, and the Dialogue of Genres: Icelandic Legends of the *Kraftaskáld.*" *Rethinking Context.* Ed. Alessandro Duranti and Charles Goodwin. Cambridge: Cambridge UP, 1992. 125–45.

———. "Differential Identity and the Social Base of Folklore." Paredes and Bauman 31–41.

———. "Disclaimers of Performance." *Responsibility and Evidence in Oral Discourse.* Ed. Jane H. Hill and Judith T. Irvine. Cambridge: Cambridge UP, 1993. 182–96.

———. "The Nationalization and Internationalization of Folklore: The Case of Schoolcraft's 'Gitshee Gauzinee.'" *Western Folklore* 52 (1993): 247–69.

———. "Performance." *Folklore, Cultural Performances, and Popular Entertainments.* Ed. Bauman. New York: Oxford UP, 1992. 41–49.

———. "Performance and Honor in Thirteenth-Century Iceland." *Journal of American Folklore* 99 (1986): 131–50.

———. *Story, Performance, and Event: Contextual Studies of Oral Narrative.* Cambridge: Cambridge UP, 1986.

———. *Verbal Art as Performance.* Prospect Heights: Waveland, 1977.

Bauman, Richard, and Roger D. Abrahams, with Susan Kalčik. "American Folklore and American Studies." *American Quarterly* 28 (1976): 361–67.

Bauman, Richard, and Charles L. Briggs. "Poetics and Performance as Critical Perspectives on Language and Social Life." *Annual Review of Anthropology* 19 (1990): 59–88.

Bauman, Richard, and Joel Sherzer, eds. *Explorations in the Ethnography of Speaking.* 2nd ed. Cambridge: Cambridge UP, 1989.

Belcher, Stephen. "Framed Tales in the Oral Tradition: An Exploration." *Fabula* 35 (1994): 1–19.

Bell, Michael J. "No Borders to the Ballad Maker's Art: Francis James Child and the Politics of the People." *Western Folklore* 47 (1988): 285–307.

———. "William Wells Newell and the Foundation of American Folklore Scholarship." *Journal of the Folklore Institute* 10 (1973): 7–22.

Ben-Amos, Dan. "Analytical Categories and Ethnic Genres." *Genre* 2 (1969): 275–301. Rpt. in Ben-Amos, *Folklore Genres* 215–42.

———, ed. *Folklore Genres*. Austin: U of Texas P, 1976.

———. "Generic Distinctions in the Aggadah." Talmage 45–71.

———. "The Myth of Jewish Humor." *Western Folklore* 32 (1973): 112–31.

———. "Toward a Definition of Folklore in Context." Paredes and Bauman 3–15.

Ben-Amos, Dan, and Kenneth S. Goldstein, eds. *Folklore: Performance and Communication*. The Hague: Mouton, 1975.

Bender, Mark. "'Felling the Ancient Sweetgum': Antiphonal Folk Epics of the Miao of Southeast Guizhou." *CHINOPERL Papers* 15 (1990): 27–44.

Bendix, Regina. "Diverging Paths in the Scientific Search for Authenticity." *Journal of Folklore Research* 29 (1992): 103–32.

Benedict, Ruth. "Introduction to Zuni Mythology." *Studies on Mythology*. 1935. Ed. Robert A. Georges. Homewood: Dorsey, 1968. 102–36.

———. *Patterns of Culture*. Boston: Houghton, 1934.

———. *Zuni Mythology*. Columbia Contributions to Anthropology 21. 2 vols. New York: Columbia UP, 1935.

Beowulf with "The Finnsburg Fragment." Ed. C. L. Wrenn. 3rd ed. Rev. Whitney F. Bolton. New York: St. Martin's, 1973.

Bergren, Ann L. T. "Language and the Female in Early Greek Thought." *Arethusa* 16 (1983): 69–95.

Berleant, Arnold. *The Aesthetic Field: A Phenomenology of Aesthetic Experience*. Springfield: Thomas, 1970.

Bernal, Martin. *Black Athena*. New York: Free Assn., 1987.

Bernheimer, Charles, ed. *Comparative Literature in the Age of Multiculturalism*. Baltimore: Johns Hopkins UP, 1995.

Bessinger, Jess B., Jr., and Robert F. Yeager. *Approaches to Teaching* Beowulf. Approaches to Teaching World Lit. 4. New York: MLA, 1984.

Bethe, Monica, and Karen Brazell. *Dance in the Noh Theatre*. 3 vols. Cornell U East Asian Papers 29. Ithaca: China-Japan Program, Cornell U, 1982. Videotapes available.

Bettelheim, Bruno. *The Uses of Enchantment: The Meaning and Importance of Fairy Tales*. New York: Random, 1976.

Betz, Hans Dieter. "The Literary Composition and Function of Paul's Letter to the Galatians." *New Testament Studies* 21 (1975): 454–79.

The Bhagavad-Gita. Trans. Barbara Stoler Miller. New York: Bantam, 1986.

Bidney, David. *Theoretical Anthropology*. New York: Schocken, 1973.

Biebuyck, Daniel, and Kohombo Mateene, trans. *The Mwindo Epic*. Berkeley: U of California P, 1969.

Bierhorst, John. *The Mythology of South America*. New York: Morrow, 1988.

———. *The Red Swan: Myths and Tales of the American Indians*. New York: Farrar, 1976.

———. *The Sacred Path: Spells, Prayers, and Power Songs of the American Indian*. New York: Quill, 1984.

bin Gorion [Berdichevsky], Micha Joseph. *Mimekor Yisrael: Classical Jewish Folktales*. Ed. Emanuel bin Gorion and Dan Ben-Amos. Trans. I. M. Lask. Bloomington: Indiana UP, 1990.

———. *Mimekor Yisrael: Selected Classical Jewish Folktales*. Bloomington: Indiana UP, 1990.

Birch, Carol. *IMAGE-ination: The Heart (and True Art) of Storytelling*. Little Rock: August, 1996.

Birch, Carol, and Melissa Heckler, eds. *Who Says? Essays on Pivotal Issues in Contemporary Storytelling*. Little Rock: August, 1996.

Birch, Cyril, ed. *Anthology of Chinese Literature: From Early Times to the Fourteenth Century*. New York: Grove, 1965.

———, trans. *Stories from a Ming Collection: The Art of the Chinese Storyteller*. New York: Grove, 1958.

Bitter Melons. Dir. John Marshall. Documentary Educ. Resources, 1966.

Blackburn, Stuart H. "Creating Conversations: The Rāma Story as Puppet Play in Kerala." *Many Ramayanas: The Diversity of a Narrative Tradition in South Asia*. Ed. Paula Richman. Berkeley: U of California P, 1991. 156–72.

———. "Domesticating the Cosmos: History and Structure in a Folktale from India." *Journal of Asian Studies* 45 (1986): 527–43.

Bleek, Dorothea, ed. *The Mantis and His Friends*. Capetown: Miller, 1923.

Bliss, A. J., ed. *Sir Orfeo*. Oxford: Clarendon, 1966.

Bloom, Harold. *The Anxiety of Influence: A Theory of Poetry*. New York: Oxford UP, 1973.

Boas, Franz. *Kwakiutl Culture As Reflected in Mythology*. Memoirs of the Amer. Folklore Soc. 28. New York: Stechert, 1935.

Boccaccio, Giovanni. *The Decameron*. Trans. G. H. McWilliam. New York: Penguin, 1972.

Bodek, Evelyn Gordon. "Salonières and Bluestockings: Educated Obsolescence and Germinating Feminism." *Feminist Issues* 3 (1976): 185–95.

Boggs, Beverly B., and Daniel W. Patterson. *An Index of Selected Folk Recordings*. Chapel Hill: U of North Carolina P, 1984.

Bonjour, Adrien. "*Beowulf* and the Beasts of Battle." *PMLA* 72 (1957): 563–73.

———. *The Digressions in* Beowulf. Medium Aevum Monographs 5. Oxford: Soc. for the Study of Mediaeval Langs. and Lit., 1950.

The Book of the Icelanders (Islendingabok) by Ari Thorgilsson. Ed. and trans. Halldór Hermannsson. Ithaca: Cornell U Lib.; London: Oxford UP, 1930.

Booth, Wayne C. *The Rhetoric of Fiction*. 2d ed. Chicago: U of Chicago P, 1983.

Borroff, Marie, trans. *Sir Gawain and the Green Knight*. New York: Norton, 1967.

Bourdieu, Pierre. *The Rules of Art: Genesis and Structure of the Literary Field*. Trans. Susan Emanuel. Stanford: Stanford UP, 1992.

Bowden, Betsy. *Chaucer Aloud*. Philadelphia: U of Pennsylvania P, 1986.

Boyarin, Jonathan, ed. *The Ethnography of Reading*. Berkeley: U of California P, 1993.

Bradbury, Nancy Mason. "The Poetics of Middle English Romance." Amodio, *Oral Poetics* 9–69.

Bradley, S. A. J., ed. and trans. *Anglo-Saxon Poetry*. London: Dent; Rutland: Tuttle, 1982.

Brady, Margaret K. *"Some Kind of Power": Navajo Children's Skinwalker Narratives*. Salt Lake City: U of Utah P, 1984.

Braid, Donald. "The Construction of Identity through Narrative: Folklore and the Travelling People of Scotland." *Romani Culture and Gypsy Identity*. Ed. Thomas Acton and Gary Mundy. Hatfield, Eng.: U of Hertfordshire P, 1997. 38–66.

———. "The Negotiation of Cultural Identity through Narrative: The Travelling People of Scotland." *Texts and Identities: Proceedings of the Third Kentucky Conference on Narrative*. Ed. Joachim Knuf. Lexington: Narrative Studies Group, 1995. 87–99.

———. "The Traveller and the Hare: Meaning, Function, and Form in the Recontextualization of Narrative." *Folklore Forum* 26 (1993): 3–29.

Brault, Gerald J., ed. and trans. La Chanson de Roland: *A Student Edition, with English and Old French*. University Park: Pennsylvania State UP, 1984.

Brewer, Derek. "Some Metonymic Relationships in Chaucer's Poetry." *Chaucer: The Poet as Storyteller*. London: Macmillan, 1984. 37–53.

Briggs, Charles L. *Competence in Performance: The Creativity of Tradition in Mexicano Verbal Art*. Philadelphia: U of Pennsylvania P, 1988.

———. *Learning How to Ask: A Sociolinguistic Appraisal of the Interview in Social Science Research*. Cambridge: Cambridge UP, 1986.

Briggs, Charles L., and Richard Bauman. "Genre, Intertextuality, and Social Power." *Journal of Linguistic Anthropology* 2 (1992): 131–72.

Briggs, Charles, and Julián Josué Vigil. *The Lost Gold Mine of Juan Mondragón: A Legend from New Mexico Performed by Melaquías Romero*. Tucson: U of Arizona P, 1990.

Bright, William. "A Karok Myth in 'Measured Verse': The Translation of a Performance." *Journal of California and Great Basin Anthropology* 1 (1979): 117–23.

Brockington, J. L. *Righteous Rama: The Evolution of an Epic*. Delhi: Oxford UP, 1984.

Bronner, Simon J. *Piled Higher and Deeper: The Folklore of Student Life*. 1990. Little Rock: August, 1995.

Bronson, Bertrand Harris. *The Ballad as Song*. Berkeley: U of California P, 1969.

———, ed. *The Singing Tradition of Child's Popular Ballads*. Princeton: Princeton UP, 1976.

———, ed. *The Traditional Tunes of the Child Ballads*. 4 vols. Princeton: Princeton UP, 1959–72.

Brook, G. L., and Roy F. Leslie, eds. *Laȝamon: Brut*. 2 vols. Early English Text Soc. os 263, 277. Oxford: Oxford UP, 1963, 1978.

Brooks, Gwendolyn. *Gwendolyn Brooks Reading at Wheeler Auditorium, University of California, Berkeley*. Audiocassette. San Francisco: Amer. Poetry Archive, 1997.

Brooks, Peter. "Must We Apologize?" Bernheimer 97–106.

Brower, Robert H., and Earl Miner. *Japanese Court Poetry*. Stanford: Stanford UP, 1961.

Brown, Mary Ellen. "Thoughts on the Ballad Genre." Porter and del Guidice 130–32.

Brown, Michael. *Tsewa's Gift: Magic and Meaning in an Amazonian Society*. Washington: Smithsonian Inst., 1985.

Bruner, Edward M. *Text, Play, and Story: The Construction and Reconstruction of Self and Society*. 1983 Proc. of the Amer. Ethnological Soc. Prospect Heights: Waveland, 1984.

Brunvand, Jan H. *The Choking Doberman*. New York: Norton, 1986.

———, ed. *The Study of American Folklore: An Introduction*. 1968. New York: Norton, 1986.

———. *The Vanishing Hitchhiker: American Urban Legends and Their Meanings*. New York: Norton, 1981.

Brunvand, Jan H., and Paddy Bowman. *A Teacher's Guide to Folklife Resources for K–12 Classrooms*. Washington: Amer. Folklife Center, Lib. of Congress, 1994.

Buchan, David. *The Ballad and the Folk*. Boston: Routledge, 1972.

Bunzel, Ruth. *Zuni Texts*. Pubs. of the Amer. Ethnological Soc. 15. New York: Stechert, 1933.

Burke, Kenneth. "Literature as Equipment for Living." *The Philosophy of Literary Form*. Baton Rouge: Louisiana State UP, 1941. 293–304.

Burns, Allan F. *An Epoch of Miracles: Oral Literature of the Yucatec Maya*. Austin: U of Texas P, 1983.

Burns, Thomas A. "Folkloristics: A Conception of Theory." Oring, *Folk Groups* 1–20.

Burton, Thomas G., ed. *Some Ballad Folks*. Boone: Appalachian Consortium, 1978.

Bushnaq, Inea. *Arab Folktales*. New York: Pantheon, 1986.

Cameron, Deborah, ed. *The Feminist Critique of Language: A Reader*. New York: Routledge, 1990.

Campa, Arthur L. *Los Comanches: A New Mexican Folk Drama*. U of New Mexico Bulletin Lang. Ser. 7.1. Albuquerque: U of New Mexico, 1942. 5–42.

———. *Sayings and Riddles in New Mexico.* U of New Mexico Bulletin Lang. Ser. 6.2. Albuquerque: U of New Mexico, 1937.

———. *Spanish Religious Folktheatre in the Spanish Southwest.* U of New Mexico Bulletin Lang. Ser. 5.1–2. Albuquerque: U of New Mexico, 1934.

Campbell, Joseph. *The Hero with a Thousand Faces.* New York: Pantheon, 1949.

Campbell, Lyle. *American Indian Languages: The Historical Linguistics of Native America.* New York: Oxford UP, 1997.

Campbell, Lyle, and Marianne Mithun, eds. *The Languages of Native America: Historical and Comparative Assessment.* Austin: U of Texas P, 1979.

Cancel, Robert. *Allegorical Speculation in an Oral Society.* Berkeley: U of California P, 1989.

Canfora, Luciano. *The Vanished Library: A Wonder of the Ancient World.* Berkeley: U of California P, 1990.

Carruthers, Mary J. *The Book of Memory: A Study of Memory in Medieval Culture.* New York: Cambridge UP, 1992.

Cartwright, Christine A. "Johnny Faa and Black Jack Davy: Cultural Values and Change in Scots and American Balladry." *Journal of American Folklore* 93 (1980): 397–416.

Catalán, Diego. "The Artisan Poetry of the Romancero." Webber, *Balladry* 1–25.

Caton, Steven C. *"Peaks of Yemen I Summon": Poetry as Cultural Practice in a North Yemeni Tribe.* Berkeley: U of California P, 1990.

Caws, Mary Ann, and Christopher Prendergast, eds. *The HarperCollins World Reader.* New York: Harper, 1994.

Cazelles, Brigitte, ed. and trans. *The Lady of Saint: A Collection of French Hagiographic Romances of the Thirteenth Century.* Philadelphia: U of Pennsylvania P, 1991.

Chadwick, John. *Linear B and Related Scripts.* Berkeley: U of California P, 1987.

Cham, Mbye. "Structural and Thematic Parallels in Oral Narrative and Film." Okpewho, *Oral Performance.*

Chambers, Raymond W., et al., eds. *The Exeter Book of Old English Poetry.* London: 1933.

Chaucer, Geoffrey. *The Canterbury Tales.* Trans. Nevill Coghill. New York: Penguin, 1977.

———. *The Riverside Chaucer.* Ed. Larry D. Benson. 3rd. ed. Boston: Houghton, 1986.

Chaytor, H. J. *From Script to Print: An Introduction to Medieval Literature.* Cambridge: Cambridge UP, 1945.

Chickering, Howell D., Jr., ed. and trans. *Beowulf: A Dual-Language Edition.* Garden City: Anchor, 1977.

Child, Francis James, ed. *The English and Scottish Popular Ballads.* 5 vols. Boston: Houghton, 1882–98. New York: Dover, 1965.

Church, F. F. "Rhetorical Structure and Design in Paul's Letter to Philemon." *Harvard Theological Review* 71 (1978): 17–33.

Civrieux, Marc de. *Watunna: An Oronoco Creation Cycle*. Trans. D. Guss. San Francisco: North Point, 1980.

Clanchy, Michael T. *From Memory to Written Record: English, 1066–1307*. 2nd ed. Oxford: Blackwell, 1993.

———. "Looking Back from the Invention of Printing." *Literacy in Historical Perspective*. Ed. Daniel P. Resnick. Washington: Lib. of Congress, 1983. 7–22.

Clements, Robert J. *Comparative Literature as Academic Discipline*. New York: MLA, 1978.

Clements, Robert J., and Joseph Gibaldi, eds. *Anatomy of the Novella: The European Tale Collection from Boccaccio to Cervantes*. New York: New York UP, 1977.

Cline, Ruth Harwood, trans. *Yvain; or, The Knight with the Lion*. By Chrétien de Troyes. Athens: U of Georgia P, 1975.

Clinton, Bill. "Remarks in Apology to African-Americans on the Tuskegee Experiment." *Weekly Compilation of Presidential Documents* 19 May 1997: 718–20.

Clover, Carol J. "The Long Prose Form." *Arkiv för nordisk filologi* 101 (1986): 10–39.

Clover, Carol J., and John Lindow, eds. *Old Norse-Icelandic Literature: A Critical Guide*. Islandica 45. Ithaca: Cornell UP, 1985.

Coffin, Tristram Potter. *The British Traditional Ballad in North America*. 2nd ed. Supp. by Roger deV. Renwick. Austin: U of Texas P, 1977.

Cohen, J. M., ed. *The Penguin Book of Spanish Verse*. 1956. New York: Viking-Penguin, 1988.

Colby, Benjamin, and James Peacock. "Narrative." *Handbook of Social and Cultural Anthropology*. Ed. John J. Honigmann. Chicago: Rand, 1973. 613–33.

Coleman, Janet. *Medieval Readers and Their Writers*. New York: Columbia UP, 1981.

Coleman, Joyce. *Public Reading and the Reading Public in Late Medieval England and France*. Cambridge: Cambridge UP, 1996.

Coley, John Smartt, trans. *Le Roman de Thèbes (The Story of Thebes)*. New York: Garland, 1986.

Colophons de manuscrits occidentaux des origines au xvie siècle. Spicilegii friburgensis subsidia 2–7. Fribourg: Editions Universitaires, 1965– .

Color: A Sampling of Contemporary African American Writers. Videocassette and study guide. San Francisco: Amer. Poetry Archive, 1994.

Connelly, Bridget. *Arab Folk Epic and Identity*. Berkeley: U of California P, 1989.

Conner, Patrick W., Marilyn Deegan, and Clare A. Lees. "Computer-Assisted Approaches to Teaching Old English." *Old English Newsletter* 23.2 (1990): 30–35.

Coote, Mary P. "Serbocroatian Heroic Songs." *Heroic Epic and Saga*. Ed. Felix Oinas. Bloomington: Indiana UP, 1978. 257–85.

Cosentino, Donald. *Defiant Maids and Stubborn Farmers: Tradition and Invention in Mende Story Performance*. Cambridge: Cambridge UP, 1982.

———. "Midnight Charters: Musa Wo and Mende Myths of Chaos." *Creativity of Power*. Ed. W. Arens and Ivan Karp. Washington: Smithsonian Inst., 1989. 21–38.

Country to Town. Wilmette: Film, 1976.

Cray, Ed. "Barbara Allen': Cheap Print and Reprint." *Folklore International: Essays in Literature, Belief, and Custom in Honor of Wayland Debs Hand*. Ed. D. K. Wilgus. Hatboro: Folklore Assocs., 1967. 41–50.

———, ed. *The Erotic Muse: American Bawdy Songs*. 2nd ed. Urbana: U of Illinois P, 1992.

Creed, Robert Payson. *Beowulf*. Audiocassette. New York: RadioArts, n.d.

———. "Sutton Hoo and the Recording of *Beowulf*." *Voyage to the Other World: The Legacy of Sutton Hoo*. Ed. Calvin B. Kendall and Peter S. Wells. Medieval Studies at Minnesota 5. Minneapolis: U of Minnesota P, 1992. 65–75.

Cressy, David. *Literacy and the Social Order: Reading and Writing in Tudor and Stuart England*. Cambridge: Cambridge UP, 1980.

Crosby, Ruth. "Oral Delivery in the Middle Ages." *Speculum* 11 (1936): 88–110.

Crowley, Daniel J., ed. *African Folklore in the New World*. Austin: U of Texas P, 1977.

———. *I Could Talk Old-Story Good: Creativity in Bahamian Folklore*. Berkeley: U of California P, 1966.

Crowne, David K. "The Hero on the Beach: An Example of Composition by Theme in Anglo-Saxon Poetry." *Neuphilologische Mitteilungen* 61 (1960): 362–72.

Culley, Robert C., ed. *Oral Tradition and Old Testament Studies*. Semeia 5. Missoula: Scholars, 1976.

Cummins, John G. *The Spanish Traditional Lyric*. Oxford: Pergamon, 1977.

Cushing, Frank H. *Zuñi Folk Tales*. New York: Putnam's, 1901.

Dance, Daryl C. *Shuckin' and Jivin': Folklore from Contemporary Black Americans*. Bloomington: Indiana UP, 1978.

Dauenhauer, Nora Marks, and Richard Dauenhauer, eds. *Haa Shuka, Our Ancestors: Tlingit Oral Narratives*. Seattle: U of Washington P, 1987.

David-Neel, Alexandra, and Lama Yongden, trans. *The Superhuman Life of Gesar of Ling*. New York: Kendall, 1934.

Davis, Gerald L. *I Got the Word in Me and I Can Sing It, You Know: A Study of the Performed African-American Sermon*. Philadelphia: U of Pennsylvania P, 1989.

Dawood, N. J., trans. *"Aladdin" and Other Tales from the* Thousand and One Nights. Baltimore: Penguin, 1957.

———. *Tales from the* Thousand and One Nights. Baltimore: Penguin, 1973.

de Caro, Francis A., comp. *Women and Folklore: A Bibliographic Survey*. Westport: Greenwood, 1983.

Dégh, Linda. *American Folklore and the Mass Media*. Bloomington: Indiana UP, 1994.

Deleuze, Gilles, and Felix Guattari. *A Thousand Plateaus: Capitalism and Schizophrenia*. Trans. and foreword by Brian Massumi. Minneapolis: U of Minnesota P, 1987.

Deleuze, Gilles, and Claire Parnet. *Dialogues*. Trans. Hugh Tomlinson and Barbara Habberjam. New York: Columbia UP, 1987.

Derrida, Jacques. *Of Grammatology*. Trans. Gayatri Chakravorty Spivak. Baltimore: Johns Hopkins UP, 1976.

———. "Signature Event Context." Trans. Samuel Weber and Jeffrey Sussman. *Glyph: Johns Hopkins Textual Studies* 1 (1977): 172–97.

Dickey, Dan William. *The Kennedy Corridos: A Study of the Ballads of a Mexican American Hero*. Austin: U of Texas Center for Mexican Amer. Studies, 1978.

Dictionary of the Middle Ages. Ed. Joseph R. Strayer. New York: Scribner, 1982–89.

Doane, A. N. "Performance as a Constitutive Category in the Editing of Anglo-Saxon Poetic Texts." *Oral Tradition* 9 (1994): 420–39.

Dolby, William. *Eight Chinese Plays, from the Thirteenth Century to the Present*. London: Elek, 1978.

———. *A History of Chinese Drama*. London: Elek, 1976.

Donaldson, E. Talbot, trans. *Beowulf*. New York: Norton, 1966.

Donoghue, Daniel G. *Style in Old English Poetry: The Test of the Auxiliary*. New Haven: Yale UP, 1987.

Dorsey, J. O., A. S. Gatschet, and S. R. Riggs. "Illustrations of the Method of Recording Indian Languages." *First Annual Report of the Bureau of American Ethnology*. Washington: GPO, 1879–80. 581–89.

Dorson, Richard Mercer. *America in Legend: Folklore from the Colonial Period to the Present*. New York: Pantheon, 1973.

———. *American Folklore*. 1959. Chicago: U of Chicago P, 1970.

———, ed. *American Negro Folktales*. 1958. New York: Fawcett, 1968.

———. "The Eclipse of Solar Mythology." *Journal of American Folklore* 68 (1955): 393–416. Rpt. in Dundes, *Study* 57–83.

———, ed. *Folklore and Folklife: An Introduction*. Chicago: U of Chicago P, 1972.

Douglas, Mary. *Purity and Danger: An Analysis of the Concepts of Pollution and Taboo*. London: Routledge, 1966.

Douglass, Frederick. *My Bondage and My Freedom*. 1855. New York: Dover, 1969.

Dronke, Peter. *The Medieval Lyric*. 2nd ed. London: Hutchinson, 1978.

Dronke, Ursula, ed. and trans. *Heroic Poems*. Oxford: Clarendon, 1969.

DuBois, Cora. *The People of Alor*. Minneapolis: U of Minnesota P, 1944.

DuBois, Thomas. *Finnish Folk Poetry and the Kalevala*. New York: Garland, 1995.

Dugaw, Dianne M., ed. *The Anglo-American Ballad: A Folklore Casebook*. New York: Garland, 1995.

———. "Anglo-American Folksong Reconsidered: The Interface of Oral and Written Forms." *Western Folklore* 43 (1984): 83–103. Rpt. in Dugaw, *Ballad* 249–68.

———. *Warrior Women and Popular Balladry, 1650–1850*. Cambridge: Cambridge UP, 1989.

Duggan, Joseph J. "Social Functions of the Medieval Epic in the Romance Literatures." *Oral Tradition* 1 (1986): 728–66.

———. *The Song of Roland: Formulaic Style and Poetic Craft*. Berkeley: U of California P, 1973.

Duke University Library. *Folk Ballads*. Ed. Henry M. Belden and Arthur Palmer Hudson. Durham: Duke UP, 1952. Vol. 2 of *The Frank C. Brown Collection of North Carolina Folklore*. 7 vols. 1952–64.

———. *The Music of the Ballads*. Ed. Jan Philip Schinhan. Durham: Duke UP, 1957. Vol. 4 of *The Frank C. Brown Collection of North Carolina Folklore*. 7 vols. 1952–64.

Dunaway, David King. *How Can I Keep from Singing: Pete Seeger*. New York: McGraw, 1981.

Dunbar, Paul Lawrence. "An Ante-bellum Sermon." Hill et al. 604–06.

Duncan, Marion H. *Harvest Festival Dramas of Tibet*. Hong Kong: Orient, 1955.

Dundes, Alan. "The American Concept of Folklore." *Journal of the Folklore Institute* 3 (1966): 226–49.

———, ed. *The Blood Libel Legend: A Casebook in Anti-Semitic Folklore*. Madison: U of Wisconsin P, 1991.

———. *Cracking Jokes: Studies of Sick Humor Cycles and Stereotypes*. Berkeley: Ten Speed, 1987.

———. "The Devolutionary Premise in Folklore Theory." *Journal of the Folklore Institute* 6 (1969): 5–19.

———. "Earth-Diver: Creation of the Mythopoeic Male." *American Anthropologist* 64 (1962): 1032–50. Rpt. in Dundes, *Sacred Narrative* 270–94.

———, ed. *Every Man His Way: Readings in Cultural Anthropology*. Englewood Cliffs: Prentice, 1968.

———. "The Hero Pattern and the Life of Jesus." *Interpreting Folklore*. Ed. Dundes. Bloomington: Indiana UP, 1980. 223–61.

———. *Life Is like a Chicken Coop Ladder: A Portrait of German Culture through Folklore*. New York: Columbia UP, 1984.

———. "The Making and Breaking of Friendship as a Structural Frame in African Folktales." *The Structural Analysis of Oral Tradition*. Ed. P. Maranda and E. Maranda. Philadelphia: U of Pennsylvania P, 1971. 171–85.

———. "On the Structure of the Proverb." *Proverbium* 25 (1975): 961–73.

———. "Oral Literature." *Introduction to Cultural Anthropology: Essays on Scope and Method of the Science of Man*. Ed. James Clifton. Boston: Houghton, 1968. 117–29.

———. "The Psychoanalytic Study of Folklore." *Annals of Scholarship* 3.3 (1985): 1–42.

————. "The Psychoanalytic Study of the Grimms' Tales with Special Reference to 'The Maiden without Hands' (AT 706)." *Germanic Review* 62 (1987): 50–65. Rpt. in *Folklore Matters*. Ed. Dundes. Knoxville: U of Tennessee P, 1989. 112–50.

————, ed. *Sacred Narrative: Readings in the Theory of Myth.* Berkeley: U of California P, 1984.

————. "Structural Typology in North American Indian Folktales." Dundes, *Study* 206–16.

————, ed. *The Study of Folklore.* Englewood Cliffs: Prentice, 1965.

————. "Ways of Studying Folklore." *Our Living Traditions: An Introduction to American Folklore*. Ed. T. P. Coffin. New York: Basic, 1968. 37–46.

Dundes, Alan, and Roger Abrahams. "On Elephantasy and Elephanticide: The Effect of Time and Place." *Psychoanalytic Review* 56 (1969): 225–41. Rpt. in Dundes, *Cracking* 41–54.

Dundes, Alan, and Robert Georges. "Toward a Structural Definition of the Riddle." *Journal of American Folklore* 76 (1963): 111–18.

Eagleton, Terry. *Literary Theory: An Introduction.* Minneapolis: U of Minnesota P, 1983.

Eastman, Carol M. "An Ethnography of Swahili Expressive Culture." *Research in African Literatures* 15 (1984): 313–40.

Eberhard, Wolfram, ed. *Folktales of China.* Chicago: U of Chicago P, 1965.

Edmonson, Munro S. *The Book of Counsel: The Popol Vuh of the Quiche Maya of Guatemala.* Berkeley: U of California Extension Center for Media and Independent Learning, 1989.

Edwards, Mark W. "Homer and Oral Tradition." *Oral Tradition* 1 (1986): 171–230; 3 (1988): 11–60; 7 (1992): 284–330.

Egerton, Clement, trans. *The Golden Lotus.* 4 vols. London: Routledge, 1939.

Egil's Saga. Trans. Hermann Pálsson and Paul Edwards. Harmondsworth, Eng.: Penguin, 1976.

Egils saga Skalla-Grímssonar. Ed. Sigurður Nordal. Íslenzk fornrit 2. Reykjavík: Hið Íslenzka Fornritafélag, 1933. 258–67.

Eisenstein, Elizabeth L. *The Printing Revolution in Early Modern Europe.* New York: Cambridge UP, 1983.

El-Abbadi, Mostafa. *The Life and Fate of the Ancient Library of Alexandria.* Paris: UNESCO/UNDP, 1990.

Elbow, Peter. *Writing without Teachers.* New York: Oxford UP, 1973.

Ellis, Bill. "*De Legendis Urbis*: Modern Legends in Ancient Rome." *Journal of American Folklore* 96 (1983): 200–08.

Ellison, Ralph. *Invisible Man.* New York: Random, 1947.

El-Shamy, Hasan M., ed. and trans. *Folktales of Egypt.* Chicago: U of Chicago P, 1979.

————. *Folk Traditions of the Arab World: A Guide to Motif Classification.* 2 vols. Bloomington: Indiana UP, 1995.

Emmerson, Richard K., ed. *Approaches to Teaching Medieval English Drama.* Approaches to Teaching World Lit. 29. New York: MLA, 1990.

Encyclopedia of Islam. Leiden: Brill, 1913–38. 2d ed. London: Luzac, 1956– .

Erdoes, Richard, and Alfonso Ortiz, eds. *American Indian Myths and Legends*. New York: Pantheon, 1984.

Evans, David. *Big Road Blues: Tradition and Creativity in the Folk Blues*. Berkeley: U of California P, 1982.

———. "Structure and Meaning in the Folk Blues." Brunvand, *Study* 563–93.

Falassi, Alessandro. *Folklore by the Fireside: Text and Context of the Tuscan Veglia*. Austin: U of Texas P, 1980.

Fanon, Frantz. *The Wretched of the Earth*. New York: Grove, 1963.

Faral, Edmond. *Les jongleurs en France au moyen âge*. Paris: Champion, 1910. Geneva: Slatkine, 1970.

Farb, Peter. *Word Play: What Happens When People Talk*. 1974. New York: Vintage, 1993.

Farrer, Claire R., ed. *Women and Folklore: Images and Genres*. 1975. Prospect Heights: Waveland, 1986.

Febvre, Lucien, and Henri-Jean Martin. *The Coming of the Book: The Impact of Printing, 1450–1800*. Trans. David Gerard. London: NLB, 1976.

Feinstein, Sascha, and Yusef Komunyakaa, eds. *The Jazz Anthology*. Bloomington: Indiana UP, 1991.

Feld, Steven. *Kaluli Weeping and Song*. LP. Kassel, Ger.: Musicaphon, 1987.

———. *Sound and Sentiment: Birds, Weeping, Poetics, and Song in Kaluli Expression*. Philadelphia: U of Pennsylvania P, 1982.

Felson-Rubin, Nancy. *Regarding Penelope: From Character to Poetics*. Princeton: Princeton UP, 1994.

Ferrante, Joan, trans. *Guillaume d'Orange: Four Twelfth-Century Epics*. New York: Columbia UP, 1974.

Feuser, Willfried. Rev. of *Comparative Literature as a Distinct Discipline: A Superfluity*, by S. Ige. *Research in African Literatures* 19 (1988): 377–80.

Fine, Elizabeth C. *The Folklore Text: From Performance to Print*. Bloomington: Indiana UP, 1994.

Fine, Gary Alan. *Manufacturing Tales*. Knoxville: U of Tennessee P, 1992.

Finnegan, Ruth. *Literacy and Orality: Studies in the Technology of Communication*. Oxford: Blackwell, 1988.

———. *Oral Poetry: Its Nature, Significance, and Social Context*. Cambridge: Cambridge UP, 1977. Rev. ed. Bloomington: Indiana UP, 1992.

Fish, Stanley. *Is There a Text in This Class? The Authority of Interpretive Communities*. Cambridge: Harvard UP, 1980.

Foley, John Miles. "Folk Literature." *Scholarly Editing: A Guide to Research*. Ed. D. C. Greetham. New York: MLA, 1995. 600–26.

———. "*Guslar* and *Aoidos*: Traditional Register in South Slavic and Homeric Epic." *Transactions of the American Philological Association* 126 (1996): 11–41.

———. *Immanent Art: From Structure to Meaning in Traditional Oral Epic*. Bloomington: Indiana UP, 1991.

———. *Oral-Formulaic Theory and Research: An Introduction and Annotated*

Bibliography. New York: Garland, 1992. Updated version at ⟨http://www.missouri.edu/~csottime⟩.

———. "Oral Tradition and Its Implications." *A New Companion to Homer.* Ed. Ian Morris and Barry B. Powell. Leiden: Brill, 1997. 146–73.

———. *The Singer of Tales in Performance.* Bloomington: Indiana UP, 1995.

———. *The Theory of Oral Composition: History and Methodology.* Bloomington: Indiana UP, 1992.

———. *Traditional Oral Epic: The* Odyssey, Beowulf, *and the Serbo-Croatian Return Song.* Berkeley: U of California P, 1993.

Foley, John Miles, and Barbara Kerewsky-Halpern. "*Udovica Jana*: A Case Study of an Oral Performance." *Slavonic and East European Review* 54 (1976): 11–23.

Folkways: The Original Vision: Recordings by Woody Guthrie and Leadbelly, 1940–47. LP and CD. Smithsonian Folkways Records SF 40001. Distr. Rounder. Cambridge, 1989.

Folkways: A Vision Shared: A Tribute to Woody Guthrie and Leadbelly. LP and CD. Columbia OC 44034. New York, 1988.

Foote, Peter. "Sagnaskemtan: Reykjahólar 1119." *Saga-Book of the Viking Society* 14 (1955–56): 226–39. Rpt. with supp. in *Aurvandilstá: Norse Studies* Ed. Foote. Odense, Den.: Odense UP, 1984. 65–83.

The Forest Book of the Ramayana of Kampan. Trans. George L. Hart and Hank Heifetz. Berkeley: U of California P, 1988.

Foster, Deborah. "The Pauper's Daughter." Scheub, *African Storyteller* 448–71.

Fowler, David C. "Ballads." *A Manual of the Writings in Middle English.* Ed. Jonathan Severs and Albert E. Hartung. Vol. 6. New Haven: Acad. of Arts and Sciences, 1980. 1753–1808, 2019–70.

———. *A Literary History of the Popular Ballad.* Durham: Duke UP, 1968.

Fox, Everett, trans. *The Torah of Moses: Genesis, Exodus, Leviticus, Numbers, Deuteronomy.* New York: Schocken, 1995.

Fox, Jennifer. "The Creator Gods: Romantic Nationalism and the Engenderment of Women in Folklore." Hollis, Pershing, and Young 29–40.

Foxfire: Twenty-Five Years. Ed. Eliot Wigginton. New York: Anchor, 1991.

Franklin, C. L., and Jeff Todd Titon. *Give Me This Mountain: Life History and Selected Sermons.* Urbana: U of Texas P, 1989.

Frere, Mary. *Old Deccan Days; or, Hindu Fairy Legends Current in Southern India.* 1868. New York: Dover, 1967.

Freud, Sigmund. *Totem and Taboo.* Trans. James Strachey. New York: Norton, 1950.

Friedman, Albert B. "The Formulaic Improvisation Theory of Ballad Tradition: A Counter-Statement." *Journal of American Folklore* 74 (1961): 113–15.

———. "The Oral-Formulaic Theory of Balladry: A Re-rebuttal." Porter 215–40.

———, ed. *The Viking Book of Folk Ballads of the English-Speaking World.* 1956. New York: Viking, 1982.

Fries, Maureen, and Jeannie Watson, eds. *Approaches to Teaching the Arthurian Tradition*. Approaches to Teaching World Literature 40. New York: MLA, 1992.

Fry, Donald K. "The Hero on the Beach in 'Finnsburh.'" *Neuphilologische Mitteilungen* 67 (1966): 27–31.

———. *Norse Sagas Translated into English: A Bibliography*. New York: AMS, 1980.

———. "Old English Formulaic Statistics." *In Geardagum* 3 Dec. 1979: 1–6.

Fugard, Athol. *Statements: Two Workshop Productions*. 1974. Oxford: Oxford UP, 1986.

Gaines, Ernest. *The Autobiography of Miss Jane Pittman*. New York: Bantam, 1971.

Gates, Henry Louis, Jr. *The Signifying Monkey: A Theory of African-American Criticism*. New York: Oxford UP, 1988.

Gates, Henry Louis, Jr., and Nellie Y. McKay, eds. *The Norton Anthology of African American Literature*. New York: Norton, 1997.

Geertz, Clifford. "'From the Native's Point of View': On the Nature of Anthropological Understanding." Geertz, *Local Knowledge* 55–70.

———. *The Interpretation of Cultures*. New York: Basic, 1973.

———. *Local Knowledge*. New York: Basic, 1983.

———. "Thick Description: Toward an Interpretive Theory of Culture." Geertz, *Interpretation* 3–33.

Genovese, Eugene D. *Roll Jordan Roll: The World the Slave Made*. New York: Vintage, 1974.

Gentleman, Hugh, and Susan Swift. *Scotland's Travelling People: Problems and Solutions*. Edinburgh: HMSO, 1971.

Georges, Robert. "Toward an Understanding of Storytelling Events." *Journal of American Folklore* 82 (1969): 313–28.

Gerould, Gordon Hall. *The Ballad of Tradition*. New York: Oxford UP, 1957.

Gibaldi, Joseph, ed. *Approaches to Teaching Chaucer's* Canterbury Tales. Approaches to Teaching World Literature 1. New York: MLA, 1980.

Gilbert, Sandra M., and Susan Gubar. *The Madwoman in the Attic: The Woman Writer and the Nineteenth-Century Imagination*. New Haven: Yale UP, 1979.

Girardot, N. J. "Initiation and Meaning in the Tale of Snow White and the Seven Dwarfs." *Journal of American Folklore* 90 (1977): 274–300.

Glassie, Henry. *All Silver and No Brass: An Irish Christmas Mumming*. Bloomington: Indiana UP, 1975.

———. *Passing the Time in Ballymenone: Culture and History of an Ulster Community*. Philadelphia: U of Pennsylvania P, 1982. Bloomington: Indiana UP, 1995.

Goffman, Erving. *Frame Analysis*. New York: Harper, 1974.

Goldin, Fredrick, ed. and trans. *Lyrics of the Troubadours and Trouvères*. Gloucester: Smith, 1983.

———, trans. *The Song of Roland*. New York: Norton, 1978.

Goody, Jack. *The Domestication of the Savage Mind*. Cambridge: Cambridge UP, 1977.

———. *The Interface between the Written and the Oral*. New York: Cambridge UP, 1987.

———. *The Logic of Writing and the Organization of Society*. Cambridge: Cambridge UP, 1986.

Gossen, Gary H. "Chamula Genres of Verbal Behavior." *Journal of American Folklore* 84 (1971): 145–68. Rpt. in Bauman, *Verbal Art* 81–115.

Gouiran, Gérard, and Robert Lafont, eds. *Roland occitan*. Paris: 10/18, 1991.

Gower, Herschel. "Jeannie Robertson: Portrait of a Traditional Singer." *Scottish Studies* 12 (1968): 113–26.

———. "Wanted: The Singer's Autobiography and Critical Reflections." *Tennessee Folklore Society Bulletin* 39 (1973): 1–7.

Graham, Laura. *Performing Dreams: Discourses of Immortality among the Xavante of Central Brazil*. Austin: U of Texas P, 1995.

Graham, William A. *Beyond the Written Word: Oral Aspects of Scripture in the History of Religion*. Cambridge: Cambridge UP, 1987.

Graves, Donald H., and Bonnie S. Sunstein. *Portfolio Portraits*. Portsmouth: Boynton-Heinemann, 1992.

Green, Archie. "A Folk Music Exhibition." Porter 97–127.

Green, Rayna. "'It's Okay Once You Get It past the Teeth' and Other Feminist Paradigms for Folklore Studies." Hollis, Pershing, and Young 1–8.

———. "Magnolias Grow in Dirt: The Bawdy Lore of Southern Women." *Radical Teacher: A News Journal of Socialist Theory and Practice* 6 (1977): 26–31.

Greenfield, Stanley B. "The Formulaic Expression of the Theme of 'Exile' in Anglo-Saxon Poetry." *Speculum* 30 (1955): 200–06.

———, trans. *A Readable* Beowulf: *The Old English Epic Newly Translated*. Carbondale: Southern Illinois UP, 1982.

Gregory, Steward, ed. and trans. *Tristan*. By Thomas of Britain. New York: Garland, 1991.

Grettir's Saga. Trans. Denton Fox and Hermann Pálsson. Toronto: U of Toronto P, 1974.

Grinnell, George Bird. *Blackfoot Lodge Tales*. Lincoln: U of Nebraska P, 1962.

Groden, Michael, and Martin Kreiswirth, eds. *The Johns Hopkins Guide to Literary Theory and Criticism*. Baltimore: Johns Hopkins UP, 1994.

Gummere, Francis B. *Germanic Origins: A Study in Primitive Culture*. New York: Scribner's, 1892.

Gumperz, John. *Discourse Strategies*. Cambridge: Cambridge UP, 1982.

Gunkel, Hermann. *The Legends of Genesis: The Biblical Sagas and History*. Trans. W. H. Carruth. 1907. New York: Schocken, 1964.

Gunn, David M. "Narrative Inconsistency and the Oral Dictated Text in the Homeric Epic." *American Journal of Philology* 91 (1970): 192–203.

Gutman, Amy, ed. *Multiculturalism*. Princeton: Princeton UP, 1994.

Haboucha, Reginetta. *Types and Motifs of the Judeo-Spanish Folktales*. New York: Garland, 1992.

Haddawy, Husain, trans. *The Arabian Nights*. New York: Norton, 1990.

———. *The Arabian Nights II: "Sindbad" and Other Popular Stories*. New York: Norton, 1995.

Haley, Alex. *Roots*. New York: Doubleday, 1976.

Halpern, Joel. *A Serbian Village*. New York: Harper, 1967.

Halpern, Joel, and Barbara Kerewsky-Halpern. *A Serbian Village in Historical Perspective*. New York: Holt, Rinehart, 1972.

Halpert, Herbert. "American Regional Folklore." *Journal of American Folklore* 60 (1947): 355–66.

Hamilton, Martha, and Mitch Weiss. *Children Tell Stories: A Teaching Guide*. Katonah: Owen, 1990.

Hamilton, Virginia. *The People Could Fly: American Black Folktales*. New York: Knopf, 1985.

Hand, Wayland, ed. *American Folk Medicine: A Symposium*. Berkeley: U of California P, 1976.

Handelman, Don. "Inside-out, Outside-in: Concealment and Revelation in Newfoundland Christmas Mumming." Bruner 247–77.

Handler, Richard, and Jocelyn Linnekin. "Tradition, Genuine or Spurious." *Journal of American Folklore* 97 (1984): 273–90.

Hanning, Robert, and Joan Ferrante, trans. *The Lais of Marie de France*. New York: Dutton, 1978.

Harker, Dave. *Fakesong: The Manufacture of British "Folksong," 1700 to the Present Day*. Keynes: Open UP, 1985.

Harris, Joseph. "Saga as Historical Novel." *Structure and Meaning in Old Norse Literature: New Approaches to Textual Analysis and Literary Criticism*. Ed. John Lindow, Lars Lönnroth, and Gerd Wolfgang Weber. Odense, Den.: Odense UP, 1986. 187–219.

Harris, Trudier. *Fiction and Folklore: The Novels of Toni Morrison*. Knoxville: U of Tennessee P, 1991.

Harrison, Regina. *Signs, Songs, and Memory in the Andes: Translating Quechua Language and Culture*. Austin: U of Texas P, 1989.

Harrison, Robert, ed. and trans. *Gallic Salt: Eighteen Fabliaux Translated from the Old French*. Berkeley: U of California P, 1974.

Hasan-Rokem, Galit, and Alan Dundes, eds. *The Wandering Jew: Essays in the Interpretation of a Christian Legend*. Bloomington: Indiana UP, 1986.

Havelock, Eric A. *The Muse Learns to Write: Reflections on Orality and Literacy from Antiquity to the Present*. New Haven: Yale UP, 1988.

———. *Preface to Plato*. Cambridge: Harvard UP, 1987.

Head, Thomas, gen. ed. *Medieval Christian Hagiography: A Sourcebook*. New York: Garland, forthcoming.

Heisley, Michael. *Annotated Bibliography of Chicano Folklore from the Southwestern United States*. Los Angeles: Center for the Study of Comparative Folklore and Mythology, UCLA, 1977.

Henderson, Hamish, ed. *The Muckle Sangs: Classic Scots Ballads*. Scottish Tradition 5. LP. Tangent TNGM 119/D. London, 1975.

Henderson, Stephen. *Understanding the New Black Poetry: Black Speech and Music as Poetic References*. New York: Morrow, 1973.

Hendricks, Janet Wall. *To Drink of Death: The Narrative of a Shuar Warrior*. Tucson: U of Arizona P, 1993.

Herrera-Sobek, María. *The Mexican Corrido: A Feminist Analysis*. Bloomington: Indiana UP, 1990.

———. *Northward Bound: The Mexican Immigrant Experience in Ballad and Song*. Bloomington: Indiana UP, 1993.

Herskovits, Frances, and Melville Herskovits. *Dahomean Narrative*. Evanston: Northwestern UP, 1958.

Herskovits, Melville J. *Man and His Works: The Science of Cultural Anthropology*. New York: Knopf, 1948.

Hesiod. Theogony *and* Works and Days. Trans. and introd. M. L. West. Oxford: Oxford UP, 1988.

Hieatt, Constance B., Brian Shaw, and Duncan Macrae-Gibson. *Beginning Old English: An Elementary Grammar for Use with Computerized Exercises*. Old English Subsidia 21. Kalamazoo: Medieval Inst., 1994.

Hill, Jonathan. *Keepers of the Sacred Chants: The Poetics of Ritual Power in an Amazonian Society*. Tucson: U of Arizona P, 1993.

Hill, Patricia Liggins, et al., eds. *Call and Response: The Riverside Anthology of the African American Literary Tradition*. Boston: Houghton, 1998.

Hobsbawm, Eric. *Bandits*. New York: Dell, 1969.

Holbek, Bengt. *Interpretation of Fairy Tales: Danish Folklore in a European Perspective*. Folklore Fellows Communications 239. Helsinki: Suomalainen Tiedeakatemia, Academia Scientiarum Fennica, 1987.

———. "The Language of Fairy Tales." *Nordic Folklore: Recent Studies*. Ed. Reimund Kvideland et al. Bloomington: Indiana UP, 1989. 40–62.

Hollis, Susan Tower, Linda Pershing, and M. Jane Young, eds. *Feminist Theory and the Study of Folklore*. Urbana: U of Illinois P, 1993.

Holloway, John, and Joan Black, eds. *Later English Broadside Ballads*. London: Routledge, 1975.

The Holy Bible: New Revised Standard Version. New York: Amer. Bible Soc., 1989.

Hornberger, Nancy H. "Verse Analysis of 'The Condor and the Shepherdess.'" Swann, *On the Translation* 441–69.

Hrafnkel's Saga and Other Stories. Trans. Hermann Pálsson. Harmondsworth, Eng.: Penguin, 1971.

Hudson, Arthur Palmer, ed. *Folksongs of Mississippi*. Chapel Hill: U of North Carolina P, 1936.

Hughes, Langston. *The Voice of Langston Hughes: Selected Poetry and Prose Read by the Author*. Washington: Smithsonian Folkways, 1995.

Hult, David F. "The Limits of Mime(sis): Notes toward a Generic Revision of Medieval Theater." *L'Esprit Créateur* 23.1 (1983): 49–63.

Hurreiz, Sayyid Hamid. "Manasir and Ja'aliyyin Tales." *African Folklore*. Ed. Richard M. Dorson. Bloomington: Indiana UP, 1972. 367–86.

Hurston, Zora Neale. "High John de Conquer." *Mother Wit from the Laughing Barrel*. Ed. Alan Dundes. Englewood Cliffs: Prentice, 1973. 541–48.

———. *Mules and Men*. 1935. New York: Harper-Perennial, 1994.

————. *Their Eyes Were Watching God*. 1934. Urbana: U of Illinois P, 1979.

Hustvedt, Sigurd Bernhard. *Ballad Books and Ballad Men*. Cambridge: Harvard UP, 1930.

Hymes, Dell. "Breakthrough into Performance." Ben-Amos and Goldstein 11–74.

————. "Folklore's Nature and the Sun's Myth." *Journal of American Folklore* 88 (1975): 345–69.

————. *Foundations in Sociolinguistics: An Ethnographic Perspective*. Philadelphia: U of Pennsylvania P, 1974.

————. "The General Epistle of James." *International Journal of the Sociology of Language* 62 (1986): 75–103.

————. *"In Vain I Tried to Tell You": Essays in Native American Ethnopoetics*. Philadelphia: U of Pennsylvania P, 1981.

————. "Objectives and Concepts of Linguistic Anthropology." *The Teaching of Anthropology*. Ed. David G. Mandelbaum, Gabriel W. Lasker, and Ethel M. Albert. Memoir 94. Washington: Amer. Anthropological Assn., 1963. 275–302.

————. "Particle, Pause, and Pattern in American Indian Narrative Verse." *American Indian Culture and Research Journal* 4 (1980): 7–51.

————. "Some North Pacific Coast Poems: A Problem in Anthropological Philology." *American Anthropologist* 67 (1965): 316–41.

————. "Use All There Is to Use." Swann, *On the Translation* 83–124.

Hymes, Virginia. "Warm Springs Sahaptin Narrative Analysis." *Native American Discourse: Poetics and Rhetoric*. Ed. Joel Sherzer and Anthony C. Woodbury. Cambridge: Cambridge UP, 1987. 62–102.

Irving, Edward B., Jr. *Rereading* Beowulf. Philadelphia: U of Pennsylvania P, 1989.

Irwin, Bonnie D. "What's in a Frame? The Textualization of Traditional Storytelling." *Oral Tradition* 10 (1995): 27–53.

Ives, Edward D. *Joe Scott: The Woodsman-Songmaker*. Urbana: U of Illinois P, 1978.

————. *Larry Gorman: The Man Who Made the Songs*. Bloomington: Indiana UP, 1964.

————. *Lawrence Doyle: The Farmer-Poet of Prince Edward Island*. Orono: U of Maine P, 1971.

Jacobs, Melville. *The Content and Style of an Oral Literature: Clackamas Chinook Myths and Tales*. New York: Wenner-Gren Foundation for Anthropological Research, 1959.

Jakobson, Roman. "Closing Statement: Linguistics and Poetics." *Style in Language*. Ed. Thomas A. Sebeok. New York: Wiley, 1960. 350–77.

James, Thelma G. "The English and Scottish Popular Ballads of Francis J. Child." *Journal of American Folklore* 46 (1933): 51–68. Rpt. in *The Critics and the Ballad*. Ed. MacEdward Leach and Tristram P. Coffin. Carbondale: Southern Illinois UP, 1961. 12–19.

Janelli, Roger, and Kim Dawn-Hee Janelli. *Ancestor Worship and Korean Society*. Stanford: Stanford UP, 1982.

Jansson, Sven B. F. *Runes in Sweden*. Trans. Peter Foote. Stockholm: Gidlunds, 1987.

Jayyusi, Lena, trans. *The Adventures of Sayf Ben Dhi Yazan: An Arab Folk Epic*. Bloomington: Indiana UP, 1996.

Jewett, Robert. "Romans as an Ambassadorial Letter." *Interpretation* 36 (1982): 5–20.

Jews and the Media. Ed. Jeffrey Shandler. Spec. issue of *Jewish Folklore and Ethnology Review* 16.1 (1994): 1–69.

Johnson, Clifton H., ed. *God Struck Me Dead: Religious Conversion Experiences and Autobiographies of Ex-Slaves*. Philadelphia: Pilgrim, 1969.

Johnson, David, Andrew J. Nathan, and Evelyn S. Rawski, eds. *Popular Culture in Late Imperial China*. Berkeley: U of California P, 1985.

Johnson, James Weldon, Aaron Douglas, and C. B. Falls, eds. *God's Trombones: Seven Negro Sermons in Verse*. New York: Penguin, 1990.

Johnson, John William, trans. *The Epic of Son-Jara: A West African Tradition*. By Fa-Digi Sisòkò. Bloomington: Indiana UP, 1986.

Johnson, John William, Thomas A. Hale, and Stephen Belcher, eds. *Oral Epics from Africa: Vibrant Voices from a Vast Continent*. Bloomington: Indiana UP, 1997.

Jones, James H. "Commonplace and Memorization in the Oral Tradition of the English and Scottish Popular Ballads." *Journal of American Folklore* 74 (1961): 97–112.

Jones, Steven Swann. *The Fairy Tale: The Magic Mirror of Imagination*. New York: Twayne, 1995.

———. "Fertile Imagery in the Legend of Santa Claus." *Papers in Comparative Studies* 2 (1982–83): 39–60.

Jones, Suzi, and Jarold Ramsey, eds. *The Stories We Tell: An Anthology of Oregon Folk Literature*. Corvallis: Oregon State UP, 1994.

Jordan, Rosan A., and Susan J. Kalčik, eds. *Women's Folklore, Women's Culture*. Philadelphia: U of Pennsylvania P, 1985.

Jost, François. *Introduction to Comparative Literature*. Indianapolis: Pegasus, 1974.

Kakridis, Ioannis. *Homeric Researches*. Lund, Swed.: Gleerup, 1989.

Karadžić, Vuk Stefanović. *Srpske narodne pjesme*. Vienna, 1841–62. Belgrade: Nolit, 1975.

Kardiner, Abram. *The Individual and His Society*. New York: Columbia UP, 1939.

Katz, Israel J. "The Traditional Folk Music of Spain: Explorations and Perspectives." *Yearbook of the International Folk Music Council* 6 (1974): 64–85.

Kay, Matthew W. *The Index of the Milman Parry Collection, 1933–1935: Heroic Songs, Conversations, and Stories*. New York: Garland, 1995.

Keene, Donald, trans. *Major Plays of Chikamatsu*. New York: Columbia UP, 1961.

Kelber, Werner. "Language, Memory, and Sense Perception in the Religious and Technological Culture of Antiquity and the Middle Ages." *Oral Tradition* 10 (1995): 409–50.

———. *The Oral and the Written Gospel*. Philadelphia: Fortress, 1983. Rev. ed. Bloomington: Indiana UP, 1997.

———. Personal correspondence to John Foley. 11 Dec. 1996.

Kellogg, Robert. "What Is a Saga?" *Sagnaþing helgað Jónasi Kristjánssyni sjötugum 10. apríl 1994*. vol. 2. Reykjavík: Hið Íslenska Bókmenntafélag, 1994. 497–503.

Kendall, Laurel, and Griffin Dix, eds. *Religion and Ritual in Korean Society*. Berkeley: U of California P, 1987.

Kendall, Laurel, Mark Peterson, and Martina Deuchler, eds. *Korean Women: View from the Inner Room*. New Haven: East Rock, 1983.

Kendall, Peter. "Urban Yarn of 'Mall Slasher' Just Won't Die." *Chicago Tribune*. 10 Oct. 1991. Chicagoland sec. 1+.

Kennedy, Peter. *Folksongs of Britain and Ireland*. London: Cassell, 1975.

Kennedy, Peter, and Alan Lomax, eds. *The Folksongs of Britain*. 10 vols. LP. Caedmon, TC 1142–51, 1961–67.

Kerewsky-Halpern, Barbara. "Text and Context in Serbian Ritual Lament." *Canadian-American Slavic Studies* 15 (1981): 52–60.

Key, Mary Ritchie, ed. *Language Change in South American Indian Languages*. Philadelphia: U of Pennsylvania P, 1991.

Kiernan, Kevin S. Beowulf *and the Beowulf Manuscript*. New Brunswick: Rutgers UP, 1981.

Kingston, Maxine Hong. *The Woman Warrior: Memoirs of a Girlhood among Ghosts*. 1976. New York: Knopf, 1989.

Kinkade, M. Dale. "Bluejay and His Sister." *Recovering the Word: Essays on Native American Literature*. Ed. Brian Swann and Arnold Krupat. Berkeley: U of California P, 1987. 255–96.

Kirshenblatt-Gimblett, Barbara. "Bibliographic Survey of the Literature on Speech Play and Related Subjects." *Speech Play*. Ed. Kirshenblatt-Gimblett. Philadelphia: U of Pennsylvania P, 1976. 179–223.

———. "The Concept and Varieties of Narrative Performance in Eastern European Jewish Culture." *Explorations in the Ethnography of Speaking*. Ed. Richard Bauman and Joel Sherzer. New York: Cambridge UP, 1974. 283–308.

Klaeber, Frederick, ed. Beowulf *and* The Fight at Finnsburg. 3rd ed. Boston: Heath, 1950.

Kluckhohn, Clyde, and William H. Kelly. "The Concept of Culture." *The Science of Man in the World Crisis*. Ed. Ralph Linton. New York: Columbia UP, 1945. 78–106.

Knight, Douglas A., and Gene M. Tucker, eds. *The Hebrew Bible and Its Modern Interpreters*. Chicago: Scholars, 1985.

Kodish, Debora. "Absent Gender, Silent Encounter." Hollis, Pershing, and Young 41–50.

Koljević, Svetozar. *The Epic in the Making*. Oxford: Clarendon, 1980.

Koschmann, J. Victor, Keibo Oiwa, and Shinji Yamashita, eds. *International Perspectives on Yanagita Kunio and Japanese Folklore Studies*. Ithaca: China-Japan Program, Cornell U, 1985.

Koskoff, Ellen, ed. *Women and Music in Cross-Cultural Perspective*. Urbana: U of Illinois P, 1989.

Kraul, Edward Garcia, and Judith Beatty, eds. *The Weeping Woman: Encounters with La Llorona*. Santa Fe: Word Process, 1988.

Kristjánsson, Jónas. *Eddas and Sagas: Iceland's Medieval Literature*. Trans. Peter Foote. Reykjavík: Hið Íslenska Bókmenntafélag, 1988.

Lacy, Norris J., ed. and trans. *Romance of Tristan*. By Béroul. New York: Garland, 1989.

Lang, Andrew. *Myth, Ritual, and Religion*. 1887. 2 vols. New York: AMS, 1968.

Langen, Toby C. S. "Translating Form in Classical American Indian Literature." Swann, *On the Translation* 191–207.

La Pin, Deirdre. "A Girl Marries a Monkey." Abrahams, *African Folktales* 336–43.

———. "Monkey Steals a Drum." Abrahams, *African Folktales* 45–55.

Larson, Jennifer. *Greek Heroine Cults*. Madison: U of Wisconsin P, 1995.

Lattimore, Richmond, trans. *The Four Gospels and the Revelation*. New York: Farrar, 1979.

Laws, G. Malcolm. *American Balladry from British Broadsides*. Philadelphia: Amer. Folklore Soc., 1957.

———. *Native American Balladry: A Descriptive Study and a Bibliographical Syllabus*. Rev. ed. Philadelphia: Amer. Folklore Soc., 1964.

Laxdæla Saga. Trans. Magnus Magnusson and Hermann Pálsson. Harmondsworth, Eng.: Penguin, 1969.

Leach, MacEdward. *The Ballad Book*. New York: Harper, 1955.

Lester, Julius. *Black Folktales*. New York: Baron, 1969.

Levine, Lawrence. *Black Culture and Black Consciousness: Afro-American Folk Thought from Slavery to Freedom*. Oxford: Oxford UP, 1977.

Lévi-Strauss, Claude. *From Honey to Ashes*. Vol. 2 of Lévi-Strauss, *Introduction*.

———. *Introduction to a Science of Mythology*. 4 vols. Trans. John Weightman and Doreen Weightman. New York: Harper, 1969–81.

———. *The Naked Man*. Vol. 4 of Lévi-Strauss, *Introduction*.

———. *The Origin of Table Manners*. Vol. 3 of Lévi-Strauss, *Introduction*.

———. *The Raw and the Cooked*. Vol. 1 of Lévi-Strauss, *Introduction*.

———. "The Story of Asdiwal." *The Structural Study of Myth and Totemism*. Ed. Edmund Leach. London: Tavistock, 1967. 1–47.

Levy, Ian H., trans. *The Ten Thousand Leaves: A Translation of Man'Yōshū, Japan's Premier Anthology of Japanese Poetry*. Vol. 1. Princeton: Princeton UP, 1981.

Li, Shujiang, and Karl W. Luckert. *Mythology and Folklore of the Hui: A Muslim Chinese People*. New York: State U of New York P, 1994.

Lim, Shirley Geok-lin, ed. *Approaches to Teaching Kingston's* The Woman Warrior. Approaches to Teaching World Lit. 39. New York: MLA, 1991.

Lindahl, Carl. *Earnest Games: Folkloric Patterns in the* Canterbury Tales. Bloomington: Indiana UP, 1987.

———. "The Festive Form of *The Canterbury Tales. ELH* 52 (1985): 531–74.

Lindfors, Bernth, ed. *Approaches to Teaching Achebe's* Things Fall Apart. Approaches to Teaching World Lit. 37. New York: MLA, 1991.

Lindow, John. *Swedish Legends and Folktales.* Berkeley: U of California P, 1978.

Livo, Norma J., and Sandra A. Rietz. *Storytelling: Process and Practice.* Littleton: Libs. Unlimited, 1986.

Lockwood, Yvonne R. *Text and Context: Folksong in a Bosnian Muslim Village.* Columbus: Slavica, 1983.

Lodge, David. *The Modes of Modern Writing: Metaphor, Metonymy, and the Typology of Modern Literature.* Ithaca: Cornell UP, 1977.

Lomax, Alan. "Appeal for Cultural Equity." *Journal of Communication* 27 (1977): 125–38.

———. *Folk Song Style and Culture.* With Edwin E. Erickson. AAAS Pub. 88. Washington: Amer. Assn. for the Advancement of Science, 1968.

———. *The Folk Songs of North America in the English Language.* Garden City: Doubleday, 1960.

Lönnrot, Elias. *Kalevala.* 1835. Trans. Francis P. Magoun. Cambridge: Harvard UP, 1963.

Lönnroth, Lars. Njáls Saga: *A Critical Introduction.* Berkeley: U of California P, 1976.

Lord, Albert Bates. *Epic Singers and Oral Tradition.* Ithaca: Cornell UP, 1991.

———. "Homer as Oral Poet." *Harvard Studies in Classical Philology* 72 (1968): 1–46.

———. *The Singer of Tales.* Harvard Studies in Comparative Lit. 24. 1960. Cambridge: Harvard UP, 1981. New York: Atheneum, 1968 et seq.

———. *The Singer Resumes the Tale.* Ithaca: Cornell UP, 1995.

———. "Yugoslav Epic Folk Poetry." *Journal of the International Folk Music Council* 3 (1951): 57–61. Rpt. in Dundes, *Study* 265–68.

Lovell, John, Jr. *Black Song: The Forge and the Flame.* New York: Macmillan, 1972.

Low, D. H., trans. *The Ballads of Marko Kraljević.* Westport: Greenwood, 1968.

Lutgendorf, Philip. *The Life of a Text: Performing the* Ramcaritmanas *of Tulsidas.* Berkeley: U of California P, 1991.

Lüthi, Max. *The European Folktale: Form and Nature.* Trans. John D. Niles. Bloomington: Indiana UP, 1982.

Lutz, Catherine. "Emotion, Thought, and Estrangement: Emotion as a Cultural Category." *Cultural Anthropology* 1 (1986): 287–309.

Lyle, E. B. "The Ballad *Tam Lin* and Traditional Tales of Recovery from the Fairy Troop." *Studies in Scottish Literature* 6 (1969): 175–85.

———. "The Opening of 'Tam Lin.'" *Journal of American Folklore* 83 (1970): 33–43.

Lyons, M. C. *The Arabian Epic: Heroic and Oral Storytelling.* 3 vols. Cambridge: Cambridge UP, 1995.

Ma, Y. W., and Joseph S. M. Lau, eds. *Traditional Chinese Stories: Themes and Variations*. New York: Columbia UP, 1978.

MacColl, Ewan, and Peggy Seeger. *The Long Harvest: Some Traditional Ballads in Their English, Scottish, and North American Variants*. LP. Argo ZDA 66–75. 1967–68.

MacDonald, Margaret Read. *The Storyteller's Start-Up Book*. Little Rock: August, 1993.

Mack, Maynard, ed. *Anthology of World Masterpieces: Expanded Edition*. 6th ed. 2 vols. New York: Norton, 1995.

Mack, Robert L., ed. *Arabian Nights' Entertainment*. Oxford: Oxford UP, 1995.

Macrorie, Ken. *The I-Search Paper*. Portsmouth: Boynton-Heinemann, 1988.

———. *Uptaught*. New York: Hayden, 1970.

Magoun, Francis Peabody, Jr. "The Theme of the Beasts of Battle in Anglo-Saxon Poetry." *Neuphilologische Mitteilungen* 56 (1955): 81–90.

The Mahabharata. Books 1–5. Trans. J. A. B. van Buitenen. Chicago: U of Chicago P, 1980–83.

Mahdi, Muhsin, ed. *The* Thousand and One Nights (Alf Layla wa-Layla) *from the Earliest Known Sources*. Leiden: Brill, 1984.

Mair, Victor, ed. *The Columbia Anthology of Traditional Chinese Literature*. New York: Columbia UP, 1994.

———. *Tang Transformation Texts: A Study of the Buddhist Contribution to the Rise of Vernacular Fiction and Drama in China*. Cambridge: Harvard UP, 1989.

Malherbe, Abraham. *Paul and the Thessalonians*. Philadelphia: Fortress, 1987.

Malinowski, Bronislaw. *Argonauts of the Western Pacific*. 1922. New York: Dutton, 1961.

———. *Coral Gardens and Their Magic II: The Language of Magic and Gardening*. 1935. New York: Dover, 1978.

Mallery, Garrick. "Sign Language among North American Indians Compared with That among Other Peoples and Deaf Mutes." *First Annual Report of the Bureau of American Ethnology*. Washington GPO, 1879–80. 263–549.

Malone, Kemp, ed. *The Nowell Codex: British Museum Cotton Vitellius A. xv. Second Manuscript*. Early English Mss. in Facsimile 12. Copenhagen: Rosenkilde, 1963.

Malory, Sir Thomas. *Le Mort D'Arthur*. New York: Random, 1993.

Manelis Klein, Harriet, and Louisa Stark, eds. *South American Indian Languages: Retrospect and Prospect*. Austin: U of Texas P, 1985.

Manimekalai. Trans. Alain Daniélou. New York: New Directions, 1989.

Marie, Sister Joseph. "The Role of the Church and the Folk in the Development of the Early Drama in New Mexico." Diss. U of Pennsylvania, 1948.

Marjanović, Luka. *Hrvatske narodne pjesme*. Zagreb: Matica Hrvatska, 1898.

Martin, Richard P. "Hesiod, Odysseus, and the Instruction of Princes." *Transactions of the American Philological Association* 114 (1984): 29–48.

———. *The Language of Heroes: Speech and Performance in the* Iliad. Ithaca: Cornell UP, 1989.

————. "Telemachus and the Last Hero Song." *Colby Quarterly* 29 (1993): 222–40.

Mason, Eugene, trans. Aucassin and Nicolette *and Other Mediaeval Romances and Legends*. London: Dent, 1910.

Mathers, Edward Powys, trans. *Thousand Nights and One Night*. 4 vols. New York: Routledge, 1995.

Matthias, John, and Vladeta Vučković, trans. *The Battle of Kosovo*. Athens: Swallow, 1987.

May, Rollo. *The Cry for Myth*. New York: Norton, 1991.

McCarthy, Terence. "Malory and the Alliterative Tradition." *Studies in Malory*. Ed. James W. Spisak. Kalamazoo: Medieval Inst., 1985. 53–85.

McCarthy, William Bernard. *The Ballad Matrix: Personality, Milieu, and the Oral Tradition*. Bloomington: Indiana UP, 1990.

McCullough, Helen Craig, trans. *Kokin Wakashū': The First Imperial Anthology of Japanese Poetry, with* Tosa Nikki *and* Shinsen Waka. Stanford: Stanford UP, 1985.

————, trans. *The Tale of the Heike*. Introd. McCullough. Stanford: Stanford UP, 1988.

McDougall, Bonnie S., ed. *Popular Chinese Literature and Performing Arts in the People's Republic of China, 1949–1979*. Berkeley: U of California P, 1984.

McDowell, John H. *Children's Riddling*. Bloomington: Indiana UP, 1979.

————. "The Community-Building Mission of Kamsá Ritual Language." *Journal of Folklore Research* 27 (1990): 67–84.

————. *Sayings of the Ancestors: The Spiritual Life of the Sibundoy Indians*. Lexington: UP of Kentucky, 1989.

————. *"So Wise Were Our Elders": Mythic Narratives of the Kamsá*. Lexington: UP of Kentucky, 1994.

McGillivray, Murray. *Memorization and the Transmission of the Middle English Romances*. Albert Bates Lord Studies in Oral Tradition 5. New York: Garland, 1990.

McLoughlin, T. O. "Reading Zimbabwean Comic Strips." *Research in African Literatures* 20 (1989): 217–41.

McLuhan, Marshall. *The Gutenberg Galaxy*. New York: Signet, 1969.

Meale, Carol M., ed. *Readings in Medieval English Romance*. Cambridge: Brewer, 1994.

Medieval Scandinavia: An Encyclopedia. Ed. Phillip Pulsiano et al. New York: Garland, 1993.

Medjedović, Avdo. *The Wedding of Smailagić Meho*. Ed. and trans. Albert B. Lord. Cambridge: Harvard UP, 1974. Vol. 3 of *Serbo-Croatian Heroic Songs*.

Menéndez Pidal, Ramón. *Romancero hispánico: Hispano-portugués, americano y sefardí*. 2 vols. Madrid: Espasa Calpe, 1953.

Merriam, Alan. *The Anthropology of Music*. Evanston: Northwestern UP, 1964.

Metcalf, Allan A. "Ten Natural Animals in *Beowulf*." *Neuphilologische Mitteilungen* 64 (1963): 378–89.

Michael, Ian, ed. *The Poem of the Cid*. New York: Penguin, 1984.

Middleton, John. *The World of the Swahili*. New Haven: Yale UP, 1992.

Miller, Elaine K. *Mexican Folk Narrative from the Los Angeles Area*. Austin: U of Texas P, 1975.

Miller, Lucien, ed. *South of the Clouds: Tales from Yunnan*. Trans. Guo Xu, Miller, and Xu Kun. Seattle: U of Washington P, 1994.

Miller, Miriam Youngerman, and Jane Chance, eds. *Approaches to Teaching* Sir Gawain and the Green Knight. Approaches to Teaching World Lit. 9. New York: MLA, 1986.

Miller, Susan. *Rescuing the Subject: A Critical Introduction to Rhetoric and the Writer*. Carbondale: Southern Illinois UP, 1989.

Mills, Margaret. "Feminist Theory and the Study of Folklore: A Twenty-Year Trajectory toward Theory." *Western Folklore* 52 (1993): 173–92.

———. *Rhetorics and Politics in Afghan Traditional Storytelling*. Philadelphia: U of Pennsylvania P, 1991.

Minnis, A. J. *The Medieval Theory of Authorship*. 2nd ed. Philadelphia: U of Pennsylvania P, 1988.

Miron, Dan. "Folklore and Antifolklore in the Yiddish Fiction of the Haskala." Talmage 219–49.

Mirza, Sarah, and Margaret Strobel, eds. and trans. *Three Swahili Women*. Bloomington: Indiana UP, 1989.

Mitchell, Margaret M. *Paul and the Rhetoric of Reconciliation: An Exegetical Investigation of the Language and Composition of 1 Corinthians*. Tubingen: Mohr, 1991.

Mitchell, Stephen A. *Heroic Sagas and Ballads*. Ithaca: Cornell UP, 1991.

Momaday, N. Scott. *The Way to Rainy Mountain*. Albuquerque: U of New Mexico P, 1974.

Morgan, Kathryn. *Children of Strangers: The Stories of a Black Family*. Philadelphia: Temple UP, 1980.

Morioka, Heinz, and Miyoko Sasaki. *Rakugo, the Popular Narrative Art of Japan*. Harvard East Asian Monographs 138. Cambridge: Council on East Asian Studies, Harvard U, 1990.

Morrison, Toni. *Beloved*. New York: Knopf, 1987.

———. *Song of Solomon*. 1978. London: Campbell, 1995.

Morton, Robin. *Come Day, Go Day, God Send Sunday: The Songs and Life Story, Told in His Own Words, of John Maguire*. London: Routledge, 1973.

Mtoro bin Mwinyi Bakari. *The Customs of the Swahili People*. Ed. and trans. J. W. T. Allen. Berkeley: U of California P, 1981.

Muhawi, Ibrahim, and Sharif Kanaana. *Speak Bird, Speak Again: Palestinian Arab Folktales*. Berkeley: U of California P, 1989.

Mulder, Martin Jan, ed. *Mikra: Text, Translation, Reading, and Interpretation of the Hebrew Bible in Ancient Judaism and Early Christianity*. Philadelphia: Fortress; Assen: Van Gorcum, 1988.

Munro, Ailie. *The Folk Music Revival in Scotland*. London: Kahn, 1984.

Murdock, George Peter. "An Outline of Cultural Materials." Dundes, *Every Man* 160–79.

Myerhoff, Barbara. *Number Our Days*. 1978. New York: Meridian, 1994.

Myrsiades, Kostas, ed. *Approaches to Teaching Homer's* Iliad *and* Odyssey. Approaches to Teaching World Lit. 13. New York: MLA, 1987.

Nagler, Michael N. *Spontaneity and Tradition: A Study in the Oral Art of Homer*. Berkeley: U of California P, 1974.

Nagy, Gregory. *The Best of the Achaeans: Concepts of the Hero in Archaic Greek Poetry*. Baltimore: Johns Hopkins UP, 1979.

———. *Pindar's Homer: The Lyric Possession of an Ancient Past*. Baltimore: Johns Hopkins UP, 1990.

Narayan, Kirin. *Storytellers, Saints, and Scoundrels: Folk Narrative in Hindu Religious Tradition*. Philadelphia: U of Pennsylvania P, 1989.

Navarre, Marguerite de. *The Heptameron*. Trans. P. A. Chilton. New York: Penguin, 1984.

Naylor, Gloria. *Mama Day*. New York: Random, 1988.

Nelson, Kristina. *The Art of Reciting the Qur'an*. Austin: U of Texas P, 1985.

Neuburg, Victor E. *Popular Literature: A History and Guide*. Harmondsworth, Eng.: Penguin, 1977.

Neugroschel, Joachim. *Great Tales of Jewish Occult and Fantasy: "The Dybbuk" and Thirty Other Classic Stories*. 1976. New York: Wings, 1991.

Neulander, Judith S. "Creating the Universe: A Study of Cosmos and Cognition." *Folklore Forum* 25 (1992): 3–18.

Ngũgĩ wa Thiong'o. *Decolonising the Mind: The Politics of Language in African Literature*. London: Currey, 1986.

The Nibelungenlied. Trans. A. T. Hatto. Baltimore: Penguin, 1965.

Nida, Eugene. *Toward a Science of Translating*. Leiden: Brill, 1964.

Niditch, Susan. *Folklore and the Hebrew Bible*. Minneapolis: Fortress, 1993.

———. *Oral World and Written Word: Ancient Israelite Literature*. Louisville: Knox, 1996.

Niles, John D. "Context and Loss in Scottish Ballad Tradition." *Western Folklore* 45 (1986): 83–106.

———. "The Role of the Strong Tradition-Bearer in the Making of an Oral Culture." Porter and del Guidice 231–40.

———. "*Tam Lin*: Form and Meaning in a Traditional Ballad." *Modern Language Quarterly* 38 (1977): 336–47.

Niles, Susan. *South American Indian Narrative: An Annotated Bibliography*. New York: Garland, 1981.

Njal's Saga. Trans. Magnus Magnusson and Hermann Pálsson. Harmondsworth, Eng.: Penguin, 1960.

Noble, Sally A. "The Tamil Story of the Anklet: Classical and Contemporary Tellings of *Cilappatikaram*." Diss. U of Chicago, 1990.

Nordal, Sigurður, ed. *Egils saga Skalla-Grímssonar*. Íslenzk fornrit 2. Reykjavík: Hið Íslenzka Fornritafélag, 1933.

Novak, William, and Moshe Waldoks, eds. *The Big Book of Jewish Humor*. New York: Harper, 1981.

Nowak, Margaret, and Stephen Durrant. *The Tale of the Nisan Shamaness: A Manchu Folk Epic*. Seattle: U of Washington P, 1977.

Noyes, George Rapall, and Leonard Bacon. *Heroic Ballads of Servia*. Boston: Sherman, 1915.

O'Barr, William M. *Culture and the Ad*. Boulder: Westview, 1994.

O'Donnell, James Joseph. *Avatars of the Word: From Papyrus to Cyberspace*. Cambridge: Harvard UP, 1998.

O'Keeffe, Katherine O'Brien. *Visible Song: Transitional Literacy in Old English Verse*. Cambridge: Cambridge UP, 1990.

Okpewho, Isidore. *African Oral Literature: Backgrounds, Character, and Continuity*. Bloomington: Indiana UP, 1992.

———, ed. *The Oral Performance in Africa*. Ibadan, Nigeria: Spectrum, 1990.

Olrik, Axel. "Epic Laws of Folk Narrative." *Zeitschrift fur deutsches Altertum* 51 (1909): 1–12. Rept. in Dundes, *Study* 129–41.

Olsen, Alexandra H. "Guthlac on the Beach." *Neophilologus* 64 (1980): 290–96.

———. "Oral-Formulaic Research in Old English Studies I." *Oral Tradition* 1 (1986): 548–606.

———. "Oral-Formulaic Research in Old English Studies II." *Oral Tradition* 3 (1988): 138–90.

———. *Speech, Song, and Poetic Craft: The Artistry of the Cynewulf Canon*. New York: Lang, 1984.

Olshen, Barry N., and Yael S. Feldman, eds. *Approaches to Teaching the Hebrew Bible as Literature in Translation*. Approaches to Teaching World Lit. 25. New York: MLA, 1989.

Ong, Walter J. *Orality and Literacy: The Technologizing of the Word*. New York: Methuen, 1982.

———. "Writing Is a Technology That Restructures Thought." *The Written Word: Literacy in Transition*. Ed. Gerd Baumann. Wolfson College Lectures 1985. Oxford: Clarendon, 1986. 23–50.

Opie, Iona, and Peter Opie. *The Classic Fairy Tales*. 1974. Oxford: Oxford UP, 1992.

Opland, Jeff. *Anglo-Saxon Oral Poetry: A Study of the Traditions*. New Haven: Yale UP, 1980.

Orenstein, Gloria Feman. "The Salon of Natalie Clifford Barney: An Interview with Berthe Cleyrergue." *Signs: Journal of Women in Culture and Society* 4 (1979): 484–96.

Oring, Elliott, ed. *Folk Groups and Folklore Genres: A Reader*. Logan: Utah State UP, 1989.

———. "The People of the Joke: On the Conceptualization of a Jewish Humor." *Western Folklore* 42 (1983): 261–71.

Orsini, G. N. G. "Genres." *Princeton Encyclopedia of Poetry and Poetics*. Ed. Alex Preminger, Frank J. Warnke and O. B. Hardison, Jr., assoc. ed. Princeton: Princeton UP, 1974. 307–09.

O'Sullivan, M. I., ed. Firumbras *and* Outel and Roland. Early English Text Soc. 198. London: Oxford UP, 1935.

Oxford English Dictionary. 12 vols. Oxford: Oxford UP, 1933.

Ozick, Cynthia. "The Pagan Rabbi." *"The Pagan Rabbi" and Other Stories.* New York: Dutton, 1983. 1–37.

Page, Christopher. *Voices and Instruments of the Middle Ages: Instrumental Practice and Songs in France, 1100–1300.* Berkeley: U of California P, 1986.

Palmer, Robert. *Deep Blues.* New York: Viking, 1981.

Palmer, Roy. *A Ballad History of England.* London: Batsford, 1979.

Paredes, Américo. "Folk Medicine and the Intercultural Jest." *Spanish-Speaking People in the United States.* Ed. June Helm. Proc. of the 1968 Annual Spring Meeting of the Amer. Ethnological Soc. Seattle: U of Washington P, 1968. 104–19.

———. *A Texas-Mexican Cancionero: Folksongs of the Lower Border.* Urbana: U of Illinois P, 1976. 2nd ed. Austin: U of Texas P, 1995.

———. *"With His Pistol in His Hand": A Border Ballad and Its Hero.* Austin: U of Texas P, 1958.

Paredes, Américo, and Richard Bauman, eds. *Toward New Perspectives in Folklore.* Austin: U of Texas P, 1972.

Parks, Ward. "The Oral-Formulaic Theory in Middle English Studies." *Oral Tradition* 1 (1986): 636–94.

———. "Oral Tradition and the *Canterbury Tales.*" Amodio, *Oral Poetics* 149–79.

Parry, Milman. *The Making of Homeric Verse: The Collected Papers of Milman Parry.* Ed. Adam Parry. 1971. New York: Oxford UP, 1987.

———. "Studies in the Epic Technique of Oral Verse-Making I: Homer and Homeric Style." *Harvard Studies in Classical Philology* 41 (1930): 73–147.

Parsons, Elsie Worthington Clews. *Folk-lore of the Sea Islands, South Carolina.* Cambridge: Amer. Folklore Soc., 1923.

———. *Kiowa Tales.* New York: Amer. Folklore Soc.; Stechert, 1929.

———. *Pueblo Mothers and Children: Essays, 1915–1924.* Ed. Barbara A. Babcock. Santa Fe: Ancient City, 1991.

———. *Tewa Tales.* New York: Amer. Folklore Soc.; Stechert, 1926.

Patai, Raphael. *Gates to the Old City.* New York: Avon, 1980.

Patterson, J. R., trans. *Stories of Abu Zeid the Hilali in Shuwa Arabic.* London: Kegan, 1930.

Pavlic, Edward. *The African-American Experience.* CD-ROM. Research, Woodbridge, 1995.

Peacock, James L. *Rites of Modernization: Symbolic and Social Aspects of Indonesian Proletarian Drama.* 1968. Chicago: U of Chicago P, 1987.

Pelton, Robert. *The Trickster in West Africa.* Berkeley: U of California P, 1980.

Peña, Manuel. *The Texas-Mexican Conjunto: History of a Working-Class Music.* Austin: U of Texas P, 1985.

Penick, Douglas J., and Magyel Pomra Sayi Dakpo. *The Warrior Song of King Gesar.* Boston: Wisdom, 1996.

Pennington, Anne, and Peter Levi, trans. *Marko the Prince: Serbo-Croat Heroic Songs.* London: Duckworth; New York: St. Martin's, 1984.

Perloff, Marjorie. "'Literature' in the Expanded Field." Bernheimer 175–86.

Perrin, Michel. *The Way of the Dead Indians: Guajiro Myths and Symbols.* Trans. Michael Fineberg. Austin: U of Texas P, 1987.

Personal Narratives Group, ed. *Interpreting Women's Lives: Feminist Theory and Personal Narratives.* Bloomington: Indiana UP, 1989.

Pfeiffer, Rudolf. *History of Classical Scholarship: From the Beginnings to the End of the Hellenistic Age.* Oxford: Clarendon, 1968.

Philippi, Donald L., trans. and ed. *Kojiki.* Tokyo: U of Tokyo P, 1968.

Ponce, Mary Helen. *Hoyt Street: An Autobiography.* Albuquerque: U of New Mexico P, 1993.

Popol Vuh. Trans. Dennis Tedlock. New York: Simon, 1985.

Popol Vuh: The Creation Myth of the Maya. Videocassette. Prod. and dir. Patricia Amlin. U of California Extension Center for Media and Independent Learning, 1991.

Popović, Tatyana. *Prince Marko: The Hero of South Slavic Epics.* Syracuse: Syracuse UP, 1988.

Porter, James, ed. *The Ballad Image: Essays Presented to Bertrand Harris Bronson.* Los Angeles: Center for the Study of Comparative Folklore and Mythology, UCLA, 1983.

Porter, James, and Luisa del Guidice, eds. *Ballads and Boundaries: Narrative Singing in an Intercultural Context.* Los Angeles: Dept. of Ethnomusicology and Systematic Musicology, UCLA, 1995.

Porter, James, and Herschel Gower. *Jeannie Robertson: Emergent Singer, Transformative Voice.* Knoxville: U of Tennessee P, 1995.

Prahlad, Sw. Anand. "'All Chickens Come Home to Roost': The Function of Proverbs in Gloria Naylor's *Mama Day.*" *Proverbium: Yearbook of International Proverb Scholarship.* Forthcoming.

———. *African-American Proverbs in Context.* Jackson: U of Mississippi P, 1996.

Propp, Vladimir. *Morphology of the Folktale.* 1928. Austin: U of Texas P, 1968.

Purves, Alan C., Joseph A. Quattrini, and Christine I. Sullivan. *Creating the Writing Portfolio.* Lincolnwood: NTC, 1995.

Quinn, Shelley Fenno. "How to Write a Noh Play: Zeami's *Sandō.*" *Monumenta Nipponica* (1993): 53–88.

Quinn, William A., and Audley S. Hall. *Jongleur: A Modified Theory of Oral Improvisation and Its Effects on the Permanence and Transmission of Middle English Romance.* Washington: UP of America, 1982.

Rabinowitz, I. *A Witness Forever: Ancient Israel's Perception of Literature and the Resultant Hebrew Bible.* Bethesda: CDL, 1993.

Radin, Paul, ed. *African Folktales.* Princeton: Bollingen, 1970.

Radner, Joan Newlon, ed. *Feminist Messages: Coding in Women's Folk Culture.* Urbana: U of Illinois P, 1993.

Rael, Juan B. *The Sources and Diffusion of the Mexican Shepherds' Plays.* Guadalajara: La Joyita, 1965.

Raffel, Burton, trans. *Beowulf.* New York: Mentor, 1963.

Raglan, Fitzroy Richard Somerset. *The Hero: A Study in Tradition, Myth, and Drama.* New York: Vintage, 1956.

————. "The Hero of Tradition." *Folklore* 45 (1934): 212–31. Rpt. in Dundes, *Study* 142–57.

The Ramayana of Valmiki: An Epic of Ancient India. Trans. Robert P. Goldman et al. 5 vols. Princeton: Princeton UP, 1985–97.

Ramsey, S. Robert. *The Languages of China.* Princeton: Princeton UP, 1987.

Randolph, Vance. *Ozark Folksongs.* Ed. and abr. by Norm Cohen. Urbana: U of Illinois P, 1982.

————. *Ozark Folksongs.* 4 vols. Rev. ed. Columbia: U of Missouri P, 1980.

————. *"Who Blowed Up the Church House?" and Other Ozark Folk Tales.* New York: Columbia UP, 1952.

Rank, Otto. The Myth of the Birth of the Hero *and Other Writings.* Ed. Philip Freund. New York: Vintage, 1959.

Reed, Ishmael. *Chattanooga.* New York: Random, 1973.

Rehfisch, Farnham, ed. *Gypsies, Tinkers and Other Travellers.* London: Academic, 1975.

Reichel-Dolmatoff, Gerardo. *Amazonian Cosmos: The Sexual and Religious Symbolism of the Tukano Indians.* Chicago: U of Chicago P, 1977.

Reichl, Karl. *Turkic Oral Epic Poetry.* New York: Garland, 1992.

Renoir, Alain. *A Key to Old Poems: The Oral-Formulaic Approach to the Interpretation of West-Germanic Verse.* University Park: Pennsylvania State UP, 1988.

————. "Oral-Formulaic Rhetoric: An Approach to Image and Message in Medieval Poetry." *Medieval Texts and Contemporary Readers.* Ed. Laurie A. Finke and Martin B. Shichtman. Ithaca: Cornell UP, 1987. 234–53.

Renza, Louis A. "Influence." *Critical Terms for Literary Study.* Ed. Frank Lentricchia and Thomas McLaughlin. Chicago: U of Chicago P, 1990. 186–202.

Reynolds, Dwight Fletcher. *Heroic Poets, Poetic Heroes: The Ethnography of Performance in Arabic Oral Epic Tradition.* Ithaca: Cornell UP, 1995.

Ricard, Alain. "The Concert Party as a Genre: The Happy Stars of Lomé." *Forms of Folklore in Africa.* Ed. Bernth Lindfors. Austin: U of Texas P, 1977. 222–36.

Richardson, Nicholas. "Aristotle's Reading of Homer and Its Background." *Homer's Ancient Readers.* Ed. R. Lamberton and J. Keaney. Princeton: Princeton UP, 1992. 30–40.

Richmond, W. Edson. *Ballad Scholarship: An Annotated Bibliography.* New York: Garland, 1989.

Riffaterre, Michael. *Text Production.* Trans. Terese Lyons. New York: Columbia UP, 1985.

The Rig Veda: An Anthology. Trans. Wendy Doniger O'Flaherty. New York: Penguin, 1981.

Rissanen, Matti. "The Theme of 'Exile' in 'The Wife's Lament.'" *Neuphilologische Mitteilungen* 70 (1969): 90–104.

Ritzke-Rutherford, Jean. "Formulaic Microstructure: The Cluster." *The Alliterative Morte Arthure.* Ed. Karl Heinz Göller. Cambridge: Brewer, 1981. 70–82.

Robe, Stanley L., ed. *Hispanic Folktales from New Mexico: Narratives from R. D. Jameson*. Berkeley: U of California P, 1977.

Roberts, John M., and Michael L. Forman. "Riddles: Expressive Models of Interrogation." *Directions in Sociolinguistics*. Ed. John J. Gumperz and Dell Hymes. New York: Holt, Rinehart, 1972. 180–209.

Roberts, John W. *From Trickster to Badman: The Black Folk Hero in Slavery and Freedom*. Philadelphia: U of Pennsylvania P, 1989.

Roeder, Beatrice A. *Chicano Folk Medicine from Los Angeles, California*. Berkeley: U of California P, 1988.

Roemer, Kenneth, ed. *Approaches to Teaching Momaday's* The Way to Rainy Mountain. Approaches to Teaching World Lit. 17. New York: MLA, 1988.

Roman de Troie. 6 vols. Paris: Firmin-Didot, 1904.

Romeralo, Antonio Sánchez. "El romancero oral ayer y hoy: Breve historia de la recolección moderna (1782–1970)." *El Romancero hoy: Nuevas fronteras*. Ed. Romeralo, Diego Catalán, and Samuel G. Armistead. Davis: U of California; Madrid: Cátedra–Seminario Menéndez Pidal, 1979. 15–51.

Rosenberg, Bruce A. *Can These Bones Live? The Art of the American Folk Preacher*. Rev. ed. Urbana: U of Illinois P, 1988.

———. "The Complexity of Oral Tradition." *Oral Tradition* 2 (1987): 73–90.

———. "The Message of the American Folk Sermon." *Oral Tradition* 1 (1986): 695–727.

Rosenberg, Donna, ed. *World Mythology: An Anthology of the Great Myths and Epics*. Lincolnwood: NTC, 1994.

Rosenberg, S. N., and H. Tischler, eds. *Chanter M'Estuet: Songs of the Trouvères*. London: Faber, 1981.

Rosenthal, Franz, trans. *The Muqaddimah*. By Ibn Khaldūn. 3 vols. London: Routledge, 1967.

Rothenberg, Jerome, and Diane Rothenberg, eds. *Symposium of the Whole: A Range of Discourse toward an Ethnopoetics*. Berkeley: U of California P, 1983.

Rothenberg, Jerome, and Dennis Tedlock. "The Ways of *Alcheringa*." *Alcheringa* ns 1.1 (1975): 2–3.

Rowe, John. "Linguistic Classification Problems in South America." *Native South Americans: Ethnology of the Least Known Continent*. Ed. Patricia Lyon. Boston: Little, 1974. 43–50.

Ruch, Barbara. "Medieval Jongleurs and the Making of a National Literature." *Japan in the Muromachi Age*. Ed. John Whitney Hall and Toyoda Takeshi. Berkeley: U of California P, 1977. 279–309.

Ruiz, Juan. *Book of True Love: Bilingual Edition*. Trans. Saralyn R. Daly. Ed. Anthony N. Zahareas. University Park: Pennsylvania State UP, 1978.

Running at the Edge of the Rainbow: Laguna Stories and Poems. Videocassette. Prod. Larry Evers. With Leslie Marmon Silko. Tucson: U of Arizona P.

Ruoff, A. LaVonne Brown. *American Indian Literatures: An Introduction, Bibliographic Review, and Selected Bibliography.* New York: MLA, 1990.

Russell, Ian, ed. *Singer, Song, and Scholar.* Sheffield, Eng.: Sheffield Academic, 1986.

Russo, Joseph A. "Homer against His Tradition." *Arion* 7 (1968): 275–95.

Ryder, Arthur W. *The Panchatantra.* Chicago: U of Chicago P, 1964.

Saaraba. Videocassette. Prod. and dir. Amadou Saalum Seck. 1988. San Francisco: California Newsreel, 1991.

Sadler, Glenn Edward, ed. *Teaching Children's Literature: Issues, Pedagogy, Resources.* New York: MLA, 1992.

Sadoff, Dianne F., and William E. Cain, eds. *Teaching Contemporary Theory to Undergraduates.* New York: MLA, 1994.

Saenger, Paul. "Silent Reading: Its Impact on Late Medieval Script and Society." *Viator* 13 (1982): 367–414.

The Saga of Gisli. Trans. George Johnston. With notes and essay by Peter Foote. London: Dent; Toronto: U of Toronto P, 1971.

The Saga of Hallfred: The Troublesome Scald. Trans. Alan Boucher. Reykjavík: Iceland Review, 1981.

The Saga of the Faroe Islanders. Thrand of Gotu: Two Icelandic Sagas. Trans. George Johnston. Erin: Porcupine's Quill, 1994. 17–143.

The Saga of þorgils and Hafliði. Shorter Sagas. Trans. Julia H. McGrew and R. George Thomas. New York: Twayne: American-Scandinavian Foundation, 1974. Vol. 2 of *Sturlunga Saga.*

The Saga of the Volsungs: The Norse Epic of Sigurd the Dragon Slayer. Trans. Jesse L. Byock. Berkeley: U of California P, 1990.

The Sagas of Kormák and the Sworn Brothers. Trans. Lee M. Hollander. Princeton: Princeton UP, 1949.

Salomon, Frank, and George Urioste, eds. *The Huarochrí Manuscript: A Testament of Ancient and Colonial Andean Religion.* Austin: U of Texas P, 1991.

"Salons: How to Revive the Endangered Art of Conversation and Start a Revolution in Your Living Room." *Utne Reader* Mar.-Apr. 1991: 66–88.

Sampley, J. P. "Paul, His Opponents in 2 Corinthians 10–13, and the Rhetorical Handbooks." *The Social World of Formative Christianity and Judaism: Essays in Tribute to Howard Clark Kee.* Ed. J. Neusner. Philadelphia: Fortress, 1988. 162–77.

Sands, D. B., ed. *Middle English Verse Romances.* Exeter: U of Exeter P, 1986.

Sapir, Edward. *Language.* New York: Harcourt, 1921.

———, ed. *Wishram Texts, Together with Wasco Tales and Myths, Collected by Jeremiah Curtin.* Pubs. of the Amer. Ethnological Soc. 2. Leiden: Brill, 1909.

Sawyer, Ruth. *The Way of the Storyteller.* New York: Viking, 1942.

Schach, Paul. *Icelandic Sagas.* Boston: Twayne, 1984.

Scheub, Harold. *The African Storyteller: Stories from African Oral Traditions.* Dubuque: Kendall, 1990.

———. "A Review of African Oral Traditions and Literature." *African Studies Review* 28.2–3 (1985): 1–72.

———. *The Xhosa "Ntsomi."* Oxford: Clarendon, 1975.

Schier, Kurt. *Sagaliteratur.* Sammlung Metzler 78. Stuttgart: Metzler, 1972.

Schoemaker, George H. *The Emergence of Folklore in Everyday Life.* Bloomington: Trickster, 1990.

Scholes, Robert. *Textual Power.* New Haven: Yale UP, 1985.

Schultes, Richard, and Albert Hofmann. *Plants of the Gods: Origins of Hallucinogenic Use.* New York: McGraw, 1979.

Scollon, Ron, and Suzanne B. K. Scollon. Personal conversation with Barre Toelken, 1982.

Seeger, Anthony. *Why Suya Sing: A Musical Anthropology of an Amazonian People.* New York: Cambridge UP, 1987.

Seforim, Mendele Mocher. *The Travels and Adventures of Benjamin the Third.* Trans. Moshe Speigel. New York: Schocken, 1968.

Segal, Ronald. *The Black Diaspora.* New York: Farrar, 1995.

Seitel, Peter. *See So That We May See: Performances and Interpretations of Traditional Tales from Tanzania.* With Sheila Dauer. Bloomington: Indiana UP, 1980.

Sekaquaptewa, Helen. "Iisaw: Hopi Coyote Stories." *Words and Place: Native Literature from the American Southwest.* Prod. Larry Evers. Videotape. Tucson: U of Arizona, 1978.

Serbo-Croatian Heroic Songs / Srpskohrvatske junačke pjesme. Vols. 1–4, 6, 8, 14. Collected, ed., and trans. by Milman Parry, Albert Lord, and David Bynum. Cambridge: Harvard UP; Belgrade: Serbian Acad. of Sciences, 1953– .

Shapiro, Sidney, trans. *Outlaws of the Marsh.* By Luo Guanzhong and Shi Nai'an. Beijing: Foreign Langs., 1988.

Shepard, Leslie. *The Broadside Ballad.* Hatboro: Legacy, 1978.

Sherman, Josepha. *A Sampler of Jewish American Folklore.* Little Rock: August, 1992.

Sherzer, Joel. *Kuna Ways of Speaking: An Ethnographic Perspective.* Austin: U of Texas P, 1983.

Sherzer, Joel, and Greg Urban, eds. *Native South American Discourse.* Berlin: Mouton de Gruyter, 1986.

Shields, Hugh. *Shamrock, Rose and Thistle: Folk Singing in North Derry.* Belfast: Blackstaff, 1981.

Shive, David. *Naming Achilles.* Oxford: Oxford UP, 1987.

Short, Ian, et al., eds. *The Song of Roland.* Berkeley: U of California P, forthcoming.

Shuldham-Shaw, Patrick, and Emily B. Lyle, gen. eds. *The Greig-Duncan Folk Song Collection.* 6 vols. Aberdeen: Aberdeen UP, 1981– .

Silverstein, Michael, and Greg Urban, eds. *The Natural History of Discourse.* Chicago: U of Chicago P, 1996.

Simons, Elizabeth Radin. *Student Worlds, Student Words: Teaching Writing through Folklore.* Portsmouth: Boynton-Heinemann, 1990.

Simpson, Jacqueline. *The Northmen Talk: A Choice of Tales from Iceland*. London: Phoenix; Madison: U of Wisconsin P, 1965.

———. *Scandinavian Folktales*. New York: Penguin, 1988.

Singer, Isaac Bashevis. "The Mirror." *"Gimpel the Fool" and Other Stories*. New York: Noonday, 1958. 78–88.

Singer, Milton. *When a Great Tradition Modernizes*. New York: Praeger, 1972.

Slobin, Mark, ed. *Old Jewish Folk Music: The Collections and Writings of Moshe Beregovski*. Trans. Slobin. Philadelphia: U of Pennsylvania P, 1982.

———. *Tenement Songs: The Popular Songs of Jewish Immigrants*. Chicago: U of Illinois P, 1982.

Slyomovics, Susan. "The Death-Song of Amir Khafaji: Puns in an Oral and Printed Episode of *Sīrat Banī Hilal*." *Journal of Arabic Literature* 18 (1987): 62–78.

———. *The Merchant of Art: An Egyptian* Hilali *Oral Epic Poet in Performance*. Berkeley: U of California P, 1987. Videotape available from author.

———. "Performing *A Thousand and One Nights* in Egypt." *Oral Tradition* 9 (1994): 390–419.

———. "Ritual Grievance: The Language of Woman?" *Women and Performance: A Journal of Feminist Theory* 5 (1990): 53–60.

Smith, Anna Deavere. *Fires in the Mirror*. New York: Doubleday, 1993.

Smith, H. Daniel. *Reading the Ramayana: A Bibliographic Guide for Students and College Teachers*. Syracuse: Maxwell School of Citizenship and Public Affairs, Syracuse U, 1983.

Smith, John D. *The Epic of Pabuji: A Study, Transcription, and Translation*. Cambridge: Cambridge UP, 1991.

Smitherman, Geneva. *Talkin and Testifyin: The Language of Black America*. Detroit: Wayne State UP, 1986.

Snorri Sturluson. *Heimskringla: History of the Kings of Norway*. Trans. Lee M. Hollander. Austin: U of Texas P, 1964.

Sowayan, Saad Abdullah. *Nabaṭi Poetry: The Oral Poetry of Arabia*. Berkeley: U of California P, 1985.

Spacks, Patricia Meyer. *Gossip*. Chicago: U of Chicago P, 1986.

Spiro, Melford E. "Cultural Relativism and the Future of Anthropology." *Rereading Cultural Anthropology*. Ed. George E. Marcus. Durham: Duke UP, 1992. 124–51.

Spivak, Gayatri Chakravorty. *In Other Worlds: Essays in Cultural Politics*. New York: Methuen, 1987.

Spurgeon, Caroline. *Five Hundred Years of Chaucer Criticism and Allusion*. 3 vols. New York: Russel, 1960.

Staal, Fritz. *The Fidelity of Oral Tradition and the Origins of Science*. Amsterdam: North-Holland, 1986.

Steblin-Kaminskij, M. I. *The Saga Mind*. Trans. Kenneth H. Ober. Odense, Den.: Odense UP, 1973.

Steckmesser, Kent. "Robin Hood and the American Outlaw: A Note on History and Folklore." *Journal of American Folklore* 79 (1966): 348–55.

Steere, Edward. *Swahili Tales*. London: Soc. for Promoting Christian Knowledge, 1900. New York: AMS, 1992.

Stock, Brian. *The Implications of Literacy: Written Language and Models of Interpretation in the Eleventh and Twelfth Centuries*. Princeton: Princeton UP, 1983.

———. *Listening for the Text: On the Uses of the Past*. Baltimore: Johns Hopkins UP, 1990.

Stoeltje, Beverly J., ed. *Feminist Revisions in Folklore Studies*. Spec. issue of *Journal of Folklore Research* 25 (1988): 141–242.

———. "'A Helpmate for Man Indeed': The Image of the Frontier Woman." Farrer 25–41.

Stoeltje, Beverly J., and Richard Bauman. "The Semiotics of Folkloric Performance." *The Semiotic Web, 1987*. Ed. Thomas A. Sebeok and Jean Umiker-Sebeok. Berlin: Mouton de Gruyter, 1988. 585–99.

Stone, Brian, trans. *King Arthur's Death*. New York: Penguin, 1988.

Stone, Elizabeth. *Black Sheep and Kissing Cousins: How Our Family Stories Shape Us*. New York: Penguin, 1989.

Storms, G. *Anglo-Saxon Magic*. The Hague: Nijhoff, 1948.

Summerfield, Judith, and Geoffrey Summerfield. *Frames of Mind: A Course in Composition*. New York: Random, 1986.

Sutton-Smith, Brian, ed. *The Folkgames of Children*. Pubs. of the Amer. Folklore Soc. Austin: U of Texas P, 1972.

Sutton-Smith, Brian, and John M. Roberts. "The Cross-Cultural and Psychological Study of Games." Sutton-Smith 331–40.

Sutton-Smith, Brian, John M. Roberts, and Adam Kendon. "Strategy in Games and Folk Tales." Sutton-Smith 341–58.

Swann, Brian, ed. *On the Translation of Native American Literatures*. Washington: Smithsonian Inst., 1992.

Taggart, James M. *Enchanted Maidens: Gender Relations in Spanish Folktales of Courtship and Marriage*. Princeton: Princeton UP, 1990.

The Tale of an Anklet: An Epic of South India. Trans. R. Parthasarathy. New York: Columbia UP, 1993.

Talmage, Frank, ed. *Studies in Jewish Folklore*. Cambridge: Assn. for Jewish Studies, 1980.

Tanna, Laura. *Jamaican Folktales*. Kingston: Inst. of Jamaica, 1989.

Tannen, Deborah. *You Just Don't Understand: Women and Men in Conversation*. New York: Morrow, 1990.

Taylor, Archer. *The Black Ox*. Folklore Fellows Communications 70. Helsinki: Suomalainen Tiedeakatemia, 1927.

Taylor, Charles. "The Politics of Recognition." Gutman 25–73.

Tedlock, Dennis, trans. *Finding the Center: Narrative Poetry of the Zuni Indians*. Lincoln: U of Nebraska P, 1978.

———. "On the Translation of Style in Oral Narrative." *Journal of American Folklore* 84 (1971): 114–33.

———. *The Spoken Word and the Work of Interpretation*. Philadelphia: U of Pennsylvania P, 1983.

Terry, Patricia, and Nancy Vine Durling, eds. and trans. *The Romance of the Rose; or, Guillaume de Dole*. By Jean Renart. Philadelphia: U of Pennsylvania P, 1993.

Third Sister Liu (Liu sanjie). Dir. Su Li. Changchun, 1961.

Thiselton-Dyer, T. F. *Folk-Lore of Women as Illustrated by Legendary and Traditional Tales, Folk-Rhymes, Proverbial Sayings, Superstitions, Etc.* 1905. Williamstown: Corner, 1975.

Thompson, Stith. *The Folktale*. Berkeley: U of California P, 1977.

———. *Motif-Index of Folk-Literature: A Classification of Narrative Elements in Folktales, Ballads, Myths, Fables, Mediaeval Romances, Exempla, Fabliaux, Jestbooks, and Local Legends*. 6 vols. Rev. ed. Bloomington: Indiana UP, 1989.

———, ed. *One Hundred Favorite Folktales*. Bloomington: Indiana UP, 1968.

———. "The Star Husband Tale." Dundes, *Study* 416–74.

Thormann, Janet. "Variations on the Theme of 'The Hero on the Beach' in *The Phoenix*." *Neuphilologische Mitteilungen* 71 (1970): 187–90.

Tiwary, K. M. "Tuneful Weeping: A Mode of Communication." *Frontiers* 3.3 (1978): 24–27.

Toelken, Barre. "Culture and Narrative Meaning: Narrative and Cultural Meaning." *Dona Folcloristica*. Ed. Leander Petzoldt and Stefaan Top. Frankfurt: Lang, 1990. 235–45.

———. *The Dynamics of Folklore*. New York: Houghton, 1979. Rev. ed. Logan: Utah State U, 1996.

———. *Morning Dew and Roses: Nuance, Metaphor, and Meaning in Folksongs*. Urbana: U of Illinois P, 1995.

———. "The 'Pretty Language' of Yellowman: Genre, Mode, and Texture in Navaho Coyote Narratives." *Genre* 2 (1969): 211–35.

Toelken, Barre, and Tacheeni Scott. "Poetic Retranslation and the 'Pretty Languages' of Yellowman." *Traditional Literatures of the American Indian: Texts and Interpretations*. Ed. Karl Kroeber. Lincoln: U of Nebraska P, 1981. 65–116.

Trachtenberg, Joshua. *Jewish Magic and Superstition: A Study in Folk Religion*. 1939. New York: Atheneum, 1974.

Tsinąąbąąs Yazzie (Little Wagon). Personal account, taken by dictation by Barre Toelken, Montezuma Canyon, UT, 5 Dec. 1954.

Tucker, John, ed. *Sagas of the Icelanders: A Book of Essays*. New York: Garland, 1989.

Tully, Marjorie F., and Juan B. Rael. *An Annotated Bibilography of Spanish Folklore in New Mexico and Southern Colorado*. Albuquerque: U of New Mexico P, 1950.

Tulsidas: The Holy Lake of the Acts of Rama. Trans. W. D. P. Hill. Bombay: Oxford UP, 1952.

Turner, Patricia A. *I Heard It through the Grapevine: Rumor in African American Culture*. Berkeley: U of California P, 1993.

Turner, Sharon. *The History of the Anglo-Saxons from the Earliest Period to the Norman Conquest*. 6th ed. Vol. 3. London: Longman, 1836.

Tutuola, Amos. *My Life in the Bush of Ghosts*. New York: Grove, 1954.

———. *The Palm Wine Drinkard*. London: Faber, 1952.

Tyler, Lee Edgar. "Annotated Bibliography to 1985." *Oral Tradition* 3 (1988): 191–228.

Tyler, Lee Edgar, Juris Dilevko, and John Miles Foley. "Annotated Bibliography (1983)." *Oral Tradition* 1 (1986): 767–808.

Tyler, Royall, ed. and trans. *Japanese Tales*. New York: Pantheon, 1987.

Tylor, Edward B. *Primitive Culture*. 1871. Vol. 1. London: Murray, 1929.

University of Glasgow Library. *The Euing Collection of Broadside Ballads in the Library of the University of Glasgow*. Glasgow: Glasgow U Pub., 1971.

Urban, Greg. "Ceremonial Dialogues in South America." *American Anthropologist* 88 (1986): 371–86.

———. *A Discourse-Centered Approach to Culture: Native South American Myths and Rituals*. Austin: U of Texas P, 1991.

Valenciano, Ana. "Survival of the Traditional *Romancero*: Field Expeditions." *Oral Tradition* 2 (1987): 424–50.

Vanderwerth, W. C., ed. *Indian Oratory*. Norman: U of Oklahoma P, 1971.

van Gennep, Arnold. *The Rites of Passage*. 1909. London: Routledge, 1960.

Vitz, Evelyn Birge. *Orality and Performance in Early French Romance*. Forthcoming.

———. "Orality, Literacy, and the Early Tristan Material: Béroul, Thomas, Marie de France." *Romanic Review* 78 (1987): 299–310.

———. "Rethinking Old French Literature: The Orality of the Octosyllabic Couplet." *Romanic Review* 77 (1986): 307–21.

———. "Romans Dir et Contar." *Cahiers de littérature orale* 36 (1995): 35–63.

Vivante, Paolo. *The Epithets in Homer: A Study in Poetic Values*. New Haven: Yale UP, 1982.

Vries, Jan de. *Heroic Song and Heroic Legend*. Trans. B. J. Timmer. London: Oxford UP, 1963.

Warner, Anne. *Traditional American Folk Songs from the Anne and Frank Warner Collection*. Syracuse: Syracuse UP, 1984.

Wasson, George B., Jr. "Coyote and the Strawberries." Jones and Ramsey 125–30.

Watson, Duane F. "A Rhetorical Analysis of *Philippians* and Its Implications for the Unity Question." *Novum Testamentum* 30.1 (1988): 57–88.

Wax, Rosalie H. *Magic, Fate, and History: The Changing Ethos of the Vikings*. Lawrence: Coronado, 1969.

Webber, Ruth H. "The *Cantar de Mio Cid*: Problems of Interpretation." *Oral Tradition in Literature*. Ed. John Miles Foley. Columbia: U of Missouri P, 1986. 65–88.

———, ed. *Hispanic Balladry Today*. Albert Bates Lord Studies in Oral Tradition 3. New York: Garland, 1989.

Webster's New Twentieth-Century Dictionary. 2nd ed. Springfield: Merriam 1979.

Wehse, Rainer. "Broadside Ballad and Folksong: Oral Tradition versus Literary Tradition." *Folklore Forum* 8 (1975): 324–34.

———. *Schwanklied und Flugblatt in Grossbritannien*. Las Vegas: Lang, 1979.

Weigle, Marta. *Creation and Procreation: Feminist Reflections on Mythologies of Cosmogony and Parturition*. Philadelphia: U of Pennsylvania P, 1989.

———. *Spiders and Spinsters: Women and Mythology*. Albuquerque: U of New Mexico P, 1982.

Wertheim, Margaret. "The Medieval Consolations of Cyberspace." *Sciences* Nov.-Dec. 1995: 25.

West Africa: Two Lifestyles. Videocassette. Santa Monica: BFA Educ. Media, 1970.

West, Stephen H., and Wilt L. Idema, eds. and trans. *The Moon and the Zither: The Story of the Western Wing*. By Wang Shifu. Berkeley: U of California P, 1991.

West, Stephanie, ed. *The Ptolemaic Papyri of Homer*. Cologne: Westdeutscher, 1967.

Whaley, Diana. *Heimskringla: An Introduction*. London: Viking Soc. for Northern Research, 1991.

Whisnant, David E. *All That Is Native and Fine: The Politics of Culture in an American Region*. Chapel Hill: U of North Carolina P, 1983.

Whiting, B. J., ed. *Traditional British Ballads: A Selection*. New York: Appleton, 1955.

Wilgus, D. K. *Anglo-American Folksong Scholarship since 1898*. New Brunswick: Rutgers UP, 1959.

Wilhelm, James J., ed. *Lyrics of the Middle Ages: An Anthology*. New York: Garland, 1990.

Williams, Alfred, ed. *Folk-Songs of the Upper Thames*. London: Duckworth, 1923.

Williams, Raymond. *The Long Revolution*. Rev. ed. New York: Harper, 1961.

Wilson, William A. "Herder, Folklore, and Romantic Nationalism." *Journal of Popular Culture* 6 (1973): 818–35. Rpt. in Oring, *Folk Groups* 21–37.

Wire, Antoinette Clark. *The Corinthian Women Prophets: A Reconstruction through Paul's Rhetoric*. Minneapolis: Fortress, 1990.

Witherspoon, Gary. *Language and Art in the Navajo Universe*. Ann Arbor: U of Michigan P, 1977.

Wolgamott, Susan Wasson. "The Girl Who Married a Sea Otter." Jones and Ramsey 262–63.

Wood, Michael. *In Search of the Trojan War*. New York: Facts on File, 1985.

Wuellner, Wilhelm. "Paul's Rhetoric of Argumentation in Romans: An Alternative to the Donfried-Karris Debate over Romans." *The Romans Debate*. Ed. K. P. Donfried. Minneapolis: Augsburg, 1977. 152–74.

Würtzbach, Natascha. *The Rise of the English Street Ballad, 1550–1650*. Trans. Gayna Walls. Cambridge: Cambridge UP, 1990.

Yanagita, Kunio. *About Our Ancestors: The Japanese Family System*. New York: Greenwood, 1980.

————. *The Legends of Toono*. Tokyo: Japan Foundation, 1975.

Yang, Gladys, trans. *Ashima*. Beijing: Foreign Langs., 1957.

Yeats, William Butler. *Celtic Twilight and a Selection of Early Poems*. New York: NAL, 1962.

Yu, Anthony C., ed. and trans. *The Journey to the West*. Chicago: U of Chicago P, 1977.

Yung, Bell. *Cantonese Opera: Performance as Creative Process*. Cambridge: Cambridge UP, 1989.

Zeitlin, Steven J. "The Wedding Dance." *A Collection of American Family Folklore*. Ed. Zeitlin, Amy J. Kotkin, and Holly Cutting Baker. Cambridge: Yellow Moon, 1982.

Zeitlin, Steven J., Amy J. Kotkin, and Holly Cutting Baker, *A Celebration of American Family Folklore*. New York: Pantheon, 1982.

Zenani, Nongenile Masithatu. *The World and the Word: Tales and Observations from the Xhosa Oral Tradition*. Collected and ed. by Harold Scheub. Madison: U of Wisconsin P, 1992.

Zink, Michel, ed. *Les chansons de toile*. Paris: Champion, 1977.

Zolbrod, Paul. *Dine Bahane: The Navajo Creation Story*. Albuquerque: U of New Mexico P, 1984.

Zong, In-Sob. *Folk Tales from Korea*. 1952. New York: Grove, 1983.

Zumthor, Paul. *La lettre et la voix: De la "littérature" médiévale*. Paris: Seuil, 1987.

————. *Oral Poetry: An Introduction*. Trans. K. Murphy-Judy. Minneapolis: U of Minnesota P, 1990.

————. *Speaking of the Middle Ages*. Trans. Sarah White. Lincoln: U of Nebraska P, 1986.

————. "The Text and the Voice." *New Literary History* 16 (1984): 67–92.

————. *Toward a Medieval Poetics*. Trans. Philip Bennet. Minneapolis: U of Minnesota P, 1992.

Zumwalt, Rosemary Lévy. *American Folklore Scholarship: A Dialogue of Dissent*. Bloomington: Indiana UP, 1988.

————. "The Complexity of Children's Folklore." *Children's Folklore: A Source Book*. Ed. Brian Sutton-Smith, Jay Mechling, Thomas W. Johnson, and Felicia R. McMahon. New York: Garland, 1995. 23–47.

Zupitza, Julius, ed. Beowulf *Reproduced in Facsimile from the Unique Manuscript British Museum Ms. Cotton Vitellius A. xv*. 2nd ed. Introd. Norman Davis. Early English Text Soc. os 245. London: Oxford UP, 1959.

Name Index

Note: Name indexes may include, in addition to names of persons, titles of anonymous works. Since most works from oral tradition are effectively anonymous (the performer being the principal agent of only one version rather than a singular author in the usual literary or textual sense), I have incorporated an extensive listing of oral traditional works mentioned in this volume.

Aarne, Antti, 79, 86, 92, 94n10, 227, 293
Abbott, Claude Colleer, 375
Abimbola, Wande, 455
Abraham, Roy Clive, 455
Abrahams, Roger D., 42, 44, 45n2, 60, 87, 94n10, 122n2, 176, 179, 180, 181, 184, 190, 195, 284, 297n1, 364, 411, 426, 435n5, 435n6, 452, 453
Abramovich, Shalom Jacob, 234, 235
Abrams, M. H., 352
Abu-Lughod, Lila, 270
Achebe, Chinua, 179, 187
Acker, Paul, 390n2
"The Adventures of Mrile," 452

Aertsen, Henk, 371
"Against a Dwarf," 55–56
Ajuwon, Bade, 455
Aland, Kurt, 335
Alberti, 205
Alcuin, 353
Aleichem, Sholom. See Rabinowitz, Shalom
Alexander, Ronelle, 93n7, 248, 272n3, 386
Alexiou, Margaret, 345
Alfonso VI, 210
Alfred, King of Wessex, 352–53
Ali, Muhammad, 192
Allen, Richard F., 385
Allen, Rosamund, 103, 371
Allen, Woody, 237